From Cold War to Democratic Peace

Syracuse Studies on Peace and Conflict Resolution
Louis Kriesberg, *Series Editor*

Other titles in Syracuse Studies on Peace and Conflict Resolution

An American Ordeal: The Antiwar Movement of the Vietnam Era. Charles DeBenedetti; Charles Chatfield, assisting author

Building a Global Civic Culture: Education for an Interdependent World. Elise Boulding

The Coming Age of Scarcity: Preventing Mass Death and Genocide in the Twenty-First Century. Michael N. Dobkowski and Isidor Wallimann, eds.

Cooperative Security: Reducing Third World Wars. I. William Zartman, ed.

Give Peace a Chance: Exploring the Vietnam Antiwar Movement. Melvin Small and William D. Hoover, eds.

Interactive Conflict Resolution. Ronald J. Fisher

Intractable Conflicts and Their Transformation. Louis Kriesberg, Torrell A. Northrup, and Stuart J. Thorson, eds.

Making Peace Prevail: Preventing Violent Conflict in Macedonia. Alice Ackermann

Organizing for Peace: Neutrality, the Test Ban, and the Freeze. Robert Kleidman

Polite Protesters: The American Peace Movement of the 1980s. John Lofland

Preparing for Peace: Conflict Transformation Across Cultures. John Paul Lederach

The Strangest Dream: Communism, Anti-Communism, and the U.S. Peace Movement, 1945–1963. Robbie Lieberman

Timing the De-escalation of International Conflicts. Louis Kriesberg and Stuart Thorson, eds.

A World Without War: How U.S. Feminists and Pacifists Resisted World War I. Frances Early

From Cold War to Democratic Peace

Third Parties, Peaceful Change, and the OSCE

Janie Leatherman

SYRACUSE UNIVERSITY PRESS

First Edition 2003
03 04 05 06 07 08 6 5 4 3 2 1

The paper used in this publication meets the minimum requirements of American National Standard for Information Sciences—Permanence of Paper for Printed Library Materials, ANSI Z39.48–1984.∞™

Library of Congress Cataloging-in-Publication Data

Leatherman, Janie, 1959–
From Cold War to democratic peace : third parties, peaceful change, and the OSCE / Janie Leatherman.— 1st ed.
p. cm.—(Syracuse studies on peace and conflict resolution)
Includes bibliographical references and index.
ISBN 0–8156–3007–7 (cloth : alk. paper)—ISBN 0–8156–3032–8 (pbk. : alk. paper)
1. Europe, Eastern—Politics and government—1989– 2. Democracy—Europe, Eastern. 3. Organization for Security and Co-operation in Europe. 4. Europe—Politics and government—1989– I. Title. II. Series.
DJK51.L43 2003
341.3'094—dc21 2003008565

Manufactured in the United States of America

To my parents, who taught me about world peace,
and in memory of Urpu, whom we all loved

Janie Leatherman is associate professor of international relations and codirector of peace and conflict resolution studies in the Department of Politics and Government at Illinois State University, where she has been teaching since 1997. Dr. Leatherman is the lead author of *Breaking Cycles of Violence: Conflict Prevention in Intrastate Crises* (1999). She also has contributed chapters to several books and published numerous articles on conflict early warning and prevention in periodicals including the *Journal of Group Rights* and the *Nordic Journal of Conflict and Cooperation.* Her research and field work have been supported through grants and fellowships from such sources as the Social Science Research Council, the United States Institute of Peace, the Swedish Government, Fulbright-Hayes, and the American-Scandinavian Foundation.

Contents

Preface *ix*

Author's Note *xiii*

1. The Dawning of a New Era *1*
2. A Normative Theory of Mediation *25*
3. From Cold War to Multilateral Détente *50*
4. Catalyzing Peaceful Change *77*
5. Laying the Groundwork for a New East-West Order *103*
6. Building Consensus on a New Normative Order *131*
7. Putting Principles into Practice *157*
8. Institutionalizing Peaceful Change *193*
9. Promoting Democratic Peace *225*

Appendix: *Government of Finland's European Security Conference Memorandum of May 5, 1969* *251*

Glossary *253*

References *257*

Index *275*

Figures

1. CSCE/OSCE Conferences, Summits, and Meetings 1973–99 *3*

2. CSCE/OSCE Expert Meetings 1978–91 *4*

3. CSCE/OSCE Human Dimension Meetings and Seminars *5*

4. Third-Party Normative Influence *33*

5. Third-Party Mechanisms for Normative Change *46*

6. Organization for Security and Cooperation in Europe Organigram: *Structures and Institutions* *230*

Preface

THE END OF THE COLD WAR caught by surprise most policymakers and scholars alike. But one forum where practitioners saw the ground shifting under their feet well before the wave of political change swept communist governments from office across Central Europe and the Soviet Union was the Conference on Security and Cooperation in Europe (CSCE). These diplomats had been engaged in a dialogue and consensus-building process since the early 1970s on the future normative order of East-West relations. In 1990 they convened in Paris to sign a new charter for Europe, heralding peace, democracy, and free-market economies. It was an extraordinary moment, followed all too quickly by what was not anticipated: intrastate crises and the outbreak of violence in many transitional states, including ethnic cleansing, internal wars, and the spillover of conflict into regional conflagrations. The bloc system had managed to suppress these tensions, but now in its wake the race was on within the CSCE and other international organizations to find new tools and mechanisms to provide legitimate political institutions and security within the domestic and regional contexts. The CSCE confronted the situation by changing itself from a multilateral diplomatic process into an international organization (thus the new name, Organization for Security and Cooperation in Europe, or OSCE) devoted to "soft security." Its new mission was focused on conflict early warning and prevention and, as circumstances soon demanded, also post-conflict rehabilitation and democratization.

I have had the opportunity of following these developments since the late 1980s, thanks initially to support from Fulbright-Hayes and the American-Scandinavian Foundation for doctoral research in Finland and Sweden on the third-party role of the neutral and nonaligned states in the CSCE. The University of Helsinki hosted my stay in 1987–88, as well as on many subsequent occasions, and for this I owe a debt of gratitude to Professor Raimo Väyrynen, who also served as a committee member on my doctoral thesis and provided expert advice. I also want to thank Martha Cottam, who served as a committee member, and Thomas Rowe, who served as chair, at the University of Denver, for their support and direction over many years. I also benefited from the assistance and warm reception of the Finnish Institute of International Affairs, then under the direction of Kari Möttölä. I am grateful for access to the Institute's extensive archival materials and documents on the CSCE.

This study on the OSCE's contribution to the establishment of a post-cold war democratic order has been nurtured over the years by the advice of many scholars, numerous interviews with OSCE diplomats and practitioners, and several grants and opportunities to collaborate on related projects. I would like to express my gratitude to Timothy Sisk and the United States Institute of Peace, as well as the Swedish Government and the Swedish Institute for International Affairs for funding and hosting me as a guest researcher. This enabled me to carry out field research to visit OSCE missions in Estonia and Latvia, as well as in Macedonia in 1994–95. Collaboration with Barnett Rubin, who led the South Balkans Working Group at the Center for Conflict Prevention at the Council on Foreign Relations (New York), also provided opportunities to visit the region in the mid-1990s and to deepen my understanding of the challenges there along with local and international responses. I am also grateful to Professor William Zartman for his help over the years and invitations to collaborate on projects at the Brookings Institution and the Austrian Institute for Applied Systems Analysis, which helped me to understand the OSCE's mission in light of the contributions of other regional organizations and their evolution.

I would like to express my gratitude to Raimo Väyrynen and various Finnish scholars who have provided assistance over the years, including Pertti Joeniemi, Harto Hakovirta, and Kirsti and Raimo Lintonen. I also want to give special thanks to Bengt Sundelius for his support and guidance, as well as to Arie Bloed and Ron Zaagman, with whom I had both opportunities to collaborate on research projects on the OSCE and numerous occasions to discuss the OSCE's development. I would also like to give special thanks to Erika Schlager and Robert Hand at the United States Commission on Security and Cooperation in Europe for generously sharing their insights and for providing help with OSCE documents and resources. I owe much of my understanding of the OSCE to these individuals, and I am especially grateful for the many hours they spent sharing their expert knowledge with me.

I would also like to emphasize my appreciation to the dozens of OSCE diplomats, practitioners, and leaders from nongovernmental organizations who I was able to interview at OSCE meetings, including the 1992 review conference; seminars sponsored by the Office on Democratic Elections in Warsaw, Poland; visits to OSCE missions in the field and to the Office of the High Commissioner on National Minorities in The Hague and to OSCE headquarters in Vienna. Most of these people are anonymous in this study, but their voices have been central to the understandings and analytical perspectives I have developed.

Thanks also to Robert and Ruthann Johansen, together with Raimo Väyrynen and Father Theodore Hesburg, for their support of this research while I was a visiting fellow at the Kroc Institute for International Peace Studies at the University of Notre Dame. I would also like to express my appreciation for summer research funding from Illinois State University and the support of the Department of Government and Politics under the able leadership of Jamal Nassar. I would also like to thank friends and colleagues for their helpful comments on the manuscript, including Patricia Davis, who guided me on issues relating to the German Question, and Carlos Parodi, who made helpful suggestions for setting out the study in the first chapter. I also owe a debt of gratitude to two scholars who reviewed the draft manuscript for Syracuse University Press, Louis Kriesberg and John Paul Lederach, who gave me many helpful and important suggestions for improving the study for publication.

Mary Selden Evans, my editor at Syracuse, has been a constant source of encouragement and enthusiasm throughout the revisions and preparation of the book, and I would like to express to her my deep appreciation for her understanding, kind words, good cheer, and support.

Finally, I would like to thank my family members and friends for their loving support and encouragement. Two of my students also deserve special recognition: Aaron Walters and Christine Wolf, who have been of great assistance in the final research phases and preparation of the manuscript. Finally, I would like to thank Marius Mates, who very kindly offered to prepare the tables, and Sarah Walczynski at Illinois State University's Laboratory for Integrated Learning and Technology for her good humor and readiness to help with the final formatting of the manuscript.

In so many ways the individuals and institutions I mentioned above share in the credit for this study, but I am solely responsible for any of its shortcomings.

Author's Note

THE ORGANIZATION on Security and Cooperation in Europe (OSCE) began as the Conference on Security and Cooperation in Europe (CSCE). Throughout the book, I have referred to the CSCE whenever this was historically appropriate, including from its inception in the early 1970s through 1994. Otherwise, I have referred to it as the OSCE, following the name change that took effect in 1995.

From Cold War to Democratic Peace

1 The Dawning of a New Era

ON NOVEMBER 19, 1990, the participating states of the Conference on Security and Cooperation in Europe (CSCE) gathered in Paris to sign the Charter of Paris and celebrate an end to the cold war. But how did the thirty-five CSCE countries, which included the United States, Canada and all of Western and Eastern Europe (except Albania), the Soviet Union, and the neutral and nonaligned states, escape the clutches of the cold war without a violent confrontation, a devastating conventional war, or even a nuclear holocaust? How was it possible that communist regimes could be swept from office throughout the Soviet bloc without Soviet tanks moving in to restore new hard-line Soviet sympathizers? How did East and West manage to overcome decades of political, economic, social, cultural, and military rivalry to herald democracy and universal human rights as the path to a common future? What ideas and normative commitments propelled these revolutionary transformations? Who were the key agents? And what platform and mechanisms of change did they use?

One East-West institution that played a key role in shaping the normative foundations for these wholesale changes is the Conference on Security and Cooperation in Europe (since 1995 renamed the Organization for Security and Cooperation in Europe, or OSCE). By forging an understanding of cooperative security and by embracing the protection of human rights and the primacy of democratic government and free-market economies, the CSCE led the participating states from cold war confrontation toward a democratic peace. In 1990, the CSCE states together faced the dawning of a new era, if not yet the reality of a "Europe Whole and Free."

The diplomatic origins of the OSCE are often traced back to the 1954 Soviet-led efforts to convene an all-European conference to deal with the outstanding issues of World War II, including disarmament, the immutability of borders, and the status of the two Germanies. However, when the CSCE took off in Helsinki in the early 1970s, it encompassed not only Soviet concerns but also Western demands relating to liberal notions of human rights. In contrast to the original Soviet proposal, not only European states but also the United States and Canada participated. The comprehensive and exhaustive rounds of multilateral negotiations that led to the signing of the 1975 Helsinki Final Act were focused on three "Baskets" containing a decalogue of principles on international relations, some provisions for economic and scientific cooperation, and issues of human rights and cultural cooperation. Paradoxically, the Helsinki Accords helped both to stabilize expectations among NATO, the Warsaw Pact, and other participating states, *and* sow the seeds of change. But the far-reaching transformations engendered by the Helsinki agreement took many years and rounds of negotiations to reach fruition. Despite rudimentary instructions and worsening East-West relations, the participating states found the means and political will to continue the Helsinki process through follow-up meetings in Belgrade (1977–78), Madrid (1980–83), and Vienna (1986–89), as well as through various expert meetings. These included the first Conference on Disarmament in Europe (CDE) held (Stockholm, 1984–86), which dealt with Confidence and Security Building Measures (CSBMs). Its on-site inspection provisions paved the way for major breakthroughs in bilateral U.S.-Soviet nuclear arms reductions agreements by the second half of the 1980s. This and other CSCE follow-up and expert meetings culminated in the 1990 Charter of Paris, putting the CSCE on the path to becoming an international organization.[1] Subsequently, the first post-cold war CSCE follow-up meeting was held in Helsinki in 1992 and was followed by three other review conferences in Budapest (1994), Lisbon (1996), and Ankara (1999) (see tables 1–3). The demise of the Soviet Union and Eastern bloc and the end of the cold war are intensely debated among scholars of East-West conflict. However, in some of the prevailing realist accounts, there is an element of uncritical reflection that locates the causes of the end of the cold war in the same basic convictions with which realists argued the Soviet challenge had to be countered. For these scholars "the Cold War's death is essentially synonymous with the Soviet Union's retreat and fragmentation"

1. At the Charter of Paris the unification of Germany reduced the number of CSCE participating states to thirty-four. Subsequently, the number rose to fifty-three states, including (since 1990) the Baltic States, and finally also Albania and the newly formed republics of the former Soviet Union, of which all solicited membership immediately except Georgia. These ten new states entered the CSCE at the January 1992 Prague meeting of the Council of Foreign Ministers. As in other international fora, Russia retained the seat of the former Soviet Union as its successor state. Before opening the March 1992 Helsinki Follow-up, three new states joined: Croatia, Slovenia, and Georgia. The December 1992 Meeting of the CSCE Council of Foreign Ministers prepared the entry of the government of the Slovak-Czech Republic as the other successor state to the Czech and Slovak Federal Republic. One participating state (the former Yugoslavia) was suspended from CSCE participation at the Helsinki Follow-up Meeting in 1992. The Republic of Macedonia became a full participating state of the OSCE in 1995, its membership having been blocked by Greece over a dispute with the name of this former Yugoslav republic.

Helsinki Consultations

November 22, 1972–June 8, 1973

Conference on Security and Cooperation in Europe

Helsinki–Geneva–Helsinki
July 3, 1973–August 1, 1975

Follow-up Meetings (and Summit)

Belgrade: October 4, 1977–March 9, 1978
Madrid: November 11, 1980–September 9, 1983
Vienna: November 4, 1986–January 19, 1989
Paris (Summit): November 19–21, 1990
Helsinki: March 24–July 8, 1992

Review Conferences

Budapest: October 10–December 2, 1994
Lisbon: November 4–22, 1996
Vienna/Istanbul: September 1–20, 1999

Figure 1. CSCE/OSCE Conferences, Summits, and Meetings 1973–1999

(Kegley 1994, 12). Hence, the West's success can be summed up by "peace through strength." The West won through its heavy investment in defense and military preponderance based on assured nuclear destruction, its superior technology and economic resources, and its extensive alliance system. These were the ingredients needed to pull down the communist system (Gaddis 1989; Einhorn 1985). Other realists contend that the system was in any case fatally flawed and destined to collapse from within, having suffered from imperial overreach (Oye 1995; Bunce 1985).

But some scholars argue we should look at a combination of factors to gain a basic understanding of the forces at play in this period of historic change, including the role of new institutions, norms, and rules developed during the post-World War II period that promoted an open world economy, and its multilateral management (Ikenberry 1996; Lebow 1994); the domestic economic and social crises in the Soviet Union (Blacker 1993); international structural factors such as the declining Soviet position in the world (Deudney and Ikenberry 1991–92); and new ideas changing the predominant norms influencing Soviet leadership (Evangelista 1999). Some explanatory frameworks integrate

Peaceful Settlement of Disputes

Montreux: October 31–December 11, 1978
Athens: March 21–April 30, 1984
Valletta: January 15–February 8, 1991

Mediterranean

Valletta: February 13–March 26, 1979
Venice: October 16–26, 1984
Palma de Mallorca: September 24–October 19, 1990

Scientific, Cultural and Economic and Other Issues

Scientific Forum, Hamburg: February 18–March 3, 1980
Environment, Sofia: October 16–November 3, 1989
Economic Cooperation, Bonn: March 19–April 11, 1990
Cultural Heritage, Cracow: May 28–June 7, 1991
National Minorities, Geneva: July 1–19, 1991
Democratic Institutions, November: 4–15, 1991

Military and Security Affairs

Seminar on Military Doctrines January 16–February 5, 1990
Second Seminar on Military Doctrines October 8–18, 1991

Figure 2. CSCE/OSCE Expert Meetings 1978–1991

international and domestic levels of analysis (Checkel 1997, 1993) to assess the impact of peace movements, epistemic communities, and political leadership on change in the Soviet Union and East-West relations (cf. Cortright 1993; Haas 1992; Grosse Stein 1994; Herman 1996). Risse-Kappen (1994), for example, has emphasized the role of transnational coalitions as conveyors of new ideas, especially relating to common security, who aligned with domestic coalitions or decision makers (and thus gained access to the political leadership) to influence their values, norms, interests, or policy choices. Focusing on West Germany, the Soviet Union, and the United States, Risse-Kappen found that domestic structures played a role in determining how successful transnational coalitions were in getting access to key decision makers.

One aspect of the cold war's transformation that these explanatory frameworks have not investigated systematically is the evolution of international consensus on norms for peaceful change. In the aftermath of World War II, there was a considerable gulf between Western and Soviet conceptions of how to deal

CSCE Human Dimension Meetings

Ottawa Meeting on Human Rights and Fundamental Freedoms: 1985
Budapest Cultural Forum: 1985
Bern Meeting on Human Contacts: 1986
London Information Forum: 1989

Conference on the Human Dimension

Paris	May 30–June 23, 1989
Copenhagen	November 19–21, 1990
Moscow	July 9–10, 1992

Human Dimension Implementation Meetings
Office for Democratic Institutions and Human Rights, Warsaw, Poland

September 27–October 15, 1993
October 2–19, 1995
October 12–28, 1997
October 26–November 6, 1998
October 17–27, 2000
September 9–19, 2002

Human Dimension Seminars
Office for Democratic Institutions and Human Rights, Warsaw, Poland

Tolerance: November 1992
Migration: April 1993
National Minorities: May 1993
Free Media: November 1993
Early Warning: January 1994
Migrant Workers: March 1994
Human Dimension in Central Asia: April 1994
Local Democracy: May 1994
Roma: September 1994
Freedom of Association and NGOs: April 1995
Rule of Law: November–December 1995
Freedom of Religion: April 1996
Administration and Observation of Elections: April 1997
The Promotion of Women's Participation in Society: October 1997
Ombudsman and National Human Rights Protection: May 1998
Human Rights: the Role of Field Missions: April 1999
Children and Armed Conflict: May 2000

Figure 3. CSCE/OSCE Human Dimension Meetings and Seminars

with a divided Europe. The Soviet Union wanted a European Security Conference as a surrogate World War II peace treaty to lend its control over Eastern Europe (and especially East Germany) the legitimacy it lacked. The United States would accede to nothing of the sort, not least because of what such an outcome would mean to its key ally, West Germany, which endeavored to keep German reunification on the table. Many Western European countries and the United States pushed to include issues relating to human contact on any agenda dealing with European security issues. For the West, this meant promoting direct contacts between people—not state-led controls on cooperation, as the Soviet bloc insisted. The neutral and nonaligned countries wanted to use the occasion to dismantle the bloc divisions and military alliances to create common security for all of Europe, but most of them also supported the West on the human-contact issues. Although they saw the conference on European security as an opportunity to promote a political process outside the bloc-based structures, this was a prospect neither the United States nor the Soviet Union wanted to entertain. In fact, in the late 1960s and early 1970s, both the Soviet Union and the United States worked hard to increase alliance cohesion within their respective blocs and minimize the centrifugal forces that détente threatened to unleash. Soviet tanks rolling into Czechoslovakia in 1968 played the role of demonstration effects for the Brezhnev Doctrine. The United States worked closely with its allies to hammer out a common NATO policy for détente, which was encapsulated in the Harmel Report. And the European Union launched its first efforts to cooperate on foreign policy with a mechanism known as European Political Cooperation.

In spite of its modest beginnings, the CSCE became an institution that was greater than the sum of its parts. The dynamics of multilateral negotiations produced agreements that often went well beyond what anyone envisioned. For example, the 1975 Final Act brought unimagined costs to the Soviets on human-rights questions along with an unexpected political bonanza for the West. The CSCE's institutional development is itself a story full of surprises, including the fact that one of the more vulnerable and isolated countries of the cold war—Finland—managed to play an extraordinary role in launching the entire process. The expectations its early initiatives created for third-party assistance proved critical for getting a consensus agreement in Helsinki—and for keeping East and West at the table when the post-Helsinki follow-up negotiations became increasingly polemical and specific guidelines for the follow-up process had yet to be agreed upon.

President Gerald Ford signed the Helsinki Accords with great reluctance in the face of newspaper headlines imploring "Gerry don't go." But in little time the Basket III commitments on human rights became a rallying cry for dissidents across the Soviet bloc, so that Ford's successor, Jimmy Carter, made the refusniks' plight a cause célèbre. Thus, the CSCE's early development took many unanticipated twists and turns to make the United States into a committed partner under the Carter presidency, whereas only a few years earlier Richard Nixon had given the launching of the CSCE such scant attention that the United States would have been the last speaker to open the CSCE talks in Helsinki had it not been for the gracious Finns, who as the host state ceded their place on the list.

In contrast the Soviets made sure their delegate cued up in the early morning hours outside the Finnish Foreign Ministry to be first on the list of speakers. They introduced in their opening statement what was essentially a complete draft for a final agreement. They wanted little in the way of negotiations and instead aimed to get a declaratory, symbolic agreement in hand in quick order before human-dimension issues could become a focus of discussion. But the Soviets greatly underestimated their possibilities of controlling the dynamics of the multilateral process of consensus building.

There are more puzzles, too. Why did Western conceptions of human rights rather than socialist interpretations of international law prevail? Did the West simply win, or did the Soviet Union capitulate from within? Alternatively, was the multilateral dialogue and consensus-building process among the thirty-five participating states itself important for shaping a new normative framework? If so, how could a diplomatic process that relied on the "mobilization of public shame" to scrutinize Soviet and East European noncompliance with the 1975 Helsinki Final Act stay at the forefront of universal standard setting in human rights? Why were major breakthroughs in post-cold war security negotiations—such as on-site inspection—first achieved in the CSCE rather than in bilateral negotiations? And how did human rights come to be linked with and made an integral part of security relations between states, so that the military-security principles justifying on-site inspection could open the door to intrusive human-rights monitoring as well? Why did the so-called "suicide theory" or self-destruction of the CSCE never materialize, despite the fact that the cold war tensions flared in its meetings perhaps as in no other fora? What accounts for the initiation, durability, and impact of the OSCE? How did it come to be a tool for peaceful change?

This study argues that the outcome of the cold war would have been different if left to the superpowers alone. Outside the CSCE, superpower relations continued to evolve along a different set of expectations—largely as had been set out in the Basic Principles Agreement of 1972 (BPA). However, in contrast to the CSCE the BPA was based on "norms of aversion," which over time failed to inhibit increases in superpower competitiveness and unilateral advantage-seeking. Thus, superpower cooperation based on the principles of the BPA proved destabilizing in the long term. As the BPA illustrates, the superpowers defined détente in their bilateral relationship in terms of *limits* on their confrontation and competition. They committed themselves to *preventing* the development of situations capable of causing a dangerous exacerbation of their relations; to doing their utmost to *avoid* military confrontation; and to recognizing that efforts to obtain unilateral advantages are *inconsistent* with these objectives (Wilson 1983, 237–38). Thus their reference point was the status quo, not increases in cooperation as had been intended in the multilateral CSCE process.

The principles that guided the U.S. approach to bilateral détente with the Soviets during the Nixon-Kissinger, Ford, and Carter administrations encouraged the framing of cooperation on the basis of simple reciprocity rather than on institutionalized cooperation. The preoccupation with securing at least equal sacrifices and equal outcomes in a negotiation process with the Soviets was simplistic and constraining (Clemens 1990, 260). For Kissinger, any advantage for one side resulted in a loss for the other—an argument he based on the assumption that in a bipolar system outcomes are zero-sum (Welch Larson 1991, 355). This meant cooperation depended on a political or technical definition of equality but not necessarily on increasing trust or common understandings. Thus, if agreements were necessary, they had to be carefully balanced; and because the Russians could not be trusted, the agreements also had to be independently verifiable.

There were also important, persistent differences in the way East and West interpreted détente, for which the BPA provided no mechanisms to resolve. For Brezhnev, superpower détente meant "a certain trust and ability to take one another's legitimate interests into account" (Jowitt 1977, 203). However, détente did not mean that the larger conflict between the two systems would end but rather that the conflict would not erupt in war. The main purpose of the policy of coexistence was to shift the class and ideological struggle to the nonmilitary sector. For Soviet military leaders, their armed forces represented "an effective factor promoting the development of progressive social processes," deterring the aggressor, protecting the socialist community, and limiting the activities of the imperialists in other regions of the world. But the Soviets were less prepared to realize that these policies increased Western European insecurities and gave rise to demands for reinforcing the U.S. nuclear guarantee. Moreover, Western Europeans feared that "the negation of American superiority would deprive the USA of leverage vis-à-vis the USSR, which the Americans undoubtedly had during the Cuban missile crisis" (Haslam 1990, 44). They also feared that U.S.-Soviet détente might evolve into a U.S.-Soviet enténte at the expense of their own security.

During détente, the way the superpowers framed the issues in contention also tended to undermine, rather than facilitate, more cooperation. For example, Henry Kissinger maintained that arms did not cause tensions; political differences did. This argument downplayed the psychological impact of the arms race and perceived threats between East and West on the escalation of conflict and tensions. It also allowed Kissinger and Nixon to argue that, because the Soviet nuclear arms build-up promised to negate U.S. superiority in any case, it was strategically advantageous to use negotiations on parity to get Soviet concessions on other issues. Hence, Kissinger initially subordinated arms control with the Soviets to resolving the political issues of a divided Europe, Vietnam, and the Middle East. This approach tended to link highly intractable issues without creating any incentives for solution. In fact, this realization led him to later abandon the strategy (Larson 1991).

In contrast, despite the destabilizing effect of renewed superpower tensions on international fora from the late 1970s to the mid-1980s, multilateral East-West cooperation continued to develop within the CSCE process based on the Helsinki norms and principles. This fact suggests that multilateralizing cooperation afforded some means of insulating East-West relations from the vagaries of superpower confrontation while gradually giving rise to a new basis for their relationship.

The principle objective of this study is to develop a normative account of the role played by third parties in this process of peaceful change. The focus is two-fold. It looks at how the neutral and nonaligned countries helped to end the cold war by (1) acting as intellectual entrepreneurs and (2) underpinning the CSCE's institutionalization. The normative transformation of conflict involves changing the mechanisms and rules by which adversaries relate to each other as well as forging consensus on new principles and purposes for working together (cf. Kriesberg, Northrup, and Thorson 1989; Väyrynen 1991; Kratochwil 1989). Norms play a key role in conflict because they serve as guidance devices or standards by which decisions can be made and appropriate evaluations of action judged (Finnemore and Sikkink 1998; March and Olsen 1998, 1989).

Norms allow people to relate to each other along a range of actions. They "allow people to pursue goals, share meanings, communicate with each other, criticize assertions, and justify actions" (Kratochwil 1989, 11). However, not all norms are the same where conflict transformation is concerned. In fact we can distinguish between different classes of norms, some of which trap adversaries into conflict spirals and others of which transform.[2] For example, some

2. Here I am following Kratochwil's discussion (1989) of different classes of norms rooted in distinctions between first, second, and third-party law. The first concerns such speech acts as threats or commands, like the Monroe Doctrine. The second-party context deals with strategic behavior among parties related to the recognition of mixed motives, or interdependence of decision making, as occurs in such problematic social situations as the prisoner's dilemma. The third-party context

norms can trap parties in a structure of confrontation, with each side attempting to impose its own will on the other. This is the case with norms underpinning such institutions as genocide, ethnic cleansing, the nuclear arms race, or slavery—which norms justify the total imposition of one party's will on another. However, other kinds of norms can transform conflict by providing adversaries with standard solutions that help them mutually define and pursue their interests. In this case, norms can be instruments of peaceful change. They can shape expectations about acceptable and appropriate ways to govern behavior and manage change nonviolently. Kratochwil suggests that norms that have this transforming capacity act as "implicit" third parties (1989, 81).

Norms can provide a range of solutions to social problems. Some classes of norms are aimed at putting limits on unacceptable behavior, while others build up trust to work out specific areas of joint interest or engender cooperative relations more comprehensively (Ayer 1994). For example, norms underpinning *aversion* agreements do not require any change in the level of trust between the parties. Rather, the agreement is based on the parties' tacit or explicit commitment to avoid situations that could exacerbate tensions and lead to dangerous confrontation. Hence such agreements have the function of expressing salient limits that the parties commit themselves not to exceed and of mitigating conflict escalation. De-escalatory measures are typical of aversion agreements. They may include a tacit or explicit recognition of spheres of influence or arrangements to regulate competition over them—as in the case of the 1973 Basic Principles Agreement signed between the United States and the Soviet Union. Cease fires, troop withdrawals, the establishment of hot lines, or advance scheduling of military exercises are other examples.

Reassurance agreements, in contrast, are based on the recognition of some minimal degree of shared interests among the parties. Such normative solutions can help build trust among adversaries by calling for limited or incremental cooperative acts, such as confidence-building measures (Ayer 1994). However, these agreements tend to be issue specific, and thus ad hoc arrangements. They aim at relieving tensions more than at transforming adversarial relations in a comprehensive fashion. These agreements are also based on norms of simple reciprocity, meaning that "specified partners exchange items of equivalent value in a strictly delimited sequence." Any obligations are clearly specified in terms of rights and duties of particular actors (Keohane 1989, 134).

A third type of norm underpins *institutional* agreements. They set standards for acceptable practices and pattern behavior. Institutional cooperation

---

deals with the use of preexisting rules to settle or mediate a dispute. Kratochwil's analysis points to how norms emerge to solve different kinds of problems of coordination and collaboration, and highlights the role of institutional norms for solving obstacles to cooperation.

has three additional normative mechanisms lacking in aversion—and convergence-type agreements. Institutional cooperation is based on (1) norms of diffuse reciprocity that build up trust and guide conduct; (2) commitments that are internalized in the parties' belief systems; and (3) governance mechanisms, such as tools for monitoring and sanctioning. Diffuse reciprocity means there is a reduction in contingency as the condition for cooperation (Keohane 1989, 134). A rough equivalence is the general rule. The contingent nature of obligations under diffuse reciprocity has both a past dimension (reciprocation in response to the benefits conferred by others in the past) and a future dimension, since at times actors will have obligations that are yet to be fulfilled. Gouldner argues this contributes substantially to the stability of social systems (1960, 175). In addition, the shared conception of the moral rectitude of repayment and of complying with one's obligations sustains diffuse reciprocity.

Institutional norms guide cooperation by shaping commitments that encompass shared understandings. Commitments are *internalized* when they become part of the members' social practices and belief systems, as reflected in grassroots, legislative, judicial, or foreign-policy decision-making processes, principles, and aims. The commitments should be both indivisible and universal. That is, all participating states should be under the same obligations. For example, there should not be a separate body of international law only for socialist states, as the Soviets sought to create in the CSCE. There should not be special considerations, such as a limited geographic scope, or functional obligations for some parties and not others (Caporaso 1993, 73). Institutionalization occurs when commitments become deeply embedded so that "the behavior of those engaged in [the institution] can be corrected by an appeal to its own rule" (Keohane 1989, 163). Violations should be the exception, and they should not jeopardize the rule-effectiveness of the institution (Rittberger and Zürn 1990, 16). Institutionalized cooperation aims both to channel conflict behaviors constructively and to keep in check developments that might undermine the parties' relations.

Just because there is a need for a new norm does not mean that it will be supplied. Someone has to see the need for a new response and agree to provide it, promote it, or get others to mutually accept it (Thomson 1993, 78). Finnemore and Sikkink (1998) treat the emergence of institutional norms in international relations as a three-stage process that moves from the emergence of a norm to broad norm acceptance to internalization. The first stage involves persuasion by norm entrepreneurs, who "attempt to convince a critical mass of states (norm leaders) to embrace new norms. The second stage is characterized more by a dynamic imitation as the norm leaders attempt to socialize other states to become norm followers." Finnemore and Sikkink argue that "the exact motivation for the second stage where the norms 'cascade' through the rest of the population (in this case, of states) may vary." However, they find that "a combination of pressure for conformity, desire to enhance international legitimation, and the desire of state leaders to enhance their self-esteem facilitate norm cascades." Norms are internalized when they are taken for granted and thus are no longer a matter for public debate (1998, 895). Norm entrepreneurs are motivated by empathy, altruism, and ideational commitments to campaign for new standards of conduct. To carry this out, they engage in activities to frame the norm in ways to compete with prevailing social behaviors. They also use organizational platforms, which may involve the mobilization of a social movement, establishment of transnational networks, international organizations, or combinations of these (Finnemore and Sikkink 1998, 896–99).

How did the CSCE come to serve as a platform for East and West to agree on a set of norms and principles for resolving the cold war conflict? There is no doubt that the main antagonists faced many obstacles to reaching such agreements. Even though the Soviet Union proposed the idea of dealing with the cold war by convening a European Security Conference in 1954, there were many problems that blocked the initiative, including such basic questions as who should participate? Under what set of rules? In what kind of forum? To deal with which issues?

One factor that has not been closely examined in the literature is the role of third parties as norm entrepreneurs and facilitators in promoting the CSCE's development. Did they act as precursors or catalysts to promote peaceful change? Did their contributions help supply the kind of metanorm that Axelrod (1986) considers essential for the institutionalization of cooperation? In the CSCE, the third parties in question were the neutral and nonaligned European states (especially Austria, Finland, Sweden, Switzerland, and Yugoslavia—the core members of the CSCE neutral and nonaligned [N+N] grouping). The N+N themselves had a stake in overcoming the divisions of the cold war. Continued East-West confrontation and competition did nothing but further exacerbate their own sense of insecurity. Yet because of their neutral or nonaligned status, they were useful to both East and West. Both superpowers sought to use the third-party states' influence potential with the other bloc to promote their own interests. This translated into N+N leverage, which helped the third parties, despite their small size, to build consensus agreements and propel the CSCE process forward toward each subsequent follow-up meeting. In fact, the greater the East-West tensions, the more difficult the situation but also the more critical the N+N role was in getting all the parties to a final consensus agreement in most CSCE meetings.[3]

3. While the focus in this study is primarily on the N+N as mediators, other states intervened on occasion in the East-West conflict, too, especially Poland in relation to its promotion of the Rapacki plan (Kriesberg [1992] calls this a "quasi-third party role") and Romania as a bridge between the N+N and the Eastern bloc, and also as the most independent of the Warsaw Pact countries. In addi-

A variety of resources shaped the N+N's influence potential as third parties. The countries differed among themselves in terms of the doctrinal basis of their foreign-policy orientation and identity or standing between East and West as neutral or nonaligned states. These differences often had a basis in historical experiences, as well as varying national capabilities and sensitivities to East-West conflict. As a result, the N+N tended to exercise different types of leadership roles as third parties in the CSCE. These differences shaped in significant ways their influence on the outcomes to the negotiations, including their capacity to build consensus, or alternatively, to influence the substantive nature of the agreements in directions more favorable to their own security concerns and stakes in the East-West conflict.

After the formal CSCE negotiations began in 1973, the N+N began to intervene in the CSCE as a grouping of countries, coordinating their third-party initiatives and efforts. Together they were often able to exploit their own strengths and minimize the limitations of their different styles of mediation. This fact helps account for their third-party successes in the CSCE. Indeed, most experts agree that the influence of these countries was disproportionate to their size or importance. Nevertheless, the literature on third-party mediation has not looked closely at how differences in third-party intervention may influence the normative outcomes of conflict transformation. The principle assumption in this study is that the extent and nature of the outcome achieved depends on both (1) the third party's behavior, conceptualized in terms of its strategy and the type of actions its intervention involves (e.g., coercive, instrumental, and facilitative approaches); and (2) certain situational variables (including the third parties' capabilities and the type of conflict issues and dilemmas the third party must resolve).

Do mediators play key roles in the genesis and spread of norms and their institutionalization? Can mediators be a surrogate for the missing metanorm or mechanisms needed for cooperation to emerge and stabilize? To answer these questions, Part 1 of this study develops a theoretical framework for understanding the normative potential of third-party mediation for transforming conflict. As we shall see in chapter 2, coercive, instrumental, and facilitative mediators all impact conflict normatively, but with different implications for the possibilities for institutionalizing cooperation. *Coercive* mediators tend to impose agreements rather than engender them. The norms governing the parties' behavior are supplied and enforced from the outside, not internalized by the

---

tion, the European Community often provided alternative proposals to Western positions (generally those forwarded by NATO or the United States) and its own initiatives at various points in the CSCE negotiations. Finally, although not part of the N+N grouping and also not a member of the Western alliance until 1986, Spain intervened at key junctures in CSCE negotiations as a third party—and especially during the second follow-up meeting in Madrid, which Spain hosted.

parties themselves. While this type of intervention impedes the institutionalization of cooperation, it can be effective for producing important intermediate results (e.g., preventing a relapse to violence). In contrast, facilitative and instrumental mediators, which are the types of third-party intervention found in the CSCE, contribute to the institutionalization of cooperation, but in different ways. Building on Princen (1992), we find that facilitators' intervention can lead to institutionalized outcomes because they promote the direct interaction of adversaries. Their role as norm precursors rests especially in their ability to persuade others to change. They lay the groundwork for this by forging agreements on rules for communicating and interacting, by building up trust, and by creating consensus on common understandings. *Instrumental* mediators have clear ideas about alternative approaches and innovations; this mediator's approach succeeds because other actors are persuaded by the merits of its diagnosis and its ability to get them to redefine their goals or political agenda (see also Hermann 1993 on types of leadership; Young 1991). Their role as a norm entrepreneur is focused on criticizing other states for failing to adopt the new norm, on constructing frames to promote the new norm, or on calling attention to issues at stake. They take their campaign headlong into the "highly contested normative space where they must compete with other norms and perceptions of interest" (Finnemore and Sikkink 1998, 897).

In the absence of institutional mechanisms, these third-party functions can extend into the postagreement phase of international negotiations (cf. Spector and Zartman, 2003; Underdal 1994). Obviously, coercive mediators impose settlements and then continue to enforce their implementation. But the subsequent intervention of instrumental and facilitative third parties can also be critical for the further development of cooperation, for mitigating the return to competitive behaviors, and ultimately for institutionalizing principles and mechanisms of peaceful change. However, the more it advocates its ideas, the less the instrumental mediator can shape consensus on substance. And the more the facilitative mediator adjusts its own position as it takes cues from the negotiation context about where the consensus is emerging, the more it risks being perceived as weak and taking orders from one or another of the adversaries. This situation can undermine the legitimacy and trust it enjoys, thus eroding its power or influence potential.

Unlike traditional third-party mediation, in the development of the CSCE the source of third-party intervention came from within the system of East-West conflict, not from outside it. This is different from the notion of a mediator as an "outsider-neutral" contracted to help resolve the conflict. Indeed, it is commonly assumed that the outsider mediator's effectiveness, legitimacy, and fairness has to do with its "externality," that is, its lack of connection or commitment to either side in the conflict or to the issues at stake. Because it has no investment in the outcome except in helping the parties reach a settlement, the outsider mediator can be neutral and make unbiased judgments (Wehr and Lederach 1996, 55–56).

The effectiveness of an "insider-partial" mediator role, by contrast, depends on "its internality and partiality." Its "acceptability to the conflictants is rooted not in distance from the conflict or objectivity regarding the issues, but rather in connectedness and trusted relationship with the conflict parties" (Wehr and Lederach 1996, 58). Trust comes partly from the fact that the mediator has to live with the consequences of the outcome, just as do the disputants. The insider-partial gains entry to the dispute through trust and its effectiveness is rooted in its knowledge of the conflict, the parties, and the problems. While trust is important in mediation in general, it is the key criterion for selecting insider-partials. Wehr and Lederach have studied the "insider-partial" as a type of mediator likely to be associated with "traditional cultural settings, where primary face-to-face relations continue to characterize political, economic, and social exchange, and where tradition has been less eroded by modernity" (1996, 59). However, multilateral contexts like the CSCE also present settings within which the conditions of internality are paramount in the selection of third parties. For both the instrumental and facilitative mediators, conflicting parties must trust the mediator in order for it to be accepted and maintain effectiveness.

Parts 2 and 3 of this study survey the origins of East-West conflict and the 1954 Soviet idea for a European security conference. This time frame encompasses the emergence of the CSCE through its post-cold war restructuring. The transformation of East-West conflict was a long-term incremental process of adjustment in adversarial relations, from confrontation to essentially ad hoc, or tacit, cooperation to institutionalized cooperation in the CSCE/OSCE.

Finland's 1969 initiative to host the CSCE, along with its role as a facilitator, helped clarify basic questions of institution building and thus laid the groundwork for launching the CSCE. Together with other nonbloc states, Finland intervened to build consensus on the CSCE Blue Book. It set out the basic CSCE modalities, rules of procedure, and normative commitments to be negotiated in the main CSCE meeting that produced the 1975 Helsinki Final Act. The N+N continued to intervene as third parties in the follow-up meetings, even while laying the groundwork for CSCE supervisory functions and for the CSCE's continuity. This fact helped secure the institutionalization of the CSCE and mitigate the destabilizing effects of the superpowers' manipulation of the rules of procedure to gain unilateral advantage. Such polemics threatened to end the CSCE at its first follow-up meeting and on many later occasions.

The Helsinki Final Act was widely publicized in the Eastern bloc as a monumental achievement in securing the legitimacy of post-World War II borders. However, the Helsinki Accords had an impact on domestic society in Eastern

Europe and the Soviet Union that was never anticipated. By confirming the right of the individual to know and act upon his or her human rights, the Final Act provided a legitimizing framework around which groups throughout the Eastern bloc mobilized and monitored their government's compliance. This situation ensured that the institutionalization of the Helsinki Final Act would be anything but routine and cooperative. The dissidents' activity raised the stakes of the first follow-up meeting at Belgrade in 1977 and influenced calculations among all the participating states about the political utility of the CSCE. Under the leadership of the new Carter administration, the United States adjusted its strategy to emphasize Basket III, and made the promotion of human rights a pillar of its foreign policy.

For the Soviets, too, the importance of the CSCE changed over time. Initially it was all they had in the way of international recognition of the post-World War II borders. But the fact that the Soviets put up with having detailed accounts of human-rights abuses laid out before the international community underscores the overriding importance they also attached to achieving a reduction in the level of military preparedness in Europe and of relieving the pressures of military spending on the Soviet domestic economy. This is a future-oriented dimension of the Soviet investment in the CSCE, evident both in its 1980 proposal for convening a conference on disarmament in Europe and in its proposal to replace the Mutual and Balanced Force Reduction talks (MBFR) with a multilateral approach to arms reductions under the umbrella of the CSCE.

The Soviet investment in the past achievements of the CSCE and expectations of its future potentialities was a key source of leverage for the West. However, by the 1986 Vienna meeting, there was still another shift in the Soviet evaluation of the CSCE: Gorbachev could use it to demonstrate to the West that "new thinking" was real (cf. Grosse Stein 1994; Risse-Kappen 1994; Checkel 1993). At the same time, he could use the CSCE to justify to hard-liners in Moscow the necessity of perestroika and glasnost. Even Schevardnadze intimated in Paris in October 1988 that the Soviet proposal to host the third phase of the CSCE Human Dimension meeting in Moscow "would assist the Gorbachev regime to correct international human rights abuses, resolve questions on political prisoners, and alter its penal code" (Korey 1993, 245). In effect, it was much more difficult for Gorbachev to push through the human-rights agreements in Moscow than to get agreement in Vienna on the CSCE with the West.[4] It was for such reasons that neutral drafts in the Vienna Follow-up negotiations on CSCE principles and Basket III, and later on the N+N comprehen-

4. Ambassador Oleg Grinevsky, interview by author, tape recording, Embassy of the Russian Federation, Stockholm, Sweden, Dec. 20, 1994.

sive draft document, were useful to the Eastern countries; coming from the neutrals, the Eastern bloc diplomats could more easily sell stronger human-rights commitments to their capital (Lehne 1991, 118–21).[5]

Eventually, the CSCE paved the way for historic breakthroughs in East-West diplomacy. From the experience of having U.S. inspectors on Soviet soil under the confidence and security-building measures regime negotiated at the 1984–86 Stockholm CDE, Russian military officials could confirm firsthand that nothing disastrous happened by opening up and cooperating; they could see the Soviet Union still existed. As Ambassador Oleg Grinevsky explains, this was a profound breakthrough psychologically. It was also imperative politically. It was impossible for Gorbachev to introduce economic and democratic reforms without first reassessing the threat from the West.[6]

For the Soviet Union and the Eastern bloc countries, the CSCE definition of security represented a revolution in ideology, which had been promoted across the bloc lines by other actors through other channels as well. Gorbachev himself was influenced by the approach of the arms-control community in the West advocating greater transparency, as well as by proposals for common security promoted in the Palme Commission report, and by Egon Bahr, which also had found support among the peace research community, the peace movement, and social democrats in Western Europe, who incorporated them into their party platforms (cf. Risse-Kappen 1994).[7] By February 1986 Gorbachev had concluded that

> Security cannot be built endlessly on fear of retaliation, in other words, on the doctrines of "containment" or "deterrence." . . . In the context of the relations between the USSR and the USA, security can only be mutual, and if we take international relations as a whole it can only be universal. The highest wisdom is

5. See also Commission on Security and Cooperation in Europe, United States Congress, Phase III and IV of the Vienna Review Meeting of the Conference on Security and Cooperation in Europe, May 5-July 31, 1987, and Sept. 22-Dec. 18, 1987. Washington, D.C.: U.S. Government Printing Office, 1988: 7, 9.

6. Ambassador Oleg Grinevsky, interview by author, tape recording, Embassy of the Russian Federation, Stockholm, Dec. 20, 1994.

7. On reading the Palme Commission report, Gorbachev discovered a useful basis for launching foreign-policy reforms: the report came from a neutral country, but it represented a consensus already achieved politically among social democrats and liberals, including the United States (which was represented by Cyrus Vance) and political leaders from the East and the Third World. Political possibilities existed for the reception of such ideas. Thus, Gorbachev determined to pick up this consensus and build on it because the Palme Commission report laid the groundwork (conceptually and politically) and it enhanced the likelihood of a positive response to changes in Soviet policy drawing on common security principles. Anders Fehrm (former Secretary-General, Palme Commission), written notes, telephone interview, Stockholm, Dec. 19, 1994.

> not in caring exclusively for oneself, especially to the detriment of the other side. It is vital that all should feel equally secure. . . . In the military sphere we intend to act in such a way as to give nobody grounds for fear, even imagined ones, about their security. (as quoted in Rissse-Kappen 1994, 200–01)

As Gorbachev came to endorse many of the principles of common security, he brought to the fore "a new face and content to Soviet military and foreign policy." This new thinking included the recognition that

1. The needs of all humanity take priority over class, national, or other interests.

2. All countries are now interdependent even while contradictions remain among them.

3. Security must be mutual between the Soviet Union and the United States; among all nations it must be universal.

4. War, in the nuclear age, cannot be an effective way to "continue" politics. Even local wars can escalate. Political dialogue and compromise are the proper way to resolve disputes.

5. Military parity between the superpowers and the threat of nuclear retaliation do not guarantee peace; therefore, arms levels must be reduced and nuclear arms gradually eliminated.

6. Military deployments should be guided by "reasonable sufficiency"—adequate for defense but inadequate to threaten others.

7. Comprehensive "security" must include economic as well as military-political dimensions. In short, the "all-human problems" facing the "whole of civilization" demand cooperation from and with all countries. (Clemens 1990, 168)

The Soviet withdrawal from Eastern Europe and then from East Germany was thus the result of a "comprehensively revised conception of security," where the common interests of humankind and the tools of dialogue, cooperation, and interaction replaced class struggle and informed a determination to come to a modus vivendi with Germany (Adomeit 1991, 546). Consequently, solutions to cold war conflict in Europe came not from unilateralism and strength, but rather from the superpowers' decision to work through multilateral arrangements and structure their relations on the basis of mutually agreed norms. Multilateral fora like the CSCE process contributed new information, as well as new perspectives that increased the participating states' knowledge about the problems at stake. The process also contributed to cognitive evolution, yielding more holistic and more interconnected understandings and principles (see also Haas 1990, 192). This fact helped diminish perceptions of threat between East and West, which is a fundamental factor attributed to the development of new thinking in the Soviet Union (Hermann 1992). Gradually the

West tested and became convinced that glasnost, perestroika, and democratization meant real change on the Soviets' part.

The nature of rule-making in the CSCE also contributed to these normative changes. The drawbacks of not having a more fully developed institutional structure (with a permanent secretariat and CSCE bureaucracy) must be judged against the advantages of the more flexible structure and process that came to define the CSCE process between 1973 and 1990. First, the light institutional structure, coupled with the decision to make CSCE agreements politically but not legally binding, meant the CSCE enjoyed a high degree of political significance. It also meant that the CSCE was immediately valid and in force as of the signature of the heads of state in Helsinki in 1975; there was no waiting period for national legislatures to ratify it.

Second, the drafting style of the CSCE in comparison to other international instruments dealing with human rights may also help explicate the CSCE's capacity to adapt rapidly to changing conditions on the ground in Eastern Europe and thus to remain relevant as Europe underwent a far-reaching process of transformation from the mid-to-late 1980s. Whereas traditional human-rights instruments "tend to proclaim a series of general principles, a limited number of specific rules, and some exceptions," the CSCE began with Principle VII of the Helsinki Final Act's Basket I, which provides a general statement on human rights (Buergenthal 1993, 6). Each succeeding CSCE agreement has added to the body of the human-dimension commitments, making them increasingly specific and spelling out the meaning of earlier commitments by creating more rules and clarifying the scope of their application. As Buergenthal notes (1993, 6), "this type of interpretive rule-making takes the place of judicial interpretation. While not adjudicatory in character, it serves to anticipate and resolve disputes about the specific meaning of CSCE commitments. It also promotes compliance by eliminating or weakening legal arguments that have been or might be advanced to excuse nonperformance." The West used this approach to "plug loopholes and redress textual ambiguities utilized by the former Soviet Union and its allies to avoid complying with the CSCE commitments" (6).

Buergenthal argues that the flexibility of this "legislative approach" worked so well because it was not subject to domestic constraints, it could dramatically transform and expand the human-dimension commitments, and it could rapidly take advantage of the changing political climate throughout Eastern Europe. In his view,

> these achievements would, on the whole, have been impossible had the participating states been drafting and voting on treaty provisions. Not only is the treaty-making process very slow—it takes a long time for a treaty to be drafted and adopted, and longer yet to enter into force—treaty provisions tend also to

> be less susceptible to evolution, particularly if no judicial or quasi-judicial bodies exist with jurisdiction to interpret and apply them on a regular basis. (Buergenthal 1993, 7; 1991)

These observations account for the degree to which the CSCE was able to score pioneering breakthroughs on human-dimension commitments (e.g., national minority rights in Copenhagen in 1990) even as the East-West system was changing underfoot.

Third, the CSCE was also quite transparent as a political process; the periodic follow-up and expert meetings facilitated direct contact between diplomats and NGOs. As a result, it was easier for dissidents and human-rights groups to get the attention of Western governments and the diplomatic community, and hence to get their issues on the agenda. The political importance of the process, while yielding polemics that exacerbated the negotiations, also underscored the importance of the contacts between delegation members and human-rights groups and dissidents.

Fourth, the fact that the actual monitoring of the Helsinki Final Act was carried out primarily by the dissidents themselves—not by bureaucrats within an organizational structure—also enhanced the political significance of the CSCE. The CSCE was dynamic and transformative because it directly challenged the legitimacy of communist regimes and led to the creation of independent voices within these societies. These voices were harbingers of a new era, calling for and ultimately galvanizing revolution throughout most of the Eastern bloc.

In the mid-1980s, the argument that the United States had more to gain by using the CSCE to press the East for changes than by renouncing the CSCE carried the day. Signs of such long-term commitment helped cast a shadow of the future over East-West cooperation. The intersessional meetings leading up to the 1986 Vienna Follow-up meeting sustained the continuity of the CSCE between the review conferences and provided an important instrument for ongoing monitoring and political accountability. The United States took advantage of the 1985 Budapest and 1986 Bern meetings to work out numerous bilateral human-rights cases with the Soviet Union. These meetings also had an information function in that they provided an opportunity for the West to gauge the ongoing changes in the Soviet Union. For sceptics, such as Congressman Steny Hoyer, the changes were not having a real impact on the fate of human rights in the Soviet Union and Eastern Europe, but rather were tactical or diversionary—a means of reinvigorating a passive public in order to stimulate the stagnant Soviet economy. Like the Soviet who went to the doctor and asked to see two specialists, one an ear, nose, and throat doctor and the other an eye doctor, some U.S. officials also claimed they did not see what they heard.

However, by 1987 it was clear to some experts that the reorientation of Soviet policy was more than "merely words." As Garthoff noted, the important question was whether the West would have the necessary patience to "test and determine how far the Soviet Union will now go."[8] The CSCE afforded the West the opportunity of such a test in an environment where changes in Soviet policy and action could be probed, measured, encouraged, and legitimized. He advocated a policy of constructive engagement.

Thus, even though Reagan administration officials argued the CSCE was important for the smaller NATO countries to negotiate human rights with the Soviets—but the United States could do this directly (see Korey 1993), the CSCE remained a key source of legitimacy for these claims and also a means for the United States to leverage Soviet compliance. Paradoxically, by using a linkage strategy to leverage Soviet cooperation on human rights, the United States was gradually drawn into accepting the multilateralization of security arrangements for Europe. This process was intensified with the 1984–86 Stockholm CDE, which later led to the decision to bring the MBFR talks (ongoing in Vienna since 1973) under the CSCE and finally to the creation of a CSCE Forum for Security Cooperation. This multilateralist orientation is also evidenced by NATO's eastward reach in the post-cold war era, which resulted in the creation of the North Atlantic Cooperation Council, the establishment of Partnership for Peace, and finally the expansion of NATO membership itself (Yost 1998).

By the mid-1980s, a number of developments pointed to the increasing institutionalization of the CSCE and its governing capacity, independent of N+N intervention. In fact, by the start of the 1986 Vienna Follow-up there were no longer any questions about "whether to meet at all." The question was rather "where, when, and under what conditions follow-up meetings will occur." Thus the durability of the CSCE process was secured institutionally rather than by means of third-party intervention. The progress achieved in the 1986 Stockholm CDE agreement on the CSBMs pointed to a greater common understanding between East and West on improving security. By the Vienna CSCE meeting there was a growing commonality of views between East and West on the human dimension of the CSCE and common interpretation of CSCE commitments in this area, too, which gave rise to a widening basis of consensual knowledge.

Lessons on Peaceful Change and Securing a Democratic Peace

The key theoretical findings and lessons of this study are as follows. First, the possibilities for promoting institutionalized outcomes among adversaries may

8. "Soviet Policy, Eastern Europe, and American Policy," statement by Ambassador Raymond Garthoff, Hearing Before the Commission on Security and Cooperation in Europe. One Hundredth Congress, First Session, Gorbachev, "Glasnost" and Eastern Europe, June 18, 1987. Washington, D.C.: Government Printing Office, 1987: 15.

be determined in important ways by the type of third-party strategy and its normative capacity to effect peaceful change. Second, institutionalizing peace processes is an important means of transforming conflicts. It facilitates incremental change, lays the foundation for alternative relationships, and allows opportunities to enhance and adjust rule-effectiveness to changing political circumstances. By promoting a largely transparent multilateral process, détente was turned into a phenomenon from both above and below.

Linking human rights and security over the years in the CSCE negotiations proved an important means of shaping a new understanding of East-West security rooted in cooperation. Cooperative security came to be defined by principles of transparency in interstate affairs and of mutual consent, including the right of states to hold other states accountable for the treatment of their citizens (Nolan 1994). In this way, the Palme Commission's promotion of common security, a simple idea with radical implications, acquired concrete expression in the CSCE (Independent Commission on Disarmament and Security Issues 1982). The CSCE approached the subject in terms of the indivisibility and comprehensiveness of security.

Third, postagreement negotiations function as a means to continuously refine initial agreements, monitor implementation, and clarify ambiguities or violations. Here again the continued presence and intervention of third parties using instrumental and facilitative strategies can stabilize the process and secure the internalization of norms. Their intervention can help mitigate the return to competitive or conflict-oriented behaviors that could undermine the process and the adversaries' achievements.

Nevertheless, conflict serves multiple functions—not only the explicit purposes of the parties concerned but also potentially the suppression of other conflicts or their displacement. The attempt to transform conflict may not adequately deal with all these aspects, and thus may bring in its wake unintended consequences. To the extent possible, secondary or latent functions of conflict should be anticipated with contingency plans to minimize over the short and long term the potential for destabilization and violence. The CSCE, like most other international organizations, was not equipped to deal with the unexpected consequences of the cold war's transformation, which led to the collapse of empires and states and to the proliferation of interethnic conflicts. If the CSCE was influential in delegitimizing communist governments, it was substantially unprepared to manage intrastate violence. Chapter 9 analyzes CSCE/OSCE efforts to reform its institutional competencies to manage the outbreak of internal conflicts in the 1990s, along with the relatively weak security structure that emerged. Special attention is given to its efforts to develop mechanisms for conflict early warning and prevention, which have been innovative, if limited, security tools. But as we shall see, they are largely premised on the kinds of facilitative and instrumental forms of third-party intervention that were key to the CSCE's own development.

This study of the transformation of East-West conflict through institutionalized cooperation is timely for a number of reasons. First, understanding how conflict outcomes are shaped by different types of third-party strategies and the timing of their intervention is all the more relevant given post-cold war efforts to make regional organizations such as the Association of Southeast Asian Nations (ASEAN), the Organization for American States (OAS), or the African Union better conflict managers (Caballero-Anthony 1998; Simon 1998; Muñoz 1998; Vaky 1993; Shifter 1997; Deng and Zartman 2002). The new emphasis on early warning and conflict prevention also means that, to be effective, facilitative strategies must be introduced very early (cf. Boutros-Ghali's 1992 *Agenda for Peace*). Although the OSCE is still somewhat of a novel organization today, there have been several proposals to develop similar multilateral institutions in other parts of the world to overcome animosity and stabilize relations (Commission on Security and Cooperation in Europe 1995). For example, the Soviets have long advocated a CSCE-type conference for Asia (Youtz and Midford 1992; Korey 1993, 221). Likewise, proposals have circulated to launch CSCE-type processes in the Middle East, among the littoral states of the Mediterranean, and among the states of Africa (von Groll and Meyer 1996; Ghebali 1993; Schimmelfennig 1993; Deng and Zartman 2002). Such proposals point to possibilities for the further institutionalization of international politics and to the nonhierarchical, decentralized type of international governance to which institutions like the OSCE contribute (Mayer, Rittberger, and Zürn 1993).

BARNETT, FINNEMORE, AND ADLER refer to these as security communities in formation (1998). Already experiencing significantly decreased fears of their former bloc enemies, OSCE states may be considered an "ascendant security community." However, the OSCE states have yet to reach the mature stage of shared identity and future where there is little or no probability that conflicts will lead to wars. Indeed, regional and subregional tensions have presented new security challenges in many of the former communist areas, including in the Balkans, Transcaucasia, the Baltic states (especially Latvia and Estonia), and Eurasia. Further comparative studies of other emergent security communities would delineate more precisely the explanatory power of the present analysis for identifying patterns of conflict transformation and causes of success or failure for institutionalizing cooperation among former adversaries in regional contexts. Such studies may also help us understand how the international community is becoming increasingly networked through overlapping institutional arrangements and how this may contribute to more transparency and democratic governance. Institutions like the OSCE seem to be rewriting key aspects of the Westphalian system, legitimizing the right of the international community to hold states accountable for their treaty obligations and normative commitments while also transnationalizing control of the means and use of force, which monopoly used to be the sovereign state's exclusive prerogative (Kaldor 2000).

2 A Normative Theory of Mediation

ARE DIFFERENCES IN THIRD-PARTY STRATEGIES at all consequential for the normative outcome achieved by mediation? Despite the importance of this question, there has been little systematic research relating the normative transformation of conflict to differences in mediators' motivations and strategy or approach. There are several reasons for this fact. First, most of the studies on international mediation have not been explicit about the international-relations theories on which they are based. Most of the international-relations literature would agree that third parties supply key motives and mechanisms for conflict management and resolution. But realists, pluralists, structuralists, or critical theorists of international relations would use different evaluative criteria to explain the impetus for and outcomes of third-party intervention. A second and related theoretical problem is that most studies that deal with mediation are not explicit about the relationship between conflict dynamics and conflict management and resolution (Kleiboer 1998; Stern and Druckman 2000; Sandole 1993).

Such motivations as the exercise of authority, altruism, empathy, or ideational commitments are important for both the enforcement of existing norms and the emergence of new ones. Third parties draw on such motivations to persuade others of the rightness of their cause. But the mediator's role as a mechanism for normative change can vary along a spectrum of conflict transformation (cf. Väyrynen 1991; Fisher and Keashly 1991). Mediators sometimes focus on turning parties from violent to nonviolent means or lowering the level of violence or risk of escalation. Alternatively, mediators may focus on engendering trust between adversaries; creating constructive patterns of communication; and developing substantive commitments based on shared understandings, values, or new belief systems. In some instances, mediator efforts may go as far as to help restructure the adversaries' entire relationship.

As this brief list suggests, not all mediators play the same kind of role. It is important to recognize this fact because different types of mediators have different avenues for controlling or transforming conflict, and this includes the normative dimension. This chapter develops three models of mediation highlighting variations in the mediator's capacity to normatively influence conflict and engender cooperation. The approach differentiates among *coercive, instrumental,* and *facilitative* mediation. Coercive mediators, or power brokers acting as mediators, are involved in strategic calculations whose aim is to ensure the stability of the status quo. Hence, they unilaterally impose norms rather than engender new ones. Their main role is in enforcing the existing norms. Neorealist and structuralist accounts of international relations are helpful for discerning the kinds of third-party motivations and mechanisms of conflict management involved (Keohane 1986, 1984; Rapkin 1990; Cox 1987; Axelrod 1986). Instrumental and facilitative mediators promote alternative norms that challenge the parties' prevailing world views and, at times, the basic structure of the international system. They may develop and use international institutions as a platform to promote norm acceptance and internalization. Through regime-building and postagreement processes, they promote the legitimacy of new norms while helping to ensure that noncompliance will result in costs in reputation and other areas. Thus, facilitative and instrumental third parties can play a key role in promoting the socialization and learning that turn new norms into customary practices. Institutionalist and the human-needs theories of international relations are most helpful for understanding the kind of transformative and potentially emancipatory role that instrumental and facilitative mediators can play (Finnemore and Sikkink 1998; March and Olsen 1998; Kratochwil 1989, 1993; Burton 1985, 1988, 1990; Lederach 1995, 1997). As we shall see, there are limits to the kind of normative change coercive mediators promote. But parallel interventions by facilitative and instrumental mediators in the same institutional setting can help mitigate some of the limitations of each of their influence potential, while maximizing their collective normative impact.

The Normative Aspect of Mediation: A Missing Link

The literature on mediation has few starting points for theorizing about the normative role of third parties. Most references to such a role are cursory. Rubin and Brown claim that mediators are capable of generating pressures toward a sense of commitment to norms of fairness, responsibility, reciprocity, and equity (1975, 56–59). Similarly, Kelman explains that negotiations under the guidance of facilitators in workshop settings vary from the traditional context of international negotiations, in which disputants are typically called on "to express their group's grievances and to proclaim its historical and legal rights as firmly and militantly as possible" (1990, 206). In contrast, the role of the facilitators in a workshop setting is "to establish and enforce certain norms and ground rules, designed to permit and encourage communication oriented to new learning" (Kelman 1990, 206). In his seminal analysis of third parties, Young (1967, 72–78) argues that intermediaries play a role in guaranteeing peace agreements by verifying, inspecting, monitoring, and supervising the adversaries' compliance. The mediator plays a normative role by backing up effective sanctioning systems.

Working from a more explicit comparative framework, Princen's analysis of mediation hints that the third party's normative influence may vary with its interests and power base (1992). His approach merits some elaboration here. Building on Touval and Zartman's (1985) work on mediators, Princen differentiates between *principal* and *neutral* mediators in terms of (1) their interests and resources and, as a consequence, (2) their bargaining relationship with the disputants. Concerning the issues in conflict, principal mediators have indirect interests; they do not have a direct interest in the issue itself, but they do have a stake in promoting a given outcome to the conflict. Principal mediators also draw on substantial resources with which they can influence the payoff structure of the conflict. In contrast, neutral mediators have no interests at stake and practically no resources to alter the payoff structure. How mediators target their intervention depends on their resources and interests. Principals (who have indirect interests at stake and considerable resources) target the nature of the bargain (its structure and payoffs to the disputants). This also means principal mediators are primarily *outcome oriented.* Neutrals (who have no interests at stake and few resources) target the disputants' interaction by exploring modes of exchanging information, clarifying perceptions and intentions, identifying interests, recognizing fundamental concerns, and exploring options. They are primarily *process oriented.*

Thus, principal mediators limit the disputants' interaction, instead controlling the flow of communication with each disputant bilaterally. In contrast, neutrals promote the direct interaction of the disputants. The differences between these two third-party approaches have a profound impact on the outcome of the conflict. In particular, Princen notes that neutral mediators may be better positioned than principals to promote institutionalized outcomes, such as conventions, regimes, and organizations.

> Because, in an intermediary intervention, the disputants must negotiate not only over the disputed issues, but over the role and procedures advocated by the intermediary, the results of the procedural negotiations help lay the groundwork for more regularized relations on other issues. An intermediary can thus be a critical seed for establishing the negotiating expectations necessary to create more durable institutions. The extent to which this occurs will depend critically on the nature of the intervention. Interveners who detract from the direct

> interaction between disputants, what is called "principal mediators" . . . will be less likely to set such precedents. (Princen 1992, 227–28, n. 10)

Theories of political leadership and of leadership roles in multilateral negotiations are also helpful for relating how mediators' interests and resources affect their capacity to influence normatively conflict outcomes (cf. Hermann 1993; Underdal 1994; Young 1991; Zartman 1994; Sjöstedt 2003; Rubin, Pruitt, and Kim 1994; Touval 1989). The main assumption in this literature is that the type of leadership role an actor plays is likely to vary with its resources and identity (or status), which is also related to its sensitivity to the political context of the dispute.[1] Political sensitivity concerns the parties' own interests and goals and their degree of dependence or independence vis-à-vis the disputing parties. Small and medium states are likely to have greater political sensitivity to disputes in their region than would larger states or states outside the region. France, Great Britain, Germany, or Russia had greater political sensitivities to the conflicts in the former Yugoslavia than did the United States, for example, which had neither the geographical proximity nor the closer historical, cultural, religious, and political ties that existed among the European states. Like political actors in general, the third party's degree of sensitivity will be important in shaping the way it intervenes and determining its influence potential. Its degree of political sensitivity will also influence how open it is likely to be to discrepant information from the environment and ability to remain flexible and search for a variety of possible solutions. Thus, not only a mediator's interests and resources but also its sensitivities shape to what extent and in what ways it can influence adversaries to change their behavior or consider alternative solutions to their problems.

These considerations are important not only for understanding the third party's capabilities for building agendas and intervening in bilateral negotiations. They are also important for understanding the mediator's role in laying the groundwork for and intervening in multilateral negotiations, where the third party may be present also as another negotiator. Kressel and Pruitt have referred to such intervention as "emergent mediation," where "the parties and the mediator are part of a continuing relational set, with enduring and encompassing ties to one another" (1985, 189). According to these authors, "whereas in contractual mediation, entry into a dispute tends to require little initiative on

1. In the discussion that follows, I use the term "mediator" to describe a type of leadership role. In particular, I draw from Hermann (1993) and Underdal (1994). However, Hermann is concerned with leaders' roles in changing the direction of foreign policy, while Underdal focuses on the role of leadership provided by national delegations in influencing processes and outcomes in multilateral negotiations.

the mediator's part, in emergent mediation gaining entry appears to be a ubiquitous strategic issue. Any member of the relational set can, at some point, find itself playing or wishing to play the role of mediator in conflicts involving other members" (1985, 189). Despite the fact that such mediation is likely to be more prevalent than the contractual variety, in which the parties bring in mediators for the specific purpose of helping resolve their dispute, very little attention has been given to this situation in the formal literature. Another important point is that emergent mediation may very well extend the precursor functions of third parties by continuing to engender commitments and secure institutionalized outcomes as the institutional arrangements unfold in successive postagreement negotiations.

Emergent mediation in multilateral negotiations is important because of the tendency for an hierarchy of roles among the participants to develop, starting with the role of the most powerful actors who can exercise "process control" to influence the outcome.[2] They can block agreement and protect their freedom of action, which they often do on a limited number of issues (Zartman 1994, 5). Whether other states that take the initiative by proposing alternative proposals or new solutions can help drive the process forward depends on their capacity to influence the disposition of the veto holders. The process involves simplification, structuring, and direction. Simplification means the parties reduce the elements or complexity of issues to the most important aspects. Structuring means the issues are put into some kind of priority or relationship to each other; direction refers to the process of moving these issues toward some kind of policy goal or outcome. The roles and objectives of parties helps determine how they deal with this process. As Zartman explains, "parties work to shape the values attached to various issues and also to manipulate the other parties and their roles in order to come to an agreement" (1997, 11). Conducting and driving are the strategies that best fit regime building. But a state that conducts is best able to promote negotiations if it subordinates its own interests to building consensus among the rest. Zartman concludes that "the multilateral conference nature of negotiations weighs in favor of a more disinterested leader to provide order to the proceedings" (1997, 12).

States that intervene in third-party capacities to assist with simplifying, structuring, and giving direction to the process of multilateral negotiations

2. I am indebted to Gunnar Sjöstedt for clarifications on these points. See also Sjöstedt (1993, esp. 68–71). Zartman, following Sjöstedt, notes that "parties select from a limited list of roles that differ in nature. They can drive, conduct, defend, brake, or cruise" (1994, 5). Thus, the process of reaching a multilateral agreement is far less complex than the number of participants suggests, because only a few states take on really key roles; most states are "cruisers" or filler.

must work within the constraints imposed by the veto holders, the drivers, cruisers, and brakers or defenders. Their normative influence potential depends partly on their power base. It can be made up of reward, coercion, referent, legitimacy, expertise, and information resources (Bercovitch 1992, 19–20). *Reward* resources relate to the mediator's capacity to provide tangible benefits or incentives, as well as promises of approval and support. The use of "carrots" falls into this category. *Coercive* resources are the "sticks." They depend on mediator threats, including the possibility of increasing the disputants' costs for noncompliance and the threat of withdrawal of support, or of the mediation sponsorship.

Referent resources derive from the "sense of mutual identity between a mediator and the disputing parties, and a desire to see things similarly" (Bercovitch 1992, 20). Ideologies, values, beliefs, and common goals may be important factors that enhance the mediator's status and hence its ability to gain the trust of the disputants, control the mediation process, and influence outcomes. Similarly, *legitimacy* resources are related to the disputants' evaluation of the mediator's right and obligation to assume a third-party role. By virtue of being a neutral state or adhering to a policy of neutrality, for example, or by occupying a particular office or position, a third party may enjoy greater legitimacy in the eyes of the disputants. *Expertise* and *information* resources relate to the disputants' belief that the mediator possesses the skills, judgment, sensitivity, and knowledge to intervene effectively, and also has the capability to uncover or provide valuable information that may enhance the disputants' understanding of each other's reservation point. Thus, the mediator may be influential in helping the parties identify common interests and mutually beneficial joint gains, and also in drafting potential compromise proposals and agreements.

Modeling Mediation Outcomes

While there is substantial literature analyzing third-party resources, strategies, and methods of intervention, there is less clarity concerning standards for evaluating outcomes (Stern and Druckman 2000). This is partly because analysts have rarely been explicit about the ways they relate mediation with conflict dynamics. Another problem is that studies of international mediation are rarely explicit about the theoretical models within which they are operating. As a result, there is a tendency to assert criteria for the success or failure of mediation in terms of unstated assumptions, or on a case-by-case basis, rather than according to solid normative standards rooted in specific theoretical traditions within the study of international relations. Kleiboer (1998) addresses this gap by developing a mediation theory that contrasts four models of mediation based on different international-relations theories. She treats the model of mediation as (1) power brokerage in the context of a neorealist approach, mediation as (2) political problem solving in terms of the school of political psychology, mediation as (3) domination from the perspective of structuralist accounts of international relations, and mediation as (4) restructuring relationships within the context of a human-needs perspective (Kleiboer 1998, 39–87).

By breaking down mediation into four different theoretical models, Kleiboer is explicit about the different ways we can analyze mediators' motivations, strategies, and impact on conflict settlement and resolution. This division is helpful for developing a normative theory of international mediation because her approach is explicit about the kinds of control mechanisms versus change and transformative purposes that various kinds of mediation strategies entail. For example, consistent with neorealist assumptions, she argues that the mediator as power broker aims at restoring and maintaining the balance of power. Thus its normative role is oriented to maintenance of the status quo system; it provides mechanisms that shape relationships of domination-subordination among states. Mediators as problem solvers mostly work within the prevailing order, too, but they help promote conflict resolution by encouraging trust among adversaries (for the most part) at the elite level by influencing perceptions, communication, and understanding of the issues at stake, etc. Not unlike cases of mediation as power brokers, mediation as dominance is also concerned with preserving the status quo in a world shaped by center-periphery relations and patterns of exploitation dictated by a global capitalist system. From a structuralist perspective, conflict management is focused on manifest forms of conflict (i.e., direct violence), occasionally between elites in the center-periphery relationship, but more typically to control conflict between elites in the periphery. It is not about addressing the latent conflict or structural violence inherent in a global system based on relations of privilege and deprivation, inclusion and marginalization, wealth and poverty, health and disease, employment and unemployment, etc.

In contrast, the model of mediation as restructuring relationships emphasizes the rationale for conflict management as a means for seeking consensual social change. The purpose of addressing human needs is to transform the root causes of conflict, including its latent sources. The objective is to go beyond a merely pragmatic solution to resolve the underlying causes of conflict. Here the mediator accepts conflict as a mechanism for social change and becomes a means of channeling it constructively (Kleiboer 1998, 71–72). As we can also see from Kleiboer's four theoretical models of mediation, the various definitions of conflict settlement or resolution that appear in the literature are more meaningfully delineated when we take into account the different assumptions of related international-relations paradigms.

Mediator Strategies and Normative Influence

Drawing from the work of Kleiboer (1998), Princen (1992), and Touval and Zartman (1985), we can develop a model of three different types of mediators, highlighting the mechanisms each uses to exercise normative influence. The first type, the *coercive* mediator, builds on the model of mediation as a dominant third party and power broker, while the second and third types, *instrumental* and *facilitative* mediators, build especially on the model of mediation from institutionalist, political psychology, and human-needs perspectives. We will also differentiate all three types of mediators in terms of their resource base, political sensitivities, and interests in the issues at stake. As a power broker, the coercive mediator has low sensitivity, high resources, and indirect interests in the conflict. The instrumental mediator has a moderate level of sensitivity, moderate resources, especially tangible resources, and indirect interests in the conflict. In contrast, a facilitative mediator has high sensitivity, low resources (except some intangible resources), and no direct interests or stake in the conflict. Different world views, capacities, sensitivities, and interests have implications for each third party's potential for normative influence. The coercive mediator is essentially a norm enforcer; it has the motivation and resources to keep things as they are according to prevailing patterns of power and authority in the international system. The instrumental mediator has the motivation but not the resources for imposing its vision of world order, so its role is important as a norm entrepreneur. Because of its political sensitivities, the facilitative mediator avoids the kind of position-taking adopted by a norm enforcer or entrepreneur, but it serves important normative functions by being a mechanism for norm acceptance and internalization.

A coercive mediator is a strong advocate of its position and objectives; it is generally a state that has a predominant position within the field of activities involved and is well-endowed where national resources are concerned (see also Underdal 1994, 187). The power broker is a great power, either within the international system as a whole or regionally. Hence, it is the least sensitive. The coercive mediator draws from substantial tangible and intangible resources (i.e., reward, coercive, referent, legitimacy, expertise, and information, and such tangible carrots and sticks as military and economic power and incentives). The coercive mediator aims both to protect its status in the system and to extend its influence. It may welcome the opportunity to intervene in some conflicts as a means of defending or extending its influence (Kleiboer 1998; Touval and Zartman 1985). Its main objective is to control conflict. Peace settlements aim at maintaining the system as a whole. The disputants, depending on their relationship with the power broker, may stand to gain in the negotiations with its help. At the same time, to refuse its intervention as a third party may entail unacceptable risks. In any event, the coercive mediator can deploy its resources

Type of Mediation	Resources	Motivation	Focus of Intervention
Coercive (e.g., great powers, super powers, powerful alliances)	Highly endowed • Tangible (e.g., economic, military tools such as sanctions & incentives) • Intangible (e.g., legitimacy, status, expertise)	• Promote own ideology, cause, or problem to ensure stability • Protect, defend, or expand own status in system • Maintain status quo	• Prevent, contain, limit, or reverse overt violence • Control interaction of conflicting parties, especially at level of elite by imposing its own governing system
Instrumental (e.g., medium-sized states, IOs, NGOs and their leaders)	Medium level of endowment: • Tangible (limited) • Intangible (expertise, political competence, organizational skill)	• Challenge prevailing worldview and ideational commitments • Advocate new solutions, approaches, and rules • Promote dynamic view of international system	• Redress root causes of injustice, oppression, or violence • Outcome oriented to promote substantive changes
Facilitative (e.g., small states, less powerful IOs, NGOs and their leaders, individuals)	Low Level of Endowment: • Tangible (fewer or none) • Intangible (e.g., skill, reputation, acceptability, empathy, unique experience in geopolitical position)	• Promote problem-solving approaches (e.g., help manage conflict in system) • Promote human needs (e.g., influence normative belief systems of others to redress problems of oppression, violence and injustice)	• More process than outcome oriented • Ensure durability and governability of results through trust building and institutionalization

Figure 4. Third-Party Normative Influence

in a threatening or highly manipulative fashion. Thus its intervention creates a high-risk environment for the disputants.

A coercive mediator attempts to control, or govern the interaction of the disputants so that communication is through the third party and not between the disputants themselves. Its approach is essentially judgmental and manipulative. As great powers, mediators in the role of power brokers are likely to be principled and motivated by an ideology, cause, or problem they want to solve to ensure stability. They are also likely to be susceptible to *selective perception;* that is, seeing what they want to see in the environment (Hermann 1993, 4). This situation can obviously limit their effectiveness; however, transforming the disputants' interaction, relationship, patterns of communication, or perceptions are not priorities in the coercive mediator's intervention.

Mediators who are *more* sensitive to the environment break down into two categories. First, there are instrumental mediators. Like coercive mediators, *instrumental* mediators have a position on the issues at stake, or clear ideas about alternative approaches and ways to innovate. Such leadership is often described as being of a strategic (Hermann 1993, 4) or instrumental nature (Underdal 1994, 187). Although the instrumental mediator lacks the resources relative to the disputants (which a coercive mediator may draw on), the instrumental mediator does have considerable status. Small and medium-sized countries, or other actors (such as international organizations or transnational movements and networks, as were behind the ban on land mines), may play this type of third-party role.

Instrumental leaders "have a sense of direction—and use contextual cues to ascertain when the time is right for making a move or what the appropriate means are to an end. These leaders take advantage of the situations they find themselves in by letting the context define how something is done rather than what is done" (Hermann 1993, 4). A third party whose approach is based on instrumental leadership succeeds because other actors are persuaded by the merits of its diagnosis—although energy and status are also important factors (Underdal 1994, 87–88). They can also be described as "intellectual entrepreneurs," that is, as promoters of new ideas (Young 1991; see also Finnemore and Sikkink 1998). They are influential in setting the agenda in international negotiations.

As a norm entrepreneur, the instrumental mediator is a powerful critic of the status quo. It challenges the prevailing rules of the game. As Sweden discovered in the 1960s and 1970s, when it championed Third-World development and disarmament and campaigned against the war in Vietnam, the norm entrepreneur is likely to be attacked by the prevailing powers for inappropriate, unbecoming, and ill-timed conduct and ideas.[3] Such behaviors are risky because

3. Finnemore and Sikkink (1998, 897) note that the "efforts to promote a new norm take place within the standards of 'appropriateness,' defined by prior norms. To challenge existing logic of ap-

they can diminish the third party's acceptability in the eyes of those it most wants to influence. Nevertheless, instrumental mediators aim at winning over adversaries by the appropriateness of their prescriptions, vision and initiative-taking, and skill in mobilizing others to help construct such an alternative (Underdal 1994, 188). The instrumental mediator thus sees conflict as an opportunity for promoting consensual change and redressing the root causes of injustice, oppression, or violence in the international system. The norm entrepreneur takes a dynamic view of the current structure of the international system. It inquires "normatively where changes are needed and empirically whether they are possible and how they can be achieved" (Kleiboer 1998, 69). Politics is not a struggle for survival, but rather emancipatory action. Such instrumental mediation requires the actor's expertise and interest in the subject matter or political competence, a skilled staff and organizational support, and the availability of human resources to see projects through from conception to implementation.

To succeed, an instrumental mediator needs to promote solutions that respond to both substantive and political criteria. However, the skills for accomplishing these tasks are quite different. Instrumental mediators are best at "articulating and postulating the need for and direction of change" (Hermann 1993, 6). When there is any challenge to its goal, the more internalized the instrumental mediator's vision or objective, the more it is likely to face personal stress and assume a rigid position. In short, instrumental mediators are not the best-positioned actors to engender the consensus needed to achieve their goals (Hermann 1993; Underdal 1994, 189). However, the instrumental mediator may play an important role in transforming conflict by influencing the content of the normative belief systems of other actors.

The most sensitive type of mediator (and generally also the most resource-poor) is the *facilitative* mediator. The facilitative mediator draws mostly from intangible resources that its structural position, status, identity, and opportunities as a mediator afford. Facilitative mediators tend to be small states, or even private individuals or nongovernmental organizations. Thus, the facilitative mediator's influence is not derived from its capacity to manipulate directly the costs or benefits the parties encounter for negotiating or not negotiating, or for agreeing or not agreeing on a solution. Rather, the skill, reputation, trustworthiness, and acceptability of the facilitative mediator are its key resources. Typical initiatives involve organizing problem-solving workshops to generate ideas for negotiations (Kelman 1990) or to promote skills training (Babbitt 1997). Alternatively, interventions may focus on building bridges among divided com-

propriateness, activists may need to be explicitly 'inappropriate,' " as the suffragettes were, for example, in carrying out acts of civil disobedience.

munities (Project on Ethnic Relations 1996), or overcoming psychological barriers to reconciliation (Neu and Volkan 1999). The role of the Norwegian foreign minister in facilitating the 1993 Palestinian-Israeli peace accords provides another example of facilitation. His intervention is in stark contrast to the multi-billion-dollar aid the United States gave to Egypt after it signed the Camp David accords with Israel in 1978, or to Jordan after entering into a nonbelligerency pact with Israel in July 1994.

What is the facilitative mediator's source of influence if it has few resources and avoids taking a position? The facilitative mediator's primary resource is its skill in trying to figure out who supports what ideas, and therefore what should be done in response to a problem. It is essentially a "cue-taker," meaning it lets others in the situation and the nature of the situation shape the position it takes and what it does. Unlike that of other mediators, the influence of the facilitative mediator is based on its capacity to empathize and its skill at creating a consensus concerning the need for change and at putting into place a new approach. Hence, it plays a key role in supplying mechanisms needed to identify, generate, and facilitate the acceptance and internalization of new norms (Hermann 1993).

The facilitative mediator may adopt a problem-solving or an emancipatory approach. In international mediation, a problem-solving approach often attempts to change the dynamics of conflict at the level of disputants' elite leadership by fostering trust, assisting with the establishment of new channels of communication, creating new grounds rules for their interaction, and helping create a consensus on areas for substantive agreement (cf. Fisher and Ury 1991; Pruitt and Carnevale 1993; Moore 1996). The rationale for conflict management is to intervene to inhibit conflict escalation that poses a threat to the international system and people's well-being. Conflict is treated more as a function of human interaction and foibles, rather than an endemic feature of the international system. Systemic change itself is not the objective. The objective is to make peaceful, rather than violent, means the norm for dealing with conflict (Kleiboer 1998, 58).

This contrasts with facilitation as a means for conflict management and resolution from a human-needs perspective, where conflict is a means for emancipation from illegitimate social relationships (Lederach 1995, 1997). As Kleiboer argues, "both conflict settlement (mitigating destructive consequences of violent conflict behavior) and resolution (e.g., helping to establish legitimate relationships between government and governed) are possible with third party assistance" (1998, 77, table 3.4). But here mediation success is measured by more than achieving changes in world views or consensus on areas for cooperation. Instead, the emphasis is both on process results (getting the maximum amount of participation and power-free communication among the parties concerned, including their constituents at all levels of society) and the outcomes (achieving durable social change that all parties support). One of the reasons why there is considerable controversy among scholars of the Middle East peace process is that, while from a problem-solving perspective such agreements as the Camp David or Oslo Accords were a success, from a human-needs perspective they were a failure. They failed to fundamentally change the structural conditions of oppression under which the Palestinians in particular have continued to live (Kleiboer 1998, 90–100; Shikaki 1999).

Whether facilitation proceeds under a problem-solving or a human-needs rubric of international affairs, personal experience or accumulated political experience in a given arena of foreign affairs will enhance a leader's repertoire of possible behaviors and approaches and evaluation of what types of mediation initiatives will succeed or fail under a given set of circumstances. As Hermann notes, "experience makes leaders more aware of discrepancies between what was planned and what is happening. It also attunes them to nuances in behavior that may permit change to be successful or have an effect. And experience increases the willingness to see situations and problems in a more complex fashion, inviting more context-specific solutions" (1993, 8–9). Thus unique experiences that other leaders have not had may give a specific leader a particular advantage in making initiatives that others would not entertain. Particular geopolitical and historical experiences gave Finland's President Urho Kekkonen (who held the office continuously from 1956 to 1982) both insight and expertise into how to manage an initiative such as launching the CSCE, which may have allowed him to succeed where other leaders failed. Finally, how accountable a leader is to his or her constituency can also impact on the conditions under which initiatives involving important foreign-policy changes can be initiated. For example, President Kekkonen had considerable latitude in setting Finland's foreign-policy agenda because he maintained a tight grip over the office of the presidency as well as control of domestic politics.

Of the three types of mediators, facilitative mediators are likely to make the greatest adjustments in their position-taking. What the facilitative mediator considers skilled maneuvering to achieve a consensus some actors may interpret as a sign of weakness, or as evidence that one of the adversaries has succeeded in manipulating the mediator to change its position or to move in a certain direction. On the other hand, because the facilitative mediator does not clearly stake out its own position at the outset, it is better positioned to gain the trust of all parties. Nevertheless, because its position-taking may change with time, the facilitative mediator may also have to work constantly to retain the adversaries' confidence and trust.

The facilitator's approach is primarily process oriented, regarding both the process of getting an agreement and the ability to ensure it promotes durable change. Facilitators have as their main objective promoting direct interaction among the parties and their efforts to reach a negotiated solution. The facilitative mediator remains in an advisory capacity and keeps the parties themselves focused on the issues and the search for solutions. The facilitative mediator desists from assessing blame or imposing any rights, obligations, or conditions on the parties. Its role is essentially noncoercive, and its intervention creates a low-risk environment. Of the three approaches to mediation, facilitative mediation is most likely to establish the groundwork to underpin the institutionalization of cooperation. The role of the facilitative mediator in building consensus is fundamental. As Hermann argues,

> the cue-takers once they have sensed the direction significant others want to go with regard to a problem have some idea about where people's positions are and what the compromise or consensus position may be. In reaching their own position, they have helped to build a consensus among those involved with an issue. As a result, there is already some momentum toward implementation since there is a shared sense of direction—at least until the nature of the situation changes and the cue-taker notes a new approach is needed. (1993, 7)

Third Parties as Mechanisms for Norm Genesis and Acceptance

The process of transforming conflict normatively involves the genesis of norms and their acceptance and internalization by the parties. However, mediation is not always transformative. Coercive mediators supply normative mechanisms of control that inhibit further conflict or control its dynamics, but they do not transform the underlying causes or roots of conflict. The coercive mediator supplies unilateral norms that it imposes on the parties. Its normative impact stems from its enforcement action. The measures the power broker takes have more to do with protecting its own interests than with the interests of the adversaries. As Kleiboer notes, neutrality, which is often considered key to mediator success, is not the issue here. In fact, it "may even be an undesirable or even impossible prerequisite." The parties are interested in the mediator because of its leverage and ability to induce them to restrain their conflict. Here, "power is what makes mediation successful" (1998, 45).

Coercive mediators have a variety of resources available to make threats or offer incentives to bring disputants to an agreement that favors the coercive mediator's normative preferences or goals. They can back up their norms with side payments to balance an agreement or with sanctions to make nonagreement more costly. Obviously, threats are costly to the mediator only when the adversaries call its bluff, whereas inducements are always costly. The use of threats carries certain risks, however, as we have seen in numerous post-cold war uses of sanctions to enforce peace agreements (Cortright and Lopez 2000; Haass 1998). Through positive and negative sanctions the coercive mediator may succeed in forcing the adversaries to cooperate even when they do not trust each other, and even when they lack adequate information about each other's reservation point. The carrots and sticks approach allows the third party to use its influence potential to promote agreements when the structures of conflict (such as in arms races or identity-based conflicts) make collectively optimal solutions difficult to achieve. Yet the purpose of such intervention is less to ascertain the will of the disputants than to promote the third party's strategic interests. Cases in point include the U.S. interventions in Bosnia and Kosovo (Chomsky 1999; Bilder 1999).

On the other hand, coercive mediators can stabilize ad hoc solutions to conflict. They can change the parties' expectations about a possible settlement, take responsibility for concessions, make the parties aware of the costs of nonagreement, supply and filter information, and control the interaction of the adversaries. The third party functions as a norm enforcer through mechanisms of dominance and control. The coercive mediator can exercise such influence in a variety of ways, including through direct interactions with the disputants and by convening conferences among the concerned parties. During the post-cold war period, leading states have frequently convened such conferences to deal with intrastate conflicts. For example, Arab states, led by Syria, convened conferences on many occasions to find solutions to the conflict in Lebanon; states in the Horn of Africa did the same in 1991 and 1992 to search for a solution to the Somali crisis; the United States organized conferences in 1993 to try to solve the Haitian crisis and in 1995, at Dayton, to find peace for Bosnia. In cases of successful convocations, the mediators have not been satisfied with a cease fire, nor have they left outcomes to the devices of the conflicting parties. Instead, the mediators have sought also to "create confidence-building measures during and after the intervention to build trust and enable the parties to check on their progress as they move from conflict to reconstruction," and they have included agreements to deal with domestic power allocation and institutional structuring (Zartman 1997, 16).

Third parties have sometimes called on international observers to support peace agreements. For example, the political transitions in South Africa, Cambodia, and El Salvador have counted on such support to ensure the safety of the voters and to validate the legitimacy and fairness of the postconflict elections (Hampson 1996). Coercive third parties can use such resources to translate their mechanisms of dominance and control into the acceptance and internalization of the peace agreement. But if the agreement is imposed, then its durability will depend on the third party's commitment to police and enforce it, and there will be problems with acceptance and internalization. In contrast, Rothstein (1999) emphasizes that the conditions for transforming relationships involve a positive conception of peace. It depends on the parties' sense of mutual acceptance and reconciliation, a sense of security and dignity, a pattern of cooperative interaction between communities, and the institutionalization of a dynamic process of problem solving.

The *instrumental* mediator is better able to help transform relations because it has ideational commitments to spreading new norms that address problems of injustice, inequality, oppression, violence, and other obstacles to positive peace. It does this by proposing new solutions or alternative ways of framing conflict issues, offering new perspectives on the situation, or redirecting the attention of the adversaries to more peripheral issues that may be more easily resolved than core incompatibilities. The confidence and security-building measures (CSBMs) negotiated in the CSCE served these purposes when other arms-control negotiations broke down between the superpowers in the early to mid-1980s. The neutral and nonaligned countries worked to get a consensus on meaningful CSBMs because they were unable to secure agreement on other security measures that would have challenged the prevailing order more fundamentally, such as nuclear disarmament.[4]

While coercive mediators may seek multilateral approaches to conflict management to control violence, instrumental and facilitative mediators can use such fora to promote conflict transformation. Multilateral venues are an important means for conflict resolution for several reasons. First, by increasing the number of players and coalition-forming possibilities, multilateralism diminishes the instrumental and facilitative mediators' power disparities vis-à-vis the disputants. They also introduce a different set of incentives for cooperation. An intellectual entrepreneur can use a multilateral forum as a platform to promote alternative ideas and get them onto the negotiation agenda. For example, throughout the 1960s, Sweden, Switzerland, Romania, Yugoslavia, and many other small, neutral, nonaligned, or bloc states used various multilateral fora to promote their own agenda for ending East-West conflict.

The *facilitator* works to change the confrontation among the adversaries by promoting their direct interaction. The facilitator, unlike the coercive or instrumental mediator, is not primarily an advocate of a particular outcome, although it does work for the durability of cooperation. The facilitator is focused on assisting the parties to reach an agreement largely within the framework of the terms they propose. Its normative influence stems from its function as a mechanism for launching negotiations and giving definition to the rules of procedure. It can help restructure relationships by who it invites to participate in negotia-

4. Ambassador Oleg Grinevsky, interview by author, tape recording, Embassy of the Russian Federation, Stockholm, Dec. 20, 1994.

tions, by the nature of the agenda that is to be under discussion, and by the rules. It works by engendering commitments or serving as a precursor to cooperation. It provides the missing link needed to generate a new relationship among the parties.

To act as a third party, the facilitator must be invited to mediate, unless it can successfully appeal to the parties to accept its call to provide good offices or to carry out similar activities such as fact finding. These efforts can help minimize misunderstandings and misinformation and reduce tensions while positioning the facilitator to monitor conditions. Unlike the coercive mediator, the facilitative intermediary has no tangible resources relative to the adversaries with which to impose a settlement or change their incentives about whether to cooperate or continue their confrontation. Thus the entry of the facilitator into the conflict depends on whether the conflicting parties come to the realization that de-escalation and accommodation are preferable to continued conflict. If the facilitative mediator is operating from a problem-solving world view, then its overarching objective is to influence the adversaries' thinking normatively in the direction of the importance of managing and resolving their conflict through cooperative means. If it is operating from a human-needs perspective, it aims more comprehensively at restructuring their relationship, especially to transform illegitimate, oppressive, exploitative, or unjust social relationships.

A facilitative mediator may be motivated to pursue a problem-solving approach with adversaries if it has considerable sensitivities to the political context of the dispute. Then it will seek first to enhance stable cooperation among the parties, minimizing potential sources of confrontation or competition detrimental to its own (national) interests. One of the problems mediators face helping adversaries make the transition from confrontational and competitive behaviors to cooperation is asymmetry in the level of interest among the disputants to change their relationship. This situation can lead to a stalemate. As Zartman and Berman point out, it is important for the party that first favored negotiations to influence the other parties' decision in the same direction (1982, 69). Facilitators can intervene both procedurally and substantively to find an acceptable "transition formula" that can mitigate adversaries' asymmetries and reluctance to appear to be conceding. The facilitative mediator can enhance channels of communication and information among the parties, legitimizing their gestures of goodwill and willingness to negotiate. Thus facilitative mediators engender adversaries' commitment to participate by placing a positive value on increasing evidence of cooperation and by setting deadlines or threatening to exit. Through these mechanisms the facilitator engenders normative change and serves as a catalyst or precursor to a new relationship among the parties.

As sponsors or potential hosts of a multilateral conference or negotiation process, facilitators can normatively influence the prenegotiations or agenda-building negotiations by emphasizing common interests, devising innovative policy options to overcome bargaining impediments, making deals and lining up support for salient options, and proposing concessions and offering face-saving proposals. They may also prepare procedural and decision-making rules and other conference modalities with an underlying substantive or practical nature. Thus the facilitative mediator shapes the parties' basic expectations as early as the pre-agenda phase of negotiations. Its early intervention establishes precedents that can help channel behaviors constructively. These are among the key ways it lays the groundwork for later institutionalized cooperation.

THE FACILITATOR may also help parties get beyond prenegotiation obstacles when the order for treating the issues at stake is in question, including the procedures for doing so. Different political and social-cultural characteristics may give rise to different approaches to negotiation. In the context of proposals leading to the founding of CSCE, radically different East and West approaches to negotiation were evident, stemming from their different ideological points of departure and different normative or principled conceptions of the issues at stake (Maresca 1985, 55–63). This situation was most notable in the East's tendency to begin from a deductive perspective versus the West's essentially inductive approach (see also Zartman and Berman 1982, 89–94). The United States in particular emphasized a pragmatic approach calling for specific, tangible solutions. The Soviets sought legal principles that would legitimize their regional interventions (for example, in Czechoslovakia and later Afghanistan); this policy required using legal formulations as the basis for international agreements. Moreover, the Soviets viewed the CSCE process, both in their initial proposals and throughout the negotiations leading up to the Helsinki Final Act, as their surrogate World War II peace treaty. Thus, for them, the CSCE process had imminent political-legal significance, whereas for the West it initially presented and continued to offer a forum through which the Soviets could be pressed for concessions, especially on human rights. The neutral and nonaligned countries played key roles, in part as facilitators, that led the CSCE incrementally to the kinds of normative and ideological changes that eventually favored the approach of the West.

In the main negotiations, facilitative mediators typically focus on two kinds of tasks: procedural and substantive coordination of the process. The main task of the procedural coordinator is to make the negotiating process itself work. This is a key role, especially in negotiations that proceed by the rule of consensus. Reaching decisions on the basis of consensus entails laborious discussions. However, at some point it is essential to organize the work and give impetus to the process of drafting agreements. Facilitative mediators can propose modalities and procedural mechanisms for organizing this process, and they can also defend these arrangements should the parties try to use procedural matters as a means of blocking negotiations, which they often do. This action is often vital to ensuring the continuity of the negotiations and to laying the foundation for cooperating in good faith.

The facilitator can also contribute to norm emergence by making the consensus rule work. It coordinates the substantive aspects of consensus building by collecting proposals from the disputants, chairing the discussions in working groups, and preparing draft documents. These interventions help to identify where difficulties in reaching an agreement may lie and how these can be bridged. The facilitative mediator can seek to overcome such impasses by presenting package deals or brokering compromises during the final rounds, although there are generally limits to how many times the mediator can do this without losing its credibility. It can also use deadlines or threats to exit to challenge the existing logic of appropriateness (see Finnemore and Sikkink 1998, 897) and get the parties to accept agreements. Both the substantive and procedural mediator may accept responsibility for negotiating failures and for concessions, compromises, and missed deadlines. These face-saving interventions keep in play the process of norm emergence and acceptance by the participants.

Promoting the Internalization of Norms

The process of the normative transformation of conflict involves the genesis of new norms as well as their acceptance and internalization. Finnemore and Sikkink argue that socialization is a "dominant mechanism of a norm cascade—the mechanism through which norm leaders persuade others to adhere" (1998, 902). But how socialization works, and whether it entails the normative transformation of conflict or the reinscription of status quo norms, depends on the third-party strategy in question. Mediators as power brokers serve as mechanisms of norm enforcement, so there are limits in this approach to the transformation of conflict. The parties may retain different views on what the issues are or were, or on what principle was set. This poses certain risks: peace settlements that are perceived as imposed and unjust can spawn new issues of contention and the fragmentation of the main parties; such perceptions have complicated the process of reaching a comprehensive peace between Israelis and Palestinians, for example (Shikaki 1999).

Coercive mediators can attempt to promote and enforce norms through direct acts of intervention as well as demonstration effects (Bilder 1999). For example, by acting as a power broker in disputes involving "rogue states," the coercive mediator can send signals to other states about the costs of noncompliance with the prevailing order, principles, and rules. Thus power brokers can selectively intervene in conflicts to socialize other states to the maintenance of the status quo. In describing mediation as domination, Kleiboer (1998) draws from structuralist accounts of international relations to paint a similar picture of socialization through system dominance. The main objective of the dominant powers or their agents (and these can be their allies, client states in the periphery, or international organizations working at the dominant power's behest) is to mitigate excessive violence in the periphery. Preserving order and stability serves the interests of the leading powers.

Norms integral to the prevailing world order that are backed up by the dominant mediator often are so deeply embedded in the logic and rules of that prevailing world order that they are seen as natural, customary, or necessary. The dominant mediator may also appropriate other emerging norms to justify its action, thereby jeopardizing the original moral standing of the norm (Bilder 1999). The emerging norm of humanitarian intervention in the 1990s could be seen from this perspective. Enforcement action, such as limited conflict prevention and crisis management, and the new imperative of rescuing populations at risk (cf. Leatherman et al. 1999; Jentleson 2000; Weiss and Minear 1993) may be a part of a pervasive socialization effort by the leading powers to ensure that other actors will buy into the norms and constraints of the current world order. The message is that states that do not conform risk losing the esteem and respect of the rest of the international community, and much more.

Instrumental mediators play a role in socializing states to new norms, but by quite different means than those available to the coercive mediator. The legacy of instrumental mediators lies in the emergence of consensual knowledge, what Ernst Haas calls "generally accepted understandings about cause-and-effect linkages about any set of phenomena considered important by society" (1991, 65). This concerns both scientific and nonscientific information that is considered authoritative by the interested parties. In postagreement negotiations, instrumental mediators contribute to the further development of consensual knowledge by working to close loopholes, clarify ambiguities, or fill in omissions in the agreement. They may also continue their role as agenda setters by reintroducing proposals considered too radical in earlier rounds or by contributing more new concepts and ways of conceiving issues. Instrumental mediators can also serve as a mechanism for socialization by promoting the transparency of institutions to integrate ideas and challenges from other norm entrepreneurs, such as nongovernmental organizations, epistemic communities, and social-movement activists. These actors can be important coalition partners for instrumental mediators: they bring expertise and scientific or technical understanding to bear both at the level of the multilateral endeavor and on the decision-making processes and practices within their home governments and bureaucracies (P. Haas 1992; E. Haas 1990). For instrumental mediators, these other norm entrepreneurs can help legitimize international norms and serve as a transmission belt for their acceptance and internalization at the domestic level. Such processes of domestication are crucial for stabilizing international cooperation (cf. Cortell and Davis 2000).

Facilitative mediators play a role in socializing states to new norms by serving as mechanisms for durable cooperation on new commitments. They can do this by helping ensure the rule effectiveness of institutional commitments. If the test of an institution's robustness is the ability of the participants to use its rules to sanction violators, then a key role facilitative mediators can play in the socialization of states to their new obligations is to ensure regime governance. This includes facilitating the development and functioning of compliance and sanctioning mechanisms.

Multilateral regimes like the CSCE create complex networks of obligations with both past and future dimensions, which make defection, despite dissatisfaction with the behavior of an important participating state, more difficult with time. In addition, continued participation may do more to stabilize expectations and achieve compliance than defection, which may itself be a source of new instabilities—not only as concerns the target state but also other friendly governments (including allies). Hence, withdrawing from international agreements and institutions brings its own reputational costs and other potentially destabilizing side effects. Facilitative mediators can help convey to other participants the significance of these costs while also working to secure their renewed compliance. Institutions provide legitimate standards against which to judge and by which means to collect and interpret information about compliance. It may be preferable to seek improvements on institutional arrangements working from within the institution than pursuing foreign-policy objectives unilaterally outside them. Facilitative mediators can reinforce these arguments through third-party efforts that help ensure both costs for noncompliance as well as efforts to help parties save face, win new concessions, and gain new legitimacy and esteem.

Summary of Hypotheses

Third parties draw on a variety of both tangible and intangible resources to transform different types and dimensions of conflict. The coercive mediator has a wider range of sources of influence than do other mediators. The coercive mediator has the tangible resources and ability to influence the parties' stakes in the conflict and or settlement—including over issues that are often perceived as intractable, like status or security. However, the coercive mediator manipulates the adversaries' stakes. The coercive mediator may also seek to influence the do-

Type of Mediation	Source of Norms	Means for Promoting Norm Acceptance	Means for Promoting Internalization of Norms
Coercive	• Unilateral (e.g., derived from third party enforcement action and assertion of dominance and control)	• Create high-risk environment • Guarantee or enforcement role • Assess blame; impose rights, duties, penalties, and obligations on parties	• Manipulate cost of noncompliance and rewards for compliance • Demonstration of effects • Socialization through system dominance by the great powers or agents
Instrumental	• Ideational commitments to spread new norms, to redress problems of injustice, violence, inequality, and other obstacles to peace	• Create politically challenging environment • Entrepreneurship • Agenda setting • Coalition building	• Promote consensual knowledge • Promote transparency • Build more institutions and commitments for democratic governance
Facilitative	• Engender commitments • Serve as catalyst or precursor to cooperation or emergence of trust • Create new expectations and new precedents	• Create low-risk environment • Promote understanding and reconciliation • Lay groundwork for consensus on normative charge • Supply trust-building interventions • Give legitimacy to adversaries' concessions and commitments	• Promote charge at all levels of conflict system (elite to grass roots) • Monitor agreements • Ensure rule effectiveness • Facilitate implementation of agreements

Figure 5. Third Parties as Mechanisms for Normative Change

mestic constituency of one or more of the antagonists, especially their evaluation of continuing the conflict or agreeing on a settlement. It may also threaten to exit. This threat can be an important source of leverage, especially when one or more of the disputants considers that its possibilities for getting the kind of agreement it prefers are enhanced by the power broker's intervention. Thus, unlike instrumental and facilitative mediators, its influence potential is not necessarily limited when the adversaries do not express a need for its intervention.

However, the coercive mediator's capacity to generate and spread new norms is constrained by the unilateral or self-imposed quality of the norms it invokes, and by its mode of operation. Socialization to its norms is through mechanisms of dominance, not emancipation and empowerment. The coercive mediator faces substantial limitations in transforming adversaries' relationship and in underpinning the emergence of a genuinely cooperative regime. In fact, the paradox is that the very power and resources that may enable it to pressure adversaries into ceasing their hostilities may also make them suspicious of attempts by the coercive mediator to promote peace.

THE INSTRUMENTAL and facilitative mediators rely primarily on their reputation, on gaining the trust and confidence of the parties, on being evaluated as reliable and fair, and on being needed to exercise influence and be persuasive. Instrumental and facilitative mediators' leverage can also be increased through political backing from their own governments and by other governments or by the international community. A strong show of support from an international organization or other authoritative body can boost the status of the third party without undermining its acceptability to the parties.

Like coercive and instrumentalist mediators, facilitators can also threaten to exit. However, such threats have to be exercised judiciously so as not to undermine the parties' trust and confidence in the third party's reliability and commitment to a constructive process of reaching and implementing an agreement. Rather than continue at the risk of a further deterioration of the environment or the parties' political will to seek a peaceful settlement, the facilitative mediator can propose as an alternative a temporary suspension or break in the negotiations or peace process. Generally, third parties retain more leverage when, before breaking off negotiations, they secure agreement on the dates and terms for continuing the process in the future. The facilitative mediator also does everything in its power to make sure the disputants perceive the process as a politically credible means for working out fair and acceptable solutions.

Of the three types of mediators, the facilitative mediator may have the most important role to play in the internalization of new norms. The facilitative mediator succeeds by enhancing the parties' understanding and information about the other's interests, needs, and objectives, and by its efforts to work out the procedural arrangements that allow them to establish a process or framework for resolving the conflict. To this end it can help them (1) define the action and rules they want to include under a cooperative arrangement, and (2) reduce the cost of bargaining—i.e. minimize psychological bias and reduce cognitive complexity and communication and information-processing problems (Tetlock 1991). Its influence in these areas is strongly predetermined by the agenda-building aspects of its role—who it brings to the table, whose participation it legitimizes, under what rules, etc. Thus, the facilitative mediator may contribute to the issue, rule, and structural dimension of conflict transformation. However, its effectiveness can also be limited when the adversaries have no need for its services and when it is too sensitive to the core issues at stake or predominant parties.

Instrumental mediators may also facilitate institutionalized outcomes by contributing novel ideas and new principles containing diagnoses or solutions that are more acceptable politically to adversaries by virtue of coming from the third party (cf. Touval 1989; Princen 1992; Heymann 1973, 804). While facilitative mediators may help lay the groundwork for new customary practices by building consensus, instrumentalists are important in shaping the normative beliefs (ideas, principles, or moral rectitude) that allow actors to communicate about their grievances on the basis of shared understandings and identify new areas where they can develop customary practices.

The question of whether the power broker's threats can be used in combination with facilitative and instrumental methods of third-party intervention to bring escalated conflicts under control and the parties into a process of resolving their conflict should be more closely studied. Because coercive mediation depends on credible threats, it limits the mediator's possibilities to gather the trust and confidence of the adversaries, which is often needed to bring them into direct negotiations. In any event, it is doubtful that the same third party would succeed by pursuing simultaneously coercive, instrumental, and facilitative types of third-party intervention. It may be for such reasons the United Nations was at risk of undermining both its credibility as a neutral mediator and the impartiality of its peacekeeping forces when, for example, it engaged in peace enforcement in Bosnia (albeit through NATO) as a parallel course of action. Notably, NATO suffered also a loss of credibility because of the constraints it faced in operating in deference to UN impartiality.

Conclusions

Because East-West conflict involved, at its apex, superpower confrontation, the possibilities of resolving their confrontation excluded the kind of mediation as power brokerage that both the United States and the Soviet Union engaged in throughout much of the cold war in the Third World. But as we shall see in subsequent chapters, the CSCE benefited instead from the combination of instrumental and facilitative third-party strategies that the neutral and nonaligned countries brought to bear on East-West relations. The fact that these different third parties worked together may have enhanced their influence potential for promoting the transformation of East-West conflict. Their joint action had an impact on the substance of agreements in at least two ways: (1) because Switzerland, Sweden, and Austria in particular tended to side with the West on matters of human rights, the Soviets were less able to control the extent to which this landed far-reaching human-rights commitments; and (2) the N+N, because they prepared the final draft text, were always able to make certain that it contained their own basic interests, also ensuring that they could draw on their own normative beliefs to shape the type of commitments and actions agreed.

Throughout the CSCE negotiations, the superpowers engaged in a tug-of-war over the N+N in an attempt to get them to tilt toward their own side on any number of crucial issues. It can be assumed that the leverage this gave to the N+N was useful not only in working out agreements but also in reducing the superpowers' incentives to defect. Defection (unilaterally dropping out of the CSCE) by one party could also risk pushing the third party into the opponent's camp. This possibility was significant in the CSCE in light of the superpowers' competition to win fence riders (like neutrals) over to their side. The West wanted the N+N squarely on its side where human rights were concerned, but it also sought N+N support for its positions on military-security issues. The East was most keen on the N+N interest in disarmament proposals, such as nuclear weapons-free zones or nuclear disarmament, if only for political reasons. In a two-way conflict, there is no need to justify defection to one's opponent. However, the CSCE succeeded in institutionalizing East-West cooperation. The multilateralism and new norms changed the stakes and the rules of the game for the superpowers. Here, finally, they had to consider their relationship to the group, including the neutral and nonaligned states. As we shall see in detail in the chapters that follow, the presence of both instrumental and facilitative mediators in the CSCE played important, if subtle roles in initiating and sustaining the new norms for cooperation among cold war adversaries. Ultimately, this helped to restructure East-West relations and pave the way for a peaceful end to the cold war divisions.

3 From Cold War to Multilateral Détente

THE CONFERENCE ON SECURITY AND COOPERATION IN EUROPE can trace its origins to a 1954 Soviet proposal for a European Security Conference (ESC). But it took a couple of decades for momentum to build to convene such a meeting. Khrushchev's policy of "peaceful co-existence," Johnson's "bridge-building," France's policy of "rapprochement," West Germany's "Ostpolitik," and proposals from the nonbloc states were part of numerous efforts that led to détente and laid the groundwork for a security conference. Nevertheless, by the late 1960s East-West relations were approaching a stalemate. Both superpowers became increasingly suspicious of the political risks posed by multilateralism. They used their preponderant position in their own military alliance to channel and control East-West relations by means of an inter-bloc dialogue. Their objective was to stabilize the status quo and avert any losses. Their resistance to a cross-bloc approach contributed to the political deadlock at the end of the decade. Finding a way out depended on resolving competing perspectives on the key questions for a ESC: Should such a conference take place? What kind of forum or fora should it be? Under what rules? Who should participate? What issues should and could be included? The search was on for a transitional formula to which all concerned parties could commit.

The Cold War's Conflict Dynamics

In the aftermath of World War II, Allied disputes over the administration of a divided Germany and the set of unresolved problems to which German dismemberment gave rise (including the status of Berlin, German unification, and, in its absence, the legal status of the two Germanies) were among the core elements of cold war conflict. The reconstruction of a devastated Europe also became another field in which the superpowers struggled to influence the continent's economic and security needs, as well as political-ideological ones. This also made the cold war an "imaginary war," powerful because "an identity based on abstract values, freedom or equality, seemed more progressive than an identity based on racial or cultural characteristics, which had been so discredited in two world wars" (Kaldor 1990, 5).

With the formation of the military alliances (NATO in 1949 and the Warsaw Pact in 1956) and economic communities in East and West (Comecon in 1949 and the European Economic Community in 1956), the cold war assumed the dimensions of bloc-to-bloc confrontation. These organizations set in motion conflict dynamics at the regional level, which deepened the divisions in Europe. Traditional cultural, social, and economic patterns of trade and cooperation were severed and reoriented along bloc lines. Families were divided and communication lines cut off, so that East-West confrontation was played out also as a social and personal conflict.

The cold war also encompassed residual conflict issues from World War II regarding both Germany and more generally borders and minority questions throughout the continent. However, border problems between East Germany and Poland (the Oder-Neisse), or East Germany and Czechoslovakia, or between France and West Germany (over the Saar), for example, produced no overt conflicts within the blocs. As a general rule, such intra-bloc tensions were suppressed (Grosse-Juette 1977, 61). In contrast, residual conflicts between member states of different blocs "became part of the confrontation and acquired a significance that transcended the national concerns" (Grosse-Juette 1977, 61). They were treated as ideological issues and as evidence of continued threat. The nonrecognition of borders and the insistence on or denial of treaties formed part of this dimension of conflict. The fact that national and bloc-level conflicts were interchangeable impeded efforts at finding solutions to East-West conflict.

The cold war was carried out by a variety of means, including economic and social competition, military showdowns and brinkmanship over Berlin, and an arms race—which, in the view of some scholars, was increasingly impelled less by the real threat situation than by the "self-dynamics" that the arms race developed (Grosse-Juette 1977, 59). The ideological nature of the cold war confrontation meant that, theoretically, joint interests could not exist. This also led to negative evaluations of whatever behavior the adversary engaged in, even if it was not directly confrontational. "The cumulative effect of these dispositions resulted in a principle 'nonnegotiability' of all kinds of conflicts" (Grosse-Juette 1977, 56).

However, Stalin's death in 1953 opened a window of opportunity for rapprochement, initiated in part by Soviet gestures that led to the recognition of a neutral Austria and the early and unilateral withdrawal of Soviet forces from overseas "bases" in Hanko, Finland, and also Darien in Manchuria (Garthoff 1985, 7; Larson 1987). The 1950s were marked nevertheless by contradictory situations and "rapid swings" from a thaw to a freeze in East-West relations.

Among the more promising initiatives were the 1956 Geneva Conference; the first Soviet proposal for an all-European Security Conference; the first agreements on inner-German cooperation (resulting in trade agreements in 1957 and 1960); the 1957 Rapacki Plan for a nuclear-free zone in Central Europe; the tripartite talks among the United States, Great Britain, and the USSR on the prohibition of nuclear testing; the eighteen-nation Disarmament Committee in Geneva; and the Antarctic Treaty (1959)—the first multilateral treaty in the field of arms control (Aćimović 1981, 28–31). These activities had a positive effect on world affairs as a whole.

But this period was also marked by confrontations in Berlin that started in 1958 and lasted through the construction of the Berlin Wall in August 1961. The cold war culminated in the Cuban Missile Crisis, which took the world to the brink of a nuclear conflagration in October 1962. The crisis brought home to the U.S. and Soviet leadership a central message: the interdependence of East and West even in the pursuit of confrontational means to settle their disputes. Among the most salient lessons learned was the need to avoid situations that could lead to such confrontation in the future. Thus, considerable importance was attached to managing East-West conflict by means of conflict avoidance and crisis management. These means were the primary instruments of superpower détente.

Superpower Détente: Maintaining the Status Quo

The experience of the Cuban Missile Crisis forced a cognitive crisis in the United States concerning both its values and strategies. Throughout the crisis decision makers "acted as if the perceived risks of escalation were such that avoiding any direct U.S.—Soviet conflict would take priority over all but the most central state interests" (Weber 1991, 795). At each stage, President Kennedy chose the most moderate of military options available to contain the Soviet threat and retained an open trade on the missiles in Turkey as a fallback position. As Weber concludes, "in future superpower crises, governments could be expected to worry less about manipulating credibility, perceptions of commitment, and resolve than about using the resources that had been built up in these areas to extract themselves from the crisis without provoking war" (1991, 795). For the United States, nuclear weapons transformed the superpower military relationship from a zero-sum game to a mixed-motive game; that is, reducing the opponent's security did not necessarily result in more security for oneself. This new approach had profound implications for unilateral security policies and arms control because it meant that, despite the persistence of competition, there was room for some cooperation (Weber 1991, 795).

The fact that the superpowers perceived this interdependence helped create the conditions for détente, the second postwar phase. Yet as the spiralling arms race and a second cold war in the 1980s attested, superpower détente did not lead directly to stable or wholly mutual forms of cooperation. As Jervis (1988, 331) notes, "for decision makers, the question is never cooperation or defection, but rather what goals to seek and the tactics that will be most apt to reach them." Bilateral agreements helped regulate superpower competition but did not transform their conflict. Weber (1991, 797) concludes that the Strategic Arms Limitation Talks (SALT I and II) did not represent a fundamental convergence of policy goals, values, or preferences between the United States and the Soviet Union, but rather "a coincidental overlapping of second tier hypotheses." However, because the agreements had provisions for monitoring and consultations, they eventually produced "some growth in mutual understanding of strategic models, as well as some joint research into the problems and possibilities that would be raised by emerging weapons technologies" (Weber 1991, 803).

Superpower attempts to regulate their competition through the 1972 Basic Principles Agreement and later consultations on the subject of crises that threatened to escalate to nuclear war proved less successful. This situation was partly because "the formal documents masked significant disagreement and differences in interpretation. If anything, the unrealistic expectations they aroused, the dispute over interpretation of the agreements, the consequent allegations of cheating and defection, and the ensuing distrust and anger exacerbated the management of the conflict between the two nuclear adversaries" (Stein 1991, 438). Over the short term, tacit agreements fared somewhat better. The largely tacit superpower commitments that emerged out of the Cuban Missile Crisis did survive repeated mini crises like the 1970 controversy over Soviet construction of a naval base in Cuba and its attempts to lessen the constraints the United States had imposed on Soviet stationing of offensive weaponry on the island (Garthoff 1985, 77–79). Nevertheless, along with misunderstandings generated by more explicit agreements, these tacit agreements may have contributed in the long term to undermining bilateral détente. Superpower competition in the Third World throughout the 1970s and renewed cold war by the beginning of the 1980s also reinforced negative images.[1]

1. Herman similarly argues that the BPA became a "casualty of continuous superpower efforts to shape political outcomes in the Third World for unilateral advantage." However, liberal thinkers who laid the groundwork for Gorbachev's New Thinking came to recognize "the transformative but wasted potential of the BPA." The problem, according to these foreign-policy revisionists, was not that superpower détente had been overambitious. On the contrary, détente had been too timid; it had neglected to address the root causes of the cold war conflict, thereby foregoing any chance to move from managed rivalry to full-fledged collaboration (1996, 191–92).

For the most part, multilateral agreements dealt with matters peripheral to superpower competition or an asymmetry of interests (George 1988). The objective was to avoid or reduce competition in a given dimension or area of the security relationship by removing an existing or potential source of conflict (Austrian State Treaty; Antarctica Treaty; 1962 Laos Neutralization Agreement; Quadrapartite Agreement of 1971; 1960s tacit agreement regarding reconnaissance).

These various security arrangements were intended to limit the harmful effects of unrestrained competition for enhanced security and influence. Although evidence of the preconditions and effectiveness of shared norms of competition is "episodic and unsatisfactory" (Stein 1991, 439), we may draw a few conclusions. First, where common interests were at stake, agreements lacking institutionalization were more likely to break down since there were no regularized means for clarifying ambiguities under nonthreatening conditions, for reassessing interpretations of the commitments, or for applying the norms in novel situations. However, Rittberger and Zürn have found that at least "controlled conflict management," in which the disputants have access to an informational forum that allows for communication between them, may be an important development in the progression toward more institutionalized forms of cooperative conflict management. This may help account for the relative stability of agreements like SALT I and SALT II (Rittberger and Zürn 1990).

Although most of the multilateral agreements in the cold war dealt with peripheral matters that did not fundamentally alter the status quo, a few were more central to East-West conflict. They contributed to the transformation of conflict between the superpowers in several ways. First, to the extent that multilateral agreements like the Quadrapartite Agreement on Berlin, which was one of the West's preconditions for convening the CSCE, removed a key source of tension between the superpowers, this helped stabilize their relations and create a basis for further initiatives. Second, some multilateral agreements emerged out of concerns from bloc member states to avert a superpower condominium: France's policy of rapprochement, West Germany's Ostpolitik, as well as the plan of the European Economic Community (ECC), the newly developed European Political Cooperation, intended to promote ECC foreign-policy coordination. There were also various third-party initiatives in the UN and in Europe. Much of this regional activity became focused on a proposal for a European Security Conference first proposed by Soviets in 1954 and reintroduced in the 1960s.

Third, the fact that the superpowers tried to realize joint gains (collusion) while also seeking to avert a relapse into another round of cold war and brinkmanship led other members of the East-West system to work to alter the stakes so that accommodation would include their interests rather than come at their expense. Fourth, the investment that other states in the East-West system made in multilateral alternatives also created its own dynamics. Alliance members' commitments to multilateral solutions tied the superpowers into the process. And finally, the entry of third parties (both alliance members and nonaligned members) into the debate on how to transform the cold war also enhanced the possibilities for working out the question of institutional supply in favor of the comprehensive treatment of outstanding issues and the search for joint gains. However, a number of obstacles impeded efforts to multilateralize and institutionalize détente in the 1960s and early 1970s.

Origins of a European Security Conference

The idea for a European Security Conference (ESC) stems from the 1954 Berlin conference of the Four Great Powers to resolve the status of the two Germanies. Molotov proposed a "Draft General European Treaty" on collective security in order to avoid the onus of failure after having rejected a plan by the British Foreign Secretary Anthony Eden (Stanley and Whitt 1970, 25). The Soviet proposal encompassed four principal obligations: (1) refrain from the threat or use of force; (2) consult in the event of a danger of armed attack in Europe; (3) ensure collective security guarantees to any states attacked, such that an aggression against one was an aggression against all other states party to the treaty; and (4) abstain from taking part in any coalition or alliance with aims contrary to those of the treaty (Borawski 1988, 1–2). Periodic review conferences were to be convened to hold consultations, and permanent political and military consultative committees were to be established.

The West found Molotov's initiative unacceptable. It was seen as a means to thwart the French-led plan for a European Defense Community, and when it failed, the entry of West Germany in NATO. The proposed conference would lead to the dissolution of NATO and would relegate the United States to a secondary status in the continent. The proposal was rejected outright, and also the Soviet's follow-on note of March 31, 1954, which sanctioned U.S. participation in the European security system.

The Molotov proposal was also unacceptable given the West's commitment to free elections in Germany. The Soviet plan, however, would have led to enforced limitations on German self-determination, as implied by the Soviet's demand to make Germany neutral (Stanley and Whitt 1970, 25). The United States also treated the subsequent October 23, 1954, Soviet note on the question of convening a security conference as a "deceptive fascade" (Borawski 1988, 20), even though the Soviets hinted they would discuss Western proposals for all-German elections, as well as the Austrian peace treaty and atomic disarmament, on the condition that West German militarization be abandoned (Ulam 1974, 557–56). The United States set forth a number of preconditions (considered essential to German unification) for convening a European conference, including ratification of the Paris agreements, agreement on the Austrian State Treaty, and clarification on the Soviet's position on all-German free elections (Borawski 1988, 3). Ultimately, the four powers were unable to reach agreement on a procedure for calling elections and dissolving the separate German governments. In any case, the West questioned whether the Soviets were really prepared to sacrifice East Germany for a united, neutral Germany (Stanley and Whitt 1970).

The result of these failed attempts in 1954 led to the deeper division of the blocs. The Soviets' attempt to establish a European security system was reduced to a meeting of Communist-bloc states (with China sending an observer), which led to the founding of the Warsaw Pact and East German membership in it. From this point on, the West moved to negotiate from a position of strength, while the Soviets adopted a policy of two Germanies, which "included the recognition of the status quo by extension of diplomatic recognition to the Federal Republic and an invitation to its Chancellor to visit Moscow" (Stanley and Whitt 1970, 26). Russia insisted the West reciprocate its gesture by recognizing East Germany, but the West would neither recognize its legitimacy nor the existence of a divided Europe with mutually exclusive spheres of influence.

The Berlin meeting was followed by the 1955 Geneva Summit, which was the first encounter among the Four Powers at the level of heads of state since the 1945 Potsdam meeting. The West presented the second Eden Plan, which called for a demilitarized area between East and West on the eastern frontier of Germany. This idea and Eden's call for a security pact were picked up by the Soviet bloc and advocated in Soviet proposals calling for disengagement, a collective security pact to replace the military alliances, and the mutual renunciation of force as well as a freeze on existing levels of armed forces (Stanley and Whitt 1970). These ideas were invoked in later proposals for the disengagement of the two military blocs, including the 1957 plan by Adam Rapacki, the Polish foreign minister who called for a nuclear-free zone in Central Europe; and the Gomulka Plan of 1960, which proposed the creation of a denuclearized area encompassing the two Germanies, Poland, and Czechoslovakia (Stanley and Whitt 1970; Aćimović 1981; Ghebali 1989). The Eden plan and subsequent proposals in the same vein contained several measures that foreshadowed the future negotiations on Confidence and Security Building measures in the CSCE (Borawski 1988, 3).

By way of French initiative, the 1955 Geneva Summit was used by the West to put the development of human contacts on the agenda of East-West negotiations. The West's objective was to eliminate the barriers that impeded the free flow of information, communication, and trade between the people of East and West, and to promote freer contacts and exchanges to the mutual benefit of all the people and countries concerned (Ghebali 1989, 267). But the Soviets refused to entertain ideas that they did not believe were subject to a multilateral approach (including the reciprocal establishment of centers of information and diffusion and exchange of information, films, or students). On other points the Soviets insisted on collective or state and officially sponsored exchanges, which did not accord with the spontaneous, free movement of millions of private, individual citizens as intended by Western proposals. While there was no possibility of reaching a comprehensive agreement in 1955, the West argued that "the Soviet bloc system is based upon artificial conditions which cannot withstand free contact with the outer world," and concluded that " 'the terrible thing is that the Russian Government fears our friendship more than our enmity' " (as quoted in Ghebali 1989, 271).

The Geneva Summit and subsequent Conference of Foreign Ministers framed the two blocs' mutually opposing policy positions on European security and cooperation, which persisted for the next fifteen years (Stanley and Whitt 1970, 25). However, these ideas for improving the military-security and human dimension of East-West relations re-emerged in the mid- to late 1960s in conjunction with renewed Eastern bloc proposals and Western counterproposals to initiate a European security conference (Stanley and Whitt 1970, 25–27; Ghebali 1989, 272). During détente these ideas were pursued in the context of a much broader multilateral debate.

Eastern Bloc Proposals

Following up on the original Soviet call for an ESC, in July 1966 the Warsaw Pact issued the "Bucharest Declaration on Strengthening Peace and Security in Europe." The declaration called for the negotiation of a security regime based on cooperation between states of different social systems and on disarmament measures. The 1960s presented new dangers but also new opportunities to renew the Soviet initiative. U.S. intervention in Vietnam posed the threat of increased capitalist aggression and danger to peace in Europe. However, it was also an opportunity to erode U.S. influence in Europe while the United States was distracted with problems elsewhere. The Soviets stepped up their détente policy with Western Europe, although not with West Germany.

Détente posed political risks for both bloc leaders. As early as September 1965, Brezhnev called for the strengthening of the Warsaw Pact, including the creation of machinery for consultations on pressing problems. In response to these initiatives, including similar calls from Soviet leaders at the 23rd Congress of the CPSU, Nicolae Ceausescu, Romanian communist party general secretary, condemned the military blocs and emphasized the importance of the free development of economic, cultural, scientific, and political ties between all countries regardless of social systems. And while Ceausescu called for further developing co-fraternal relations among communist bloc nations, he rejected increased military preparedness. To this end he renewed Romania's demand for the liquidation of the military blocs and bases. For Ceausescu, the high priority Brezhnev gave to obtaining recognition of the status quo in Central Europe and preventing West German "revanchists" from getting access to nuclear weapons was much less urgent (Birnbaum 1970, 51).

The Bucharest Declaration of 1966 encompassed compromise language on these intra-bloc differences, focusing on both the dangers and opportunities of the European situation. The declaration invoked the dangers of aggressive (revanchist) forces, as well as opportunities to further the interests of peace and security. It called for "the renunciation of the threat of force or the use of force," for the "settlement of disputes only by peaceful means . . . based on the principles of sovereignty and national independence, equality and noninterference in domestic affairs, and on respect of territorial inviolability," and for the abandonment "of claims for the frontiers of Europe to be carved up again."[2] At the same time the declaration called for movement on specific matters, including (1) the creation of a post-NATO and Warsaw Pact system of European security, (2) the abolition of foreign bases, (3) the withdrawal of foreign forces from foreign territories to national frontiers, (4) the reduction of armed forces of both Germanies and the establishment of nuclear-weapon free zones, and (5) the recognition of "the immutability of frontiers" as the "foundation of a lasting peace in Europe."

The Eastern European members of the Warsaw Pact did not share all of the Soviet priorities and objectives. This situation produced certain inconsistencies in the Bucharest Declaration,[3] as well as differing interpretations by Warsaw Pact members of several key demands and objectives stated in the declaration. The primary Soviet objective was to prevent the development of pan-European cooperation. Yet the Bucharest Declaration notes that "it is necessary that all member States of the North Atlantic Pact and the Warsaw Treaty, and also the countries who do not participate in any military alliances, should exert efforts on a bilateral or multilateral basis" to advance the cause of European security. Although the action program that the declaration outlines omits reference to political cooperation, elsewhere it states that "there is no area of peaceful co-operation where the European states could not find opportunities for further

2. See "Extracts from 'Declaration on Strengthening Peace and Security in Europe,' Bucharest, July 1966," reproduced in Palmer (1971, 77). Although this quotation is taken from the 1966 Appeal, subsequent appeals reiterated these principles and key issues.

3. See Birnbaum (1970) for a thorough discussion of these differences in light of the declaration's main points.

mutually beneficial steps."[4] The call for strengthening political relations between states without regard to their social system (although delimited to relations aimed at defending peace) also left open the possibility of political cooperation (Birnbaum 1970, 52–57).

As concerned preconditions, the Bucharest Declaration required that cooperation should be on an equal footing, and in this context it specified the establishment of normal relations between East and West, including normal relations with both Germanies. Although the Soviet Union and East Germany sought to limit the growth of West German contacts and influence in Eastern Europe, the wording was sufficiently vague to serve competing purposes within the Warsaw Pact (Birnbaum 1970, 54). The emphasis in the text on the expansion of "good neighborly relations" was probably more an East European than a Soviet concern. Eastern European countries sought greater trade ties and technological assistance from Western Europe to help stimulate their economies. Like the Soviet Union, Poland remained cautious toward West Germany,[5] but Czechoslovakia and Hungary were more anxious to establish better relations and received an official West German envoy in January 1967. Romania went even further and agreed to exchange ambassadors on January 31, 1967, calling this "a major contribution to European security and international *détente* in the spirit of the Bucharest Declaration" (Birnbaum 1970, 60; emphasis in original). Moreover, while the Soviets interpreted consolidation of the status quo to mean fixation of post-World War II borders and the dividing line in Central Europe, for the East Europeans fixation of these borders was "important exactly because it could facilitate the loosening of Moscow's grip over Eastern Europe" (Birnbaum 1970, 57).

For the Soviets the real issue at stake was the fortification of its own position. They increasingly insisted on the deference of their allies on major issues of foreign policy as well as the right of suppression of internal processes of liberalization and democratization. The West dubbed these principles the Brezhnev doctrine, first clearly demonstrated by the invasion of Czechoslovakia and again put to the test by economic riots in Poland in 1970, when military intervention was contemplated but averted by Gomulka's ousting (Ulam 1974, 745–46). The Soviet commitment to watch over the domestic developments in Eastern Europe was a considerable burden. According to Ulam, these Eastern

4. See "Extracts from 'Declaration on Strengthening Peace and Security in Europe,' Bucharest, July 1966," reproduced in Palmer (1971, 79–80).

5. However, Gomulka used the Bucharest Declaration as a means for legitimizing his efforts to renew Poland's traditionally good ties with France. These policies, launched by de Gaulle to loosen the bloc structures, were said to coincide with the aims of the socialist countries " 'to ease tensions and dispel the threat of armed conflict in Europe' " (as quoted in Birnbaum 1970, 56).

European vassals, not other countries elsewhere in the free world, were the real potential " 'dominoes': if one totters, they all may collapse" (1974, 746).[6] Moscow's interest in promoting peaceful coexistence with the West thus revealed a powerful bias in favor of the status quo.

The Soviet position on any reconciliation with West Germany continued to depend on the latter's recognition of the status quo in Central Europe. The Soviets rigorously maintained that a "German peace settlement is in accord with the interests of peace in Europe,"[7] and more specifically that

> the interests of peace and security in Europe and throughout the world, like the interests of the German people, demand that the ruling circles of the Federal Republic take the real state of affairs in Europe into account, and this means that they take as their point of departure the existence of two German States, abandon their claims for the frontiers of Europe to be carved up again, abandon their claims to the right exclusively to represent the whole of Germany and their attempts to bring pressure to bear on States that recognize the German Democratic Republic.[8]

By late 1970, recognition of East Germany became a Soviet precondition to "security in Europe." This and other preconditions for dealing with the German questions, as well as the Warsaw Pact's own agenda for a European security conference, were stated in the 24th Congress of the CPSU in Moscow in 1971 (Chernenko 1975, 4–6).

As concerned participants, the Soviet bloc's position on the proposed ESC called for all European states to be invited.[9] In addition to the European NATO and Warsaw Pact member states, the 1966 declaration specifically called on those countries not participating in a military alliance to "exert efforts on a bilateral or multilateral basis with the objective of advancing the cause of European security."[10] Still more specifically, as to convening a European security conference, the Warsaw Pact members noted "our countries are ready to take

6. In fact Ulam (1974, 746) predicted in 1974 that the lessons of 1968 would keep Eastern European governments in line for some time, but that "it is almost inevitable that in time there will be another explosion: national aspirations cannot be repressed or contained indefinitely."

7. See "Bucharest Appeal," in Palmer (1971, 80–81).

8. See ibid., 77.

9. See ibid., 78, 80. The term "all-European" implied the United States and Canada should not be parties to the efforts of the Europeans to work out a new security arrangement. The assertion that "the European States are capable of solving the questions of relations between them without outside interference" ("Bucharest Appeal 1966," 78) further underscored suspicions in the West that these appeals were mere efforts to divide and separate the Western alliance from its American partner.

10. See ibid., 80.

part in such a conference at any time convenient to the other interested states, both members of the North Atlantic Treaty and neutrals." The declaration asserted that "neutral European countries could also play a positive rôle in the convocation of such a meeting." [11] The conclusion of the 1969 Budapest Message contained as well an implicit reference to third-party efforts, recommending that:

> a practical step towards strengthening European security would be a meeting, at the earliest possible date, of representatives of all interested European States, to establish by mutual agreement the procedure for calling the conference and also to determine the items on its agenda. *We are ready to consider at the same time any other proposal concerning the method for preparing and convening this conference.*[12]

The early Soviet bloc proposals (1954 and 1966) for convening an all-European security conference placed them in the initiator's position. To state the problem in Zartman and Berman's words, "to the party which has not (yet) decided to negotiate, the decision of the other party is a prima facie reason for the first to continue to refuse because it makes it appear that the other party is yielding" (1982, 62). The very issue of agreeing to negotiate entailed a number of considerations for the Western alliance. Kissinger held that the decision to negotiate would be a sign of weakness or concession from the West.[13] The West would risk appearing to recognize and legitimize the Eastern bloc's claim (through the organ of the Warsaw Pact and hence the hegemony of the Soviet Union) to participate in the solution of the issue, and in effect, the ratification of the East-West division.[14] The West also risked granting legitimacy to the way the East

11. See ibid., 81. Subsequent Warsaw Pact communiqués continued to include overtures to non-bloc countries as well as support for convening the European Parliamentary Conference, which could be interpreted as recognition of the efforts of the Group of Nine countries. See "Extracts from 'Statement on European Security,' Karlovy Vary, April 1967," in Palmer (1971, 84).

12. See Palmer, "Extracts from 'Message from the Warsaw Pact States to all European Countries,' Budapest, March 1969," in Palmer (1971, 86–87), emphasis added. Chapter 4 explores in detail the relationship between the Budapest communiqué and Finland's May 1969 initiative to sponsor and host the preparatory meeting and security conference. According to Vladimirov (1993), this initiative arose out of Soviet consultations with President Kekkonen during early 1969, although Jakobson (1983) gives a different account.

13. Recounting a meeting he attended with Kekkonen, Nixon, and Kissinger, Jakobson says that "Kissinger's interest in the European security conference remained lukewarm, however. He departed from the position that organizing the conference had become an end in itself to the Soviet leaders. Agreeing to it was then a concession from the US side" (1983, 286).

14. This was apparently a strong enough concern that the memorandum in which the Finnish government launched its proposal for convening multilateral consultations in Helsinki noted that

had identified the negotiable issues. The alternative was for the West to exact its own price for agreeing to the conference. Its method was to obtain as many concessions in return as possible—notably Soviet agreement on a conference on military force reductions. In this way the Alliance members challenged the nature and purpose of the conference proposed by the Soviet bloc.[15]

Western Response

New impetus for a political settlement of the divisions in Europe came with the Berlin crisis as well as the Cuban Missile Crisis. The Soviet move in August 1961 to erect the Berlin Wall revealed the lack of U.S. and Western resolve to use force and risk war to reverse the increasingly demarcated separation of the two Germanies. Willy Brandt was among the West German leaders who saw in these developments the necessity of a new Ostpolitik. Anticipating his future foreign-policy initiatives, as early as December 1961 he wrote that the great challenge for German foreign policy was to enter a "new relationship with the Great Power in the East" (Barnet 1983, 231; see also Hanrieder 1989, 171; and Baring 1984, 201–02). The Western allies were also disconcerted by the fact that, during the Cuban Missile Crisis, the United States informed them of its decisions but did not consult them (Pfetsch 1981, 153). The different détente policies NATO countries launched vis-à-vis the East in the aftermath of the Cuban Missile Crisis challenged alliance cohesion throughout the 1960s.

Under the Kennedy Administration, U.S. détente policy in Central Europe came to mean a normalization within the framework of the status quo (George, Farley, and Dallin 1988). Arms control replaced such intractable issues as German unification on the U.S.-Soviet agenda. Accommodation replaced confrontation, as the United States and the Soviet Union developed a common interest to stabilize the European state system. Washington conceded the reality of a divided Europe and sought to sustain its stability under an American-Soviet condominium, if necessary. The United States was reluctant to support German policies that would deny the recognition and legitimization of conditions maintaining the military and strategic balance in Europe, because the division of Germany was a fundamental factor in this equation (Handrieder 1989,

---

"the Finnish Government has emphasized that the participation of Governments in various stages of the present process of consultation and negotiation does not imply recognition under international law, of existing political circumstances in Europe." See "Suomen hallituksen muistio," Ulkoasian launsuntojaja Asiakirja (hereafter ULA) 1970, 73.

15. This is the strategy that Jakobson (1983, 285–86) attributes to Kissinger, with whom he met while accompanying Finnish President Urho Kekkonen on an official visit to the White House in July 1970.

172–73). The United States began to press Bonn to accept the political normalization under way, and demanded movement toward a West German modus vivendi on European problems (Haftendorn 1985, 81).

For Bonn, Washington's policies regarding a European settlement were too conservative—too concerned with maintaining the status quo—whereas de Gaulle's vision of a Europe from the Atlantic to the Urals was too far-reaching. From the West German perspective, both the United States and France were prepared for different reasons to exploit the circumstances at the Federal Republic's expense. Moreover, France's policy of rapprochement called into question Germany's long-standing premise of reunification—i.e., that Bonn would support France's European (e.g. EEC policies) and Atlantic policies in exchange for French support of Bonn's Eastern policy, thus safeguarding the Federal Republic's territorial, cultural, and historic interests. By establishing ties with the East, France undermined the legal premise of the German unification policy while it obstructed Germany's NATO-oriented security policy. As Handrieder notes, "the apparent loosening of the Warsaw Pact, which French policy sought to accelerate and exploit, and the dynamics of the bilateral accommodation between Washington and Moscow, which American policy sought to sustain, made it appear imperative that the Germans themselves take some initiative" on the Eastern questions (1989, 18). Throughout the early and mid-1960s, Bonn's emphasis on the legal and political foundations of its Eastern policy became rigid and increasingly anachronistic; by the late 1960s, West Germany became increasingly isolated from both East and West (Baring 1984, 200).

UNDER DE GAULLE the French built up their own nuclear force, withdrew French forces from the NATO command, and distanced French East-West policy from the United States politically. In 1966 De Gaulle headed to Moscow on a state visit to discuss his vision of a new Europe extending from "the Atlantic to the Urals." In France's attempt to resist U.S. influence over the European continent, Germany was rendered a "junior partner." From 1963 to the late 1960s, U.S. efforts to work out its bilateral relationship with the Soviet Union instilled fear in West German leaders that the policy of nonrecognition and strength would not bring Germany closer to reunification. U.S.-Soviet efforts to reach a nuclear nonproliferation treaty while effectively maintaining their own nuclear superiority over the heads of European allies (amid President Lyndon Johnson's decision in December 1964 to scrap the ill-fated Multilateral Force—a fleet of carriers for nuclear missiles) only served to fuel these fears. The European territorial status quo had obtained "de facto" if not "de jure" recognition among the Western powers (Handrieder 1989, 176). Germany would have to redefine the question of unity by replacing territorial demands with a policy of political rapprochement. Thus, as West Germany moved beyond the Adenauer era, Chancellor Erhard sought to balance Atlantic pressures to keep secure ties between West Germany and the United States against fears of an emerging superpower entente and the danger of being isolated.

The United States, Great Britain, and France held onto their Four Powers rights in Berlin more to retain influence over the ultimate political settlement of the German Question and to safeguard their own national interests and prestige than to achieve German unification. During the 1960s, the German Question was increasingly placed in the pan-European context of a multipartite European settlement. This was in contrast to the various proposals of the 1950s which discussed a European settlement in terms of German peace treaties and the possibility of German neutrality (Baring 1984, 230–31). Even by 1959, before embarking on his new diplomatic campaigns in the East, de Gaulle had recognized the Oder-Neisse line. "There was a growing recognition that a solution or even attenuation of Germany's division could take place only within the wider context of the European state system, that the partition of Germany and partition of Europe were intertwined in a convoluted political and historical dialectic" (Handrieder 1989, 177). This situation led to the Europeanization of the German Question.

Meanwhile, in West Germany domestic pressures on the right and left were building, creating the need for a new understanding with Eastern Europe (Pfetsch 1981, 151–54). Recognizing the post-World War II Eastern boundaries was also a necessary precondition for developing West German ties to the East. However, this required Bonn's renunciation of the 1955 Hallstein Doctrine (which banned diplomatic ties with any states, except the Soviet Union, that recognized East Germany), something neither the Adenauer government or the Erhard government was yet prepared to do. Without compromising the Hallstein Doctrine, Gerhard Schröder, foreign minister during the last years of Adenauer's government, and then foreign minister to Erhard, initiated normalization of West German relations with Eastern Europe. This led to the establishment of trade missions in Budapest, Sofia, Warsaw, and Bucharest, and the launching of the West German "Ostpolitik" (Haftendorn 1985, 120; Barnet 1983, 246). These policies were carried forward by Willy Brandt, who became chancellor in 1970. Building on his earlier initiatives (for example, the Berlin Pass Agreement of 1963) and on his strategy of achieving changes through a policy of small steps, Brandt launched a new Ostpolitik. He abandoned as unrealistic the debate of the 1960s on whether bilateral treaties with the DDR, Poland, or Czechoslovakia could be used to break the bloc system and liberalize East-West relations. Instead, he signed a nonaggression treaty first with Moscow and thereafter with Poland, the DDR, and Czechoslovakia (Pfetsch 1981, 160–61). Although these agreements did not legitimize the post-World

War II borders, they secured a commitment on both sides not to violate the borders. The immediate aim was to normalize relations with the Soviet Union and the other Eastern European states, but the long-term objective was to create the preconditions for the solution of the German Question (Haftendorn 1985, 122). The Brandt initiative became the basis for a new Soviet attitude toward Germany and brought about the beginning of Moscow's "opening policy," which led to summit meetings with President Nixon, the SALT I agreement, the ABM treaty, and finally—the crowning achievement—the 1975 Helsinki Final Act (Schmidt 1989, 25).

Specter of Structural Changes

In some Western circles, the Soviet's proposal for a security conference was seen as an attempt to prevent Western European integration and dilute the internal cooperation of the EEC. Many conservatives also believed that cross-bloc developments were especially attractive to social democrats and other liberal and leftist West European groups.[16] European-wide opposition to U.S. policies in Vietnam and the 1968 cultural revolution and student protest movements raised the specter of a West in decay and disorder (Barnet 1983, 272). The U.S. president also faced domestic legislative action by Senator Mike Mansfield, who, starting in 1966, introduced a series of amendments threatening unilateral troop withdrawals from Europe (Borawski 1988, 11).

For conservatives, these developments portended Western appeasement and revealed a lack of moral resolve. They were concerned with West Germany's accommodation toward the Soviet Union as a means of achieving reunification. Conservatives feared this would lead to West Germany's neutralization—both politically and ideologically. Détente was a thinly veiled disguise for a process leading to Europe's loss of independence—that is, to its Finlandization (Garfinkle 1978, 18–19).[17]

Despite the earlier talk of "bridge building" and the "pontifications about the need to differentiate among the individual members of the socialist camp," the United States remained concerned that the peaceful engagement of Eastern Europe would antagonize the Soviet Union. The United States policy toward

16. The United States recalled its ambassador from Stockholm for consultations when in early 1968 Olof Palme, then Swedish Education Minister, led an anti-American demonstration alongside the North Vietnamese Ambassador to Moscow (Jönsson and Petersson 1985, 82).

17. A central aspect of Garfinkle's argument is the anticipatory deference shown by such weak states as Finland toward a great power, here the Soviet Union. Scholars of Finnish foreign policy, as well as Finnish policymakers themselves, found the appropriation of the "Finlandization" metaphor unfortunate. See also Maude (1982, 4–5).

Eastern Europe during three successive administrations from presidents Eisenhower to Johnson amounted to "no policy." The more than decade-long U.S. efforts to engage the Soviet Union in an accommodative relationship precluded serious overtures to Eastern Europe, a premise which the Nixon-Kissinger doctrine did not challenge. "East Europe was perceived as adding an unnecessary factor to an already complex equation" (Korbonski 1973, 193). The gestures to Romania and Yugoslavia aside, broad-based efforts to launch pluralistic East-West relations were not on the U.S. agenda. U.S. policy was based on realpolitik and on "the premise that 'liberation' of East Europe is impossible in the foreseeable future" (Korbonski 1973, 226). In other words, the rules of the superpower relations, based on the notions of sphere of influence and the maintenance of the status quo, were not challenged (Lieber and Lieber 1979, 272–73).

West's Position on a European Security Conference

By the late 1960s, the U.S. policy of stabilization and bilateralism with the Soviet Union, France's withdrawal from the integration of NATO command and its attempts to take the lead in East-West dialogue, and the possibility of the NATO treaty's termination in 1969 contributed to political uncertainty about the alliance's future (Haftendorn 1985, 118). In spite of these centrifugal tendencies, the NATO members determined to develop a common stand and détente policy. At a June 1967 NATO ministerial meeting in Luxembourg, the members initiated a study that resulted six months later in a "landmark decision" known as the Harmel Report.[18] Presented at the 1968 North Atlantic Council meeting in Reykjavik, Iceland, the report assimilated the ideas for improving relations to the East that they had been pursuing separately, including Johnson's notion of "building bridges," de Gaulle's concept of *détente—cooperation—entente,* and Brandt's idea for a "European order of peace."

The Harmel Report was formulated in summary fashion and intended essentially as an instrument to maintain the military capability and political cohesion of the alliance (Haftendorn 1985, 120). The objective was to ensure a controlled process of East-West interaction and change, enhance the political role of NATO, and promote a peaceful settlement of issues dividing Europe (see also Nerlich 1976, 55). This also meant dealing with the German Question, but the alliance commitment "to examine and review suitable policies to achieve a just and stable order in Europe, to overcome the division of Germany and to

18. The Harmel Report to the North Atlantic Council, titled "The Future Tasks of the Alliance," was annexed to the Final Communiquè issued by the NATO Foreign Ministers on the conclusion of their meeting in Brussels, Belgium, on December 13–14, 1967. It is reproduced in Stanley and Whitt (1970, 115–18).

foster European security," proved all too vague and meager to the West Germans (Baring 1984, 230–31).

Among the other issues under study were "disarmament and practical arms control measures, including the possibility of balanced force reductions." The latter was meant to discourage domestic trends toward the unilateral reduction of forces pressed in the U.S. Congress by Senator Mansfield and also under the consideration of the newly installed Trudeau administration in Canada (Spencer 1984, 35). The report was also an effort to paper over alliance divisions occasioned by the Johnson administration's continued propagation and escalation of the Vietnam conflict and generally to limit and channel domestic détente in Europe to the system level, where it could be pursued as a controllable inter-bloc dialogue (Nerlich 1976). The report argued that "the pursuit of détente must not be allowed to split the Alliance" and that the "chances of success will clearly be greatest if the Allies remain on parallel courses" (NATO 1967, 2).

The alliance strategy was to pursue détente by working within the status quo power structures, not through a cross-bloc, inclusive, and transformative European solution. The Harmel Report set forth two principal pillars for NATO policy: deterrence and defense, and negotiation and détente, with the political dimensions mainly subordinated to preserving the defense capability of the alliance. This was evident in the NATO response to the Warsaw Pact-proposed ESC. In contrast to the latter's broad aims, the NATO proposal announced in June 1968 called for Mutual and Balanced Force Reduction (MBFR)—a narrower, more pragmatic approach. While NATO sought to satisfy certain preconditions, it stressed that only concrete measures would lend themselves to negotiation.[19] In December 1969 NATO outlined an agenda for talks on MBFR in Central Europe. The NATO list included possible accompanying measures such as prior notification of military maneuvers, the exchange of observers at such maneuvers, and other militarily significant aspects of force reductions. It also suggested that "examination of techniques and methods of inspection should also be further developed."[20]

As with its approach to security, on the issue of principles dealing with cooperation NATO emphasized practical measures, especially those reflecting a Western conception of human rights.[21] The NATO Declaration also drew atten-

19. See "Extracts from Declaration Published by the North Atlantic Council, Brussels, December 1969," reproduced in Palmer (1971, 92).

20. See ibid., 91–92.

21. See the "Final Communiqué and Declaration of December 1969," Issued by the NATO Foreign Ministers after their meeting in Brussels, Belgium, on December 4–5, 1969, reproduced in Stanley and Whitt (1970, 121–26).

tion to some substantive issues relating to an ESC, which the Warsaw Pact had raised in its appeals, among them a lasting peace settlement for Germany, technical and economic cooperation, and cultural exchanges. These goals could be achieved by "freer movement of people, ideas, and information between the countries of East and West," thus resurrecting the Western great powers' agenda presented at the 1955 Geneva conference.

The breakthrough on the alliance position vis-à-vis a European security conference came at the May 1970 Rome meeting. Noting the alliance's readiness to enter into multilateral contacts with all interested governments, the communiqué assured that "one of the main purposes of such contacts would be to explore when it will be possible to convene a conference, or a series of *conferences, on European security and co-operation*" (emphasis mine).[22] Asserting that it "will not be enough to talk of European security in the abstract," the communiqué argued, "the causes of insecurity in Europe are specific, they are deeply rooted in conflicting perceptions of State interests, and their elimination will require patient endeavour." Affirming the willingness of the alliance to negotiate those concrete issues whose resolution would enhance the security of Europe, the allies foresaw the establishment of a permanent body as one means to embark on multilateral negotiations and called for inclusion of the following subjects in particular: "(a) the principles which should govern relations between States, including the renunciation of force; (b) the development of international relations with a view to contributing to the freer movement of people, ideas and information and to developing cooperation in the cultural, economic, technical and scientific fields as well as in the field of human environment."[23]

NATO once again set out certain preconditions that would have to be secured before a European security conference could be convened (see also Borawski 1988, 2–3). By forcing the Warsaw Pact to meet these conditions (including progress on the West German negotiations with the East, the MBFR, and a Four Power agreement on Berlin), NATO could exact its own substantial price from Moscow. For its part, the U.S. approach was to point to the absence of a Soviet response to the NATO proposals for MBFR talks and progress on the situation in Berlin as a means of explaining what was a rather meager Western agenda. U.S. Secretary of State William P. Rogers himself observed that

22. See "Extracts from Declaration on Mutual Balanced Force Reductions Published by the Ministers of the Countries Participating in NATO's Integrated Defense Programme, Rome, May 1970," reproduced in Palmer (1971, 95). This can be taken as the original impetus to give the conference the name of Conference on Security and Cooperation in Europe, which emphasized its relationship to Europe but not its "all-European" character as the Soviet term "European Security Conference" implied.

23. See ibid.

> the Warsaw Pact proposals do not deal with these fundamental questions [regarding a European security system]. What is proposed cannot properly be described as a security conference at all. The Warsaw Pact countries have suggested merely (1) that a conference discuss an East-West agreement on the principle of nonuse of force—which has been a basic principle of the United Nations Charter for over 20 years, so that another pronouncement on the nonuse of force would have no meaning—and (2) increased trade and technical exchanges, for which regular diplomatic channels are always available. (as quoted in Borawski 1988, 9–10)

The substance of a CSCE agenda was not initially the primary concern of the United States. The United States pushed key issues through bilateral channels with the Soviet Union, and in the case of Berlin, among the Four Great Powers. But common positions in NATO were essential to assure alliance solidarity. Viewed from other perspectives (and certainly from the French perspective), this same strategy provided means for circumventing a plurality of alliance views, proposals, and activities aspiring to broader and deeper systemic change (Maresca 1985, 20).

Cross-Bloc Alternatives

With the reduced likelihood of direct superpower confrontation or threat of a European or global conflagration under détente, the neutral and nonaligned countries promoted pan-European cooperation through a more activist foreign policy aimed at democratizing international relations and improving collective efforts for international security (Aćimović 1981, 61; Hakovirta 1983; Binter 1985, 1989). Their initiatives on matters concerning East-West conflict and cooperation challenged the superpowers' status quo orientation. By insisting on their inclusion in a multilateral process of East-West détente with significant military-security issues, the neutral and nonaligned challenged the superpowers' control over East-West security.

EVEN THOUGH the European neutrals' political, economic, and social systems were then closely associated with Western democratic values as a whole, they shared many concerns with such nonaligned states as Yugoslavia and Malta. The commonality between the neutral and nonaligned also inhered from the fact that the traditional legal basis of neutrality as a practice in wartime was being replaced in the post-World War II period by the customary norms of neutral states emphasizing the peacetime dimension of their neutrality policy. To some extent, the neutrals shared with nonbloc states an activist orientation to foreign policy because of their similar structural position in the international system. They shared the perceived risk of increasing East-West tensions on their security, a critical stance toward the growing arms race, and the violation of the rights of small states. They also shared greater solidarity than other Western European countries with the demands of the developing world, including those on issues of colonialism and racism. In the European context, Yugoslavia served as a vital link between the global nonaligned movement and the peace policies of European neutrals (Hakovirta 1983, 60–61). The prospect of a superpower condominium, which Yugoslavia criticized on behalf of the nonaligned movement, was echoed by Sweden's Olof Palme in what became known as the Palme Doctrine. It condemned U.S. actions in Vietnam, Soviet intervention in Czechoslovakia, and the exploitation of the South, also exacerbated by the arms race between East and West.

Smaller aligned European states also maintained that solutions to East-West conflict should be inclusive and comprehensive. These states were active both within and outside their alliance, promoting greater cross-bloc contacts (Belgium, Bulgaria, Hungary, Romania, Holland), comprehensive disarmament and security measures (Switzerland, Austria, Sweden, Yugoslavia, Romania), greater security for independent communist orientations (especially Romania and Yugoslavia), and recognition of both the acceptability of neutrality and the Westerness of its practitioners—ideologically, politically, and economically—in the bipolar structure of the bloc system (Finland).

The small aligned, neutral, and nonaligned states accepted each other as legitimate stakeholders in institutionalizing détente and forwarding international agreements and cooperation in the field of disarmament (Väyrynen 1973, 101; Palmer 1971; Kirk Laux 1972). The UN was a central arena for Sweden's active neutrality policy, where it brought expertise to bear on various multilateral fora dealing with disarmament and nonproliferation (Andrén 1967; Birnbaum 1970; Huldt 1984). For Sweden, Austria, and Finland, the UN was also an important arena for offering good offices and third-party mediation and for providing peacekeeping troops (Hakovirta 1988).

A loose coalition of small aligned European states from the East (Bulgaria, Hungary, and Romania), the West (Belgium, Denmark, and after 1967 Holland), the neutral (Austria, Finland, and Sweden), and nonaligned states (Yugoslavia) came together in the early 1960s in the UN to form the Group of Nine. Its activities were among the most notable third-party efforts to expand the number of states with a stake in European détente. These countries sought to alter the range and salience of issues to be considered, and thus to influence the debate on who was to participate in the multilateralization of détente and how the issues should be distributed among the various fora proposed.

While the first initiative of the Group of Nine was launched in the UN General Assembly, the former's concerns and objectives were clearly regional and

European. Between 1965 and 1969 they came to play a prominent role working for détente, foreshadowing coordination among the grouping of neutral and nonaligned states in the CSCE that developed almost a decade later.[24] The Group of Nine's efforts also served as a catalyst for third-party initiatives and cooperation on East-West issues. Although the ties between the Group of Nine countries were limited before the group first came together in the UN in the fall of 1965, this situation was gradually transformed. If prior to 1965 only the four neutrals each had full diplomatic relations with all of the other eight countries (Kirk Laux 1972, 150), during the next four years relations among all the Group of Nine states were formalized. Their association was consolidated through numerous bilateral visits and communiqués, consultations, group resolutions, and the mutual sponsorship of resolutions in other international organizations (Kirk Laux 1972, 147, 150–51).

The Romanian delegation first raised the issue of regional cooperation in Europe for inclusion in the agenda of the fifteenth General Assembly of the UN in 1960.[25] Although it failed to receive attention at the time, the matter was reintroduced by Romania in 1963, when it was determined that international support for regional agreements was on the rise.[26] Eventually, the Romanian initiative was included in the agenda for the twentieth session and sent to the First Committee. In 1965 Romania submitted a draft for adoption in the General Assembly under the co-sponsorship of Finland and other Group of Nine countries. As suggested by its title, Resolution 2129 called for "Actions on a regional level with a view to improving good neighborly relations among European states having different social and political systems."[27] The resolution "sprang from the conviction of the sponsors that regional measures were called for in order to find solutions to specifically European problems, but that they could also have a positive effect on international relations as a whole" (Huopaniemi 1973, 8). They promoted the "transformation of the European international system away from inter-bloc relations to pluralized, inter-national relations in which all states, in principle, should participate equally" (Kirk Laux

24. For a characterization of these ten countries' individual foreign policies and their contributions to this détente process, see Davidson (1972).

25. See "Supplementary List of Items for the Agenda of the Fifteenth Regular Session of the General Assembly: Item Proposed by Romania," *Official Records of the General Assembly, Fifteenth Session, Annexes,* Agenda Item 75, Document A/4440, Aug. 18, 1960, 1–3.

26. See "Romania: Request for the Inclusion of an Additional Item in the Agenda of the Eighteenth Session," *Official Records of the General Assembly, Eighteenth Session, Annexes,* Document A/5557, Sept. 26, 1963, 1–3.

27. "Action on the Regional Level with a View to Improving Good Neighborly Relations Among European States Having Different Social and Political Systems," *Annexes,* Document A/6207, Dec. 18, 1965, 1–3.

1972, 148). They advocated respect for basic norms—such as sovereignty, equality, full participation, and cooperation—among European states rather than between the blocs.

Despite the seemingly ad hoc nature of their association, these states, in Kirk Laux's view, expressed a "consistent group 'interest' in transforming international politics away from hierarchical and interbloc relations to pluralized inter-state relations conducted on the basis of sovereign equality" (1972, 153). The appeal for equal participation by all states in European relations was rationalized by the invocation of national sovereignty (citing UN Charter principles) and was made operational by introducing draft programs or special conferences on all-European problems for representatives from all-European states. Although on October 4, 1966, the foreign ministers of the Group of Nine held a consultative meeting in New York to continue their actions, this resolution was not followed by further action in the UN. According to Aćimović, "as this project became more and more successful, the hostility and resistance of the great powers grew, and they soon managed to put a stop to it" (1981, 82).

The significance of the Group of Nine's resolution lay not with its approval in the General Assembly but in the impetus it gave to the European Security Conference idea, which gained momentum soon after the Warsaw Pact issued the Bucharest Declaration. Although the efforts of the Group of Nine were thwarted in the UN, they took up the matter in the Interparliamentary Union (IPU).[28] Between 1966 and 1970, different members of the Group of Nine made efforts in the IPU to bring about the all-European Security Conference. Despite the IPU's unanimous adoption of a 1966 Yugoslav proposal calling on the European parliaments to realize the Group of Nine's UN resolution, and the subsequent Belgian offer to host such a conference with delegates from the European member states of the IPU, the effort stalled.

The unresolved political problems of Central Europe and the negative responses from all of the socialist states left the IPU deadlocked. A key obstacle was the Belgian proposal to include on the agenda such topics as the free flow of persons and goods (Huopaniemi 1973, 8–9). On Yugoslav initiative, the national members of the Group of Nine also met in September 1966 in Belgrade and issued a joint communiqué that attempted to circumvent the dispute over an agenda for the proposed IPU all-European conference. They suggested that

28. From its founding in the late 1800s, the IPU had been a central force in bringing about peace conferences. During the first half of the twentieth century, the IPU's commitment to disarmament, the outlawing of war as a means of national policy, and the establishment of democratic parliamentary institutions had both influenced and paralleled at the governmental level international developments such as those leading to the establishment of the League of Nations and later the United Nations (Huopaniemi 1973, 4–5).

the agenda be worked out by common efforts to realize the UN resolution as well as possible. On January 9, 1967, Yugoslavia presented to all European governments "a well received memorandum" to promote cooperation among European countries in different fields, including political relations, economics, industry, agriculture, finance, transport, tourism, labor, information, culture, and science (Aćimović 1981, 82).[29]

However, this initiative and efforts within the Group of Nine and the IPU were interrupted by the 1968 Soviet military intervention in Czechoslovakia. In the aftermath of the crisis, the Group of Nine attempted to reconcile its differences at a meeting held at the UN in October 1969. Attempts were made to enlarge the group by inviting Czechoslovakia, Italy, Poland, and Turkey to attend, but these failed and the group dissolved (Palmer 1971, 10).[30]

In spite of the apparent stalemate or lack of any clear movement toward a solution to the East-West conflict, by the 1960s the moment was ripe for action. Zartman characterizes such a juncture as a "deadlock or blockage to competing unilateral solutions, a high or rising cost, valid spokesman, and an alternative way out that reduces the costs but achieves an acceptable number of the goals and interests originally sought " (1988, 213). The Cuban Missile Crisis brought home the realization that unilateral solutions posed too high a cost. The proposals for an ESC pointed to the growing recognition that ad hoc solutions also no longer sufficed and that the problems of East-West security and cooperation could only be resolved jointly.

The moment was favorable for launching multilateral negotiations between East and West also in terms of power relations. The balance of power was shifting toward equality. In the aftermath of the Czechoslovakian invasion, the Warsaw Pact was more cohesive politically and more powerful militarily. These factors indicated a consolidation of positions vis-à-vis the United States. With the strengthening and enlargement of the European Community, the underdogs of Western Europe became a more coherent voice politically and economically. In addition, the EEC loomed on the horizon as a negotiator in its own right. The Community countries brought with them a new mechanism for foreign-policy coordination, European political cooperation, for which the CSCE became the premier testing grounds (Hill 1983; Stein 1983; Stabreit 1983; Defarges 1986).

29. The issue of inviting the United States and Canada was not brought up during these debates or initiatives in the IPU and among the Group of Nine (Huopaniemi 1973, 8).

30. The IPU initiatives on a European Security Conference remained in the background until the early 1970s. They were given new impetus by the Finnish delegate Johannes Virolainen and the IPU-sponsored Conference on European Security and Cooperation, which convened in Helsinki at the level of parliamentary representation alongside the multilateral, preparatory meeting of the CSCE in 1973.

Many of the smaller, aligned European states were active both within and outside their alliance in promoting the search for a transitional formula (Palmer 1971; Kirk Laux 1972; Davidson 1972). They shared with neutral and nonaligned European states the view that solutions to East-West conflict should be inclusive and comprehensive (Väyrynen 1973, 101).

THE PROPOSALS of East, West, and the N+N called for different types of consultations and fora on different sets of issues, involving different sets of actors. Nevertheless, many of the primary disputants in the cold war were amenable to finding joint solutions for regional problems. The further ripening of the conflict for solution depended on sorting out these alternatives and the preconditions different parties attached to them. An idea had to take hold on which debate and discussion could take place so that alternatives were formulated and agreement could eventually emerge (Zartman 1988, 212).

Despite these favorable developments, by the late 1960s the superpowers became more suspect of the political risks posed by multilateralism. Their resistance contributed to the political deadlock at the end of the decade. Finding a way out depended on resolving competing perspectives on the question of institutional supply. The literature on negotiation analysis and regime theory notes that parties find it difficult to enter into commitments when there is a veil of uncertainty regarding the type of institution to be developed, the participants, the issues to be included in the negotiation agenda (or excluded from it), or the type of obligations likely to emerge. The United States and the Soviet Union each attempted to limit these ambiguities by using the status quo as their referent point. The German Question was especially problematic, and thus more of the same was preferred to fundamental changes. They sought in particular to avoid joint gains that could result in costs born asymmetrically. Unification of the two Germanies posed such a dilemma and had eluded solution since the end of World War II. The fact that the superpowers continued to compete against each other on a global scale throughout détente was also counterproductive, more so because of the linkage strategy that the United States used in the 1970s as a basis for improving relations with the Soviet Union. The superpowers' competitive moves to get unilateral gains drove out the possibilities for cooperative moves to create it jointly. Thus, the superpowers' competition limited also their allies' and the N+N's possibilities for reaching mutually acceptable terms for multilateral solutions (see also Sibenius 1992, 30).

Any attempt to change the nature of the game—that is, the structure of East-West accommodation between the superpowers— introduced a number of unknowns into the bargaining dynamics. In negotiation encounters, there is generally only imperfect information and knowledge about the full set of actual and potential players, their interests, beliefs, and issues at stake. Different parties may perceive alternative rules for behaving and they may envision different sets of agreements. The range of possible solutions may depend on which set of players gets involved in the search for solutions and which issues they bring in or exclude. This in itself can raise or lower the salience of different interests or alter the "rules" of the interaction. Thus, "the collective perception of the 'game's' configuration" depends on who is involved, who is excluded, and the course of action chosen (Sibenius 1992, 24). At the outset, "the menu of possibilities" for changing the structure of the situation may not be common knowledge (31).

Conclusions

The potential for broad-based East-West negotiations on a European Security Conference was evident in the proliferation of proposals offered by both military alliances. Still, impetus had to be given to the process so that the opportunity for multilateral negotiations could be realized. The remaining obstacles were considerable. First, the clash over NATO preconditions and the East bloc's original preference for beginning directly with a conference had to be worked out. Second, the incommensurability of the remaining stakes, which the prior resolution of the Western preconditions occasioned, would raise new questions to be addressed. From a bloc-to-bloc perspective, the proposed conference would be left to negotiate human rights, freedom of information and movement of people for the respect and recognition of the inviolability of the frontiers of all European states, and other principles of interstate relations. But this raised the question of whether real negotiation could take place on issues as incommensurate as negotiating apples for oranges.[31] It would be an agenda juxtaposing recognition of the Soviet consolidation of international socialism in Eastern Europe, and especially in East Germany, in exchange for the freer movement of peoples and ideas—the Western ideological premise for human rights and liberal democracy. For those critics of détente and negotiation who saw in this attempt a West succumbing to Soviet domination by the tactics of peaceful coexistence, the inevitable outcome was Finlandization of West Germany and Europe as a whole. What was really feared, in other words, was the specter of the Eastern Europeanization of all of Europe.

Thus, in addition to the other obstacles, it was important to establish an agenda that was at once acceptable to the ideological orientations of both East and West and broad enough to take into account the mechanisms, procedures,

31. Swedish official, interview by author, written notes, Foreign Ministry, Stockholm, May 19, 1988.

and substance for a framework to convene a conference of this type. There were no precedents on which to draw,[32] although the 1966 Bucharest Appeal had pointed to two preliminary tasks for convening the conference: identification of participants and the convocation of a preparatory meeting. Nevertheless, there were numerous differences between the blocs that impeded substantive agreement on an agenda so that multilateral negotiations could proceed.

How, then, could multilateral cooperation between East and West on a broad range of issues get started? As we shall see in the next chapter, Finland's role as a facilitative mediator proved critical in helping East and West surmount the difficulties of the cold war conflict. Its third-party involvement improved the possibilities for sorting out the merits of competing proposals and helped change adversaries' perceptions about "potentially unrealized joint gains" (Sibenius 1992, 18). Because facilitative third parties do not have disputes at stake with the main adversaries, they have different opportunities for promoting cooperative outcomes, which the adversaries may find more difficult to refuse than concessions made in response to the opponent's initiatives or demands. In this way, the entry of Finland, and later other third parties, into the debate on the ESC helped expand the menu of possibilities for changing the structure of East-West conflict.

32. On this point see "Ote Suurlähettiläs Ralph Enckellin esitelmästä Jyväskylän kesän yhteydessä 30. 6. 1970," Euroopan turvallisuuskysymys, ULA 1970, 33–36. See also Jakobson (1983, 230).

4 Catalyzing Peaceful Change

FINLAND'S IDENTITY as a European neutral country and its foreign-policy experiences as the only European liberal democracy bordering the Soviet Union are among the key factors that shaped its third-party approach to facilitative mediation. Isolated from international affairs during the early years of the cold war, Finland still was considered something of a Western outpost through the 1960s and early 1970s. However, the Finnish proposal to host the CSCE was a move as much to satisfy Finnish foreign-policy interests as to serve the general European interests, which Finland claimed to understand.[1]

Among Finnish President Urho Kekkonen's principal aims in promoting a European Security Conference was to multilateralize Finnish neutrality policy to better insulate Finnish foreign policy from Soviet pressures, and, for related reasons, to maintain unchanged Finnish ties with the two Germanies. As it turned out, the evolving status of the two Germanies during the early 1970s continued to present policy challenges for Finland, so that dealing effectively with this issue became essential for maintaining Finland's mediator readiness and for disproving suspicions in the West that Finland wanted to act like a neutral but could not.

Finland's Third-Party Identity

The post-World War II realities of a divided Europe and superpower confrontation shaped in important ways Finland's conception of the role it could play as a state seeking to remain outside of the alliances. Its overarching objective was to gain international recognition of and respect for its policy of neutrality.

A policy of neutrality has two main operative components. The more traditional component concerns the *negative dimension* of neutrality politics, which emphasizes the deterrent capability of the neutral and the costs to a belligerent of failing to respect a state's neutrality policy. This component is closely associ-

1. Finnish official, interview by author, tape recording, Foreign Ministry, Helsinki, Finland, May 12, 1988.

ated with the wartime dimension of neutrality as a security policy and with the associated neutral obligations of impartiality, rights, and responsibilities (cf. Bindschedler 1976; Binter 1989). However, the post-World War II practice of neutrality increasingly embraced a *positive dimension,* which consisted of an active peace policy. This component underscored the utility of neutrals as third parties in support of international peace and security, and it demonstrated that neutral states were no longer "doomed to remain passive outsiders in international politics on which international security and welfare depend" (Hakovirta 1988, 244).

Whereas the negative dimension is closely related to outsiders' estimation of the neutral's *credibility* based on its defensive capabilities, the positive dimension relates to outsiders' evaluations of the *acceptability* of the neutrals' policies or stands on issues. Of the two dimensions, acceptability depends on outsiders' expectations (Hakovirta 1988). If acceptability is the primary dimension of a neutral's policy, then this imposes greater self-restraints on its policy choices. For example, Switzerland chose to remain outside the United Nations, emphasizing its impartiality during peacetime and, like Sweden, the maintenance of a strong national defense. Both countries gave priority to the credibility—the national capability to deter and defend the country against threats.

On the other hand, policymakers in Austria and Finland tended to emphasize the acceptability of their neutrality policy. For Finland, as for Austria, the choice of neutrality was less an option than a "pressing existential necessity" (Binter 1989, 415). Counted among the defeated of World War II, both countries faced restraints on the acquisition of certain armaments (for Finland in the 1948 Treaty of Paris and for Austria in the State Treaty of May 1955).[2]

While Sweden used its active neutrality policy as a means to challenge the status quo and criticize the superpower condominium, Finland limited itself to working within the prevailing power structures to promote stability and change. Thus, the "active ingredient in Finnish foreign policy was not about rebellion in the periphery" (Joenniemi 1987, 1). In an implicit critique of the Swedish neutrality model, Kekkonen argued that "impassioned stances seldom change the course of events. By adopting them we may be able to still the voice of our own conscience or feel, for a moment, self-admiration at our fearless-

2. As a World War II belligerent, the Paris Peace Treaty enforced limitations on Finland's sovereignty and rearmament, including an army not to exceed 34,000 men, a navy of not more than 4,500 men and 20,000 tons, and an air force of no more than 60 aircraft and 300 personnel. Possession of bombers and submarines was banned, as was possession of nuclear weapons, guided missiles, and torpedoes. A key restriction on Finland's sovereignty was removed in 1955 when the Soviets returned to Finland the Porkkala naval base it had occupied since the 1944 Armistice. This return was accomplished in part because Finland agreed to the early extension of the 1948 Treaty of Friendship, Cooperation, and Mutual Assistance by twenty years (Jakobson 1968).

ness. But that is usually all that they accomplish. On the debit side, by contrast, they may lead to feelings of resentment against our country abroad, and this in turn can cause difficulties. A country like Finland cannot afford that" (1982, 21). Instead, Kekkonen emphasized both preventive diplomacy and the "trust factor." The idea of preventive diplomacy was to sense approaching dangers and take measures to avoid them so that as few people notice as possible (1982, 19). The trust factor was of special importance for Finland's dealings with the Eastern superpower neighbor and was consequential for its relations to the West. Kekkonen argued that the "better we can gain the trust of the Soviet Union in Finland as a peaceful neighbor, the better our opportunities for close cooperation with Western countries" (1982, 17).

Sensitivities to East-West Conflict

Finland's experience as an outpost of the Russian empire, its struggle against Russification and for national independence in 1917, and the tragedy first of the Winter War and then the Continuation War against the Soviets during World War II informed its postwar search for a secure foreign policy. These historical circumstances shaped Finland's pursuit of a neutrality policy, which came to be based on its interpretation of the 1948 Treaty of Friendship, Cooperation, and Mutual Assistance (FCMA Treaty) with the Soviet Union.

Reflecting President J. K. Paasikivi's draft wording, the Preamble to the treaty stated Finland's "desire to remain outside the conflicting interests of the Great Powers" and expressed the country's "firm endeavor to collaborate towards the maintenance of international peace and security in accordance with the aims and principles of the United Nations Organization." In order to strengthen Finland's profile as a neutral, Paasikivi and his successor, President Urho Kekkonen, tried to diminish the importance of Article I of the FCMA treaty, which obligated Finland to repel an attack against Finnish territory or Soviet territory via Finland by Germany or any ally of Germany, and instead give greater importance to the Preamble. Nevertheless, Finland remained highly sensitive to regional developments that exacerbated East-West conflict in relation to the German Question, or that heightened Soviet perceptions of the threat from "German revanchists." Thus, East-West conflict over Berlin and NATO plans to further militarize the Nordic area and carry out exercises in the Baltic contributed to two crises in Finnish-Soviet relations: the 1958 Night Frost and the 1961 Note Crisis (Väyrynen 1972, 1982; Apunen 1977).

Kekkonen extracted Finland from these crises with a determination to maintain national consensus on Finland's foreign-policy line, known as the Paasikivi-Kekkonen line, and after the 1961 crisis with a commitment to monitor regional developments. This change also marked the initiation of a more activist Finnish neutrality policy. Kekkonen's 1961 Nordic Nuclear Weapons Free Zone proposal was designed to enhance Finland's third-party role as a bridge builder and regional watchdog.[3] Among his aims were to achieve greater recognition of Finland's neutrality in the West, integrate Finland further in Western institutions, improve the country's defense capabilities, and overcome Finland's isolated position in the cold war. In order to maintain stable and predictable relations with the Soviet Union, Finnish leaders tried to insulate Finnish-Soviet relations from the fluctuations of international relations and regional tensions (Möttölä 1982, 290).

Beginning in the 1960s, Kekkonen also strove to promote and strengthen Finland's credibility as a neutral in the United Nations to help solve conflicts. At first he emphasized Finland's role as bridge builder. Accordingly, Finnish diplomats played an increasingly active role in UN disarmament negotiations, and the country gained a seat on the Security Council in 1969. Under Kekkonen, Finnish Foreign Ministry officials also lobbied actively on behalf of their colleague, Max Jakobson, as candidate for the post of secretary general of the United Nations (an initiative defeated by apparently a Soviet veto). Finland also hosted the first rounds of the U.S.-Soviet SALT talks in Helsinki. Still, the government sought a more active role by which Finland would contribute not only to the reduction of tension but also to the enhancement of confidence. Kekkonen argued that more channels were needed to institutionalize détente than bilateral accords between the superpowers.[4] This was one of his points of departure for Finland's security conference initiative.[5]

These initiatives in the UN in the late 1960s were part of Kekkonen's diplomatic operations to multilateralize Finnish neutrality policy as insurance against repercussions from the Soviets (Jakobson 1983, 246–48). He aimed in particular to improve the acceptability of Finnish neutrality in the West. Despite this *lännenpolitiikka* (literally, "Westpolitik"), Finlandization was held up in the West as emblematic of the corrosive effect of Soviet influence and the specter of a neutralist Europe (Nevakivi 1975, 84). Moreover, Jakobson's monograph, *Finnish Neutrality* (1968)—an attempt to clarify the special nature of Finnish neutrality and its Western roots—failed to win much acceptability in the West but provoked Finland's neighbor to the East. The Soviets found fault with

3. See Kekkonen's Speech to the Paasikivi Society, Helsinki, May 28, 1963, "Maanpuolustustiedotuksen Suunnittelukunta," in Maanpuolustustiedotuksen Suunnnittelukunta, ed. (1982, 89–92).

4. "Tasavallan Presidentin haastattelu televisiossa Leningradin matkan jälkeen 22. 5. 1969," ULA 1969, 163.

5. "Finland and the European Security Conference," Speech by Risto Hyvärinen, Director for Political Affairs of the Ministry for Foreign Affairs, Joensuu, July 28, 1971, ULA 1971, 71.

Finnish attempts to root the country's neutrality policy in the FCMA Treaty by diminishing its military assistance clause (Blomberg 1969, 5–7; Suomela 1971, 8).[6] Finland had the support of the Soviets for its neutrality policy in the UN as a positive factor in developing cooperation between East and West, and its recognition of Finland's desire for peace within the Nordic region.[7] However, the Soviets withheld recognition of Finnish neutrality in the regional context. In fact, after the autumn of 1969, the Soviets gradually dropped references to Finland as a neutral country in their bilateral communiqués, resorting instead to the phrase, "Finland's peace loving foreign policy, which has gotten the name Paasikivi-Kekkonen line." Some Finnish officials believed that their efforts to win Western acceptance of Finnish neutrality easily caused irritation in Moscow. They could not be certain to what extent the Soviets viewed the Czechoslovakian and the Romanian foreign-policy crises between 1967 and 1968 as prototypes of Finnish policy and political emancipation. According to Jakobson (1983), the bilateral pressures the Soviet Union used to prevent Finland's neutrality policy from gaining the confidence of the West was part of the Soviets' larger structural dilemma: they wanted to improve their relations in the West (the Chinese situation made that more imperative), but they did not want to allow this rapprochement to lead to more events like that in Czechoslovakia.

The Warsaw Pact's invasion of Czechoslovakia greatly concerned the Finnish government. Foreign Minister Karjalainen emphasized that states have an obligation to respect each other's inviolability and political independence. Negotiation, not violence, was the way to resolve international conflicts. Prime Minister Mauno Koivisto asserted that the crisis in Czechoslovakia was a grave reminder of how far such principles were from being defended in Europe.[8] In a March 1969 speech, Karjalainen asked rhetorically whether Finland had moved fast enough to solidify its international status as a neutral given the recent turn of events, and "whether the country's foreign policy has strived in good time to fortify its foundation, and to extend its circle of influence to provide against difficult times."[9]

Finland was also under pressure from the Eastern bloc to update its German policy. From the perspective of the FCMA treaty, the Finnish-Soviet rela-

6. See also Urho Kekkonen's Radio and Television Speech, July 31, 1970, reprinted in Blomberg (1972, 4).

7. "Ulkoasiainministeri Ahti Karjalaisen haastattelu Novoje Vremjassa Neuvostoliiton vierrailun aattona," ULA 1969, 149–50; and especially "Ulkoasiainministeri Ahti Karjalaisen puhe virallisella lounaalla Moskovassa 18. 2. 1969," ULA 1969, 152.

8. "Pääministeri Mauno Koiviston esitelmä Paasikivi-Seurassa Helsingissä 27. 11. 1969," Historian tulkinnasta, ULA 1969, 56.

9. "Ulkoasiainministeri Ahti Karjalaisen puhe VI valtakunnallisilla nuorisotyöntekijäpäivillä," Nuorison rooli kansainvälisessä politiikassa, ULA 1969, 29.

tionship was tied to the center of European security, especially to the fate of the two Germanies—to the questions of German sovereignty and unification.[10] Finnish officials did not fail to appreciate the importance of the German Question for making an initiative to launch the CSCE.[11] As Jakobson writes in his memoirs, in the late 1960s East Germany itself had begun to pressure Finland to change its policy on the German Question and recognize East Germany as a sovereign state. The East Germans saw Finland then as the weak point in a ring that the West German foreign policy had built around East Germany. The East Germans forwarded the thesis that recognizing both Germanies would be fully in harmony with Finnish neutrality. Yet this was also the Soviet position—its solution to an East German state that was recognized at that time only by the communist bloc. The Soviets raised the issue repeatedly with Kekkonen in an attempt to get Finland to recognize the DDR de jure (Vladimirov 1993, 164).

Surprisingly, many politicians and journalists advocated this policy change, apparently confident that Kekkonen could assume the responsibility for managing Finland's relations with the West (Jakobson 1983, 224). However, Kekkonen resisted any change of policy before matters on the German Question had been worked out in the West (Vladimirov 1993, 164). In the meantime, he grew concerned that his German policy was crumbling in the parliament. Jakobson argues "for that reason, it was important to tie our Security Conference initiative to our German policy" (1983, 224). Hosting the conference presupposed an unchanging position on the German Question (1983, 224). The shaping of this initiative, and more generally Finland's activist neutrality, involved an intense struggle among elites to influence the intellectual, strategic, and normative content of the country's foreign policy, while collecting feathers for their own caps.

Finland's Westpolitik

Within the Center Party, foreign policy was Kekkonen's exclusive domain (Kekkonen retained the presidency continuously from 1956 to 1981). However, during the late 1960s and early 1970s two groups struggled for political power and an opportunity to influence the direction and substance of Finland's active neutrality policy. On the one hand, a group of mostly Harvard-trained foreign-policy technocrats (dubbed the mandarins) advised Kekkonen on plans for "diplomatic operations" to make Finnish neutrality part of the balance of

10. Finnish official, interview by author, tape recording, Foreign Ministry, Helsinki, May 12, 1988.

11. Ibid. See also "The Foreign Policy Report of the Government to Parliament on November 5, 1970," ULA 1970, 164–65.

power structure between East and West. Notable among the mandarins were Max Jakobson (Finnish ambassador to the UN) and Risto Hyvärinen (head of the Political Division of the Foreign Ministry).

On the other hand, there was the *nappulaliiga* (the little league), a group of professional politicians from the Social Democratic Party and largely of the 1960s university generation. They included Kalevi Sorsa, Väinö Leskinen, Ahti Karjalainen, Johannes Virolainen, and Päiviö Hetemäki. The *nappulaliiga* worked to overcome its party's long-standing exclusion from foreign policy-making circles and to improve its prospects for developing a policy toward the East. The *nappulaliiga* represented the new voice of the Social Democratic Party in Finland, calling for a more active Finnish policy toward the Third World, a more active peace policy in the UN, and a cooperative relationship toward the Soviets. These were the basic elements of the party's foreign-policy platform adopted in 1969.[12]

The young Social Democrats represented a *Weltanschauung* in Finland. They provided a new realism rooted in support of a more explicit Finnish security policy, especially on Finnish-Soviet relations.[13] They criticized the older generation's tendency to follow the Paasikivi line: maintaining good relations with the Soviets at arms length without directly facing the implications of the military clause in the FCMA Treaty. They forced answers to questions about the FCMA treaty and the cooperation with the Soviets that the treaty would require.[14] They charged that the necessary policy mechanisms had failed to materialize after the Note Crisis, despite the government's commitment to be on guard against the emergence of a crisis situation in the north. They also criticized Jakobson's 1968 book, *Finnish Neutrality,* for selling Finnish neutrality to the West in part on the premise that the military assistance clause of the FCMA treaty would come into effect only after an attack on Finland had already occurred.

Based on their interpretation of the FCMA Treaty, the *nappulaliiga* called for practical norms and expectations on the basis of which Finland's Eastern relations could be regularized and normalized (Blomberg 1969, 7). The objective was to ensure mechanisms of consultation to prevent the need to move directly to military assistance in a crisis situation. Ensuring confidence in Finnish-Soviet relations would reinforce Finland's peace policy and neutrality and obviate the difficulties that assistance under the FCMA might pose. This would introduce

12. Professor Raimo Väyrynen, discussion with author, written notes, Washington, D.C., Apr. 13, 1990; see also Suomela (1971, 8–9) and Joenniemi (1978, 50).

13. The debate included counterpoints to Jakobson's (1968) *Finnish Neutrality.* Among these critics, see Blomberg (1969) and Blomberg and Joenniemi (1971).

14. See for example, Dag Anckar, "Biståndspaktens problematik," *Huvudstadbladet,* Oct. 18, 1969.

an element of stability that would allow Finland to contribute to the overall security arrangements pertaining to the East-West system.

The politicization of debate on Finnish neutrality put in question the country's security and defense policies. Eventually, Finland's defense policy came to embrace a capability of reassurance toward the Soviet Union in an effort to meet autonomously the formal security guarantees for Soviet security interests in the Finnish sector (see also Möttölä 1982).[15] The policy was designed to ensure that vital Soviet interests would not be provoked to the extent that the Soviets would find it in their interest to expand their control over the region (Ries 1988, 230). Simultaneous to this reassurance policy and in equilibrium to it, Finland pursued a deterrent policy to ensure the country's inviolability and to signal to the Soviets that any effort to infringe on Finland's sovereignty would entail substantial costs.

Ultimately, the mandarins influenced the direction of Finland's active neutrality policy by promoting their new realism under Kekkonen's approval while guarding his principles (Apunen 1984, 175). Although they appeared to maintain a low profile by letting the politicians collect their own feathers as they carried out official duties (Apunen 1984, 196), the mandarins kept the initiatives in their own hands (Apunen 1984, 175). The Finnish offer to host the proposed European Security Conference, the Finnish proposal for a German Package deal, and the internationally concerted attempt to have Max Jakobson elected secretary general of the United Nations all entailed high stakes. However, it was the little leaguers who took the responsibility for the mishandling and failure of some of these initiatives (cf. Apunen 1984, 196; Jakobson 1983, 297–359; Määttänen 1973). For his part, Kekkonen continued to manage relations with the Soviet Union often through direct personal contact with Soviet officials.

Facilitative Mediation Strategy

Finland's initiative to host the CSCE was thus informed by a set of political, economic, strategic, and cultural considerations calling for a strategy based on more active engagement. By the late 1960s, Finland's "watchdog" role of monitoring conditions in the Nordic area and, more generally, the stability of Central Europe was seen as inadequate. West Germany's Ostpolitik and France's policy of rapprochement (de Gaulle's vision of "détente, entente and coopera-

15. See "Parlamentaarisen Puolustuskomitean mientintö," Komitenamietintö n:o A 18, Helsinki, 1971; "Report of the Second Parliamentary Defense Committee," Committee Report 1976, 37, Helsinki, 1976; "Report of the Third Parliamentary Defense Committee," Helsinki, 1981. Procurement had been implemented erratically throughout the 1960s and led to more than a decade-long retooling in Finnish defense policy and capabilities (Ries 1988, 192).

tion") with the East pointed to widening political cleavages in the Western alliance, reinforced by the French withdrawal from NATO's military command. By the early 1970s, however, it became clear this depolarization was crystallizing not around a new all-European system but around a repolarization in Western Europe encompassing an enlarging EEC. This situation was also evident in the EEC members' establishment of a common West European foreign policy (European Political Cooperation).

The 1969 Hague Summit that led to the decision to enlarge the EEC also portended Britain's withdrawal from the European Free Trade Association (EFTA) and created pressures on the Nordic states to join the EEC. These developments also spurred discussions on launching a Nordic customs union, NORDEK, but this plan fell through when Norway and Denmark were offered membership in the EEC, causing Finland to back out. While Sweden was able to work out satisfactory arrangements with the EEC by signing a Free Trade Agreement (FTA) in 1972, for Finland the process of establishing ties with Western economic and cultural institutions was much more problematic—as it had been throughout the post-World War II period. Despite Finland's "wait and see" strategy (Hakovirta 1975, 415–19), sanctions from the Soviet bloc were not uncommon (Väyrynen 1972). In the immediate postwar years, Finland (like other Eastern European nations) declined the invitation to participate in the European Recovery Program and only became involved in the Organization for European Economic Cooperation (OEEC, reconstituted in 1961 as the OECD) first as an observer in 1956 and finally as a full member in 1968. Finland's relations to the Soviet Union continued to require sensitivity and patience also in matters of economic and cultural integration in Western institutions. It was only in 1971 that Finland fell in line behind the other European neutrals and negotiated a free-trade agreement with the EEC (signed in 1973)—which was balanced by further extending Finland's relations with the Comecon.

Thus, despite some elements of depolarization and cross-bloc activity, détente was giving way to an even deeper division between Eastern and Western Europe. The Soviets' success in consolidating internal cohesion and disentangling the Warsaw Pact from détente—as amply demonstrated by the 1968 invasion of Czechoslovakia—caused alarm in Finland as elsewhere. For the neutral and nonaligned countries, the accumulating political and economic pressures posed real challenges for their own course of action in working for the future of cooperation in Europe and for their own security. Kekkonen noted in his 1969 New Year's address that "when 1968 began, there existed a certain hopefulness in relaxing international tensions. Unfortunately, these expectations have not been realized. Hardly any great problem eluding international peace has been resolved, and on the contrary many open conflicts have become acute. There are new controversies, which strain cooperation between people."[16] Thus, by 1969 Finnish officials were deeply concerned about the state of détente.

The inter-bloc exchanges of positions on the future of East-West relations driven by NATO appeared to circumscribe the security aspects of the agenda of the proposed CSCE while also excluding the non-bloc states from the more militarily significant proposal for launching the MBFR talks. Moreover, it appeared that key issues would be decided in bilateral or great power negotiations preceding the conference. This left the disturbing prospect of convening an East-West security conference with little in the way of a substantive agenda left to negotiate.[17] The fulfillment of Western preconditions largely precluded discussions on more far-reaching measures, such as the Soviet proposals calling for the dissolution of the military systems, Swedish and Yugoslavian appeals to include disarmament, and the Swiss interest in a system of peaceful settlement of disputes.

In an attempt to sort out how Finland related to these debates, Finnish officials questioned what it meant to be European.[18] Where did Europe start and end?[19] And who had a right to be involved in the détente process? Finland's participation in the Group of Nine provided an important avenue to define its relationship to the rest of Europe. This helped Finland establish ties across ideological lines and draw attention to its cultural, political, economic, and social roots in the West.[20] By improving relations with the East, Finland gained possibilities for integrating further in the West. These contacts also enhanced Finland's acceptability among a core of states interested in supporting multilateral détente.

Prominent among the arguments marshaled in support of Finland's initiative to host the CSCE were those made in the government's May 1969 Memo-

16. "Ote Tasavallan Presidentin uudenvuodenpuheesta 1. 1. 1969," ULA 1969, 13.

17. In March 1972, Finnish Ambassador Ralph Enckell observed "no problem of current interest has been postponed or put aside for consideration in due time by the conference. Quite on the contary [*sic*], solutions and progress have been of late so numerous that some people have asked what would remain for the conference to do." Yet he hastened to add, "there is of course no shortage of important issues as of yet." See "Speech by Ambassador Ralph Enckell at the General Meeting of the Ecumenical Workshop," ULA 1972, 76.

18. "Pääministeri Mauno Koiviston puhe yya-sopimuksen 20-vuotisjuhlassa 6. 4. 1968," ULA 1968, 26.

19. "Opetusministeri Johannes Virolaisen esitelmä Keskustapuoleen seminaarissa Dipolissa 17. 6. 1968," Suomi ja Euroopan turvallissuuskysymys, ULA 1968, 37.

20. Compare, for example, these documents: "Ulkoasiainministeri Ahti Karjalaisen Suomen Titotoimistolle 31. 12. 1966 myöntämä haastattelulausunto," ULA 1966, 82; "Ulkoasainministeri Ivan Bachevin vierailun johdosta annettu tiedonanto 16. 5. 1966," ULA 1966, 85; "Pääministeri Mauno Koivisto puhe pääministeri Ion Georghe Maurerin ja ulkoasiainministeri Corneliu Manescun kunniaksi tarjoituilla päivällisillä, 1. 4. 1968," ULA 1968, 144–46.

randum, underscoring that Finland has "good relations with all the countries which are concerned with European security and her impartial attitude toward the most vital problem of European security, the German question, has been appreciated by different interested parties."[21] Finland's potential for working on behalf of European security lay in its special qualities: its neutral, northern European location and its good relations with all states.[22] In particular, Finnish officials emphasized Finland's balanced relations with both German states at the level of trade delegations, which made Finland the only "true" neutral in all of Europe.

Finland's more pragmatic approach also suited it better for third-party intervention in East-West affairs, at least compared with its neutral neighbor's approach (cf. Sipilä 1988; Jönsson and Petersson 1985). Sweden's policy of criticizing superpower intervention, especially with regard to Vietnam and the Czechoslovakian invasion, limited its acceptability as a third party.[23] Only exceptionally did Finland draw attention to the violations of principles it saw at stake, which it had done with regard to the Soviet intervention in Czechoslovakia; otherwise its condemnation, if any, was limited to the actual circumstances rather than being directed at the great powers or their policies.

More important, Finnish interest in holding the CSCE in Helsinki was a strategy to deflect tensions in Finnish-Soviet relations. This could be accomplished by being associated with a process that would provide a world stage on which to promote Finnish neutrality, East-West détente, and the Soviet objective of peaceful coexistence. Through such a forum, Finland stood to gain legitimate acceptance of its neutrality policy in the West. East-West relations would also be founded on greater stability, which would reduce pressure from the Soviets. Finally, initiating such a forum would institutionalize, according to international norms, cooperation between the blocs on a range of issues including economic ones, thereby reducing the bloc distinctions. In sum, hosting the

21. Finnish and Swedish experts and officials also emphasize this point. Finnish official, interview by author, tape recording, Helsinki, May 11, 1988; also Swedish official, interview by author, written notes, Foreign Ministry, Stockholm, May 19, 1988. The full text of the "Government of Finland's European Security Conference Memorandum of 5 May 1969" is reproduced in Appendix A.

22. "Opetusministeri Johannes Virolaisen esitelmä Keskustapuolueen seminaarissa Dipolissa 17. 6. 1968," ULA 1968, 36, 41.

23. United States reactions to the Swedish decision to recognize the North Vietnamese government and establish full diplomatic relations are reported in the Finnish Foreign Ministry's newspaper clippings service, which cites articles in the *Washington Post,* Jan. 13 and 14, 1969, in the *Süddeutsche Zeitung* Jan. 15, 1969, and in the *National Review* Jan. 28, 1969. See Ulkoasiainministeriö Sanomalehtiasiaintoimisto: Lehdistökatsaus, (hereafter UMSLT: LK) n:o 10/23. 1. 169 and n:o 11/27. 1. 1969 and n:o 12/17. 1. 1969 respectively.

CSCE could deflect these problems and provide Finland with greater freedom of choice in the field of foreign policy.

Third-Party Resources

The mediator's influence potential is enhanced when the disputants believe it possesses the skills, judgment, sensitivity, and knowledge to intervene effectively, and also the capability to uncover and/or provide valuable information. The Finnish initiative promised to give the Soviet idea of a security conference the neutral sponsor it had long sought and thus a stamp of legitimacy it otherwise would lack in the West. The Finnish government's expertise, information, and channels of communication with the Soviets were likewise important resources. Also significant as a referent resource was the common goals the Finnish offer to host the CSCE implied for its bilateral relations with the Soviets. As noted in chapter 2, referent resources derive from the "sense of mutual identity between a mediator and the disputing parties, and a desire to see things similarly" (Bercovitch 1992, 19–20). Common goals may be important factors that enhance the mediator's status and hence its ability to gain the trust of the disputants, control the mediation process, and influence outcomes. Similarly, legitimacy resources are related to the disputants' evaluation of the mediator's right and obligation to assume a third-party role. By virtue of being a neutral state, Finland stood to enjoy greater legitimacy in the eyes of the disputants.

The type of leadership Finnish mediation provided was important. As noted in chapter 2, how sensitive a mediator is to the political context of the dispute is also indicative of how open the mediator is likely to be to discrepant information from the environment and what kind of leadership it can offer. Thus, not only a mediator's interests and resources, but also its sensitivities to the political context of a conflict determine how it can intervene and to what extent and in what ways it can influence adversaries to adopt changes in their positions. Obviously, Finland faced significant sensitivities with respect to the core issues at stake in resolving the cold war conflict, particularly with regard to the German Question. However, these limitations were also a potential source of strength for a Finnish third-party role facilitating the initiation of a multilateral endeavor. Among Western democracies, Finland's unique experiences and political socialization under the shadow of its superpower neighbor translated into considerable political experience in dealing with the Soviets and perhaps a greater appreciation of which initiatives might succeed or fail under a given set of circumstances. Years of experience also undoubtedly helped Kekkonen to see situations and problems in a more complex fashion, inviting more context-specific solutions. Kekkonen managed the direction of Finnish foreign policy himself and was an adept and experienced "cue-taker."

Finland's 1969 Memorandum

Because the East was a *demandeur* on the issue of the European Security Conference, and because Finland apparently enjoyed Moscow's blessing on launching its third-party initiative, Finland's primary challenge was getting the commitment of the West to come to Helsinki. This meant getting some basic understanding about the West's terms, which at the same time would not be unacceptable to the East. Although Finland did not start out with any grand strategy for achieving this, its third-party activities encompassed several phases, each one ratcheting up a notch the commitments of the potential participants to initiate a multilateral conference on East-West security and cooperation. The first of these phases encompassed Finland's 1969 invitation to all interested states to convene a European Security Conference in Helsinki and diplomatic efforts to garner a positive response to the initiative.

Gaining Entry

For Finland the first challenge was to gain entry as a third party. This involved drafting a memorandum of invitation, but whether this was an independent initiative or came as a result of Soviet pressures has been a matter of considerable speculation. President Kekkonen, Max Jakobson, and other Finnish officials maintained that the decision was Finland's and was in line with Finnish foreign-policy interests. Even though the 1993 publication of a Soviet KGB's memoirs lends credence to Western suspicions that Finland acted at the behest of the Soviets, considerable evidence suggests that the decision to launch the CSCE initiative was Kekkonen's, and that he arrived at this having carefully assessed the risks and potential gains, while considering the country's qualifications for the job as a neutral. It may also be noted that the Soviets considered certain countries to be "their neutrals" while others were the West's.[24]

In preparing Finland's initiative to host the proposed European Security Conference, Kekkonen consulted with other heads of state on European security (Jakobson 1983, 215–26). In particular, during a January 1969 state visit to Paris, Kekkonen gained the support of de Gaulle for his (Kekkonen's) vision of launching a new understanding on the European realities.[25] This consultation

24. Thus the decision to alternate between Helsinki and Vienna for the SALT talks was not coincidental. A similar conclusion may also be drawn with respect to the decision to hold the agenda-building negotiations and signing of the Final Act in Helsinki, but the main negotiations in Geneva. Ambassador Oleg Grinevsky, interview by author, tape recording, Embassy of the Russian Federation, Stockholm, Dec. 20, 1994.

25. Jakobson (1983, 215) makes it clear that Kekkonen identified closely with de Gaulle's nationalistic leadership of France and that the two leaders shared similar appreciations of the Euro-

was followed in February by Foreign Minister Ahti Karjalainen's official visit to the Soviet Union. The Foreign Ministry reported that among the main subjects of discussion were several international questions of interest to both countries, and specifically that of European security. "Both states committed themselves to strive for the reduction of tensions and the protection and strengthening of peace."[26]

Shortly after Karjalainen and his Foreign Ministry delegation returned to Finland, the nature of Finland's interests in European security attracted attention in broader governmental circles and the national press. Responding to a parliamentary inquiry, Karjalainen affirmed in early March that "on the part of the Finnish government, it has in different connections been made known that we take a favorable interest in the idea of a well organized conference dealing with European security and including all concerned countries."[27] Karjalainen acknowledged that "we naturally have been and are also prepared to examine actions the implementation of which would help the organization of the conference." Regarding whether the government proposed or intended to propose Finland as the host of the European Security Conference, Karjalainen observed that "a call to hold the conference in Finland would have to come in a timely fashion in such circumstances that our country would be viewed as being suited to this endeavor." However, Finland needed to examine first whether it possessed the practical qualifications for organizing the conference.[28]

In early 1969 the Soviets judged that the prospects for organizing a general European conference were limited by the cold war dynamics that led each bloc to reject out of hand the other's proposals in order not to cede any propaganda advantage. The possibility remained that the entire project would be buried with the idea still in an embryonic stage (Vladimirov 1993, 165). However, by the 1960s the Chinese threat in the East reinforced views in Moscow of the necessity of securing the Soviet Union's Western borders and stabilizing the situation in Europe (Vladimirov 1993; Jakobson 1983; Ulam 1974). Now the issue was not simply gaining an edge in propaganda but rather achieving concrete results that would assure the Soviet Union's security on at least one of its flanks.

The Soviets decided that the initiative to convene the European Security

---

pean scene and Soviet security concerns. This fact is also echoed in Kekkonen's writings and speeches. See for example, Kekkonen (1977, 306).

26. "Ulkoasiainministeri ja rouva Ahti Karjalaisen Neuvostoliiton vierailun johdosta annettu tiedonanto 22. 2. 1969," ULA 1969, 154.

27. "Edustaja Melinin suullinen kysymys Suomen esittämisestä Euroopan turvallisuuskokouksen isäntämaaksi 7. 3. 1969," ULA 1969, 142.

28. "Karjalainen turvallisuuskokouksesta," *Suomenmaa,* in Ulkoasiainministeriö Lehdistökatsaus edustustoja varten (hereafter UM: LKEV) n:o 56, Mar. 8, 1969.

Conference should be passed on to a neutral country. According to Vladimirov (1993, 166), Finland was highly acceptable to the Soviets, bringing together the right kind of third-party identity, interests, and objectives. Finland was both nonaligned and friendly toward the Soviet Union, maintaining a foreign policy based on good relations with all countries. The Soviets judged that Finland sought to advance international political objectives rather than those of small countries or of a narrow national interest. Given these considerations, the Soviets proposed to Kekkonen that he assume and self-define the task of making a third-party initiative to host the European Security Conference (Vladimirov 1993, 166). Kekkonen had doubts about whether this would serve Finnish interests. He questioned whether the conference could ever be convened, whether Finland would be accused of forgetting its neutrality and assuming a Soviet position, and whether Finland would as a result lose the West's confidence in its foreign-policy leadership and direction. If the proposed conference should succeed, however, it would improve Finland's foreign-policy position and give impetus to international and European détente (Vladimirov 1993, 167).

According to Jakobson (1983), it was the Budapest Appeal issued by the Warsaw Pact countries on March 17, 1969, that placed before the Finnish foreign-policy officials a problem for which no self-evident design was at hand. In what the West judged to be "a diplomatic rather than agitational document" (Spencer 1984, 36), the Warsaw Pact members called with a sense of urgency for the "assembly at the earliest possible date of representatives of all interested European states for the purpose of establishing by mutual agreement, both the procedure for the convening of the conference and the questions on its agenda." A memorandum to this effect and without any preconditions was issued by the Soviets to the governments of European countries, and to the United States and Canada, although this was not stated or known to Finland at the time (Spencer 1984, 36; Jakobson 1983, 222, n. 109).[29] The memorandum was received in Finland on April 8 and pushed the matter of timing the Finnish initiative immediately to the fore. Opportunity for any further assessments of Finland's technical capabilities had run out; it was time to formulate answers to other basic questions, such as who should be invited and how the initiative should be carried out (Jakobson 1983, 220).[30] Finland could not afford to delay long in responding, perhaps, if for no other reason, because other neutrals (such as Sweden and Austria) had been approached by the Soviet Union.[31] Indeed, Aus-

29. Regarding U.S. and Canadian participation, see the editorial in the *Washington Post,* May 10, 1969.

30. For Kekkonen's account, see "Tasavallan Presidentin haastattelu televisiossa," ULA 1969, especially 162–63.

31. Regarding Sweden, see "Pohjoismaiden Ulkoministerikokous," *Die Welt* in UMSLT: LK, n:o 48, May 6, 1969.

tria expressed interest in hosting the conference (Spencer 1984, 37; Palmer 1971, 42).[32]

Preparing the Initiative

In preparing its initiative, Finland followed up on earlier discussions in France, Sweden, and Moscow with consultations among its Nordic neighbors to gain support for its potential third-party role, and input on framing the initiative. As was common practice among the Nordic community when foreign-policy issues of importance were at stake, the Finnish officials set out by exploring the latest Soviet call for the proposed conference at the biannual Nordic Council's Foreign Ministers' Meeting, which convened in Copenhagen on April 23, 1969.[33] Composed of two neutrals (Finland and Sweden) and two NATO allies (Denmark and Norway), the Nordic Council proposed its own, nonbloc framework for launching the ESC. Among other requirements for the conference, the council insisted that it (1) be well prepared, (2) be timed to offer prospects for positive results, and (3) allow all states open to a solution to the European security problem the opportunity to participate in the negotiations.[34]

The Nordic Council's proposal was important for a couple of reasons. First, it provided a set of basic principles from which Finland drew directly in formulating its reasons for its May 5, 1969, Memorandum. This preparation helped to expand the range of issues and bargaining space and also started the process of committing potential participants to the ESC.

Next, Kekkonen turned to formulating the Finnish initiative, and to this end called Jakobson to the presidential residence in Tamminiemi. While the president was certain the proposed conference was advantageous to Finland given the intention of the conference to strengthen the status quo in Europe, he realized the problem remained as to how Finland could support such an endeavor while assuring others that Finland was working to its own advantage—

32. During the couple of years that led to the convening of the preparatory stage of the CSCE in Helsinki, Austria would continue to make offers and lobby for the conference to be held in Vienna.

33. This point was also confirmed by a Swedish official close to the CSCE during its early years. Swedish official, interview by author, written notes, Foreign Ministry, Stockholm, May 27, 1988. Ten days earlier Karjalainen had visited Sweden, where he drew attention to the Nordic countries' reputation for peace work. He was quoted in the Finnish press as having stated at a luncheon address in the Swedish Foreign Ministry in Stockholm that "we [the Nordic countries] have many common interests concerning this field [of peace work]. We have supported each other in securing Northern peace, and we surely will do so in the future." *Uusi Suomi* in UM: LKEV, n:o 83, Apr. 12, 1969, 4.

34. "Kööpenhaminassa 23. -24. 4. 1969 pidetyn Pohjoismaiden ulkoministerikokouksen tiedonanto," ULA 1969, 85–88.

not on behalf of Soviet business (Jakobson 1983, 221). The task of formulating the initiative was charged to the head of the Foreign Ministry's political department, Risto Hyvãrinen, and the result was the May 5, 1969, Memorandum, which the Finns believed was balanced in its approach (see Appendix I). Finland accepted the latest Soviet position that the conference be convened without the fulfillment of preliminary conditions, but it also allowed that the participants should have the right to present their own views and proposals on European security.[35]

Other Western positions stated in the Nordic communiqué were also incorporated into the Finnish Memorandum. Foremost was Finland's decision to invite the United States and Canada along with the European states (including East and West Germany).[36] This decision was a response to political realities. While the conference was not to be a negotiation between the military alliances, Finnish officials took the position that it was equally important not to exclude any members of those alliances. "We were very strongly of the opinion that all nations participate as independent nations rather than through the vehicle of coordinated alliance policy."[37] The Finnish initiative also included invitations to all the neutral and nonaligned European countries, thus providing for participation by the European neutrals and nonaligned states in the conference and the possibility, as Brandt himself had raised, that the conference would not strictly serve to reinforce the blocs and the division of Europe. The very fact that Finland acted on the view that the neutral and nonaligned countries should have a voice in the definition of East-West relations was in itself a call for changes in the way the questions of European security were addressed.

The memorandum also specified the conference be well prepared and be convened without preconditions, because "it must not be politically biased." This in itself presupposed that the agenda would contain many issues and that, in order for it to succeed, careful preparation would be paramount. Finland called for consultations between governments and "after the necessary conditions exist, a preparatory meeting for consideration of the questions connected with the arrangement of the conference." The memorandum noted that Finland

35. This is significant to the extent that the West's approach was to require first the resolution of a number of outstanding East-West issues (e.g., four-power solutions on Berlin, progress with SALT, and bilateral negotiations between East Germany and West Germany) before a conference could be convened. Of course, Finland's support of such an approach would risk leaving the neutral and nonaligned states removed from important aspects of the resolution of the East-West conflict. These Western demands represented the cost the Soviets would have to pay for Western agreement to participate in a conference on European security and cooperation (see Palmer 1971, 74–76).

36. "Suomen hallituksen Euroopan turvallisuuskonferenssimuistio," May 5, 1969, ULA 1969, 66. See also Jakobson (1983, 222); and Aćimović (1981, 85).

37. Finnish official, interview by author, tape recording, Helsinki, May 11, 1988.

had good relations with all the countries concerned with European security and exercised "an impartial attitude towards the most vital problem of European security, the German question." The fact that these qualifications had been appreciated by different parties explained "why the Government of Finland is willing to act as the host for the security conference as well as for the preparatory meeting." In order to facilitate the process, Finland noted that it would "instruct her representatives to sound the position of these countries on the European security conference." The Finnish government committed itself to "closely follow this matter and consider what real possibilities it may have in order to take new measures on its part." On May 5, 1969, the Foreign Ministry dispatched the Finnish Memorandum.

The essence of the Finnish formula was to take the idea of a European Security Conference that had been circulating in the mid—to late 1960s, including among the Group of Nine, and turn it into "a broad framework of contacts and communications between the governments concerned." The memorandum set up procedures and conditions for convening the conference, although it did not set a deadline of any kind. Finland offered itself as a third party to help flush out the interests of the various states and to facilitate their active commitment to more concrete deliberations and their agreement on an agenda for multilateral consultations.[38] As Hyvärinen explained, the process would move from "bilateral to multilateral consultations and explanations, on which basis the possibilities for launching a preparatory meeting can be examined." He foresaw an incremental process of building commitments into an expanding set of relationships. The final outcome of the discussions launched by Finland "would depend ultimately on the achievement of the widest possible understanding between the parties involved." Hyvärinen assured that generating this understanding was "the objective of the Finnish government."[39]

Finland supported the creation of a system in which not only military-security issues could be taken care of—because this was the main subject concerned—but in which the Western interests could also be incorporated. These included the human aspects of the CSCE—more open frontiers, closer cooperation between individuals, and contacts between individuals and groups of people. In Helsinki it was felt that it was not enough to speak only of security as borders; there had to be a dynamic element as well.[40] However, agreement on these substantive matters was not of essence to Finland. Rather, the primary Finnish objectives were tied to the successful *development* of the agenda and the

38. Speech by Risto Hyvärinen, director for political affairs of the Ministry for Foreign Affairs, Joensuu, July 18, 1971, "Finland and the European Security Conference," ULA 1971, 72–73.

39. Ibid., 73.

40. Finnish official, interview by author, tape recording, Foreign Ministry, Helsinki, May 12, 1988.

multilateral process itself. This was the substance of the matter for Finland (see also Apunen 1972). The success and durability of such a conference would provide Finland with a stronger framework of European relations within which to insure its neutrality policy. This change would reduce the constraints on its foreign policy and status as a neutral imposed on it by its special relationship with and geographical proximity to the Soviet Union. A durable, regional institutional process would relieve Finland of its isolated position and facilitate its ties to the processes of European integration. These concerns were evident as well in Finland's commitment to examine how the developments under way "could be extended towards becoming a permanent arrangement," encompassing the aims and principles of the UN Charter and possibly leading toward a regional peace arrangement in Europe in accordance with chapter 8 of the Charter.[41]

In its approach to hosting the conference and promoting its realization, Finland posed as a self-styled "explorer" or catalyst[42] that would refrain from taking stands on issues of substance.[43] Ralph Enckell, appointed roving ambassador by Kekkonen to carry out the Finnish initiative, argued that for Finland the main task was to help East and West learn to get along together. This was imperative whether East and West liked one another or not.[44] In his judgment, a central problem in developing cooperation was the way East and West remained anchored on a few well-worn opinions. Enckell emphasized that past experiences may lead to wrong conclusions and to erroneous actions "when we try to act under new conditions as we used to act under past ones." He called for genuine knowledge to replace fixed stereotypes, and called on all interested parties "to avail ourselves of the great potentialities we have in Europe for achieving beneficial things through cooperation across our borders." The objective was to achieve a community of interest, a code of conduct, and the regulation both of state behavior and of a state's behavior toward its peoples.

Impact of the Memorandum

Kekkonen perceived the May 1969 initiative as a calculated political risk, which he later described as the equivalent of subjecting Finnish neutrality to the

41. Speech by Risto Hyvärinen, director for political affairs of the Ministry for Foreign Affairs, Joensuu, July 18, 1971, "Finland and the European Security Conference," ULA 1971, 73.

42. "Ulkoasiainministeri Ahti Karjalaisen lausunto moskovalaiselle Kainsainvälinen Elämä-lehdelle 5/1969," Euroopan turvallisuuskonferenssi, ULA 1969, 68.

43. "Ote valtiosihteeri Richard Töttermanin esitelmästä Paasikivi-Seuran lounaskokouksessa 24. 9. 1970," Suomen ulkopolitiikan ajankohtaisista näkymistä, ULA 1970, 49.

44. "Speech by Ambassador Ralph Enckell at the General Meeting of the Ecumenical Workshop for Information in Europe, in Espoo, March 28, 1972," *The Present Situation in Europe*, ULA 1972, 77–78.

test of an international baptism by fire (1977, 311, 332–35).[45] After the memorandum was communicated abroad, Finnish officials waited anxiously to see how it would be received. It first met with some skepticism in the West. The fact that it began with the words "the Government of the Soviet Union approached recently the Governments of European countries" led to much speculation that the Finnish initiative was issued on behalf of the Soviet Union. Finnish officials devoted considerable effort to refuting this suggestion.[46] Spencer also notes that, although the memorandum "dealt adequately with the procedural questions of North American participation and the need for careful preparation, . . .[Finland's] claim to a special role in view of the relations [it] maintained with both the Federal Republic and the GDR through commercial missions . . . appeared to endorse the WTO position on the German questions and was poles apart from the Canadian and Western stand" (1984, 38). Considering that Finland was still under suspicion in the West that she was willing—but not able—to act as a neutral, Kekkonen argued that the real test of the initiative, and hence of Finnish neutrality, lay with its "baptism" in the West.

However, Canadian officials considered the Finnish Memorandum "a decisive boost" to the proposed ESC. In spite of U.S. concern that the Finnish Memorandum "created a presumption that the conference would in fact take place," Canada insisted the Finnish initiative "provided the West with an opening to discuss the conference idea on its own merits, without involving preliminary negotiations with the USSR" (Spencer 1984, 41–41). Canada was among those alliance members (including Belgium, Italy, and West Germany) that were interested in the idea, and it urged its NATO mission to play a constructive role in NATO's study of subjects that could be dealt with in such a forum. The NATO strategy that emerged focused on making the West's cooperation with the Soviets in the future conditional on the fulfillment of Western preconditions. The West proceeded on the basis of the " 'jujitsu principle' of using an opponent's force to serve one's own ends" (Spencer 1984, 38). It turned the Soviet demand for a security conference into means of leveraging the Soviets on the West's own interests. This gave rise to the West's linkage strategy. The Soviet's fulfillment of each set of preconditions would inch the West closer toward its cooperation on the CSCE.

This linkage strategy also acquired an explicit dimension of cross-issue linkage. In the Rome communiqué of May 27, 1970, the NATO alliance sig-

45. This is from Kekkonen's articles written under the pen name "Liimatainen." See "Taikuri itsekin oli hämmästynyt" and "Suomi ja Turvallisuuskonferenssi" in Kekkonen (1977).

46. However, as one well-informed West German journalist noted, the Finnish Memorandum did not follow Soviet policy on a number of points. In particular, Finland observed it would send the Memorandum "to the Governments of all European states, to those of East and West Germany," whereas Moscow wanted Finnish recognition specifically of the German Democratic Republic as a sovereign state. See "Suomi ja turvallisuus-konferenssi; länsisaksalaisia arviointeja," *Die Welt*, May 19, 1969, in UMSLT: LK n:o 70/31. 5. 1969, 1.

naled that if satisfactory progress on Germany and Berlin were achieved in the ongoing talks, NATO would be willing "to negotiate, in any suitable forum, those concrete issues whose resolution would enhance the security of Europe" and would be ready to enter into multilateral talks "to explore when it will be possible to convene a conference, or a series of conferences, on European security and cooperation." Although not an explicit quid quo pro, the West also linked Soviet agreement on the MBFR proposal to initiating talks on the CSCE. Despite French resistance, another aspect of the West's strategy was to arrive at a common substantive position within the NATO alliance that would constitute as far as possible the terms of draft documents for a conference on security and cooperation in Europe. This was an attempt "to strengthen the West's negotiating position and to check the USSR's attempts to divide the West" (Spencer 1984, 73). The West's attention to substance stood in contrast to the Soviet position that essentially envisaged approaching the CSCE on the basis of an exchange of ideas and reaching broad, declaratory principles on interstate relations.

The development of alliance positions strengthened the allies' internal commitments to entering into multilateral consultations on the CSCE. This in turn made less likely defection by any one state, including the United States, which was probably the least enthusiastic. Thus, East and West and the nonbloc states saw their commitments envelop a widening set of relationships through ties to Finland as the third party promoting the CSCE, and to their own allies and friends in the problem-solving process, and then to the idea of the conference itself. Indeed, as Rubin argues, "a series of such small, constructive commitments can create a rhythm of concession making that is *entrapping*. Each side comes to feel that it now has too much invested in this new process (or rhythm) or movement towards agreement to give up" (1991, 242, emphasis in original).

Finland would still have to prove it had the skills and resources, including the technical knowledge, and adequate facilities to host a European security conference. Many questions remained in the West also about "the Finnish role" and the formalities—the "what, when, where, and how" of the proposed conference. These matters were complicated, however, by questions regarding the status of the two Germanies. Although the German Question would put its own obstacles in the way of Finland's bid to host the CSCE, Kekkonen judged initial reactions to its May 1969 Memorandum were quite positive. This fact led him to write that one could apply a well-known saying to the occasion: "even the magician was amazed" (1977, 311).

Maintaining Mediator Readiness

Careful management of Finland's relations to the two Germanies was critical to forwarding Finland's third-party offer to launch the CSCE. Third parties have to be available and ready to seize opportunities when adversaries arrive at critical junctures in their relationship. Changes in the relationship among the parties in the conflict, the nature of the issues at stake, or the escalation of conflict are all normal aspects of conflict dynamics. However, when such changes adversely affect the third party's interests, resources, or capacity to influence the disputants' interaction, as well as their stakes in a potential agreement, they pose serious obstacles to mediator readiness (Susskind and Babbitt 1992, 42). Preparations between the superpowers and also between West Germany and the Soviet Union in advance of the preparatory talks on the CSCE threatened to render Finland's relations with the two Germanies at the level of trade delegations a relic of the cold war, and thus jeopardize its chances of hosting the CSCE.

In June 1970 the Warsaw Pact issued from Budapest the call for all states, including East Germany and West Germany, to participate in the proposed European Security Conference "on equal footing" and with "rights equal to" other European and North American participating states.[47] This declaration put the issue of full diplomatic recognition of the two Germanies onto the agenda of bilateral issues for which Finland would have to find adequate solutions in order to protect its third-party role. The Finnish Foreign Ministry calculated that the timing of a decision to grant full diplomatic recognition was the key issue, so that Finland would derive the greatest advantage in its bid to sponsor the CSCE.

According to Jakobson, the "German Package" was generated by Risto Hyvärinen and used two Soviet policy initiatives to justify the new Finnish approach: the October 1970 address to the UN General Assembly by the Soviet Foreign Minister Gromyko, which referred to the agreement made between the German Federal Republic and the Soviet Union, and Gromyko's appeal that states organize their relations on the basis of the principle of prohibiting the use of force. In Finland this led to the calculation that, if Finland worked out an arrangement to reduce its own security threats from the two Germanies, the relevance of the military assistance clause in the FCMA Treaty could be significantly reduced.[48] Finland also saw the signing of the West German-Soviet

47. See "Extracts from Memorandum Published by the Warsaw Pact, Budapest, June 1970," reproduced in Palmer (1971, 97).

48. The objective was to obviate any possibility for consultations between the Soviet Union and Finland, as the Soviets had called for in the 1961 Note Crisis. However, in a 1972 speech given at the University of Turku, Kekkonen strongly refuted various Western interpretations of Finland's German initiative, which suggested Finland was attempting in some fashion to use the agreements to maneuver against the Soviet Union. He retorted that "Finland does not try to use roundabout ways in its relations with the Soviet Union, nor seek advantages for itself by devious routes. Finland has wanted for its own part to resolve the German issue in a way that leaves no room for return of the shadows of the past and that from the outset is appropriate for the relations of the two Germanies with Finland within the international position we have achieved." See "Speech by the President

nonaggression pact on August 20, 1970, and of the Quadrapartite Agreement on September 3, 1971, as justification for reexamining Finnish ties to the two Germanies.

Although revealing Finnish-German negotiations was a critical matter of timing, a leak to the press during the 1971 Nordic foreign minister's meeting in Copenhagen obliged Kekkonen to make a premature public announcement of the foreign-policy initiative (Apunen 1984). Kekkonen attempted to put the initiative into the best possible light. In a radio and television speech on September 11, 1971, he announced that Finland's general goals were to ensure that these favorable developments continued and that Finland's position in this changing situation would be strengthened.[49] Finland's German Package in the government's view was an integral part of the process of negotiation and change in Europe (Apunen 1977, 280–81).

Finland sought to normalize its relations with the two Germanies without changing the nature of the underlying principle of equal treatment, on which both its neutrality policy and legitimacy as a third party rested. The foreign-policy objective for Finland was to reinforce the balance and symmetry in Finland's East-West relations. To protect its third-party status, Finland assured the two Germanies that it did not seek to influence the process of negotiations between their two states.[50] Although the Finnish proposal called for the negotiation of peace treaties between Finland and each German state, which were to be identical, and presented and signed simultaneously (though separately) with both Germanies, a principal obstacle was the fact that the two Germanies had not yet worked out a negotiated agreement on the issue of their sovereignty. Because the Finnish government sought agreement on the "diplomatic recognition and the establishment of diplomatic relations between Finland and the two Germanies,"[51] the Finnish initiative took a leading position on the issue.

Seeking to contain suspicions of Finland's initiative, Ahti Karjalainen, then prime minister, explained that Finland pursued these bilateral proposals because it was not necessarily the case that all issues would fall under the purview of the Security Conference, even though the (then) current developments might

---

of the Republic on the Occasion of the 50th Anniversary of the Student Body of the University of Turku, November 8, 1972," Aspects of Finnish Foreign Policy, ULA 1972, 62. See also Jakobson (1983, 292–94), on the government's handling of the German initiative and on Leskinen's slip of the tongue, when he sought not to answer directly a reporter's question of whether the FCMA treaty was outdated, but suggested, nonetheless, that the Soviets hardly need to fear threats from Germany.

49. "Radio and Television Speech by the President of the Republic, Dr. Urho Kekkonen, 11 September 1971," ULA 1971, 64–66.

50. "Pääministeri Ahti Karjalaisen puhe 20. 9. 1971 Helsingissa," Suomen väylä historian merellä tänään, ULA 1971, 86.

51. "Communiqué of the Finnish Government, September ll, 1971," ULA 1971, 79.

lead to peace structures. The government argued the Finnish initiative on German recognition came early in the process of European negotiations because this assured their being treated as a part of the whole organization of relations.[52]

In the end, Finland arranged to establish full diplomatic relations with both Germanies as sovereign states on November 20, 1972.[53] With the signing of the East German Treaty in July 1972 and the West German Treaty in January 1973, the way was cleared for their mutual, and fully equal, participation among all other states in the proposed consultations and eventually in the conference itself.[54] According to the prevailing view in the West, the Finnish move to reach agreement first with East Germany was an indication of pressure from the Soviet Union—that is, Finlandization. In fact, the matter of reaching agreement first with East Germany was a result of West Germany's unwillingness to proceed earlier with negotiations on the Finnish proposal. This delay was a result of complications in Bonn on settling the matter of the inner-German treaties. Once the inner-German agreement was initialed in Bonn on November 8, 1972, it was possible for negotiations on the West German-Finnish agreement to move forward.[55]

Conclusions

The course Kekkonen and the mandarins set for Finland's third-party initiative to launch the proposed European Security Conference entailed high stakes for Finnish neutrality. Finland sought a balanced position on whether the ESC

52. "Pääministeri Ahti Karjalaisen puhe 20. 9. 1971 Helsingissa," ULA 1971, 87.

53. On Finland's diplomatic recognition of the two Germanies, see "Saksojen tunnustaminen," Nov. 20, 1972, *Helsingin Sanomat* UM: LKEV n:o 228/ 20. 11. 1972, 8.

54. Kekkonen suggested as much in a November 1972 speech when he noted (referring to the inner-German agreement) that "behind great decisions there are often many small details which are not without influence in bringing about the final settlement. We hope that through our initiative of last September we have at least made a small contribution towards effecting an important agreement which is going to promote the cause of peace in Europe." See "Speech by the President of the Republic on the Occasion of the 50th Anniversary of the Student Body of the University of Turku, 8 November 1972," ULA 1972, 63.

55. Kekkonen strongly denied Western accounts that attributed to Soviet pressure Finland's treaty proposal to East Germany. Kekkonen equally refuted other analyses suggesting that, in making such arrangements entailing the recognition of Finnish neutrality policy, Finland attempted to strengthen its position vis-à-vis the Soviet Union. Kekkonen refuted analyses in the same vein that connected the Finnish GDR initiative and its negotiations with the EEC, maintaining that "wrapping the recognition of the two Germanies and the EEC agreement together in one package would be such a transparent 'trick' that the Finnish government would not be party to it." See "Speech by the President of the Republic on the Occasion of the 50th Anniversary of the Student Body of the University of Turku, November 8, 1972," ULA 1972, 62.

would aim to preserve and strengthen the status quo or work toward its transformation. Karjalainen argued that, without understanding from all sides, Finland believed it would not be possible to attain outcomes or results on the questions of European security.[56] Thus it was first necessary to seek an appreciation of the state of East-West affairs that went beyond outmoded conceptions, and from this basis move forward toward greater cooperation.

While at the outset the Finnish approach was conservative and oriented toward maintaining the status quo, a process of gradual adjustment ultimately implied a different order of things in Europe. In supporting the European Security Conference, Finland's objective was to attain "more cooperation in order to build confidence and trust between opposing sides in Europe." These goals represented possibilities for Finland also "to get better and more involved in the European process as a neutral country." The basis of Finland's strategy was to call first for stability and then for an element of change. Rooting the country's neutrality policy in the changing structural relationships in Europe was directly in its interest.

Furthermore, from Kekkonen's perspective, the European Security Conference was advantageous because it would create a forum for Finland's policy of active neutrality, where Finland could prove that its neutrality was of equal value to all sides of the international community. This would show that Finnish neutrality was not limited by its special relationship to the Soviet Union as far as Finland's role in the international arena and in multilateral contexts was concerned. Finnish neutrality could be of benefit to the West—in many cases even more than to the East. The aim of Max Jakobson and others in the foreign-policy leadership was to demonstrate that Finnish neutrality was genuine and legitimate—genuine in the sense that it was not dictated by the Soviet Union; even the need to maintain a relationship of mutual confidence with the Soviet Union did not prevent Finland from acting as a Western-type neutral in accordance with certain Western, liberal, political values. The essence of this thinking was that Finnish neutrality contributed to the stability and peace of the international system and to the development of Europe. For Finland to be useful, it had to be neutral. Kekkonen drew a direct link between Finnish neutrality and expanding international cooperation, which were both important national interests (Kekkonen 1982, 129).

At the opening of the multilateral consultations on the CSCE in November 1972, Kekkonen proclaimed that "Finland's neutrality, built up through persistent efforts, has become a positive and permanent element in the balance of power in Europe."[57] Finland's historical relations with Russia and the Soviet

56. "Ulkoasianministeri Ahti Karjalaisen Stuttgarter Zeitung-lehdelle myöntämä haastattelu 7. 6. 1969," ULA 1969, 69.

57. "Speech by President Urho Kekkonen on the Opening Day of the Helsinki Consultations," Nov. 22, 1972, ULA 1972, 98.

Union and its position as an outpost in the cold war gave it an intense sensitivity to increasing East-West tensions that shaped Kekkonen's foreign policy and third-party leadership as a "cue-taker." As a facilitative mediator, Finland *engendered commitments* from adversaries to come together, and to adhere to the problem-solving and decision-making process it was helping to create, as we shall see in detail in the next chapter.

5 Laying the Groundwork for a New East-West Order

THIRTY-FOUR DELEGATIONS from the East, West, and the neutral and nonaligned states of Europe opened the Dipoli Consultations on November 22, 1972, at the Politechnic school in Otaniemi, one of the peninsulas that forms the outlying area of Helsinki. Agreement on the Final Recommendations of the Helsinki Consultations, or the Blue Book—the agenda for the negotiations on security and cooperation in Europe—was reached by consensus by thirty-four states on June 8, 1973. This achievement was facilitated by the preparations to which Finland had committed itself in the May 1969 Memorandum along with the third-party efforts of other (mostly nonbloc) states.

Altogether, it took more than three years from the time Finland first offered to host the proposed security conference in Helsinki before the Dipoli Consultations commenced. As a facilitative mediator, Finnish officials were *process-oriented.* Their efforts helped create as low-risk an environment as possible. Although they did not start out with any grand strategy for how to get the negotiations off the ground, the Finns began by engendering commitments from potential participating states and exploring where consensus on a preconference agenda might be found. This was an incremental process that encompassed first a bilateral exploratory phase followed by a "multi-bilateral" phase of intense "preconsultations" or exchange of information among the diplomatic community in Helsinki. This second phase of activity led to the opening of the Consultations among the thirty-four delegations, or the third phase.[1]

1. These thirty-four states were from the East: Bulgaria, Czechoslovakia, German Democratic Republic, Hungary, Poland, Romania, Union of Soviet Socialist Republics; the West: Belgium, Canada, Denmark, France, Federal Republic of Germany, Greece, Iceland, Ireland, Italy, Luxembourg, the Netherlands, Norway, Portugal, Spain, Turkey, United Kingdom, and the United States; and the nonbloc states: Austria, Cyprus, Finland, Holy See, Liechtenstein, Malta, San Marino, Sweden, Switzerland, and Yugoslavia. The core of the neutral and nonaligned group was formed by the four neutrals, Yugoslavia, and Malta. Ireland caucused with the West as an EC member state, yet pursued a neutralist foreign policy. Still, it was not part of the N+N grouping. Spain remained iso-

During the *first phase,* Kekkonen and other Finnish diplomats conducted bilateral explorations with leaders in capitals across the European and North American continent to gather information, maintain open channels of communication, keep the parties focused on the issues, and clarify potential areas of common interest that could become the substance of an agenda. Through shuttle diplomacy between Moscow and Washington, Kekkonen personally served as a "sounding board" for the disputants, hearing each side's point of view, its position, and interests, then representing these to the other (see also Spector and Korula 1992). The *second phase* built on these early exploratory and counseling activities and created a transition from bilateralism to multilateralism by making Helsinki the nub of activity. Thus, during more than a year before the opening of the Dipoli Consultations in November 1972, Finland conducted "multi-bilateral" consultations among heads of mission in Helsinki with Finnish Foreign Ministry officials preparing the CSCE. These contacts and preparations were sustained all the way through the opening of the *third phase,* the official multilateral consultations in Dipoli on the question of the modalities and possible agenda for a Conference on Security and Cooperation in Europe.

Finland's emphasis on consensus building was important for three reasons. First, it was a means for shaping a mutually acceptable agenda. This possibility in itself was important for engendering commitments to the negotiation process. Second, the Finnish approach to consensus building in these exploratory phases also set precedents and created expectations that laid the groundwork for the basic procedural rules and modalities that would structure the CSCE process. Third, the Finnish preparations were significant not only for the immediate solutions they helped to shape but also because they created expectations among participating states in East and West for these nonbloc states to emerge as mediators.[2] As we shall see, the Finnish consensus-building approach and procedural preparations for the Dipoli Consultations, together with the intervention of other nonbloc states in Dipoli, helped lay the normative foundation for the Blue Book and in turn for building a process of cooperation between East and West.

---

lated from the West through the early 1970s, playing something of a third-party role especially during the Dipoli negotiations, but never assumed close collaboration with the N+N. Spain joined the EC and NATO in 1986. However, it hosted the CSCE Follow-up Meeting in Madrid in 1981–83 essentially in the capacity of a state outside the military alliances. Romania also acted independently, especially during the early 1970s, and maintained contacts with the N+N through Yugoslavia in particular. Monaco participated in the CSCE from the initiation of the Helsinki Phase in 1973, thus bringing the total number of participants to thirty-five. Albania was the only European state that did not participate in the CSCE (until after the cold war ended).

2. The N+N's third-party role eventually became customary practice in the CSCE.

Phase I: Bilateralism

The Finnish third-party strategy led to initiatives that engaged the entire Finnish Foreign Ministry apparatus, including delegations abroad, those working at the Foreign Ministry headquarters in downtown Helsinki, the president, and other governmental ministry and elected officials. Even before making public its intent to promote the convening of the Security Conference, Finland based its third-party strategy on getting the commitment of its neighbors in the Nordic community, of which the support of Sweden was viewed as especially important.[3] Likewise, in the months following the announcement of its intentions to offer its capital as a host cite, Finland sought and received the support of other neutral countries.

Kekkonen also lent his own office to developing a network of ties and diplomatic support for the Finnish initiative. This effort took him on diplomatic missions to Poland, Czechoslovakia, Hungary, Romania, the Soviet Union, and England in 1969 alone. On a round of shuttle diplomacy in 1970, Kekkonen met first with Brezhnev in Moscow and then President Nixon in Washington, D.C. In discussions with Nixon and his national security adviser Henry Kissinger, Kekkonen (himself accompanied by Jakobson) sought to sell the idea of a security conference to a still-doubtful U.S. administration. Kekkonen emphasized that, in evaluating the conference, the strong interest of the small East European states should be taken into consideration. The conference setting offered an opportunity for them to reveal and strengthen their own national identity. Kekkonen assured Nixon that the Soviet Union was taking "known risks in its relations with the East European countries in its efforts to organize the security conference" (Jakobson 1983, 285).[4]

Even as early as this visit, a proposal for setting up the preliminary talks on the conference was advanced by Belgium's Foreign Minister Harmel. He called for the first phase to consist of an ambassadorial level "salon de thé" in a neutral capital such as Helsinki. In talks at the White House, the Finnish president determined that Nixon was interested in convening an ambassadorial-level

3. In Sweden the Finnish initiative was viewed as a good development for Finland and its neutrality policy. An improvement in the Finnish position, given the geopolitical environment shared by the two countries, it was also considered favorable to Sweden's neutrality posture.

4. As Spencer informs us (1984, 39), this argument had some currency among NATO states. Canada, at least, judged that the Soviets were unable to maintain their will over Eastern Europe without using force and that their decision to use the Budapest proposal to serve Soviet interests thus entailed risks that the Eastern European countries would take advantage of détente. While cooperating with the Soviets on a conference on security and cooperation in Europe could lead to a diminution of solidarity among Western governments, the risks the Soviets were taking could nonetheless be exploited by the West.

meeting. Nixon noted to Kissinger that, if a conference could provide more independence to the Eastern bloc countries and if it were a means to build peaceful developments between East and West, then it would be of great significance. However, Kissinger expressed the view that one conference would do little to change a century of Russian behavior. Indeed, he remained highly skeptical of the CSCE throughout his tenure as national security adviser and later as secretary of state under presidents Nixon and Ford (Jakobson 1983, 285–86). Kissinger referred to the proposed conference as the "Helsinki tea party" (Spencer 1984, 81).

The notion of a preconference set of consultations in Helsinki was being explored by Finnish officials through other channels as well. To promote the initiative and broad understanding, Ralph Enckell, an able diplomat and also ambassador to the OECD, was appointed roving ambassador in March 1970 (Jakobson 1983, 285). As one Finnish official later judged, "he was particularly suited for the task because of his vast experience, and much better than usual skills in that sort of sensitive game." The task would have been quite impossible to accomplish without this diplomatic effort.[5] It was Enckell who coined the phrase, "I come on a mission, but I am not a missionary." According to instructions, he was to stress "that his mission was about exploring the possibilities for a European Conference, not to sell one." It was the Finnish view that "[the conference] had to stem from the will of those who participated, and not something that was given to them in exchange for something else. It had to have its roots deep in the needs of the participating governments, rather than be in itself an object of negotiation, whether or not, for what price."[6]

By the end of June 1970, Enckell had visited thirteen capitals. These were mostly bilateral talks but also included discussions with the Nordic foreign ministers and the secretary general of the United Nations, U Thant. Assessing these visits, Enckell noted they gave opportunity for broad and thorough discussions. The matter of convening a conference had been mutually clarified and his counterparts, he reported, "have said it is very beneficial." He concluded that "through these measured contacts the matter has been forwarded and these [contacts] can be regarded as a part of the thorough preparations, to which the Finnish government in its memorandum stipulated its condition for the success of the conference."[7]

Finland had to overcome numerous challenges to secure support for the talks to be held in Helsinki. These included finding the right formula for bring-

5. Finnish official, interview by author, tape recording, Helsinki, May 11, 1988.

6. Ibid.

7. "Ote Suurlähettiläs Ralph Enckellin esitelmästä kesän yhteydessä 30. 6. 1970," Euroopan turvallisuuskysymys, ULA 1970, 35.

ing East and West into a first phase of multilateral talks. There was also competition from Austria on the matter of hosting the proposed ESC and a Romanian proposal for a preliminary meeting to discuss the formalities of a conference at the level of deputy foreign ministers (Spencer 1984, 51–52). Finland also was under pressure from the East during this period regarding its policy of equal ties to the two Germanies at the level of trade delegations.

In contrast to Finland's facilitative mediation focused on promoting the CSCE process, Austria had assumed more of an instrumental mediator role in its bid to enter the competition to host the ESC. In a July 24, 1970, memorandum, Austria urged that several conferences, not just one, would be needed, commended the idea of forming " 'mutually agreed organs or working parties between conferences,' " and offered Vienna as a conference cite. In contrast to the Finnish proposal for a multilateral phase of consultations at the level of ambassadors, Austria proposed the preparations be carried out among government experts, specifically those officials who had long been following the CSCE process (Apunen 1977, 301).

Both the Finnish and the Austrian offers were subject to certain shortcomings. The Finnish proposal called for ambassador-level talks, but the delegations represented in Helsinki were not prepared to deal with the CSCE initiative.[8] Austria, on the other hand, had entered into the discussions on the substance of the agenda and had aligned itself with a NATO position, namely that mutual and balanced force reductions be included on the agenda (Apunen 1977, 301–02). Arguing that this was a concrete measure consistent with the principle of the renunciation of the use or threat of force in mutual relations of European states, the Austrian Memorandum noted:

> on the ground of her own particular geographical and military position and on the ground of the general military situation in Europe, Austria believes that a favourable and lasting progress of *détente* can only be achieved if the conference on European security also considers and solves the question of balanced and mutual force reduction, being the focal factor of security in Europe.[9]

Because it was a facilitator, Finland's third-part strategy aimed specifically "to promote the birth of the negotiation process," and thus Finland maintained that "we do not meddle in the questions of substance." Finland judged further that "the discussion touching on the European Security Conference is a con-

8. Kekkonen and Jakobson already appreciated this at the time of their discussions with Nixon and Kissinger. See Jakobson (1983, 286).

9. See "Memorandum of the Austrian Government, Vienna, July 1970," reproduced in Palmer (1970, 99). The italics are in the original.

stantly moving process, which gives birth to new designs."[10] In arguing that there should be no preconditions, Finland left the possibility for the substance of the agenda to remain open. Austria's proposal, however, was tainted from the start not only because it meddled with substance by including the MBFR on the agenda (Apunen 1977, 301) but also because it described them as *balanced* and mutual reductions, again NATO's position.

Over time, support for Finland as the host for the consultations grew, an opportunity that Finland promoted in its November 24, 1970, proposal.[11] The idea of an informal ambassadorial-level meeting, Enckell explained, was considered "a definite possible preparatory step, which would give to the participating states a picture of the conditions by which the actual conference is to succeed."[12] Such measured steps helped to engender the interest and support of potential participating states while reducing the veil of uncertainty that surrounded the launching of the entire conference endeavor. Also, by suggesting the parties begin in Helsinki with multilateral *consultations* rather than *preparatory* talks, Finland finessed the commitments needed to launch the CSCE.

Phase II: Multi-Bilateralism

The final stages of consolidating Finland's initial third-party role in launching the CSCE depended on concretizing the process of opening the multilateral consultations. Finland continued to use its role as a sponsor of the negotiations to achieve incremental commitments through bilateral contacts, even though Finland's third-party status was still subject to considerable suspicion in the West.

But by the summer of 1972, it was reasonably clear to Finnish officials that the German situation had been clarified.[13] The last hurdles over preconditions were surmounted between the blocs in the late spring and summer of 1972. These included Bundestag approval both of the Moscow Treaty and the Warsaw Treaty on May 17 with ratification in the Bundesrat quickly following. As Spencer also notes, this change cleared the path "for the four-power protocol

10. "Ote valtiosihteeri Richard Töttermanin esitelmästä Paasikivi-Seuran lounaskokouksessa 24. 9. 1970," ULA 1970, 49.

11. The issue of adequate representation in Helsinki was resolved by agreeing to hold a preparatory stage with a plenipotentiary at the full ambassadorial level, while the governmental experts, or "CSCE-ologists," would carry out the actual negotiations in unofficial working groups. See Spencer (1984, 82), who notes that "by tacit agreement the ambassadors in Helsinki played almost no role in the work of the MPT [Multilateral Preparatory Talks] after the first few weeks."

12. "Ote valtiosihteeri Richard Töttermanin esitelmästä Paasikivi-Seuran lounaskokouksessa 24. 9. 1970," ULA 1970, 49.

13. Finnish official, interview by author, tape recording, Helsinki, May 11, 1988.

which would bring the Berlin accords into effect" (Spencer 1984, 78). On the conclusion of their foreign ministers' meeting at the North Atlantic Council in Bonn on May 30–31, 1972, the NATO members announced at last that they accepted the Finnish proposal of November 24, 1970. The green light was signaled for holding an ambassador-level meeting in preparation for entering into multilateral negotiations for the Conference on Security and Cooperation in Europe.[14] Substantial efforts had produced an alliance position on four key areas,[15] which in fact foreshadowed the actual division of the conference into "baskets." These four points encompassed: the Declaration of Principles; Certain Aspects of Military Security; the Freer Movement of People, Information, and Ideas and Cultural Relations; and finally Economic Cooperation (Spencer 1984, 75–77).

WHILE NATO was attempting to generate a common policy toward the issues for the preparatory talks, the matter of where the conference was to be held remained one on which NATO was not yet ready to take an unambiguous stand. The alliance members agreed to be reserved toward Helsinki "until the Finnish role was clarified." This policy was problematic because NATO ambassadors in Helsinki had already been meeting informally. The Canadians had expressed the view in NATO that "contacts between local heads of mission 'could be construed as [the] edge of [the] wedge' opening the way towards an eventual conference, 'whatever disclaimers might be made' " (Spencer 1984, 58). In spite of these lengthy ongoing contacts, NATO still believed it was important to determine the relationship of these activities to the Finnish government and its role as a neutral sponsor. Moreover, because "the proposed multilateral talks on the CSCE could coincide with sensitive intra-German negotiations towards a basic treaty, Canada and other NATO governments also assessed Finnish objectivity very carefully" (Spencer 1984, 73). Thus, even as preparations were under way in Helsinki to initiate the multilateral consultations in Dipoli on the Conference on Security and Cooperation in Europe, Finland was still under suspicion in the West that she was willing—but not able—to act as a neutral. As one official recalled, "Finland heard from third parties, sometimes informally, face to face, in many instances subtle references to less than convincing views that we would maintain a neutral stance in all matters. And we did subject ourselves to that test."[16]

14. "Kommuniqué der Ministertagung des Nordatlantikrates am 30. und 31. Mai 1972 in Bonn (Auszüge)," in Schram, Riggert, and Friedel (1972, 354).

15. These four key areas of agreement emerged despite difficulties in the Western alliance to coordinate its position. The four points resulted in somewhat distinct EC and NATO preparations.

16. Finnish official, interview by author, tape recording, Helsinki, May 11, 1988.

Nonetheless, on the basis of extensive multi-bilateral consultations the Finnish government had been pursuing in Helsinki, by mid-July 1972 Finland was able to convey that agreement generally existed for commencing the consultations in Helsinki on November 22, 1972.[17] At this point Finland used a deadline for the first time to keep the pressure and momentum building. The Finnish Foreign Ministry then set up two small working groups in Helsinki. One was to be responsible for the technical arrangements of the preparatory meeting, while a second worked on the political arrangements.[18] The big question was how to draft the definitive invitation. As a Finnish official close to the pre-Dipoli developments explained:

> it was politically a highly sensitive matter. And we were unwilling to discuss the text with any of the potentially invited, because they would have no doubt come with all sorts of amendments and suggestions of their own and in all probability we never would have brought any harmony into these thirty-four different sets of various proposals and ideas. And this is why we talked with people without showing them a word or a line in order to form an opinion on what would be acceptable and what would be highly objectionable—and then made a draft of our own and had it circulated—on the basis of assuming full and sole responsibility for it.[19]

The Finnish third-party approach used consensus building as the principal tool to accompany its strategy of engendering incremental commitments to overcome the problems of organizing a multilateral approach. Finnish officials considered consensus building the key to improving international affairs and promoting a new basis for cooperative relations among states.[20] It offered a normative basis for structuring relations so that the benefits commonly and mutually achieved in other spheres of international relations, such as economic spheres, could also be realized in the domain of international security, to which they gave a broad conception. The emphasis Finland placed on facilitating understanding also implied that consensus building should function as an instrument to promote learning. The integrative, learning, and the norm-generating capacity of consensus building thus carried the potential for forming an international regime to reduce threats and build peace on cooperation. The Finnish

17. It is clear from the text of a press release. See "Ulkoasiainministeriön tiedonanto 27. 7. 1972," ULA 1972, 90. The United States did not want the consultations to begin until after presidential elections.

18. Finnish official, interview by author, tape recording, Helsinki, May 11, 1988.

19. Ibid.

20. "The Finnish Memorandum of 24 November 1970, Relating to a Conference on European Security," ULA 1970, 73–74.

approach to consensus building also resonated with discussions in the West, where there was general agreement that the proposed conference should adopt a consensus rule. However, it should be emphasized that the Finnish approach was to apply this type of decision rule as a key element of its strategy to get agreement on launching the proposed ESC. As Karjalainen noted, "consensus can only be obtained through the consideration of the totality of national interests and through the adjustment of different opinions. The discussion connected to the European Security Conference is an important step in locating this consensus."[21]

It was only in late October that NATO countries announced they would be ready to come to Helsinki for the November 22 opening date.[22] NATO's commitment was tied up with the issue of who was to participate at the MBFR, and with the timing of the initiation of both the CSCE and the MBFR. The United States and its NATO allies had pushed a parallel timetable. Eventually, the matter was resolved during a visit by Kissinger to Moscow on September 10–14. The Soviets handed him a note that suggested the following sequencing: November 22, 1972, opening of Dipoli consultations, January 31, 1973, MBFR preparatory talks, and June 1973 the opening date of the CSCE. The West accepted this in principle, although in its reply to the Soviets the United States maintained that June 1973 was a reasonable date for the CSCE—because such determination actually fell under the competence of the multilateral talks themselves at Helsinki (Spencer 1984, 80–81). Clarification of these issues of timing opened the way to Dipoli. Finally, with long-sought assurances from the West, on November 9, 1972, Finland issued its formal invitation to thirty-six potential European and North American participants. It called for a four-week long period of consultations to commence on the agreed date.[23]

Phase III: The Dipoli Consultations

Just as the pre-agenda development of the CSCE had required laborious efforts, including extensive bilateral negotiations in Helsinki, prior to the multilateral, consultative phase, so too did the agenda-building process that commenced outside Helsinki on November 22, 1972. Finland's contribution to this was greatly facilitated by the manifold diplomatic contacts it promoted and pursued at all levels and the literal CSCE bank of information Helsinki was able to col-

21. "Ulkoasiainminsteri Ahti Karjalaisen puhe ulkoministeri ja rouva Waldheimin kunniaksi tarjotulla lounaalla 10.11. 1969," ULA 1969, 258.

22. See "ETYK," *Suomenmaa,* UM: LKEV n:o 210, Oct. 25, 1972, 8.

23. "Memorandum of the Ministry for Foreign Affairs, 6 November 1972," ULA 1972, 93–94.

lect through these channels.[24] The potential CSCE participants now prepared to move from the diagnostic phase to the prenegotiations. After six months of formidable discussion (and not the mere four weeks anticipated), they produced the "Final Recommendations of the Helsinki Consultations." Commonly referred to as the "Blue Book" (after its rather Finnish, sky-blue cover), the document set out the modalities and substance that breathed life into the CSCE process.

The work progressed again over various stages, the first of which took up the technical questions such as the working procedures and conference modalities, which proved inseparable from the basic principles that would be the foundation of the CSCE process. This was followed by the reading of opening statements, which lasted until December 5. On January 25, 1973, delegations resumed work at Dipoli and continued throughout the spring in three more sessions until agreement was reached on an agenda and mandate for the conference. The Blue Book was organized by "baskets" as a device to set out the framework of the agenda. The Blue Book called for a three-stage conference to open in Helsinki, which would then move to a committee-working level in Geneva and return to Helsinki, although the specifics of the third stage were left to determine in Geneva.

Interstate Principles and Modalities

Before any consultations on the substance of the negotiations for the CSCE could proceed, the rules of procedure and working methods for approaching the consultative, and subsequently the negotiating tasks in the CSCE proper, had to be settled. Inseparable from the symbolic and actual working nature of the conference modalities were the basic principles of interstate relations from which these modalities would derive. Principles of interstate relations shape in fundamental ways expectations about states' interaction. Principles establish relevant premises from which states reason with each other, and about who has a right and on what ground to make decisions. These considerations informed the set of working rules to be adopted at Dipoli, not only in terms of the method of making decisions but also concerning the procedural arrangements for deliberating and the operational approach for eventually implementing the agreements (see also Ostrom 1990, 52).

The Consultations opened with discussion first on the procedural rules. They were resolved during the week of November 22–28, 1972. By means of a compromise formulation forwarded by Belgium, it was agreed that these modalities applied to only the Helsinki Consultations. Characteristic of the ten-

24. "Ulkoasiainministeri Olavi Mattilan esitelmä Utrikespolitiska Samfundetin tilaisuudessa Helsingissä 11. 1. 1972," Turvallisuuspoliittinen tilanne Euroopassa, ULA 1972, 15.

tativeness of the entire endeavor, a decision as to the working rules, organization, and other procedural matters for the main CSCE meeting was delayed. Nevertheless, the Dipoli modalities and working rules eventually found their way into the Blue Book.[25]

As a sponsor of the negotiations, Finland had carefully examined the position and attitudes of different governments, where possible making practical proposals to bring about the convening of the Consultations, the participation of all states, and agreement on technical matters.[26] During the two weeks before the opening of the Consultations, Finland continued its efforts to reach consensus in advance as regarded the rules of procedure of the opening phase and its organization.[27] During the last two days, a final round of prenegotiations was held (Spencer 1984, 84). As candidates for the chair and vice-chair of the Consultations, the heads of mission were invited by Mr. Tscherning, the Danish ambassador and dean of the diplomatic corps, to nominate Richard Tötterman, head of the Finnish Foreign Ministry, and Jaakko Iloniemi, respectively. There was also agreement that an executive secretary from the Finnish foreign service would be named in order to facilitate the technical tasks arising during the Consultations.[28] However, these suggestions met immediately with protest from the Romanian delegation. Because the meeting had already been "declared closed" by the Finns, the Romanian position was not heard, but it soon was.[29] On the day of the opening ceremony, Finland distributed informally a draft text enumerating Finland's suggestions on procedural issues for the Consultations.[30] Romania and France followed on Thursday with their proposals. In the end,

25. On the early procedural debates, see "Dipolin Kompromissi tasoitti tien kohti yleiskeskustelua," *Helsingin Sanomat,* Dec. 2, 1972, from Ulkopoliittisen instituutin leikelmäarkisto (hereafter UILA).

26. "Etyk, kutsut," *Helsingin Sanomat,* UM: LKEV n:o 223, Nov. 13, 1972, 5. See also "Etyk," Uusi Suomi, UM: LKEV n:o 226, Nov. 16, 1972, 4; and "Extracts from Speech by Assistant Director Osmo Apunen at the Christian Peace Conference Working Committee, in Espoo, 30 September 1972," the Peaceful Future of Europe, ULA 1972, 92.

27. "Ulkoasiainministeri Kalevi Sorsan lausunto Seuratieto-lehdessä 3/1972," Euroopan turvallisuus—ja yhteistyökonferenssin koollekutsumisvalistelut, ULA 1972, 89.

28. "Etyk," *Helsingin Sanomat,* UM: LKEV n:o 229, Nov. 21, 1972, 2. See also "Etyk" *Suomenmaa,* UM: LKEV n:o 233, Nov. 27, 1972, 1; "Franskt förslag mot rumänsk," *Hufvudstadsbladet,* Nov. 24, 1972, UILA.

29. The *Frankfurt Allgemein* alleged that Finland endured a loss of prestige because of its decision to allow the meeting to stand closed. The paper speculated that the Finnish defensive maneuver had to originate from the Soviet Union, the apparent benefactor of attempts to silence Romanian demands. See Seppo Kuusisto, "Saksalaislehdet ety-kokouksesta: Suomelle arvovaltatappioita myötätuntoa Romanialle," *Uusi Suomi,* Nov. 21, 1972, UILA.

30. "Statement at the Opening by Dr. Richard Tötterman, secretary general of the Ministry for Foreign Affairs of Finland," Nov. 22, 1972, photocopy of document. See also "Dipolissa päätettiin kokouksen työajoista: Itse Asiaan vasta ensi viikolla," *Kansan Uutiset,* Nov. 24, 1972, UILA.

Tötterman's appointment was confirmed, but the matter of a vice-chair remained in question given the presentation of competing proposals on the nature of the procedural rules, which were still to be formerly adopted.

Eventually, the Finnish delegation introduced a compromise paper that took account of the earlier debate and proposals. It embraced eight points on the basic questions at hand.[31] The first of these concerned the principle of sovereign equality of all states, which met with no opposition (Sizoo and Jurrjens 1984, 56). However, Romania insisted the conditions of sovereign equality be stated so that it would hold for the states " 'independent of their belonging or not to a Military Alliance' " (as quoted in Sizzoo and Jurrjens 1984, 56).[32] While this formulation was unacceptable to the Soviet Union, the Romanian position led to the first paragraph of chapter 6 of the Rules Procedure in the Blue Book, stating that "All States participating in the Conference shall do so as sovereign and independent States and in conditions of full equality. The Conference shall take place outside military alliances." [33] This was the key founding principle for the negotiations. Sizoo and Jurrjens argue that "acceptance of the principle of equality altered the pattern of the East-West dialogue, giving way to a more egalitarian and genuinely multilateral approach as opposed to the earlier inter-bloc exchange of communiqués" (1984, 56).

Romania also argued in favor of a rule stipulating the rotation of the chairmanship in the plenary and formal committees rather than for the Finnish proposal for a vice-chair. The rule of rotation was another means by which the Romanians sought to underpin the principle that states participate independent of military alliances, and hence that the conference not be a bloc-to-bloc confrontation. The mechanisms of the balance of power were not to reside in the bloc structure but rather in the juridical equality of all states having an equal voice. Thus, the rule of rotation embodied important principles. On Romanian insistence, the "rotation principle" also extended itself to other considerations, including an agreement to rotate the conference among different host capitals.[34]

As a solution to the immediate organizational matters at hand, no vice-

31. "Dipoli kokous on pitkä askel Etyk:iin," *Helsingin Sanomat,* Nov. 19, 1972, UILA. See also "Sorsa, Karjalainen ETYK:stä," *Helsingin Sanomat,* UM: LKEV n:o 228, Nov. 20, 1972, 4.

32. See also "Töttermanista pysyvä puheenjohtaja—varapuheenjohtajuus avoin," *Suomenmaa,* Nov. 24, 1972; "Menettelytapakysymys puhutti yhtä Dipolissa Belgialta kompromissiesity," *Suomenmaa,* Nov. 28, 1972; and "De vestlige land støtter Romania," *Aftenposten* Nov. 28, 1972, UILA.

33. *Final Recommendations of the Helsinki Consultations,* chapter 6 (65).

34. As we see below and in subsequent chapters, this principle came to be applied throughout the CSCE deliberations, to the attainment of balanced progress on all the mandates, in their substance, modes of implementation, and mechanisms for review.

chair was named. Instead, the rule of rotating chairs by French alphabetical order was accepted, despite especially the West's fears that it would encumber the work of the conference (Ferraris 1979, 20). However, when the drafting in working groups began under this system of rotation in March 1973, the rule proved cumbersome, and yielded to expectations for a more extensive third-party role. To circumvent any infractions of the agreed working procedures, the formal committees were converted into "mini-groups" under a fixed chairman usually supplied by one of the nonbloc states. This method of the neutral and nonaligned states supplying a fixed chair or "coordinator" was used more extensively in Geneva and became highly customized thereafter in the CSCE (Sizoo and Jurrjens 1984, 63).

Consensus Rule

Even in its draft document circulated November 22, 1972, Finland proposed the consensus rule as the method of taking decisions,[35] defining it as "the absence of any objection expressed by a representative and put forward by him as constituting an obstacle to the taking of the decision in question."[36] The West held that consensus should be applied to substantive decisions, but majority voting should hold for procedural matters, since it also maintained the CSCE decisions were to be politically and not legally binding.[37] States would not adhere to agreements on substance reached by a majority vote to which they were in opposition, especially where this could concern their own security. Hence, decision by consensus on substance was paramount. The West's fear that a consensus rule might lead to a deadlock otherwise mitigated in favor of majority voting on procedural matters, even when the adoption of the final document might be at stake. However, any deviation from a consensus-decision rule was unacceptable to the East, since they could be outnumbered in voting by members of the Western alliance. Romania also insisted the rule of consensus was a measure of the full equality of sovereign states. An unqualified rule of consensus decision-making ensured that the great powers would not be subject to the tyranny of the small, but more numerous states, and guaranteed the latter

35. Spencer (1984, 83), citing External Affairs Documents of the Canadian Foreign Ministry, also credits the Finns with introducing and insisting on the concept of preceding by consensus only.

36. See "Statement at the Opening by Dr. Richard Tötterman, secretary general of the Ministry for Foreign Affairs of Finland," Nov. 22, 1972, photocopy of document. See also "Dipolissa päätettiin kokouksen työajoista: Itse Asiaan vasta ensi viikolla," *Kansan Uutiset,* Nov. 24, 1972, UILA.

37. However, the Soviets continued to insist on a legally binding agreement, which they wanted to result in a permanent institutional forum such as a European Security Council. See Korey (1993, 13).

that their own views would matter to the final substance (Sizoo and Jurrjens 1984, 58).[38]

Thus, chapter 6 of the Blue Book called for a "negative approach" to the consensus rule (Sizoo and Jurrjens 1984, 61). It was defined as "the *absence* of any objection expressed by a Representative and submitted by him as constituting an obstacle to the taking of the decision in question."[39] This encouraged states to withhold consent only when they resolutely objected—not when they were only partially unsatisfied. States also could enter into the record formal reservations or interpretive statements regarding decisions to be duly registered (Sizoo and Jurrjens 1984, 61).

Structuring the Working Method

During late November and early December, the Dipoli Consultations passed from debate on the basic principles and decision rules and presentation of opening statements to negotiate the mandate for the CSCE. However, there was no consensus on how to proceed and this led to the first major impasse. Remarkably, the crisis focused on whether consensus could be reached to recess the Consultations from mid-December to mid January. This question had assumed the characteristics of an ideological debate, with the Soviets pushing for a short break only over the New Year.

In order to inject some momentum into the deliberations, Tötterman, in the capacity of the presidency of the Consultations, suggested several alternatives for how they could proceed beyond the presentation of opening positions: "examining one of the various questions raised during the individual declarations; establishing a provisional agenda for the CSCE, examining the organizational aspects of the CSCE, determining priorities or a type of order of business for the Preliminaries" (Ferraris 1979, 11–12). Several other countries, including Yugoslavia, the United Kingdom, France, Poland, Hungary, and the Soviet Union, offered alternative proposals. In line with the Western inductive and pragmatic approach, the French "insisted on the necessity of going deeper into question [*sic*] of the contents of a possible agenda in an 'all-embracing and progressive' manner which should at the same time be flexible" (Ferraris 1979, 12). Meanwhile the Eastern bloc sought to keep the discussions at this juncture limited to the question of participants for the CSCE.

The Yugoslavian proposal outlined how the work could be organized. The

38. Malta tested this principle in Geneva, Belgrade, and Madrid, holding out consensus on a final document until its demands on matters relating to the Mediterranean were incorporated in some measure into the final text.

39. See the *Final Recommendations,* chapter 6 (69), emphasis added.

delegates should *first* define the type of conference, i.e. one to take place in three stages with ministerial meetings (as France had earlier proposed); *second* determine the agenda, at which point working groups could take up the mandate or detailed instructions and the rules of procedure; *third* determine the place of the conference, its time, and its participants, as well as its financial and technical organization; and *finally* take an accounting of what had been agreed to in the discussions.[40] The French interceded with a document agreed among the EEC, to explain the purpose of developing "mandates," in line with its insistence that there be a deep discussion of the contents of an agenda (Ferraris 1979, 14).

Anxious that the negotiations not become too specific and that the delegations in Dipoli not assume the tasks of negotiating the actual text, the Soviets had great difficulty acceding to the mandate approach outlined in the December deliberations (Ferraris 1979, 16). This difficulty was also an indication of the extent to which the ideological element of East-West confrontation shaped the points of departure in East and West and consequently the agenda at Dipoli. The Soviet pressure for a short recess over the New Year holiday was certainly not the key issue at stake. The real impasse stemmed from the strange bedfellows behind the negotiations. The West's position was anchored on a philosophy of liberal democracy, while the East's was based on the doctrine of international socialism. As a result, East and West had different orientations to international law, and this situation gave way to competing points of departure in their approach to negotiating the mandate.

This competition came to define the whole nature of the CSCE enterprise. For their part, the Soviets led the Eastern bloc in an attempt to protect the socialist states' policy of resisting the application of international law and agreements in any area other than between competing ideological systems. For the Soviets, this was also a means to avoid limitations on the Brezhnev Doctrine and on domestic socialist laws. Thus, universal applicability of international law as conceived in the West was challenged by the East. Moreover, the Soviets sought to elaborate special regional principles of interstate relations. On the whole, they aimed for a final document based on broad declaratory principles that would largely reinforce Soviet foreign-policy aims. However, the West resisted this approach and aimed instead to negotiate a text that would contain detailed, concrete, and practical commitments.

The Soviets' discomfiture with the French proposal to negotiate "mandates" for the CSCE meeting stemmed from its reluctance to engage in any specifics that could give legitimacy to the West's liberal demands, particularly on matters relating to human rights and humanitarian concerns. Because of their different starting points, East and West also clashed over their deductive,

40. "Jugoslavia loi pohjan jatkolle?" *Helsingin Sanomat,* Dec. 13, 1972, UILA.

versus inductive, approach to negotiating the substance. To protect the starting point, the Soviets later made known they understood a mandate to be essentially instructions ("zadanie"). In any case, by late February the more pragmatic French and Western approach essentially prevailed, whereby drafting in working groups proceeded inductively. In this way the mandates for the substantive areas of the conference were derived.[41]

Although the Yugoslav document was not formally accepted in December because of the divergence of opinion between East and West, the rest of the Dipoli discussions developed largely along the lines of the tasks it outlined. The West insisted the drafting proceed according to the Yugoslav document *as a whole* to avoid reaching agreement first on principles the Soviets sought, without also getting concrete and practical measures, particularly on human contact and issues concerning freer movement. The Yugoslav paper gave the delegates a basic framework to guide their work during the Consultations and a basic referent principle (i.e. working toward balanced progress). In the meantime, the Swiss had intervened on the issue of the holiday recess, insisting that small countries needed time to prepare for the next stage. A difficulty at Dipoli (and to some extent throughout the CSCE) had been their smaller delegation size, which presented challenges for keeping up with all the developments in each of the basket areas, especially as these became increasingly complex and required more and more specialized expertise. This face-saving argument helped to secure the necessary Soviet concession and provided for a monthlong break, rather than the short New Year's holiday the Soviets had originally proposed (Ferraris 1979, 13).

Origins of the Basket Structure

In January 1973 the delegations began to present their own projects for an agenda. Various proposals were presented from all sides, although these fell under the basic points outlined in a Belgium proposal: European security; economics and environment; and the broadening of freedom in the areas of the movement of people, information, and culture.[42] These were also still essentially the same points NATO had proposed in its December 1971 communiqué, which called for four areas of discussion: (1) questions of security, including principles governing relations between states and certain military aspects of security; (2) freer movement of people, information and ideas, and cultural relations; (3) cooperation in the fields of economics, applied science and technology, and pure science; and (4) cooperation to improve the human envi-

41. "Kolmannen vaiheen avaus: Dipolissa aloitettiin Ranskan esityksellä," *Uusi Suomi,* Feb. 27, 1973, UILA. See also Ferraris (1979, 19–20).

42. "Komiteoita Etykille," *Helsingin Sanomat,* Jan. 17, 1973, UILA.

ronment (Sizoo and Jurrjens 1984, 29). Eventually, preparations among the EC states on a common position led to the substitution of the phrase on "Freer Movement" with "Development of Human Contacts," to which the NATO allies acceded to keep a NATO consensus, but only on the understanding "that the content of discussion will be the same" (Spencer 1984, 84).

Several especially difficult debates emerged and characterized discussions throughout both Dipoli and Geneva, since much of the agenda proved ambiguous. Of central importance was debate on the principles of European security, particularly their relative importance to one another (the Soviets insisted on the primacy of the immutability of frontiers) versus the interdependence of principles (the West's position). The West also insisted that regional principles be related to universal principles to avoid the creation of special regional ones. Also at stake was the relationship between security principles and the human dimension, including the principles and specific measures on humanitarian concerns, free flow of information, and freer movement initiatives the West sought. Finally, there was the matter of the inclusion of military measures. The neutrals along with Yugoslavia and Romania began to intensify their efforts to include in the negotiations agenda measures on military security, including disarmament and mechanisms for overseeing this (Sweden, also supported by Norway); the establishment of an organ for the peaceful settlement of disputes (Switzerland); a connection between the CSCE and the MBFR (Sweden, also supported by the Netherlands); and a connection between the principles, that is political security or détente, and military security, calling for specific measures.[43]

All of this activity resulted in a proliferation of proposals and the need once again to bring more organization into the proceedings. The Belgium proposal already suggested a way to structure the substantive aspects of the agenda. However, the issue was delicate because again it exposed the fundamentally different ideological premises of East and West, which seemed inseparable from the working methods and the type of agreement by which each side stood most to gain. This search for order led to the unique concept of "basket." In a moment of inspiration a Dutch delegate imagined "in his mind's eye four baskets standing on the platform and cried out: 'On jette toutes les propositions dans un panier,' " (as quoted in Sizoo and Jurrjens 1984, 73 n. 2).[44] At one point four baskets were produced and ceremoniously placed on the platform.[45]

Spain began the process of gathering the proposals. Because the Swiss had

43. On these developments see especially Ferraris (1979, 14–40). See also S. G., "S-möte bör ta upp Mellanösternfrägan," *Hufvudstadsbladet,* Jan. 18, 1973; and "MBFR-tietoja ei haluttu kommentoida Dipolissa" *Helsingin Sanomat,* Jan. 19, 1973, UILA.

44. The reference is to the late Jhr. B. E. Quarles van Ufford. Sizoo and Jurrjens (1984, 73 n. 2) also note that the term "panier" was replaced by the use of the French "corbeille."

45. Finnish official, interview by author, tape recording, Helsinki, May 11, 1988.

first elaborated on the idea of collecting all the documents into a single compendium, they were formally requested to do so by Spain, and then again by Italy on behalf of all the delegates. For this task "generally, the Swiss ambassador was beckoned on an individual basis."[46] In conjunction with the position taken in the West, it was understood that the Swiss would prepare a synopsis, and equal weight or importance would be given to each document under the corresponding basket, which would be numbered to avoid debate over the headings (and hence over the primacy of working according to deductive versus inductive approaches). The Swiss delegation accepted the task, although later it presented the agenda in its own name, not as officially authorized by the Consultations. In the working document the Swiss "numbered and labeled the baskets as follows: basket I security; basket II economics and environment; basket III human contacts, information and cultural cooperation; basket IV follow-up" (Sizoo and Jurrjens 1984, 73 n. 2).

The Swiss intervention set a precedent for such third-party coordination to be assumed by neutral and nonaligned states. But because the task was considered difficult technically and implied position-taking of a political character, the delegations at Dipoli did not call on the Finnish hosts to carry it out.[47] The great confidence and respect the Swiss had gained by their long tradition in the practice of neutrality, and the skill of the Swiss diplomat, also qualified them to handle this sensitive procedural matter, which carried significant substantive implications. Moreover, speculation about the Soviet shadow of influence over Finland had not abated, and editorials on Finlandization actually intensified, particularly in the conservative Austrian and West German press.[48] This fact even prompted the Finnish Foreign Ministry to protest that its diplomatic efforts in Dipoli were being undermined by the ill will expressed abroad toward Finland's neutrality policy.[49]

46. "Sveitsi laatimaan luetteloa Dipolin asialistaehdotuksista," *Uusi Suomi,* Jan. 26, 1973, UILA.

47. Ibid.

48. One conservative journalist went so far as to speculate that the Soviets were rewarding the Finns for having signed the FCMA treaty in 1948 by holding the CSCE negotiations in Helsinki. See Erkki Pennanen, "Itävaltalaislehti arvosteli Suomea Etyk-isäntänä," *Helsingin Sanomat,* Jan. 29, 1973, UILA.

49. See "Kirjoittelu Suomesta närkästyttää Um: ää. Tuoviselta kirjallinen vastine," *Uusi Suomi,* Feb. 3, 1973, UILA. A February *Helsingin Sanomat* editorial observed that, at Dipoli, Switzerland practiced an aggressive policy of active neutrality, perhaps taking advantage of every opportunity to become the host of the actual CSCE meeting. Austria, too, it was recalled, was still aspiring to host the CSCE. Countering criticism from abroad for Finland's handling of the CSCE preparations, the editorial noted the Austrians had not yet gotten agreement on a final list of participants for the MBFR. Finland had settled this early in its efforts to prepare the Helsinki Consultations. See "Houkutteleva Etyk-isännyys," *Helsingin Sanomat,* Feb. 4, 1973, UILA.

In any event, with Swiss intervention the basket structure came to organize the agenda-building discussions (Ferraris 1979, 15).[50] It provided the basic cognitive structure for the CSCE negotiations and the scheme by which work in Geneva was subsequently organized. The ingenuous basket approach was successful no doubt because this working method could at once accommodate the principled Soviet and pragmatic Western objectives. As Zartman and Berman note (1982, 90), when parties have irreconcilably different perceptions or conceptions of the problem, such that they are unable to proceed deductively, this makes the construction of a substantive formula to propel the negotiations forward difficult to achieve. Although the parties may still reach some agreement on details, they are likely to attach different meanings to them. The basket method provided an intermediate accommodation: a procedural more than substantive formula.

The designation of the four baskets (Basket I, European security; Basket II, economics and environment; Basket III, humanitarian dimension; and Basket IV, the staging of the conference and any follow-up mechanisms) clearly defined the subjects of concern for the negotiations on security and cooperation in Europe. Against the position of the Soviets, who sought at Dipoli to emphasize the principles of interstate relations above all other issues, it was agreed that the principle of multiplicity and equality of all texts before all other texts in the document would be observed (Ferraris 1979, 46). This meant the substance of the negotiations should also receive equal treatment and that the rule of equality would be extended to the method by which the negotiations proceeded.

The basket formula helped to mitigate the effects of the East-West conflict in several ways. The baskets provided a cognitive structure that helped move the delegations beyond the polemics of tabling positions in a plenary setting (highly unamenable for drafting) to a working-group setting, which France formally proposed at the start of the third session in Dipoli.[51] Using the baskets, the East, West, and nonbloc state proposals were mixed together under the appropriate general subject heading. This helped get the delegates focused on the issues and beyond debate on their different ideological premises. While the placement of proposals into the baskets had the effect of mitigating the ex-

50. See also "Sveitsi ryhmittelee Dipolin ehdotukset," *Helsingin Sanomat,* Jan. 25, 1973; "Sveitsi sai tehtäväkseen Etyk-asioiden ryhmittelyn," *Suomenmaa,* Jan. 26, 1973; "Suomi kannatti neljän korin listaa ETYK:ssa," *Demari,* Jan. 26, 1973; "Sveitsi laatimaan luetteloa Dipolin asialistaehdotuksista," *Uusi Suomi,* Jan. 26, 1973, UILA.

51. France proposed this procedural approach on behalf of the EEC members in a resolution taken by the Political Committee of the Nine (EEC countries) on February 20 and on behalf of the NATO alliance. See Ferraris (1979, 19–20); see also "Kolmannen vaiheen avaus: Dipolissa aloitettiin Ranskan esityksellä," *Uusi Suomi,* Feb. 27, 1973, UILA.

tremes of East and West in terms of their respective deductive and inductive approaches, it did not require them to concede their own starting points at the outset. Thus, proposals of a principled or declaratory nature and proposals on a variety of concrete measures were treated together. This facilitated moving to dialogue and into the compromise-building aspects of the exercise—even if a genuine integration of positions would prove difficult to achieve.

The task of combining the proposals within each basket into a draft document was formidable. To facilitate the tasks at the working-group level, Spain raised several procedural points. The discussion was followed by further British elaboration and the principle was then accepted that the working meetings should be informal, open to all the participants, and presided over according to the rotation principle. This decision established the importance of the rotation principle, but in practice the challenges of drafting soon necessitated even smaller "mini-groups," which in Dipoli often resulted in cross-bloc efforts to meet and develop acceptable drafts on the various agenda points.

Still, as one Swedish CSCE official recalls, "when at the end, however, it became apparent that East and West could not come to an agreement, it was natural that the neutral and nonaligned countries should come up with a compromise to spare the superpowers from losing face, and offering the possibility that the shortcomings or failure of the recommendations could be blamed on the N+N."[52] This contribution followed from Finland's activity in preparing and hosting the negotiations at Dipoli. Other nonbloc states also stepped in to assist in basic duties (such as setting up a work schedule and timetables for when to meet and when to break). As one Finnish official recalled, "the neutrals just took up problems. Finland would say, 'Well, we have a problem here or there and then they would go about mediating.' " This in itself proved essential to keep developing and maintaining the necessary channels of communications between East and West.[53] These neutral efforts also took place alongside the considerable compromise and consensus-building efforts on the part of various other delegations, so that in many ways the cross-bloc nature of negotiations at Dipoli was sustained in producing a final set of recommendations.[54] This was really the main idea—that everyone should be independent, and that everyone was equal. Nevertheless, the Finnish preparations, the Yugoslav paper, and the

52. Swedish official, interview by author, written notes, Foreign Ministry, Stockholm, May 19, 1988.

53. Finnish official, interview by author, tape recording, Helsinki, May 11, 1988.

54. This is clear from Ferraris's detailed analysis. Crossbloc contacts characterized the nature of the discussion on preliminaries, especially as regarded work during the third and fourth phases. See Ferraris (1979, especially 19–40).

Swiss paper, along with numerous interventions of other nonbloc states, left a founding stamp on the organizational structure and even substantive nature of the CSCE.

Framing the Substance of the Agenda: The Nonbloc States as Instrumental Third Parties

Excepting Finland (for the most part), the nonbloc states were insistent on not passing over the opportunity to maintain a national profile through their own proposals. Up to three quarters of their time at Dipoli was spent on this aspect. The neutral and nonaligned states were among the most insistent—not only on lending their weight to ensure the inclusion of issues related to human contacts and other humanitarian and cultural issues, but also in tirelessly seeking to imbue the CSCE process with a mandate to deal with both military and political security.

On the military aspect, among the most active were Sweden and Yugoslavia, along with Romania acting secretly through Yugoslavia.[55] Sweden, Switzerland, and Austria argued that military and political security could not be separated from each other, a notion the Soviets opposed (Ferraris 1979, 23). Consistent with its earlier policy stands, Sweden presented in the consultations specific proposals outlining the linkage it sought between the CSCE and the MBFR. But the West was adamant in its opposition to East-West disarmament or arms-control issues being a concern of the CSCE negotiations—MBFR was for that. Along with the West, and including France, the Soviets also supplied their opposition to this point (Ferraris 1979, 23), along with strong opposition to a Finnish proposal for a system for the peaceful settlement of disputes (1979, 31). Yugoslavia and Malta in particular emphasized the need for security measures to apply to the Mediterranean; to this appeal the neutrals added their own proposals for aerial and naval maneuvers to be included in a Confidence Building Measures (CBMs) regime for the Mediterranean (Ferraris 1979, 22–23).

Sweden discovered it could not engender support for a broad disarmament agenda, and thus to its disappointment it learned that the CSCE was unlike the UN, where everything could be discussed. Eventually, Sweden (and Yugoslavia) had to decide whether to pursue their own agendas, pushing and pushing for disarmament at the risk of disrupting any possibility for consensus, or concede that a successful outcome of the Consultations was more important to them.[56] By early April there was a gradual shift among an increasing number of delega-

55. Swedish official, interview by author, written notes, Foreign Ministry, Stockholm, May 19, 1988.

56. Ibid.

tions toward restricting the extension of every military aspect of the CSCE (Ferraris 1979, 26). For the neutral and nonaligned, including Romania, in the end it was a matter of taking the CBMs—the only measures NATO would supply from its MBFR agenda.[57]

The CBMs stemmed from the concept of collateral constraints (Maresca 1985, 168 ff.), which the West had advocated in the Four Powers talks of the 1950s.[58] The West's CBMs proposal included the idea of prior notification of major military movements and maneuvers and the exchange of observers, measures which they had first proposed for the CSCE agenda a year earlier in the alliance's Bonn communiqué.[59] However, at Dipoli the allies proved unwilling to broaden beyond these measures the discussion on military aspects of security. The nonbloc states had to be satisfied with "psychological" measures aimed at reducing threat perceptions, or they would probably get nothing in security and perhaps not a conference result.[60] With Soviet opposition to previous notification of major military movements, the issue of the parameters for such measures was left to the Geneva negotiations (Ferraris 1979, 26).

The CBMs amounted to very little in contrast to what Sweden and other nonbloc states wanted on disarmament in the *Final Recommendations*. Also to the detriment of the nonbloc objectives, the French maintained their opposition to connecting the CSCE and the MBFR, but did make way for the *Final Recommendations* to affirm that "efforts aimed at disarmament complement political détente and are essential elements."[61] The Swiss succeeded in having included in the section enumerating the "Principles of Relations between States" a recommendation that proposals be studied to undertake the elaboration of a method of peaceful settlement of disputes among the participating states, but failed to achieve anything more concrete.

Among the final issues to be resolved at Dipoli were those of Basket IV—of central importance to Finland—the site of the CSCE for each of its stages. As became CSCE practice, practical arrangements for and consensus on the continuity of the CSCE process was left for last. As the Dipoli Consultations entered their final session, it was not at all certain Finland would get anything other than the first stage of the CSCE; other neutrals were still potential hosts. By

57. Swedish official, interview by author, written notes, Foreign Ministry, Stockholm, May 19, 1988.

58. For an extensive account of the origins of the CBMs, see Borawski (1988).

59. "Kommuniqué der Ministertagung des Nordatlantikrates am 30. und 31. Mai 1972 in Bonn (Auszüge), in Schram, Riggert, and Friedel (1972)." This communiqué signaled that NATO was transferring these CBM measures from their earlier communiqués calling for the MBFR talks.

60. Swedish official, interview by author, written notes, Foreign Ministry, Stockholm, May 19, 1988.

61. *Final Recommendations*, chapter 2/1 (22).

May the competition between Finland and Austria was played out at the official level. While the CSCE issue was central at that moment, the competition between these two neutrals was not only over the CSCE but also over the pending determination of the secretary general race in the UN (Austria presented Kurt Waldheim and Finland offered Max Jakobson); the SALT talks, which the two countries shared; and also, to some extent, over interpretations of appropriate domestic politics. Also at stake were the two states' efforts to get general acceptance in East and West of their active neutrality policy (Hyvärinen 1969).

As Risto Hyvärinen, a seasoned Finnish diplomat, argued, if the exceptional elements distinguishing the policies of the other European neutrals could be understood (Switzerland not belonging to the UN, or Austria not having normal diplomatic relations with Czechoslovakia or East Germany), then "why would Finland's own [special] points not be understandable?"[62] Thus, in an official state visit to Austria, Finland's Prime Minister Kalevi Sorsa claimed a "moral right" to host the CSCE meeting.[63] Despite the support of the Scandinavian countries for Finland to be host for all stages,[64] in the end the main conference negotiations for the second stage were assigned to Geneva, while Finland got the opening and closing ceremonies. Several considerations intervened, including the greater centrality of Geneva, the milder climate (the determination of which one Finnish December proved sufficient), greater practical facilities (including better communication facilities and more hotel accommodations), and "some evaluations of political opportunity." Finland "nobly" accepted the arrangement (Ferraris 1979, 39).[65]

Impact of Third-Party Intervention

Finland's initial contributions at Dipoli as a facilitative mediator, along with the procedural and substantive mediation of other nonbloc states (Switzerland, Sweden, Austria, Yugoslavia—and also Romania, which acted as a nonbloc state) helped shape and stabilize expectations on the core elements of the CSCE

62. See "Itävalta ja Suomi," *Helsingin Sanomat,* May 25, 1973, UILA. Hyvärinen (1969, 51) also points to the varieties of neutrality and differing characteristics of practicing states.

63. Austrian Chancellor Bruno Kreisky (also a social democrat) criticized the Finnish Social Democrats for entertaining the possibility of cooperation with the communist party. See "Sorsa Itävallassa: Suomella moraalinen etuoikeus Etykiin," *Helsingin Sanomat,* May 23, 1973; and "Itävalta ja Suomi," *Helsingin Sanomat,* May 25, 1973, UILA.

64. Finland sought and got the Nordic community's support at the March 1973 Foreign Ministers' meeting in Oslo. In late May the Norwegian ambassador reinvoked the Nordic community's support. See "Koko Pohjola kannattaa Suomea ETYK:in kaikkien vaiheiden isännäksi," *Suomenmaa,* May 26, 1973, UILA.

65. See also "Det blir en Helsingforskonferens," *Nya Pressen,* July 4, 1973, UILA.

in three ways. First, they facilitated agreement on the principle of the sovereign equality of states and the right to participate independent of blocs. This agreement contributed to the democratic character of the negotiating encounter and also set the foundation for overcoming the structure and logic of the bloc system as the principle guiding East-West relations. Second, they established agreement on consensus as the key decision rule and facilitated other aspects of the working methods. Third, they promoted a more universal and comprehensive treatment of security and cooperation.

Although the nonbloc states arrived in Dipoli with the aim of participating in the CSCE process on equal terms with all other states, Finland's early role in launching the CSCE process had already established precedents for third-party mediation. However, the difficulties in finding mutual interests in the positions of East and West led to impasses in the negotiations concerning both the structure of the work and the substance of the mandate. These problems led to expectations that the nonbloc states intervene as third parties to facilitate the achievement of consensus. Thus, their third-party role continued the precursor functions Finland had taken on in its initial bid to prepare and host the CSCE.

Throughout the Dipoli Consultations, the nonbloc states helped prepare agreement on procedural and decision-making rules and facilitated other aspects of the working methods (e.g., order for treating the issues, along with method, such as inductive or deductive and crafting package deals). In terms of substantive outcomes, the nonbloc states emphasized common interests, devised innovative policy options to overcome bargaining impediments, made deals and lined up support for salient options, and suggested concessions. Thus, they contributed norm-engendering and norm-supporting functions by controlling the negotiating process and facilitating agreement on the substance of the mandate for the CSCE.

Adoption of the consensus rule at Dipoli had a profound effect on multilateral decision making, and the substantive and normative outcomes in the CSCE. Whereas agreement on majority voting requires coalition building (for example, building common views within alliances and then persuading fence riders to join), consensus requires much more—a much fuller exchange of information and comprehension of positions. It means continuous dialogue, not just bargaining. Communication, the exchange of information and building knowledge among all sides, is central to drafting common texts of agreement under a consensus rule. This is a slow and incremental process. The rule of consensus is a procedural formulation referring to the whole decision-making process in a wide sense (Törnudd 1982, 168).

In a highly divided international system, especially where the parties consist of stable majorities and minorities and are perceived as indispensable supporters of a legitimate decision, the consensus rule is also useful for gaining broad support. Together with the other CSCE working principles, the consensus rule "tended to move the talks beyond the control of the blocs or individual countries, it enhanced the role of the neutral and nonaligned states, and it tended to give to the MPT [Multilateral Preparatory Talks or Consultations] a life of its own" (Spencer 1984, 86).[66] Ultimately, the consensus rule allows for an egalitarian procedure and is important for organizational learning and institution building (Buzan and Jones 1981; Törnudd 1982). As one Finnish official has noted, the discussions under Basket I presented the first opportunity ever for the thirty-five participants to examine together principles of interstate relations from the perspectives of East and West. It gave way to a "formidable discussion, a fantastic diplomatic seminar." Only through the serious and probing interaction of such a decision-making approach could real knowledge and understanding of the European situation be fully exchanged and its integrative potential for cooperation tapped.[67]

But even the negative formulation of the consensus rule created challenges for sustaining momentum. In negotiating a consensus agreement, parties must insist long and stubbornly on their own positions. The participating states at Dipoli appreciated the fact that this can lead to protracted, even perennial, negotiations, like the Conference on Disarmament in Geneva. So that Parkinson's law would not hold (i.e. "the reaching of consensus expands to fill the time available"),[68] the delegations at Dipoli had to find an active approach to the consensus rule. This effort led to the customization of the N+N role as coordinators in the CSCE, an informal arrangement that gave multilateral legitimization of their precursor functions.

As a whole, the nonbloc states (and especially Switzerland and Sweden) contributed to the West's effort to elaborate a system of CSCE governance to apply to the political-military and humanitarian dimension of relationships not only between states but *also* between people. Sweden, Switzerland, Yugoslavia, and also Romania were advocates also of a different structure of relations among the principle cold war adversaries. As intellectual entrepreneurs, they helped shape common understandings among adversaries on more universal commitments, particularly in the area of military security issues. They also helped ensure that the structure of obligations created in the CSCE would be of a multilateral and cross-bloc rather than interbloc nature. These third-party

66. For example, although Switzerland did not belong to the United Nations, Swiss officials assured that their country would be an active participant and not just a sideline observer in the CSCE. See Lauri Karén, "Sveitsiltä ehdotus Etykin ratkottavaksi," *Helsingin Sanomat,* Nov. 20, 1972, UILA.

67. Finnish official, interview by author, tape recording, Helsinki, May 11, 1988.

68. I have borrowed this point from Spencer (1984, 88).

contributions were important, if not sufficient, measures for institutionalizing East-West cooperation. The extent to which the Dipoli mandate simply papered over rather than fundamentally resolved deep differences between the blocs, however, put the credibility of these early CSCE commitments in question.

Conclusions

In many respects, the cross-bloc nature of the Consultations was sustained to the end at Dipoli, no doubt in part because the United States did not seek to assert its views over the Western alliance. The lack of Atlantic cohesion was in no small measure compensated for by the increasing political cohesion among the European Community states. The Dipoli Consultations provided them with a prime testing ground to advance a common front in the foreign-policy arena and an opportunity to gain greater legitimacy as a partner worthy of negotiations with the Soviets. As a consequence, there were two overlapping, and at times competing, Western positions, with NATO generally accommodating itself to the common positions the EEC states had worked out. The French in particular sought to establish the "appropriateness and integrity of consultations among the Nine" (as quoted in Spencer 1984, 83). Yet in the military-security field one thing was clear: neither military alliance in the East or the West, or the French for that matter, was willing to introduce broad security objectives into the CSCE.

This fact was a major disappointment for the nonbloc countries, although they managed to inject some of their ideas into the Blue Book. It was especially troubling to Sweden, which took a different approach to Finland's aim of rooting its neutrality in the balance of power in Europe. As Swedish Ambassador Ryding outlined in his opening statements at Dipoli, neutrality policy brought Sweden a basis for stability. This stability, in turn, was a condition for the development of détente, also so that neither of the two alliances could affect the direction of the security policy of any of the neutral and nonaligned countries. However, in a longer-term perspective, Sweden wished to ensure that security in Europe would be built on a foundation other than a balance between two blocs confronting one another. In the meantime, Sweden appreciated that the dissolution of the alliance system could only be effected after a period of trustful cooperation among all European states. Sweden insisted that disarmament should have a place in the discussions related to promoting these developments.[69]

The *Final Recommendations* established a weak connection between disar-

69. Svenska Ambassaden Helsingfors, "Anförande av ambassadör Ryding i general debatten vid de förberedande multilaterala överläggningarna i Helsingfors om en konferens om säkerhet och samarbete i Europa," Dec. 1, 1972. Photocopy.

mament and political détente. The possibility that other organs could be set up in the future development of the CSCE remained, however, as a close reading of the recommendations to Basket IV, "Follow-up to the Conference," illustrates: the participating states were to give effect to the decisions of the Conference, and "to further the process of improving security and developing co-operation in Europe. Having considered proposals to this effect, *including proposals of an organizational nature,* it shall make any recommendations which it deems necessary." (emphasis added)[70] These differing points of departure led Sweden, along with Yugoslavia, Romania, and Malta (especially in relation to the Mediterranean), to champion the cause of disarmament and more meaningful security measures in the CSCE, while Finland remained more concerned with encouraging the superpowers to assume responsibility and take the first steps toward disarmament themselves.

The Dipoli experience revealed the advantages under a consensus rule for countries intent on taking the initiative. Still, the novel setting required some adjustments in national strategies. In order to get a position into the concluding document, the delegations learned they had to stick by their positions long and hard. Patience was paramount. However, the upcoming Geneva negotiations would also illustrate the limitations of trade-offs that yielded mandates reduced to the least common denominator, or even worse, to ambiguous commitments, or commitments to which parties still held competing interpretations. Ideally, consensus requires an incremental process of drafting, so that as much of all the participants' positions are incorporated without incurring objections from others. In the best of worlds, this involves a process of learning and leads to final agreements based on the achievement of shared meanings or consensual knowledge. However, the nature of the ideological confrontation between East and West posed serious challenges for attaining well-integrated texts. It also posed serious questions about the credibility of the commitments into which the CSCE participating states were preparing to enter.

The tentativeness of the entire CSCE undertaking also mitigated against prejudging at Dipoli steps toward institutionalizing the process that would be the subject of debate in Geneva. Thus, just as the determination of the level of representation in various stages proved difficult to decide early in the negotiations at Dipoli, the evolution of the CSCE process itself was left to decide later. In this way, the guidelines Canada set out in a pre-Dipoli memorandum—that each phase of the CSCE process "should be seen as a continuous negotiating process with each step dependent upon the progress of the preceding one"—correctly anticipated the cautious mood that predominated (Spencer 1984, 70). The development of cooperation nonetheless proceeded on the basis of small,

70. See the *Final Recommendations,* chapter 2, 4 (53).

incremental steps, which had the effect of entrapping the blocs into a new method of conceiving and managing East-West security. However, the reluctance of the delegations at Dipoli to outline any specific obligations with an orientation to the future had important implications for the institutionalization of cooperation in the CSCE and for the role of the nonbloc states in the CSCE in Geneva and beyond.

6 Building Consensus on a New Normative Order

THE BLUE BOOK established the basic parameters for developing the institutional framework of the CSCE and took East and West one step closer to institutionalizing multilateral cooperation. Nevertheless, it was based on compromises that papered over different interpretations. Nowhere was the clash of positions and approaches to be more problematic than in the Basket III negotiations on human contacts, cultural exchange, information, and other freer movement issues. In contrast to the cross-bloc contacts sustained through much of Dipoli, in Geneva the negotiations soon became polarized around bloc positions.

The N+N countries emerged as a grouping of third-party states working to attain consensus on the document that would become the Final Act. They contributed a "neutral package deal," which proved to be a key formula that helped to tie together the entire negotiated agreement. Nevertheless, such third-party contributions had their own costs for the N+N, who had to choose whether to focus on facilitating the process of the negotiations or work as agenda setters in order to get more of their own substantive interests such as disarmament into the final document. A second issue of paramount importance concerned the follow-up to the conference. Here, too, the N+N got less than they wanted. But they established for themselves a role in sustaining the CSCE process that would prove crucial on the rocky and long road toward its institutionalization.

Bargaining Dynamics: Soviet Bloc

The Soviets came to Helsinki with one basic desire: to bring the entire Helsinki conference to a close as quickly as possible. Just to get the West to agree to open the Consultations in Dipoli, they had already made too many concessions on such issues as the German Question, the status of Berlin, and the MBFR. Moreover, by means of these preparations, the Soviets had already achieved one of their main objectives—the acceptance of the German Democratic Republic as a full-fledged member of the international community. The Soviet Union's remaining objective was to gain Western recognition of the inviolability of frontiers—and especially the primary importance of this principle. However, at Dipoli this objective had already cost them the inclusion of the West's human-rights agenda.

The CSCE endeavor had evolved so far from the original Soviet aspirations that they scaled back (and later dropped entirely) their original appeal for it to lead to a Permanent European Security Commission. In effect, the Soviets were hardly prepared to accept more costs in the short run on the expectation of future rewards. Instead, they aimed to minimize the damage by achieving a speedy agreement in Geneva (by the end of 1973—they hoped), which would give legal force to only the principles on relations between states as outlined in the Blue Book. To facilitate this action, Gromyko announced even in his opening statement in Helsinki the Soviet's draft of the final document on the first item on the agenda of the Blue Book, which was grandly titled the "General Declaration on the Foundations of European Security and the Principles of Relations Among States in Europe." Its adoption would be "of exceptionally profound international significance." This would give the Soviets legal guarantees, the surrogate World War II peace treaty they sought, and stabilize the status quo.[1]

The rest of the agreements to be reached at Helsinki would achieve other, less strident Soviet interests. Economic, scientific, technological, and trade relations would expand on the basis of the peaceful development of East-West relations, which the declaration would codify. Cooperation could proceed along bilateral contacts between governments.[2] Security could be enhanced by actions based on "a common view that the participating States will refrain from rendering political, military, economic or any other aid and assistance to any State or States commiting [*sic*] acts endangering international peace and security."[3]

1. See Mr. Gromyko, USSR, CSCE/I/PV.Z p. 16, in Conference on Security and Cooperation in Europe: Stage I Helsinki Verbatim Records: July 3–7, 1973 (Vation Painatuskeskus: Helsinki).

2. A CSCE document that circulated in Basket III noted that, whereas the West presented proposals in Basket III with the emphasis on contacts and exchanges at the individual level, the Eastern bloc's explanatory interventions on their proposals underlined exchanges at the level of governments and organizations. While the socialist countries expressed views in favor of drafting the final document in the form of general principles that could later be applied in bilateral agreements between the participating states, the Western countries wanted to see them take "the form of multilaterally binding agreements and particular measures which would be enforceable and immediately applicable." CSCE document, Committee III, 18.9–26.10.1973, 2.

3. See Mr. Gromyko, USSR, CSCE/I/PV.2, p. 14 in Conference on Security and Cooperation in Europe: Stage I Helsinki. Verbatim Records: July 3–7, 1973 (Valtion Painatuskeskus: Helsinki).

Western Europe and the United States

The EC states and NATO allies, including both the United States and Canada, made up the Western bloc. They did not always act with one voice, as EC states continued to present their own proposals and often adopted an independent position to promote European Political Cooperation (Ghebali 1989; Schoutheete 1980). The coordination of Western positions in NATO generally followed on the consensus reached in EC caucuses. The United States continued to play a low-key role, a fact amply illustrated by its delegation's failure to secure Secretary of State William Rogers an early place on the speakers' list for the opening statements in Helsinki. In its capacity as host, the Finnish government graciously ceded its slot, so the United States would not be the last to take the podium (while the Soviets had made certain to be first) (Maresca 1985, 40). The Nixon-Kissinger administration saw the CSCE as a regional enterprise that could jeopardize bilateral U.S.-Soviet accommodation on strategic nuclear issues, Vietnam, and other regional issues affecting international peace. In contrast to the EC's emphasis on human rights, the U.S. demands were limited to obtaining agreement based on mutual respect for different systems of government and nonintervention in internal affairs (Maresca 1985). The U.S. administration gave little importance to the Basket III issues. The fact that the U.S.-Soviet Basic Principles Agreement signed in 1972 made no mention of human-rights issues alienated West Europeans all the more.

In contrast to the Soviets' high expectations for the CSCE, the West was cautious. The allies were determined, however, to maintain Western cohesion and counter the Brezhnev doctrine with principles on the respect for sovereign equality, political independence, noninterference in the internal affairs of any state, and the right of the people of each European state to shape their own destinies free of external constraints (Holsti 1984, 137). For genuine improvement of East-West relations to develop, a "people first" conception of détente was vital: any East-West agreements must yield concrete benefits to individuals, both personally and in their professional lives. This was a reversal of the Soviet priorities, which held that state-to-state relations were the foundation of détente (Holsti 1984, 136).

However, the West feared the Soviets would both "nudge" the EC into greater cooperation with the East and slow the process of Western integration, or at least "deflect it from political-military forms." This occurrence would also strengthen security in the Eastern bloc. Indeed, at Helsinki, Gromyko "emphasized" that the "Soviet Union intends to establish long-term co-operation in Europe, to determine the main directions of the development of economic, scientific and technological ties for many years to come." This would strengthen the East's security, and also give them a *droit de regard* over Western Europe—two related prospects that the West sought to thwart.

The West was especially adverse to negotiating a legal document, in light of the Soviet demands for the recognition of the inviolability of frontiers, as a means of gaining international recognition of its post-World War II boundaries. Not wanting to ratify such outcomes legally (especially in light of the German Question), the West insisted on a political agreement. Although this also meant the West would have to settle on political, not legally binding, human-rights commitments, in the view of many experts, this has not diminished their relevance (Helgesen 1990). Soviet insistence on the inviolability of European borders provoked Western efforts to drive the human-rights agenda, in part to assure both Eastern governments and its own domestic audience that "security and status quo are not entirely synonymous" (Kirk Laux 1984, 259). The effect of the West's position on an agenda including freer movement initiatives (e.g., individuals, information, cultural exchanges, emigration) polarized the negotiation around many of the key debates left unresolved in the *Final Recommendations*. As the political nature of the bargain became clear to the Soviet Union, the initial enthusiasm for institutionalizing the CSCE as a European security system was greatly diminished. Instead the Soviets sought a speedy close to the negotiations and a final agreement based on vague recommendations for further cooperation.

To this end, the Soviets in particular, and the East bloc in general, adopted a number of tactics. They started out the CSCE negotiations in the role of "defenders" of the status quo, seeking specific provisions only where the legitimacy and stability of the divided Europe were concerned. However, they increasingly assumed the role of "brakers," resisting progress on issues of human rights, or conceptualizations of cooperation that implied direct contact between peoples, or proposals to support cultural affairs and exchanges that challenged a statist conception of culture. As in Dipoli, the Soviets first tried to get as much agreement on the principles as possible. For example, during the Geneva negotiations, the Soviet Union attempted first to block the reassembly of the Basket III committee before the final issues in Basket I and especially the principles on nonintervention were negotiated. Later it tried to introduce a preamble to Basket III that would have emptied the Basket's provisions of any practical significance. Finally, it tried to stonewall the negotiations, using to its advantage the consensus decision rule.

Few cross-bloc dynamics prevailed,[4] and essentially none in Basket III.

4. The Nordic countries also caucused. This group provided one arena for consultations outside military blocs. Romania often lobbied Yugoslavia. There were also some limited groupings that formed around specific issues, most notably the Mediterranean, for which Yugoslavia, Spain, and Italy in particular often took leading roles. Malta's singular interest in this issue ensured it a notorious bargaining role as a "defender," prepared as it was on more than one occasion (Geneva, Belgrade, Madrid) to hold up consensus among the other thirty-four participating states on a final document until its interest was satisfactorily taken into account. See Zartman (2003) on such negotiating roles.

Even though in the negotiations on Basket I Romania co-sponsored proposals with the N+N, and in Basket II Hungary took a more liberal position than either the GDR or USSR, in Basket III the East negotiated on the basis of bloc solidarity (Kirk Laux 1984, 258–59). Thus, the Soviets' diplomatic activity in the later rounds of negotiations leading to the Helsinki Final Act was an exercise in damage control. Their objective became to concede as little as possible for achieving the legitimization of the status quo, and particularly to limit commitments on human rights and related provisions. The West became the "drivers" of the CSCE process, attempting to produce an agreement consonant with their political interests, and increasingly in order to satisfy domestic political pressures. Complicated bargaining tactics proliferated in Geneva and soon characterized the whole meeting. Work proceeded with much of the text in brackets, as states made their commitment on any number of points conditional to agreements elsewhere in the text. Often parties reneged even on brackets, such that "texts laboriously arrived at were reopened on the insistence of one or more parties" (Holsti 1984, 150).[5]

Neutral and Nonaligned

As a whole, the nonbloc states emphasized the importance of achieving meaningful results in disarmament and gave as broad an interpretation of the Dipoli mandate as possible. In the Swedish view, it was not "reasonable that a Conference with the aim of dealing with security in Europe should ignore the important military aspects," and to this end insisted on the necessity of stressing the connection between security and disarmament in Europe and argued for considering ideas beyond the Dipoli mandate on "confidence-building measures." Finland supported a careful examination of the confidence-building measures, investigations into nuclear-free zones in particular, *and* the geographical limitation of armaments in Europe in general.[6] Yugoslavia advocated dealing with military aspects of security in Europe, including the reduction of armed forces and armaments, along with the inclusion of the Mediterranean area, which was also a main concern of Malta. Characteristic of the nonbloc perspective, Yugoslavia emphasized that security is *indivisible,* and that all states should have a full opportunity to participate in the deliberation of these issues.[7] The other

5. See also Ferraris's (1979, 99–164) account of the labyrinthian and tortuous Geneva negotiations in the First Sub-committee charged with deriving a text on interstate principles. In particular, many participants had difficulties finding adequate wording for the principles dealing with the inviolability of frontiers and peaceful change of borders.

6. "Statement by the Foreign Ministry of Finland, Dr. Ahti Karjalainen, in the General Debate of the CSCE, Helsinki, 6 July 1973," ULA 1973, 143–44.

7. Proposal by the Delegation of Yugoslavia, "Military Aspects of Security in Europe—Arms Limitation and Disarmament," CSCE/II/C/7, Geneva, Sept. 28, 1973.

neutrals supported the Swiss proposal for a system of the peaceful settlement of international disputes. The N+N countries sought to achieve as much substance from the entire process as possible, in many respects taking positions that were close to the West, particularly the EC countries (Ferraris 1979).[8]

For the neutrals, a precondition for détente was "respect for the policies of national security chosen by the various States, including the neutral and non-aligned countries."[9] Central among these expectations was the view that détente should strengthen each country's own position and identity. This meant respect for and elaboration of multiple points of contact. Finland's Foreign Minister Ahti Karjalainen also emphasized that the European neutrals "share a basic objective in their security policy, which is that they endeavor to remain outside of conflicts between the great powers." In Finland's view, one of the results of the CSCE, "should be that this objective is respected, recognized and reaffirmed."[10]

The neutral and nonaligned also supported the creation of a forum to further contacts and to facilitate the convening of more conferences. For Finland, the task of shaping the follow-up to the Conference was "especially important."[11] Likewise, Sweden, which did not regard the Conference as a "one time event," was interested in creating some forum to facilitate the convening of new conferences and kept "open the possibilities for a discussion on arms limitations measures for the entire group of States represented here." Multilateral settings such as the CSCE were essential in Sweden's view to ensure that "the search for international détente is not limited to meetings and agreements between the leaders of the two super-powers."[12]

Thus, the neutrals approached Geneva much as they had the Dipoli Consultations, focused on the main idea that everyone should be independent and that everyone was equal. The N+N were still insistent on not passing over the opportunity to maintain a national profile through their own national proposals. The frequent caucusing within the military alliances had left neutral and nonaligned sitting alone around the table. The tight bloc lines drawn in the military-security discussions also had the effect of strengthening the sense of commonality of interests among the neutral and nonaligned states. In view of the N+N's limited success in promoting their aims in especially the military-security

8. Mr. Wickman, Sweden, CSCE/I/PV.4, pp. 17, 22, in Conference on Security and Cooperation in Europe: Stage I Helsinki. Verbatim Records: July 3–7, 1973 (Valtion Painatuskeskus: Helsinki).

9. Ibid., pp. 12–15.

10. "Statement by the Foreign Minister of Finland, Dr. Ahti Karjalainen, in the General Debate of the CSCE, Helsinki, 6 July 1973," ULA 1973, 143.

11. Ibid., 146.

12. Mr. Wickman, Sweden, CSCE/I/PV.4, p. 12, in Conference on Security and Cooperation in Europe: Stage I Helsinki. Verbatim Records: July 3–7, 1973 (Valtion Painatuskeskus: Helsinki).

dimension at the Consultations in Dipoli, it was also clear that some strategy among them was necessary. In Geneva there was the understanding that, if only one N+N sponsored a proposal and submitted it (especially if it was a bit controversial), then the door was left open for the other N+N countries to suggest amendments to it. This was seen as a way of protecting the N+N interests and keeping control over the process of altering them. At first a consolidation of positions around a joint N+N proposal was not pursued because it was felt this might very well tie their hands in controlling the alterations.[13]

This strategy was of limited effect, however, especially in the security-basket negotiations at Geneva. To the extent that the N+N had performed useful services as intermediaries in Dipoli, they had built expectations that this help would be provided again in the future. As one Swedish official recalls, "this did cause problems later on in Geneva when the N+N showed that they did have their own ideas, and would pursue them. They were not willing to be around just as servants to the superpowers in order to devise compromise proposals for them." The neutrals were important, too, as secret allies of the smaller West and East European countries that sought to use them to get their positions onto the negotiating agenda.[14]

While the common interests of the N+N were consolidated in relation to the discussion in Geneva on military-security issues, coordination among the neutrals became more customary in relation to their intervention as third parties. Given the polarization between the blocs and precedents set from their third-party contributions in Dipoli, they quickly faced renewed expectations they would assume third-party tasks. Thus the N+N emerged as a grouping in Geneva whose third-party roles encompassed both instrumental and facilitative mediation. Instrumentally, their efforts helped to ensure that the final document included military-security commitments. As facilitators, they negotiated the "neutral package deal," the key agreement that tied together the whole Final Act. On the whole, the N+N's objective was to get the bloc members through negotiating impasses, to come to a consensus on a new starting point for talking through the problems of East-West security and cooperation, and to help find solutions. They were committed to empowering the superpowers to abandon old points of departure and to manage their relations in a multilateral context on the basis of a common code or "generalized principles of conduct" (Ruggie 1993). This meant the N+N had to get the East-West adversaries to see that their earlier mind-sets and decisions were not useful to them independently or mutually, and that they were not the most effective approaches for getting what they wanted. As West Germany's Foreign Minister Walter Scheel advised in his

13. Swedish official, interview by author, written notes, Stockholm, May 27, 1988.

14. Ibid.

opening statement during Phase I of the CSCE in Helsinki, "We must be clear about what we really mean. Only if we speak the same language, if we mean the same thing by the same words, will we be successful." He urged that "noncommittal generalities will not help us on. . . . We must want the same thing."

Only further down the road in the postagreement period would it be clear to what extent the commitments reached in Helsinki were *indivisible* (in terms of the costs and benefits spread across the geographic and functional aspects of cooperation among the participating states), *credible,* and *durable.* Could East, West, and the N+N secure a new foundation for East-West relations? Or, as Walter Scheel put it, would Talleyrand's assessment of the foreign ministers at the Vienna Congress apply to the CSCE: "Too frightened to fight each other and too stupid to agree"?[15]

Organizational Structure

After the presentation of opening statements in Helsinki (July 3–7, 1973), the delegations moved to Geneva for tabling proposals and debate, and eventually for drafting. The work was facilitated in part by the precedents and experience from Dipoli.[16] It was first in Geneva that the full-fledged structure of the CSCE with its principal negotiating committees was established, reflecting the basket designations. The Blue Book specified that the Conference would function by means of several different working bodies, with the Coordinating Committee as the central organ. In addition, there were to be committees and subcommittees organized along the basket structure, which could in turn establish smaller working groups.

The Dutch delegation (in consultation with the EC and NATO) presented a draft of a framework for a final text on February 11, 1974. Its substance was skeletal, but the formula met Soviet interests in several key ways: following the organization of the Blue Book, the principles were listed first, giving them a prominent place in the text (if not the special status the Soviets sought); the Dutch framework made room for preambles before each of the baskets, thus allowing for the caveats the Soviets wanted to introduce on these—particularly

15. Mr. Scheel, Federal Republic of Germany, CSCE/I/PV.3, pp. 22–25, 36–37, in Conference on Security and Cooperation in Europe: Stage I Helsinki. Verbatim Records: July 3–7, 1973 (Valtion Painatuskeskus: Helsinki).

16. Some proposals had already been presented in Helsinki during the opening statements. Most notable among these was the Soviet (Eastern bloc) proposal titled, "General Declaration on the Foundations of European Security and the Principles Guiding Relations Between States in Europe." CSCE/II/C1 Geneva, Sept. 19, 1973. It was little more than a repetition of the Recommendations. Czechoslovakia, on behalf of the Warsaw Pact, presented a "Resolution concerning the Advisory Committee on Security and Co-operation in Europe," CSCE/CC/22, Geneva, Oct. 18, 1973, which was the first to delineate the shape of the follow-up to the CSCE.

as concerned Basket III; and it committed the West to a document that was to be signed. Maresca argues that this last element was critical to the Soviets (1985, 90).

The Dutch proposal came at a crucial juncture in East-West relations—just a week after the arrest of Alexander Solzhenitsyn. His case symbolized the dilemma of détente for the West: how far should the West push human-rights standards with the Soviets, and what kind of Soviet behavior on these questions could put East-West détente in jeopardy (Maresca 1985, 89–90)? The Dutch proposal thus signaled the West's determination to proceed with negotiations at Geneva and affirmed its fundamental commitment to the Conference to reach politically significant results.

In the early phase of the CSCE process, there was no kind of preconceived third-party role. The mediation efforts by mostly nonbloc states in Dipoli were informal. Moreover, the Blue Book strictly called for the delegate of a different country to chair the meeting each new day for the Helsinki-Geneva-Helsinki stages of the negotiations. Much of the negotiating in Geneva proceeded in the committees themselves, with all thirty-five countries working together around the table;[17] this approach encumbered the discussion and drafting of principles in Basket I, although the work was facilitated through some third-party efforts by states other than the N+N. Spain brokered a critical compromise on the inviolability of frontiers principle through a procedural formula known as the "separate-piece-of-paper solution" (Maresca 1985, 92). And starting in July 1974, the Belgian delegate Laurent, on behalf of the EC, regularly presented a "mosaic" of all the proposals concerning the remaining principles, and the preamble for Basket I as a means to facilitate the discussion (Ferraris 1979, 123).

Despite the absence of any preconceived, formal third-party role for the Conference, the neutrals soon largely facilitated the practical organization of the work in Geneva. Following on their procedural interventions in Dipoli, they began in Geneva to automatically assume responsibility for developing the working programs (e.g. devising timetables for six weeks ahead; deciding how many meetings should be convened, and when the plenary would be meeting next; and determining how the working parties would be set up). The two blocs could not do it, and, because neither bloc would let the other do it, they asked the four neutrals. Later this group of four was extended to five to include Yugoslavia, and then to the other nonaligned, all of whom shared in the responsibility while "insisting all along that we are no group of N+N countries. We are just working together."[18]

17. Other informal negotiating arrangements emerged, but not to the extent they did at Belgrade and in subsequent CSCE meetings.

18. Swedish official, interview by author, written notes, Swedish Foreign Ministry, May 27, 1988.

The technical organization was only one practical aspect of the procedural facilitation the N+N provided. At the actual working level in Geneva, the need for N+N intermediary services varied among the different baskets. The contentious nature of the issues in Basket III and the polarization of the blocs around them led to the system of neutral heads of delegation facilitating not only the procedural work of the negotiations, but also its substantive aspects, guiding under their coordinatorship the various informal discussion groups (see also Ferraris 1979, 314 and 319). The term "coordinators" was used to distinguish the neutrals' tasks from the office of the chairman (Sizoo and Jurrjens 1984, 157), which the Blue Book required for each committee, subcommittee, and subsidiary body of the conference according to the rule of rotation.[19]

Although coordination was not needed in Basket I in the negotiations on interstate principles, complex bargaining tactics and impasses elsewhere eventually necessitated third-party intervention, especially to work out the compromises that would determine the relationship between the different baskets. From April to June of 1974, the Geneva negotiations bogged down on most fronts. This proved a critical impasse, which had to be resolved in a comprehensive fashion. The solution turned out to be a "neutral package deal."

Impasse on Multiple Fronts

Basket I: Interstate Principles

The Soviets approached the negotiations on principles guiding interstate relations in Basket I by pushing for a rapid agreement in an effort to merely codify the *Final Recommendations* along the lines of the "General Declaration" they had submitted during the Helsinki opening statements. This effort gave way to considerable alarm in the West. Both the Western allies and the N+N endeavored to draw out negotiations as long as possible on the key principles, especially the inviolability of frontiers and nonintervention in internal affairs, to allow progress to go forward in Basket III. For the West, this resulted in a basic trade-off in Geneva. Agreement on key Soviet principles would be extended only in exchange for a Western conception of human rights, which would emphasize concrete measures to promote the basic and universal dignity of each individual. Because of this bargaining situation, strategy and tactics were important from the outset. In Basket I the West began by slowly and laboriously moving the negotiations first through the presentation of positions, to extensive debates on each principle, then to a protracted period of presenting formulas, to

19. *Final Recommendations of the Helsinki Consultations,* (71) B (a) and (b).

efforts from all sides to find compromise language on them, and finally to the drafting and registering of texts. All this moved forward only as progress was achieved in the other baskets.

Even though it is often customary in international conferences to entrust to a small group of delegates the tasks of drafting the document, in the Basket I negotiations on the principles the drafting was conducted together among all thirty-five delegations throughout most of the Geneva stage. It was done this way particularly at Romanian insistence (Ferraris 1979, 110). The extraordinary multilateral effort this implied, along with the ingenious negotiating maneuvering on the part of all thirty-five to get as much into each of the principles as possible, encumbered the negotiations. In some instances in which one party sought to link its agreement to a favorable formulation in another basket, the only way to proceed was by placing the text in brackets. More difficult still, many of the formulas on the principles could only be registered after other issues (in Basket II or III) were cleared up first.

The slow going was further complicated by a period of Soviet intransigence from April to July 1974. It is speculated that this resulted from the Soviets' uncertainty with Nixon's then-precarious political future as president, or because of Soviet anticipation of a change in foreign-policy directives from the newly elected French and German governments, or because they began to have doubts about the shape of the formula then reached on the principle on inviolability of frontiers (Ferraris 1979, 122–23).[20]

Military-Security Negotiations

In Basket I Subcommittee C, the discussions focused on the CBMs. The two blocs began the practice of caucusing among themselves from the very start of the Geneva phase, so that the debates in Subcommittee C were largely the product of policies and proposals each side arrived at in internal consultations.[21] This exchange lasted from September 1973 until March 1974, when the differences of attitude became apparent "without ambiguity, and in fact, with sudden brutality" (Ferraris 1979, 180). It was mainly the two blocs that were

20. Despite these procedural difficulties, it was only in the last round of consolidating the text—in fact in the course of its "second reading" and very near the end of the negotiations—that a Canadian delegate was "unanimously chosen as 'co-ordinator' " of Basket I. He was to clean up the text largely along stylistic or technical lines. The selection was made "in virtue of the good reputation he acquired for his competence, common sense and objectivity" (Ferraris 1979, 162–63).

21. Ferraris (1979, 184) recounts that "in this way a situation was arrived at whereby the background of the meetings of the Sub-Committee had been pre-established down to the minutest detail."

engaged at the time, and from the neutrals' perspective, this was "an impossible situation."

As in the other baskets, the Soviets endeavored to change their opening position as little as possible, and above all in the military-security field. The Warsaw Pact maintained that no progress had occurred in military détente since the end of World War II, so they expected progress in this area to be minimal and measures limited (Ferraris 1979, 181). In a conference that the Soviets had intended to be largely political, and to which Soviet policy had directed broad statements on East-West security based on the party's peace program, this very limited posture was extraordinary.

In spite of attempts in Subcommittee C to move beyond the general debate and presentation of positions in order to commence work at the drafting level, the divide between East and West was so great that there was no ground on which to begin building common texts. All the participants in the West, including the N+N, agreed that the Soviet proposals elaborated measures of such a scale (applicable, for example, to not less than thirty thousand men) that few countries, if any, would find their military maneuvers subject to the mechanisms of notification. Furthermore, the Soviets proposed that only maneuvers of such magnitude *and* within a fifty-kilometer frontier zone be subject to notification. It was well appreciated by the Western delegations that maneuvers of thirty thousand soldiers could hardly be restricted to a fifty-kilometer band, and in the event the possibility loomed that only part of the maneuver would be reported; or worse still, no maneuvers would be subject to reporting at all given such a zonal conception (Ferraris 1979, 186). As the Italian delegate pointed out, "it would be extremely dangerous to introduce into a document on security and cooperation in Europe, at a time when détente had made enormous progress, a concept such as that of the frontier zones, which was strictly tied to the period immediately following the war and the cold war, recalling the resolution of disputes with bordering countries" (Ferraris 1979, 187).

The West endeavored to make the concept of confidence-building measures meaningful for all the participants, insisting first on an unambiguous mandate for their application; second, that all countries derive some benefit; and third, that the measures have as wide an application as possible. Thus, from the West's perspective, "the more intense the preventive notification of military activity, the greater the contribution to the process of détente" (Ferraris 1979, 180). To probe the Soviet position, the Western allies introduced five comprehensive proposals (Ferraris 1979, 188). Especially significant was the Belgium proposal to conceive of CBMs not only as a negative guarantee against misunderstandings and misinterpretations stemming from the perceived threats or a potential surprise attack, but also as a means to promote a climate of confidence (Borawski

1988, 5).[22] However, none of these attempts elicited a Soviet counterproposal. By the spring of 1974, the West began to feel that its options were exhausted. According to Ferraris (1979, 191),

> the Western delegations . . . came to the conclusion that it would be useful if, on the eve of the drafting stage, a written document were also to be presented by the neutral and nonaligned delegations; the West was perfectly well aware that a document of this kind would contain proposals which went far beyond those which they were prepared to accept (one need only think of the pre-notification of autonomous naval and air born activities, or the undertaking of self-restraint); nevertheless, it might constitute a new means of exerting pressure to induce the countries of the East to negotiate.

While the two blocs had been caucusing in Subcommittee C, the N+N countries had also begun to meet. At first only the four neutrals met, because it was felt that nine was a rather large, ineffective number and that some of the other countries were rather small and would not produce so much of their own work.[23] Thus, when the request came, preparations were already under way for a joint N+N proposal. The four neutrals and Yugoslavia had the strongest positions, although Finland was somewhat restrained in order not to compromise its role as a host for the third stage. Not obtaining a final agreement would have been, in the least, an embarrassment to Finnish diplomacy. And, as the country was seeking a permanent CSCE secretariat in Helsinki, the potential long-term benefits of a successful conference were not insubstantial. Finland would not stray from the agreed agenda for negotiations in order not to jeopardize the whole negotiation outcome. This was the case with both the CBM proposal and the Swiss proposal for peaceful settlement of disputes. The Finns were somewhat concerned that the military aspect might complicate the whole issue of reaching a final document, but they were eager about it all the same.[24]

The joint N+N proposal on CBMs, presented by Sweden on behalf of the delegations of Austria, Cyprus, Finland, Switzerland, and Yugoslavia, was well received by the West as an attempt to find a middle path between some East and West positions—while retaining a maximalist position on goals of special interest to the N+N (e.g. some disarmament measures). However, even this N+N initiative was profoundly rejected by the Eastern bloc (Ferraris 1979, 192). In the meantime, in the other subcommittee discussions on military aspects of security

22. Borawski (1988, 4 and n. 13) notes that the term "confidence-building measure" apparently first appeared in a 1955 UN General Assembly Resolution (914X) for the "Regulation, Limitation, and Balanced Reduction of All Armed Forces and All Armaments."

23. Swedish official, interview by author, written notes, Stockholm, May 27, 1988.

24. Ibid.

outside of the talks on CBMs, Sweden continued to champion disarmament, along with Yugoslavia, and in this context the N+N introduced on March 15, 1974, a second proposal. But like the work on CBMs, these negotiations, too, failed to advance (Ferraris 1979, 194–95). In view of the Soviets' attacks on the Swiss proposal for the peaceful settlement of disputes, the Swiss eventually abandoned their attempts to see a concrete agreement on this at Geneva, and instead satisfied themselves with securing in the Final Act no more than a commitment for some future meeting of experts to consider the idea (Maresca 1985, 89 and 138).

In May and June 1974, as the Conference bogged down on many fronts and as the summer target date for the conclusion of the negotiations proved entirely premature (this was already the second target, December 1973 having been the first), the West prepared to postpone or break off the negotiations (Maresca 1985, 98). The N+N remained firm in their conviction that good results be obtained or the Conference proceed later under more favorable conditions. It was also considered important not to allow the CSCE to become another perennial negotiation unable to deliver, as had happened with the UN Conference of the Committee on Disarmament in Geneva.

In an effort to break the deadlock, several neutral delegations organized an informal meeting among heads of delegation. In what Maresca describes as a "dramatic intervention" after considerable stalemate, the head of the Soviet delegation gave the signal that the Soviets were prepared to move toward serious negotiation. To demonstrate this, he announced three concessions, which touched on important issues in both Basket III and the military-security talks (1985, 99). This action paved the way for the neutrals' package deal (see below).

Basket III—The Devil Is in the Details

In Basket II, negotiations on economics, science, technology, and the environment went well without much coordination, but in Basket III the situation was quite different. Whereas in the negotiations on principles Romania consistently took positions contrary to the Eastern bloc, and much of the drafting included reasonable efforts to reach across bloc lines to find acceptable formulas, in Basket III the Geneva negotiations were polarized between East and West from the very start (Kirk Laux 1984, 259). Having conceded much in principle already at Dipoli, the Soviets used the strategy in Geneva of exerting as much influence as possible over the debate so the outcome would favor their positions. At the outset in Geneva a Swiss delegate captured the challenge for the West when he quipped: "Attention, Messieurs, le diable est dans les détails" (quoted in Ferraris 1979, 299). It was well appreciated that Basket III was in its details "a broad challenge to Soviet-style political systems as well as a negotiating counterpoint to the USSR's obsession with gaining recognition of the boundary changes which had followed World War II" (Kirk Laux 1984, 259).

The ideological confrontation between East and West led to a severe clash of negotiating strategies and tactics in Basket III especially. The East wanted to reach agreement first on the preamble, while the West went for the specifics, without prejudice to the ideologically inspired principles in which the East sought to couch the agreement at every turn. The East's strategy alternated between pushing broad, abstract political principles and seeking to negotiate word by word, with each marginal provision connected to conditions or principles that would rob it of the liberating effects the West intended. This situation resulted in the East's demand, for example, that measures intended to facilitate the expansion of cultural exchange would need to meet the test of strengthening peace and security, or the Eastern bloc insistence that even as such exchanges develop, the governments must take measures to protect their respective cultures from the "cultural pollution" of other countries. Such stipulations, limitations, or the use of ideological "filters" were utterly unacceptable to the West (Ferraris 1979, 329).

In view of these difficulties, the negotiators resorted to neutral coordinators to call together smaller, informal drafting groups, known as mini-groups. This was done, Ferraris tells us, despite the fact that the method had on a number of different occasions justifiably received criticism from various quarters. Namely, in view of the principle of equality and the rule specifying that meetings be open to all, the restricted participation that the method imposed was not well received by the smaller delegations. But at least in this way it was possible to outline the problems and facilitate greater and more rapid awareness of them (1979, 314). In Basket III, Finland coordinated drafting on culture, Sweden on education, Switzerland on information, and Austria on human contact.[25]

Neutrals' Package Deal

The coordinator's role proved crucial when it became necessary to strike compromises between Basket I and Basket III on the relationship between the principle of the sovereignty of participating states and of noninterference in the state's internal affairs. The neutrals' third-party efforts in the Basket I negotiations stemmed from their role as coordinators in Basket III. Over the spring and summer of 1974, the negotiations as a whole were stagnating under the weight of Soviet intransigence. This came as a surprise to the Western delegations, because the Soviets had produced a number of key concessions prior to the Easter

25. Finnish official, interview by author, written notes, Washington, D.C., Apr. 12, 1990.

recess in order to achieve early registration of the principle of inviolability of frontiers, which for Brezhnev (who followed this aspect of the Geneva negotiations on a daily basis) was the primary objective.

In Basket III the West had gotten the Soviets' to agree to registration of the text on "Contacts and Regular Meetings on the Basis of Family Ties" and a commitment to the dissemination of printed information, also part of the freer-movement text (Maresca 1985, 92–93). The Soviets also had made several other notable concessions in the Basket I negotiations on the principles. They agreed to an innovative Spanish compromise, which provided that the wording for the principle of peaceful change of borders be placed on a separate piece of paper, with its placement in the list of principles to be determined later. This decision also satisfied West German demands that the CSCE not prejudice its possibilities for future unification[26] and Soviet demands that the inviolability of frontiers not be defined itself in the context of peaceful changes. The Soviets also agreed to a rendering of the inviolability of frontiers principle, "which strongly suggested only violent changes in frontiers were excluded" (Maresca 1985, 92–94). However, having now achieved their principal aims, the Soviets proved intransigent and failed to produce the additional compromises in Basket III they had promised to make after the Easter recess. In effect, the West had lost much of its leverage.

After more than nine months of negotiations, there was no overall framework (although the Dutch proposal had already outlined what would come to resemble closely the Final Act's structure). There was still no general, commonly accepted referent principle to guide the bargaining and drafting. The efforts to overcome the deadlock were spurred initially by a Finnish-proposed formula (Ferraris 1979, 129). This idea helped to promote discussions, but its formula was not acceptable to the West. The negotiations stalemated over what was essentially an ideological obstacle. The West insisted on the supremacy of international law over internal laws, wishing to avoid any formulations in the negotiations that the Soviets could point to as a political-legal agreement legitimizing the "Brezhnev" doctrine. As Ferraris explains (1979, 130), the Western countries, while realizing that the CSCE was on the brink of failure, and "spurred on by America (Kissinger, by this time, seemed prepared to bring an end to a diplomatic exercise which had shown itself to be sterile and even counterproductive), examined their consciences in order to identify their minimum essential objectives: in other words, an attempt to save the salvageable." It was

26. However, Germany attached its own reservations on these points, thus making its agreement conditional to: (1) the placement of the peaceful change formula; (2) its precise formulation as well as that of the governing principle of self-determination; and (3) an agreed-upon formula on the interdependence of the principles (Maresca 1985, 93–94; Ferraris 1979, 166, 121).

in this context that the Swiss brought more balance (more of the "West") into the Finnish proposal. A package deal on this issue, along with Swedish efforts in the tenth principle, and later Finnish efforts to draft the preamble to the third basket resulted in the key package deal holding the entire CSCE Final Act together between East and West (see also Ferraris 1979, 30).

The central aspect of the package centered on the East's insistence that Basket III have a preamble. They wanted wording to the effect that national laws take "precedence" or something to say that Basket III commitments on human contact could be rendered "in accordance with national laws." The solution found by the neutrals was to transfer such a protection clause to the principles set out in Basket I (where such a provision could be balanced by or interpreted in light of the other principles) and then make a vague connection between the various sections of the final document.

Thus, the first principle of the Final Act, which addresses Sovereign Equality, not only calls on states "to respect each other's sovereign equality and individuality, . . .but also each other's right freely to choose and develop its political, social, economic and cultural systems as well as its right to determine its laws and regulations." Sweden insisted on another clause in the tenth principle, so that it came to read: "in exercising their sovereign rights, including the right to determine their laws and regulations, they [the participating states] will conform with their legal obligations under international law; they will furthermore pay due regard to and implement the provisions of the Final Act."[27] The Soviets insisted this read "legal obligations" to give them further opportunity to play on their interpretation of "legal" having reference to national laws, over "international obligations" as being rooted in international law. The Swiss contributed to the drafting of the peaceful settlement of disputes, also a component of the tenth principle.

Thus, as Jaakko Iloniemi (a member of the Finnish delegation) explains, the neutral package contained "the text of the preamble to the third basket and separate statements connected with the first and tenth principles regarding the right of states to make their own laws and in so doing to consider their international obligations" (1975, 34). The neutrals' intervention also provided the basis for the successful integration of the principles in the first basket. Moreover, the package deal not only connected these principles but also promoted progress in the summer of 1974 between the first and third baskets, and connected them to the principles.

It was an important turning point. Even though it was clear that the negotiations were far from an early conclusion, there was now a general framework

27. Swedish official, interview by author, written notes, Swedish Foreign Ministry, Stockholm, May 27, 1988. See also Ferraris (1979, 130–31).

to guide the work after a summer recess. And even if it was a tenuous basis for moving toward an agreed document, it provided some sense of momentum with which to begin pulling all the pieces together once the work resumed in September.

Basket IV: A Follow-up?

Under the heading, "Follow-up to the Conference," the *Final Recommendations* charged the delegations "to consider, on the basis of progress made at the Conference such measures as may be required to give effect to the decisions of the Conference and to further the process of improving security and developing co-operation in Europe." The conference was to consider proposals of an organizational nature and make recommendations.[28] At Dipoli the Soviets had been among the most ardent supporters of a permanent advisory organ to emerge from the Conference. At that time the United States opposed such a plan, fearing it would lead to a mini, European UN of Soviet domination. However, the experience at Geneva gave rise to new calculations on all sides about the significance of a follow-up. This issue became one of the most "delicate and uncertain" of those before the negotiators. As Ferraris explains, the "definition of the follow-up to the Conference would presuppose a definition of the synthesis of the very essence of the entire negotiating process on security and co-operation in Europe, in a political and historical perspective and, in light of its real and potential content, of the interests involved and of the functions attributed it" (1979, 341).

Which model should prevail? A model based on great power prerogatives, on the logic of the bloc structures, or, as the egalitarian and balanced structure of the Final Act itself was to suggest, on the basis of equality and the pursuit of relations outside the bloc structures?[29] Furthermore, proposals for a follow-up also had to account for how the various baskets should be treated in any institutionalization of the process. Should they continue to receive equal treatment, which had been the guiding principle already in negotiating the Blue Book and had guided the work in Geneva? Or should they allow for a division of the tasks and varying emphases, as for example, between political and military security (Ferraris 1979, 341)?

Inherent in any questions on the follow-up were the Dipoli instructions that required the participating states "give effect," that is, ensure the implementation of the agreed provisions. Measures to give effect to and further the progress

28. *Final Recommendations*, chapter 4 (53).

29. Numerous scholars also had debated these issues. See for example Galtung (1972). Sizoo and Jurrjens (1984) and Aćimović (1981) summarize these scholarly debates.

of security and cooperation would, in light of the agreements forthcoming in the various baskets (especially Basket III), favor the dynamic purposes of a follow-up. This had since become problematic for the Soviets. On the other hand, the West questioned whether a permanent organ would lend the follow-up process the kind of dynamism it sought, and thus was circumspect about the Czechoslovakian proposal. It envisaged the creation of an advisory committee to exchange views and set up working groups to prepare practical measures to strengthen security and the development of cooperation in Europe, which was "to meet whenever its members consider this advisable."[30]

Because a discussion on the follow-up would have implied an evaluation of the progress achieved in Geneva and because there was a general desire, especially in the West and among the N+N, to attain balanced results in all the basket areas, deliberations on the follow-up were not referred to a body set up for this purpose until March 1974. The main proposals on the follow-up were presented by Yugoslavia, which emphasized its periodicity,[31] and Denmark on behalf of the Nine, which called for an ad hoc arrangement. The latter foresaw a meeting of senior officials in 1977 (without yet specifying the place) and the possibility of additional expert meetings, meetings of senior officials, or a new conference as a possible means of assessing how the decisions taken by the first CSCE had been carried out.[32] Like Czechoslovakia, Finland's proposal aspired to the CSCE's permanence and built on elements of the EC draft (calling for the implementation of the conference decisions unilaterally, bilaterally, as well as multilaterally within existing international organizations and through working groups and meetings of experts). However, Finland also proposed a Committee on the Follow-up to the CSCE. It would be composed of the representatives of the participating states and have competencies to organize and coordinate agreed multilateral activities; convene meetings as indicated in the decisions of the conference; make necessary arrangements with international organizations; and decide on the rules of procedure, financing, and other questions essential to multilaterally execute the decisions of the conference. The committee would

30. Proposal submitted by the Delegation of the CSSR, "Resolution concerning the Advisory Committee on Security and Co-operation in Europe," CSCE/CC/22, Geneva, Oct. 18, 1973, p. 2.

31. Yugoslavia called for a "Continuing Committee" to meet annually, each time in another participating state, and to be "responsible for co-ordinating, initiating and reviewing activities designed to implement the decision of the Conference and further to develop co-operation among the participating States in all the areas it has considered." See Proposal Submitted by the Delegation of Yugoslavia, "Draft Resolution, Follow-up to the conference on Security and Co-operation in Europe," CSCE/CC/WG/IV/1, Geneva, Mar. 28, 1974.

32. Proposal submitted by the Delegation of Denmark, "Resolution concerning the follow-up to the Conference on Security and Co-operation in Europe," CSCE/CC/WG/IV/2, Geneva, Apr. 26, 1974.

also call a meeting of high officials to assess the implementation of the conference decisions. This meeting would study ways and means to further the process of improving security and developing cooperation in Europe, including by (a) additional multilateral activities aimed at the implementation of the decisions of the conference and (b) a new Conference on Security and Co-operation in Europe.[33]

Movement on the drafting of the follow-up began in November 1974, partly because the West considered it "inappropriate to frustrate the interests of the neutral and nonaligned countries, with the risk of cracking the attitude of solidarity which they had maintained with the positions held by the Nine [EEC states] in other sectors of the CSCE, which was becoming ever more valuable with the approach of the final phases of the Conference" (Ferraris 1979, 346). In the final analysis, it was the deliberation among the nine countries of the European Community that proved decisive in the determination of the follow-up mechanisms of the CSCE. Although NATO under the influence of the United States and its Atlanticist orientation held a mostly ambivalent attitude toward the CSCE, for the EC the matter was wholly different. In an early stage of developing its own voice and sense of European identity, especially in the field of foreign policy, the EC focused in the early to mid-1970s on the question of the relative weight that should be given to developing institutions of a pan-European nature versus efforts to consolidate the integration of Western Europe. Reluctant to give priority to any endeavors that might detract from their own opportunities and at the same time give the Soviets a *droit de regard* over the construction of pan-European affairs, the European Community pushed for an ad hoc arrangement rather than permanency as the key principle of the follow-up mechanism (Ferraris 1979, 343). This meant the more ambitious plans for institutionalization were set aside.

Several factors weighed in the deliberations. First, the Soviets had ample time at Geneva to reconsider their position. It became increasingly evident that they had not been able to exercise much control over the development of a diplomatic conference they had worked so hard to get. True to the Swiss ambassador's assertion, once formulated and agreed upon, the details reached in the third basket would bedevil the Soviets and their appreciation of the CSCE process. The last Soviet position on the follow-up called for little more than the postponement of a second conference, probably far off in the future. The neutral and nonaligned had to scale back their expectations. However, they drew a line and stated that whichever shape the follow-up should assume, the process launched in Helsinki should be "irreversible." It had to pass the test of "the sui-

33. Proposal submitted by the Delegation of Finland, CSCE/CC/WG/IV/3, Geneva, June 7, 1974.

cide theory"—any possibility of the CSCE coming to an end and bringing European relations back into the traditional bilateral context (Ferraris 1979, 344). As the centerpiece of Finnish foreign policy and as the multilateral setting that provided Finland with the opportunity to pluralize its neutrality policy and locate it in the European structure, the CSCE and it continuity were important to promote security and respectability for the policies of neutral and nonaligned states as a component of European security. Having done so much to promote the CSCE's creation, Finland's national prestige was also on the line in ensuring this project would not come to a premature end. Thus, the nonbloc states (and Romania), with the indirect support of some smaller Western countries (especially Norway), "managed to overcome all opposition and achieve their [basic] goal" (Aćimović 1981, 272).

In keeping with the West's earlier position that steps toward each new stage be based on evaluations of progress achieved, it was eventually determined that the follow-up should be tentatively launched on the basis of a review of implementation meeting in Belgrade in 1977, which should also consider means of deepening the relations, albeit in light of the progress. The EC argued for an intervening period after the conclusion of the Conference and before any new meetings of the CSCE to allow for the implementation to proceed independent of further multilateral efforts. In other words, review of the implementation of the Final Act should proceed without confusing its achievements with the new challenges of the follow-up conference. The Danish proposal of 1974 called for a follow-up to convene in 1977, thus anticipating a three-year interval. However, with agreement on the Final Act not forthcoming until the summer of 1975, less than two years elapsed before the CSCE follow-up convened in Belgrade, and this, as we shall see in the next chapter, turned out to be precipitous.

The Final Act and the Ten Principles

Among the accomplishments of the Geneva negotiations, the Final Act sets out standards and principles of security for states' behavior with regard to other states, for behavior with regard to their own people, and for behavior with regard to cooperation among the people themselves. Security among persons was introduced as a fundamental aspect of interstate security. Hence, security must also be based on the respect for human rights (Ghebali 1989, 60). The multidimensionality of the CSCE concept of security lends itself to a broader range of application and also serves to frame and empower people to demand their state's fulfillment of international obligations as well as for people to demand of their government that they hold other participating states to their obligations. This multifaceted conception of security was vital for success of the implementation of the CSCE and for its further evolution.

Even though the results on the CBMs were limited in scope (for example, valid for the whole territory of Europe, but only including a 250 kilometer border zone within the European border of the Soviet Union) and based on a voluntary regime, their importance lay elsewhere. First, they allowed security issues to be reframed in nonzero-sum terms—and military maneuvers and exercises to be regulated in terms of the principle of the security needs of both parties, rather than unilaterally in terms of status or power. The security need of the adversary was taken into account by the confidence that could be gained from the notification of maneuvers, exchange of observers, and the general transparency the regime promoted. In these ways, the CBMs devised at Geneva introduced cooperative security and a multilateral, nonbloc approach, based also on the indivisibility of security.

There are numerous, important linkages in the Final Act between security and cooperation. Cooperation is not an end in itself, but an objective "to improve mutual understanding, confidence, friendly and good-neighborly relations, international peace and justice."[34] Cooperation spanned the broad range of issues grouped under the CSCE baskets. Principle IX of the Decalogue, "Co-operation among States," recalls the special emphasis on these fields and confirms also that not only governments but also "institutions, organizations and persons have a relevant and positive role to play in contributing toward the achievement of these aims of their co-operation."[35]

The basic premise of the Final Act is that these objectives are to be met equally by all states in all fields of endeavor. It establishes a balance among its provisions juxtaposing the *universal* rules contained in the Decalogue, *declarations of intent* (such as to encourage cooperation in the Mediterranean), and *recommendations* for unilateral action on issues in Baskets I, II, and III. As Ghebali notes, "the merit [of the Final Act] resides in the interdependence which unites rigorously all its components: the program of the CSCE forms an indivisible whole that requires parallel and even progress" (1989, 62). As we shall see, this fact permitted issue linkages, and in subsequent follow-up meetings it provided a means for the West to return to a review of implementation of CSCE principles and commitments, even when the negotiators had already moved on to consider other matters, such as new commitments.

Basket I of the Final Act enumerates a Decalogue of principles guiding relations between participating states and provisions to enhance security. The Decalogue is composed of Principle I, Sovereign Equality, and Respect for the Rights inherent in sovereignty; Principle II, Refraining from the threat or use of force; Principle III, Inviolability of frontiers; Principle IV, Territorial integrity of

34. See Principle IX of the Decalogue, § 2.
35. See ibid, § 3.

States; Principle V, Peaceful settlement of disputes; Principle VI, Nonintervention in internal affairs; Principle VII, Respect for human rights and fundamental freedoms, including the freedom of thought, conscience, religion or belief; Principle VIII, Equal rights and self-determination of peoples, Principle IX, Co-operation among States; and Principle X, Fulfillment in good faith of obligations under international law.

Basket II deals with cooperation on economic, scientific, and environmental issues; Basket III covers human-dimension issues on traditional civil and political rights, and also economic, social, cultural, and humanitarian rights (Bloed 1993b); and Basket IV concerns the follow-up to the CSCE. But the Final Act's "Principles Guiding Relations Between Participating States" provided the core of the CSCE rule making. This Decalogue established the overarching principles and commitments on which basis security and cooperation in Europe and among the participating states and people were to be achieved.

These provisions were throughout imbued with tensions, stemming from differences between the West's universal conceptions of international law and the East's doctrine of socialist internationalism. At stake was the area of applicability of the Final Act. For the East only the doctrine of socialist internationalism applied to relations between socialist states. The West sought a document of universal applicability regarding not only interstate relations but also the treatment of citizens by their state. Partly for these reasons, the West made clear it would not negotiate a peace treaty, much less a special European legal order. For its part, the Soviet Union sought to give the Decalogue legal force, but not the text of the third basket on human rights.

In the end, reaching consensus on the Final Act depended on compromises between the socialist camp's insistence on the primacy of nonintervention in internal affairs (Principle VI) and the West's emphasis on human rights and international cooperation. This was accomplished by means of the neutral package deal. Thus, Principle VI is balanced with Principle X, fulfillment in good faith of obligations under international law. It reads that "in exercising their sovereign rights, including the right to determine their laws and regulations, they will conform with their legal obligations under international law; they will furthermore pay due regard to and implement the provisions in the Final Act." It states further that "all the principles set forth above [i.e., all the ten principles] are of primary significance and, accordingly, they will be equally and unreservedly applied, each of them being interpreted taking into account the others." Hence the overall equality and interdependence of the Final Act's provisions.[36]

The human-rights provisions included in Basket III and Principle VII on Re-

36. *Conference on Security and Cooperation in Europe. Stage III—Final Act* (Lausanne, Switzerland: Imprimeries Réunies, S.A., 1975).

spect for Human Rights and Fundamental Freedoms were a principal means of challenging the Soviet defense based on Principle VI and also Principle I, which recognizes the "right of every State to juridical equality" and "each other's right freely to choose and develop its political, social, economic, and cultural system as well as its right to determine its laws and regulations." As Helgesen notes, Principle I established the equality between social systems. Although from the East's perspective the CSCE was not to become an arena for debates about these different systems, this is precisely what transpired (1990, 245).

Notably, the West and N+N built into the final agreement safeguards against the East's recourse to nonintervention in internal affairs (as was discussed above) in order to avoid the implementation of human-rights provisions. Similarly, Swedish intervention provided a compromise formula for language by which the West could safeguard their rights over Berlin under such international treaties as the Quadrapartite agreement, while also avoiding exclusionary language that might have been used by the Soviet Union to justify the Brezhnev Doctrine (Ghebali 1989, 80–81). The language is found in Principle X, "The participating States, paying due regard to the principles above and, in particular, to the first sentence of the tenth principle, 'Fulfillment in good faith of obligations under international law,' note that the present Declaration does not affect their rights and obligations, nor the corresponding treaties and other agreements and arrangements." It is important also to note that the first sentence establishes that these other obligations arising from treaties or other agreements refer to "treaties or other agreements, in conformity with international law, to which [the participating states] are parties." [37]

Despite these attempts to close loopholes, the Final Act contained partial solutions to many aspects of East-West conflict. From the West's perspective (including most of the N+N), the CBMs were weak and militarily insignificant and the human-rights provisions of the Final Act had serious shortcomings. Moreover, the CBMs were only a nominal step in view of the N+N's much broader aims. The nonaligned profile Yugoslavia brought to the negotiations and the UN perspective pushed by Sweden did not prevail; their efforts to inaugurate disarmament mechanisms in a regional European context, or to establish a mechanism between the CSCE and other fora dealing with arms control or disarmament, did not find their way to concrete results in the Final Act. Voluntary notification of military maneuvers (more than twenty-five thousand troops), as was finally agreed, was a minimal measure, of relevance at the most to training exercises, which in most countries would never reach these proportions. In contrast, the more realistic threat scenario stemmed from major military movements, but these remained outside the area of consensus in Geneva except for a general recommendation that they also be reported.

37. *Conference on Security and Cooperation in Europe. Stage III—Final Act.*

Among its limitations in other issue areas, the Final Act spoke of "freer" movement, not "free" movement and contacts for people individually and collectively. It is true that Basket III dealt in a detailed and innovative fashion with many issues relating to human rights that had never been the subject of diplomacy. Many of these issues (categorized under four sections on human contacts, information, culture, and education) dealt with sensitive questions between East-West (e.g. reunification of families, emigration, binational marriages, and working conditions for journalists). Other commitments aimed at the general improvement of relations between East and West, such as travel for personal or professional reasons and improvement of conditions for tourism. Still, many of these provisions were couched in language that did not connote a high level of commitment, i.e. "the participating states will examine favorably," "they will encourage," "contribute to," "examine jointly," "consider," etc. (Helgesen 1990, 249).

Conclusions

The road to the Helsinki Final Act took numerous twists and turns: the Soviets had agreed to the West's demands for MBFR on condition the West agree to convene the European Security Conference, which would formally recognize the division of Germany, and the post-World War II frontiers. The West sought to turn this bargain to its advantage by making recognition of the Soviet control of Eastern Europe conditional on acceptance of the free flow of information, free movement of individuals, and other Western, liberal human-rights standards.

The initial reaction of the Western press to the Final Act revealed considerable dissatisfaction with the results. With its lead editorial reading "Jerry Don't Go," the *Wall Street Journal* represented the view among the public at large that President Ford should not sign the Helsinki Final Act on the grounds the West sold out to the communist states' demands for recognition of the status quo in exchange for a weak commitment to uphold human rights. By conventional wisdom, the Final Act was little more than a piece of paper with no evidence of, or means to effect, real change. In the aftermath of the 1975 Helsinki Summit, it was not at all certain the West would remain committed to the further development of the CSCE, much less to the strengthening of its human-rights content.

As for the Russians, "the CSCE was a mixed blessing. It really left them only marginally more secure than before. They had failed to obtain Western recognition of the postwar frontiers of Europe as 'unalterable' even by peaceful change; inviolable was as far as NATO would go" (Haslam 1990, 72). Second, the prominence of human rights in the Final Act was disconcerting to the KGB and Central Committee members. According to former Soviet diplomat Shevchenko,

> in various meetings of senior Foreign Ministry officials during the years I served as Gromyko's adviser, I heard several colleagues as well as KGB and Central Committee participants in the discussions caution against the trend in East-West negotiations to expand beyond Soviet goals. Their warnings went unheeded. . . . Although few Westerners recognized the success their diplomats scored in the relatively unpublicized talks, the Final Act emerged as a notable advance for their ideas and a set back of sorts for the Soviet Union. (as quoted in Haslam 1990, 72)

While Brezhnev published the Final Act in the leading Soviet press to draw attention to his foreign-policy victory that secured post-World War II borders, it was Basket III that mattered to most people. Dissidents in the Soviet Union and throughout the Eastern bloc took inspiration from the Final Act's provisions on "the right of the individual to know and act upon his rights and duties" in the field of human rights and fundamental freedoms.[38] As Haslam notes (1990, 72), "only some of the more cynical KGB officials wryly noted that 'basket three' might have the beneficial side-effect of enhancing their own role in the scheme of things."

In the West it was totally unexpected that the Final Act would have so direct and immediate impact on the lives of human-rights activists. Yet the elevation of the individual, of human rights, of openness and transparency between social systems and within the state, and the establishment of international standards of political accountability and for human-rights abuses all constituted a fundamental challenge to the East. The West's philosophical rejection of the core premises of communism had found expression in a multilateral agreement to which the communist states had acceded. The devil was indeed in the details. Human rights and humanitarian issues were now squarely on the agenda of East-West relations.

38. Principle VII, the Final Act.

7 Putting Principles into Practice

THE COMPREHENSIVE NATURE of the Final Act set it apart from other international agreements, as did its broad conception of security and treatment of human rights in the context of other basic international principles guiding relations between states. In addition, in contrast to traditional human-rights instruments of a declaratory nature, the Final Act spelled out practical, specific, and detailed human-rights commitments, which proved of immediate relevance to dissidents in the Eastern bloc. Nevertheless, the Final Act contained significant ambiguities and escape clauses limiting its obligatory character. Agreement on the Final Act was reached through numerous compromises based on carefully crafted phrases, formulas, and package deals. Only institution-building processes could mitigate these limitations, but the Final Act also lacked specific instructions for the CSCE's development.

The West's attempts to make progress in East-West relations and improvements in security conditional on the enhancement of human-rights provisions helped drive the CSCE process forward, despite the participating states' initial lack of a clear commitment to its institutionalization. Through successive negotiating rounds from 1975 through the late 1980s, many loopholes were filled in, leading to the more effective functioning of the CSCE and to extending the CSCE's institutional competencies in terms of its standard setting, obligatory character, policy goals, compliance, and monitoring capabilities. For the West, which was generally supported by the N+N, it was a matter of putting principles into practice and then seeking to improve the results with more strident principles and newer, more intrusive, practices.

We examine these aspects of institution building throughout the postagreement negotiation processes in the cold war CSCE, which spanned the follow-up meetings in Belgrade (1977–78), Madrid (1980–83), and Vienna (1986–89), as well as numerous intersessional expert meetings. The culmination of these negotiations was the November 1990 summit meeting of CSCE heads of state and the signing of the Charter of Paris, signaling an end to the bloc-based divisions between East and West and the triumph of liberal democracies and market economics. This manifesto marked the end of the cold war.

Strengthening CSCE Commitments

The United States and its West European allies shared essentially two basic objectives regarding the post-Helsinki development of the CSCE. First, they sought to draw a connection between implementation and new commitments as a means of strengthening the credibility of CSCE commitments, and hence its rule effectiveness. Second, they sought to link agreement on new military-security measures to progress in the East on human rights (in terms of both implementation and new commitments). However, there were three different approaches within the West over where the balance should be struck between using the CSCE for monitoring versus achieving newer, more exacting, commitments.

For the United States, the review of implementation of human rights was to be the main task of the CSCE; the emergence of Helsinki monitors in the East raised the stakes of the follow-up process and also prompted the United States to engage in a diplomacy of public shaming. The new emphasis in U.S. policy on human rights was also in response to the pressures of a domestic constituency that included vocal East European emigré communities from "captive nations" and leaders of human-rights groups. However, this U.S. policy invited counterattacks from the Soviet bloc and thus contributed substantially to the polemicization of the CSCE process.

The 1980s were also marked by the rise of peace movements, for which the CSCE offered the Soviets a public platform and opportunity to issue appeals for a disarmament conference (Sizoo and Jurrjens 1984; Haslam 1990). Thus, there was a strong element of self-serving demagoguery (and propaganda) in the superpowers' interventions in the CSCE during the height of the second cold war.

West Germany, Denmark, Norway, Belgium, and Ireland, along with Sweden and Austria among the N+N, approached the follow-up as a means for expanding the CSCE role in "standard setting." This second group "favoured a step by step course on more exacting normative commitments on the human dimension" (Heraclides 1993, 9). The United States argued that setting new standards was inadvisable because it undermined the importance of compliance by substituting noncompliance with new commitments. However, the West Europeans maintained that more exacting standards strengthened previous commitments and did not undermine the review of implementation. A third group of countries took a position between these two approaches—less severe in criticizing the Eastern bloc's lack of compliance, but still supportive of the development of new, more exacting, commitments. This third group of countries included the United Kingdom, the Netherlands, Canada, and occasionally Italy, France, and among the N+N, Switzerland (Heraclides 1993, 8–9).

For the Soviets, the Helsinki Final Act was the high point of political détente. In any event, the Final Act had gone well beyond their initial political objectives. However, there remained many problems of military détente, and these were of increasing concern to the Soviets in the post-Helsinki period. By the late 1970s and early 1980s, the deterioration of the Soviet economy made domestic reform increasingly imperative, but this situation posed tradeoffs between guns and butter. Thus, under Soviet influence, finding ways to improve military détente was high on the agenda of the Warsaw Pact in the late 1970s and throughout the 1980s. The N+N shared similar positions on some disarmament ideas with the Warsaw Pact. However, the N+N also wanted more concrete CBMs, and in this regard their position was closer to the West. Overall the N+N role as intellectual entrepreneurs on military-security issues helped to establish the center of gravity in the negotiations on more practical measures for East-West security cooperation, rather than on the more general, declaratory measures the Soviets promoted.

Military-Security Dimension

The 1977 Belgrade meeting opened an important debate on expanding the military-security dimension of the Helsinki Final Act. This was the first opportunity to improve the military significance of the CBMs introduced in the Final Act. However, the results of the Belgrade CSCE Follow-up were disappointing. The United States rejected the Soviet's Basket I proposals (no first use of nuclear weapons, a freeze on military spending, and the creation of nuclear weapons-free zones) as propagandistic. As had been the case in Geneva, the N+N continued to work for the establishment of a mechanism for expert meetings, the treatment of Mediterranean issues, and the introduction of militarily significant measures on European security. To promote the CBM concept, the N+N produced joint proposals reintroducing many of their Geneva proposals, including the extension of CBMs to cover air and sea forces. The N+N proposal also coincided with a West European proposal (submitted on behalf of Great Britain, The Netherlands, Norway, and Canada) to lower notification from the rather high figure of twenty-five thousand to include maneuvers above ten thousand troops and to extend the CBM regime to cover major military movements.[1] Sweden also proposed (as it had in Geneva) that all participants publish their defense budgets. Although the proposal had practically no prospect of meeting Eastern bloc acceptance, Sweden took the view that it was imperative to establish a basis of common information so that disarmament efforts could proceed in a realistic and informed fashion.[2]

1. "Proposal Submitted by the Delegations of Canada, Great Britain, The Netherlands and Norway, Confidence Building Measures," CSCE/BM/11 Belgrade, Nov. 2, 1977.

2. "Puolueettomilta uusi ehdotus: Suurista joukkojen siirroista ilmoitettava," *Helsingin Sanomat,* Oct. 29, 1977, UILA.

Both Sweden and Yugoslavia, especially the latter, worked hard on the military-security measures at Belgrade and presented extensive drafts for measures that they believed the Soviets and the East could have accepted without problems. The Americans might have accepted this, too, at the end, but U.S. Ambassador Arthur Goldberg (on behalf of President Carter, it was understood), would accept the military measures only if the Soviets conceded on human rights. Because this possibility was out for them, the CBMs were out for the Americans, and as a result, for the N+N, too.[3] Indeed, the East would not consider any new human-rights commitments, nor accept any final document that took account of the implementation debate. Thus the primary accomplishment of the Belgrade meeting was to delineate the operating methods for the follow-up meetings and parameters for continuing the CSCE process. Nevertheless, this was a significant result given the limited operational provisions of the Final Act for securing the continuity of the CSCE (see chapter 8).

The Belgrade meeting set a date and place for the next follow-up meeting to convene in Madrid in November 1980. The prospect of a new round of CSCE negotiations encouraged the participating states to remain focused on the main issues dividing them and continue to search for potential solutions. However, soon after the Belgrade meeting ended, dark clouds gathered on the horizon of East-West security negotiations. The U.S. commitment to its allies to keep American forward-based systems (FBS) out of bilateral arms-control negotiations exacerbated differences in the SALT II negotiations with the Russians, who had already tried to include these systems in SALT I and MBFR. To get an agreement on an equal aggregate level of launchers, including heavy bombers, and an equal subceiling on MIRVed missiles, Brezhnev was forced again to drop the issue of forward-based systems. In the face of strong opposition from his own military (who considered the U.S. FBS a significant threat), Brezhnev had to find compensation elsewhere and this included his decision to test the SS-20 (Haslam 1990, 57). With the SALT I interim agreement expiring October 1977 and expectations for SALT II negotiations to be concluded by then, the Soviets would need test results of the SS-20 in order to gain credible bargaining leverage (Haslam 1990, 59–60).

The years 1977 and 1978 proved a turning point in East-West relations. The change of administration in the United States introduced new difficulties in both the superpower relationship and the conclusion of a SALT II treaty, as well as in U.S.-West European relations. The new U.S. president Jimmy Carter offered the Soviets entirely new parameters for a SALT II treaty, aiming at significant reductions in strategic weapons on both sides. He personally preferred

3. Swedish official, interview by author, tape recording, Office of the Prime Minister, Stockholm, May 27, 1988.

strict controls or limits on new generations of weaponry, but backed away from the formula for counting air-to-surface cruise missiles, which the Ford administration had agreed at Vladivostok. Characteristic lack of adequate consultations with West European allies on the U.S. negotiating position, appearances of incompetence over the Carter approach to SALT II, and proposals from Cyrus Vance to Andrei Gromyko to ban the deployment of ground—and sea-launched cruise missiles (so-called GLCMs and SLCMs) aroused a strong and negative reaction from the West European allies. In addition, the West Germans were "infuriated because [Carter's] sermons on the observance of human rights in Eastern Europe jeopardised the arrangements following from the CSCE for the emigration of Germans from Russian, Polish, Romanian and East German territory" (Haslam 1990, x). It was in the context of these intra-alliance tensions and West German calls for the deployment of long-range GLCMS and SLCMS that the Soviet Union began to deploy the SS-20.

The Soviets thereby set in motion a process that would come to undermine their own security interests. They underestimated the extent to which this deployment would trigger the growth of hostility in Western Europe against Moscow. The "Americocentrism" that characterized Soviet foreign policy under Gromyko throughout the SALT years diminished their sensitivity to West European anxieties about the overkill the Soviet military capability represented on the continent. Indeed, as Haslam writes, "[the Russians] took détente with Western Europe for granted." By deploying the SS-20, they "liquidated Western Europe as a critical factor moderating the increasing assertiveness of the hawks in U.S. foreign policy making, [and] they also unwittingly drove the West Europeans into the anti-Soviet camp at a crucial moment" (1990, 93–94).

The stage was set for a seemingly intractable policy dilemma: the Soviets had no reason not to deploy the SS-20s; the West had no reason to negotiate as long as they saw the balance tilting in the favor of the Soviets. This dilemma led to NATO's so-called Track Two decision: (1) the need for the modernization of NATO long-range theater nuclear forces to close the disparity in theater nuclear forces brought about by the Soviets' introduction of the SS-20 and the Backfire bomber, and (2) the need for arms control to be pursued in parallel. The possibilities for resolving the crisis along the second of the two tracks was diminished with the election of Ronald Reagan to the U.S. presidency. He set out the rebuilding of Western military power as a precondition to any negotiations. With some pressure from West Germany and Italy, along with a growing peace movement in Western Europe, Reagan finally conceded to open negotiations with the Soviets on intermediate nuclear forces in November 1981. The U.S. position, which had been worked out among NATO allies, called for the "zero option"—that is, a commitment from the United States to cancel deployment of the Pershing II and the Cruise missile if the Soviets would dismantle their SS-20, SS-4, and SS-5 missiles, and agree to on-site inspection. The U.S. position was based less on a real commitment to negotiate than the expectation that these parameters would never be acceptable to the Soviets. When NATO proceeded as scheduled to deploy the Cruise and Pershing-II missiles in November 1983, the Soviets broke off not only Intermediate Nuclear Force Reduction (INF) talks but also Strategic Arms Reduction Talks (START) and MBFR. As a consequence, the only fora that remained for East-West dialogue was the Stockholm Conference on Disarmament in Europe (CDE), for which the CSCE participating states were convened in Helsinki at the time to prepare an agenda and procedural matters. As it turned out, they managed to push through this agreement just as all the other doors were closing.

The idea for a CDE originated with the French in 1978. Along with expectations that a SALT II treaty would put superpower relations on a new footing and improve the prospects for more meaningful disarmament measures, the opening of the first UN Special Session on Disarmament (UNSSOD) in New York in May 1978 also kept disarmament at the center of international attention. In contrast to the complete lack of initiative by the Carter administration,[4] the French used the occasion to announce a major departure from the Gaullist and Pompidou policies, which since the early 1960s had resulted in an "empty chair" approach to disarmament in the UN. Among other initiatives, French president Valéry Giscard d'Estaing presented a French proposal for a European disarmament conference to be convened among the thirty-five CSCE participating states, but outside the CSCE. This initiative emerged from an ongoing policy reevaluation, prompted in part by the upcoming French presidential elections and by the official acceptance of nuclear weapons by the Socialist Party in January 1978 (Howorth 1984, 582–83).[5] The forum would be charged with negotiations on the reduction of weapons on the European continent from the Atlantic to the Urals.[6]

Although the French intended the CDE to be independent of the CSCE process, it was decided in NATO and the EC to bring the CDE into the CSCE process and negotiate a mandate for it at the 1982 Madrid Follow-up. The alliance proposal, reflecting the original French conception, consisted of a two-phased process. The first phase, the mandate for which was to be negotiated in

4. The United States was the only major country (except China) that neglected to submit an advance policy paper to the Disarmament Preparatory Committee (Geyer 1982, 120).

5. See "French Proposals for the Special Session of the General Assembly Devoted to Disarmament, February 23, 1978," reproduced in United States Arms Control and Disarmament Agency, *Documents on Disarmament 1978* (Washington, D.C.: Government Printing Office, 1980), 95–98.

6. See Kathleen Teltsch, "Giscard, at UN, Asks Arms Monitoring by Satellite," *New York Times*, May 26, 1978, A3. On the French approach to these issues of East-West security in the context of preparations for the Madrid Follow-up, see Borawski (1988, 19–25).

Madrid, would focus on extending the CBMs to a confidence and security building (CSBM) regime (Borawski 1988, 19–25). The mandate for a second phase, which would potentially deal with arms reductions, would be determined in a future follow-up meeting in light of the results of the first phase.

The French initiative was received by the N+N as a promising development. In turn, the N+N stepped up their preparations to advance this aspect of the CSCE. Under Swedish initiative, the N+N countries began to meet to work out a common approach to security issues. In Stockholm at the general ambassadorial level, complete, would-be Madrid delegations met, with Sweden taking a leading role as an intellectual entrepreneur. After a restructuring in its foreign ministry, Sweden sought to bring its long-standing expertise on disarmament issues in the UN context to bear now on the developments in Europe. In addition to ordinary N+N meetings, subgroups also met. CBMs were initially the sole focus of discussion. Bilateral talks were also built into a national Swedish study group, starting with Finnish officials in December 1979. Experts on the CBM regime took part in meetings at various capitals, including Stockholm, Helsinki, Vienna, and Zurich. The aim was to achieve N+N acceptance of the Swedish CBM concepts.

In the meantime, Sweden also brought up its own CDE idea in an effort to build a common N+N position. Later on there arose an element of intellectual and political competition in Sweden with the line of thought on the CBM work on the one hand, and the new CDE concept on the other. This national Swedish debate was also carried to the N+N circles. After much turmoil during 1980, two different proposals were prepared for Madrid: a joint N+N CBM proposal, RM. 21; and a national, Swedish CDE proposal, RM. 34.

The first of these two proposals, RM. 21, dealt with concrete measures for improving the CBM regime, much as the N+N had tried out in Belgrade. The N+N introduced this proposal with the intention that its measures would be considered for immediate adoption on the basis of the Madrid concluding document, even as a mandate for a subsequent CDE would lead to negotiations on additional measures for implementation at a later stage. For its part, the Swedish CDE proposal also took account of the two-phase approach characteristic of the Western alliance position, which had evolved on the basis of the French proposal. However, the Swedish CDE proposal contained the explicit objective of a second phase entailing arms limitation and reduction agreements that covered conventional and nuclear weapons. This feature distinguished the Swedish proposal from the Western and Soviet bloc proposals. Sweden also secured the Nordic foreign ministers' endorsement for Stockholm to be the host site for a European disarmament conference.[7]

7. "Pohjoismaiden ulkoministerikokouksen tiedonanto Helsinginssä 27.-28. 3. 1980," ULA 1980, 35; and "Pohjoismaiden ulkoministerikokouksen tiedonanto Oslossa 1–2. 9. 1980," ULA 1980, 44.

Although it underwent some changes in an N+N meeting just before the Madrid meeting opened, the CBM proposal was mostly finalized at a neutral and nonaligned meeting in Liechtenstein at the change of the month between April and May of 1980.[8] The Liechtenstein meeting attracted Soviet attention. After the invasion of Afghanistan, the Soviets had been quiet about their response to the original French CDE proposal but were anxious to regain the initiative; to this end they invited a Swedish delegation headed by Ambassador Rappe to Moscow. They knew this was the last opportunity to contact an N+N country before the latter's Liechtenstein meeting to decide on a joint course of action for the Madrid Follow-up. "The Soviets concretely proposed to the Swedish representatives that they bless, and bring to the N+N the idea that there should be a preparatory meeting to the main Madrid Meeting besides the ordinary procedural, agenda-building preparatory meeting."[9] The Soviet objective was to set up a (parallel) expert meeting to decide on all the details of a Conference on Military Détente and Disarmament in Europe, which they had proposed at the Warsaw Pact's foreign ministers' meeting in Budapest on May 15, 1979 (Borawski 1988, 24–25). The Swedes found it "very interesting to see the way the Soviets felt that maybe through and by means of neutral and nonaligned assistance that idea could be espoused and a means [obtained] by which to regain the initiative." It was of substantial political significance at the time, but the N+N would not support the idea of a parallel discussion on a CDE, and so that part of the Soviet initiative simply fell.[10]

As the opening of the Madrid preparatory meeting neared, Sweden gave more and more emphasis to the question of a CDE—a different and broader approach that landed a national Swedish proposal when N+N negotiations on a joint CDE proposal failed. Although there were many consultations on the CDE at a high level, at the last stage of efforts to achieve a joint N+N position on it "even the Finns refrained from joining."[11] Tactically, the establishment of a CDE leading to a process that emphasized results only in the CSCE field of security would disrupt the balance among the baskets, thereby risking what could be achieved in Basket III. For Finland, the matter could be reduced to this principle.[12] With East-West bipolarization in evidence at Madrid, Finland's assessment of the N+N making rapid progress in conventional disarmament in the CSCE was also more cautious than the Swedish approach.[13] Yugoslavia had its

8. Swedish official, interview by author, tape recording, Office of the Prime Minister, Stockholm, May 26, 1988.

9. Swedish official, interview by author, tape recording, Riksdag, Stockholm, May 26, 1988.

10. Ibid.

11. Swedish official, interview by author, tape recording, Stockholm, May 26, 1988.

12. Ibid.

13. Finnish official, interview by author, written notes, Minneapolis, Minn., May 11, 1990.

own disarmament proposal, RM. 27, calling for military restraints. Although Yugoslavia was anxious that Sweden and the N+N should present a broad disarmament program that included the Mediterranean area, Sweden found it necessary not to come in too close to the Yugoslavian position. From the very start, the Swiss were hesitant about the idea of having an N+N proposal because they did not want to undermine in any way the Western CDE proposal. These differences generally characterized the extremes within the N+N: the Swiss tendency not to want to compromise the West's position, and, on the other side, the activist Yugoslavs, who behaved politically like a nonaligned country. While the Yugoslavs wanted to maintain their own profile in the disarmament question, they would have been prepared to cooperate bilaterally with Sweden on disarmament issues.[14]

Without the backing of the N+N and without support from any other N+N country, Sweden found that its proposal on the CDE was only a national proposal and as a result raised little interest in the Madrid negotiations. In addition to the demand the East-West confrontation and polemics created for N+N third-party intervention, the lack of a common N+N position on a CDE also circumscribed both Sweden's and the nonbloc states' role as intellectual entrepreneurs. The Swedish national proposal was outside the realm of debate in Madrid also for real political reasons—not the least because it pushed for disarmament and discussions that would have brought bilateral superpower negotiations on nuclear arms and other arms reduction fora under the CSCE. Thus, the Swedish interest in the CDE became focused first on coordinating the negotiations in the special working body dealing with the mandate for such a conference[15] and second on obtaining agreement on Stockholm as the host site for the conference.

Breakthrough on On-site Inspection

The West's position at Madrid on the development of a mandate for the CDE was premised on improving the shortcomings of the Helsinki CBMs, including in the area of compliance. During the review of implementation, the West acknowledged that the minimum Helsinki CBMs were generally adhered to by all the CSCE participating states, but "contrasted their willingness to observe discretionary CBM provisions, particularly the prior notification of smaller maneuvers, with the Eastern refusal to reciprocate."[16] Whereas NATO and N+N

14. Swedish official, interview by author, tape recording, Stockholm, May 26, 1988.

15. Sweden's intention to facilitate procedural matters while holding onto its substantive objectives led to a debate with Finland over the advisability of the approach, given Sweden's strong national stand on the issue.

16. The staff of the Commission on Security and Cooperation in Europe, "The Madrid CSCE Review Meeting: An Interim Report," Jan. 6, 1981, 14.

states notified of all major and most minor military maneuvers, the Warsaw Pact countries did not notify of all major maneuvers and notified only a small number of minor maneuvers. Similarly, the NATO and N+N countries "invited observers from all CSCE states to 89 and 70 percent of their large military exercises respectively, [but] the [Warsaw Pact] invited observers to only 30 percent of these activities, and those observers who were invited mostly came from neighbouring countries. Between 1979 and 1985, for instance, no western observers were invited to notified manouevres in the Soviet Union" (Efinger and Rittberger 1991, 106). In fact, the Polish crisis that led to the declaration of martial law in December 1981 was a backdrop to the whole Madrid conference and resulted in the first direct violations of the Helsinki Final Act's CBMs. The large-scale exercises held by the Soviets in the Belorussian and Baltic military districts on August 14 and on the Baltic Sea September 4–12, 1981, were not reported, and at least two other Eastern exercises (Soyuz 1981 and Shchit 1982) similarly went unnotified (Borawski 1988, 29).

In light of the problems with implementation that had been identified in the Madrid review, the United States and NATO stressed the need for a new generation of measures to contribute to the building of confidence and security between the blocs. Hence, CBMs were renamed Confidence and Security Building Measures and were to be mandatory—as well as militarily significant, verifiable, and applicable to all of Europe.[17] Military significance meant that the measures should promote openness about the size, structure, and activities of military forces; establish standards and patterns of routine military activities so that deviations from the agreed measures would be identifiable; act as constraints on the show or use of force for political intimidation; make adherence to CSBMs difficult while preparing for aggression; enhance decision making through increased information; and facilitate timely responses to warnings while preserving training action (Borawski 1988, 23).

By agreeing to the so-called functional approach to the applicability of measures related to military activity carried out in adjoining sea area and air space, NATO succeeded in gaining Soviet acquiescence to extending the geographical application to include European Russia through the Ural mountains.[18] According to this functional approach, the Madrid Concluding Document laid out the parameters for an improved regime on the Helsinki CBMs and a mandate for negotiating it at the Stockholm Conference on Disarmament in Europe to open January 17, 1984—the first of a two-phase conference negotiation on disarmament under the CSCE.

17. Ibid.

18. In the Madrid mandate for the Stockholm CDE, this geographical zone of application is referred to as covering "the whole of Europe as well as the adjoining sea area and air space." See also Borawski (1988, 27–28).

Nevertheless, when the Soviets broke off the INF negotiations in Geneva and the MBFR in Vienna in response to NATO's deployment of Cruise and Pershing-II missiles, prospects dimmed for convening the Stockholm Conference. Although the Soviets came to the 1983 Helsinki preparatory meeting willing in the long run to accept the Madrid mandate in terms of both its political and "military-technical" provisions (the East's term for the NATO-type measures), it took two rounds of neutral compromise proposals (first by the Swedes and Finns, and then by the Austrians) to produce a text acceptable to both the Soviets and the West. However, on last-minute instructions from Gromyko, Soviet head of delegation, Ambassador Oleg Grinevsky came to the opening of the CDE in Stockholm with a mandate to negotiate only on the basis of the political aspects of the Madrid mandate—he was to forget the military-technical aspects. In response to his suggestion that it would be better not to negotiate than to initiate the Stockholm Conference on this basis, Gromyko told Grinevsky that "Stockholm is the only light at the end of the tunnel. It is your task to keep this light burning." [19]

Thus, Grinevsky had the unenviable task as a diplomat to obstruct any concrete progress in the negotiations but prevent them from breaking down completely. The West's efforts to improve both the military significance of the Helsinki CBMs (which were modest and mostly voluntary, militarily insignificant, and only politically—not legally—binding) and the means of achieving compliance with them met up with obduracy from the Eastern bloc. Instead of addressing NATO's CSBM proposal, the Warsaw Pact attacked the U.S. deployment of intermediate nuclear forces. It was only in May 1984 that Grinevsky introduced the Soviet position that Gromyko had outlined in his opening address to the CDE in January. The proposal included a preamble "condemning 'the continuing deployment of new U.S. Missiles' as undermining universal confidence and security" (Borawski 1988, 45) and called for some improvements in the Helsinki Final Act's notification and observation provisions, as well as a numerical ceiling on the scale of ground-force exercises. However, its main thrust was to call for the no first use of nuclear weapons, nonuse of force generally in Europe, a freeze and subsequent reduction in military spending, nuclear-free zones, a ban on chemical weapons, and the renegotiation of the Madrid mandate for the zone of CSBM application. In effect, the Soviets sought a treaty result covering nonuse of force including chemical and nuclear forces, and also antisatellite and space-weapons systems. Although these proposals could be considered outside the Madrid Mandate, as Polish CSCE delegate Adam Rotfeld explained, the Madrid Mandate did not specify the concrete content of confidence-building measures. Thus, " 'any undertaking which

19. Ambassador Oleg Grinevsky, interview by author, tape recording, Embassy of the Russian Federation, Stockholm, Dec. 20, 1994.

can contribute to the removal of existing fears and distrust and correspond to accepted criteria is appropriate for consideration' " (as quoted in Borawski 1988, 47).

After encouraging an early Swedish initiative to move the negotiations beyond the general debate (which was highly polemical) and into working groups in May 1984, Grinevsky received orders from Gromyko now signaling his opposition. Thus, the negotiations remained stalemated through December 1985 at the level of general debate, while Grinevsky endeavored to keep them going without entering into substance on a mandate for any military-technical measures.[20] This situation did not change until Gorbachev began his general reorientation of Soviet foreign policy in late 1985 and early 1986.

During their Christmas vacation in Moscow, Gorbachev called on the Soviet Stockholm delegation to meet with him *one by one* to learn of the possibilities for an agreement and what was necessary to achieve it. Grinevsky argued for parallel discussions on technical and political matters in order for the first time to have common ground on which to proceed in the negotiations. When called a few days later by Gorbachev to report on their conversations to the Politburo, Grinevsky emphasized that the Stockholm CSBM negotiations were the least sensitive of all the arms-control talks, and thus were the best beginning for the Soviets to open doors to other negotiating fora. He argued in favor of accepting on-site inspection—a move that would be sure to result in a Stockholm agreement. Moreover, "on-site inspection would not harm Soviet security," he claimed, "if we are not planning to attack the West. But if we have concerns about U.S. and NATO intentions to invade Russia and the Soviet Union, then this would give us an opportunity to examine in advance their preparations." Among those most strongly against the proposal in the Politburo was Marshal Sergei Akhromeyev, who, turning emotional, accused Grinevsky of state treason and argued that such provisions would be politically impossible. On this point Gorbachev intervened. While acknowledging Akhromeyev's role in advising on security issues, he assured him "political problems are my business to decide." Thus Grinevsky knew he had Gorbachev's support. The major concession was signaled to the West during François Mitterand's visit to Moscow on July 8–9 for discussions with Gorbachev, and announced in principle (although somewhat ambiguously) by Ambassador Grinevsky in Stockholm on July 19 (Borawski 1988, 91). However, to signal the Soviet resolve, it was

20. According to one interpretation, in spite of the failure of an extensive Soviet effort to mobilize the Western peace movements against the Cruise and Pershing-2 to forestall their deployment, the Soviets still apparently expected that unilateral action would ensue as a consequence of the general improvement in the political climate in Europe. They could obtain political détente without any specific military commitments. Swedish official, interview by author, tape recording, National Defense Research Institute, Stockholm, May 17, 1988.

decided that Marshal Akhromeyev, chief of general staff, should introduce in Stockholm the Soviet proposal for air inspection, which the West deemed the most significant of the options for an inspection regime.[21]

Surprisingly, these turnabouts in Soviet policies permitted *more*—not less—substance to be agreed during the "end game" of the negotiations. Thus, the process of reaching a final agreement was characterized by adding more substance, or "compromising up." This meant that the N+N were not needed as third parties to sort out differences and shape a consensus on what was left. However, their joint proposals (SC. 3 and SC. 7) had already served a bridge-building function earlier in the negotiations by establishing the "center of gravity of the substance" of the Stockholm document. In effect, by not supporting the Soviets' declaratory approach, the N+N diminished this aspect of the Soviet strategy (see also Goodby 1987).[22]

However, the superpowers briefly entertained a Swiss and Austrian proposal that neutrals provide air support as a means of carrying out on-site inspection; this was the first time the neutrals offered to formally guarantee the implementation of a CSCE agreement. After having accepted conditionally, the Soviets then balked at the neutrals' suggestion. In the end, the United States agreed to host country air support (rather than national air support as it preferred) in order not to risk bringing the whole agreement apart on this last sticking point.[23] Thus, the Stockholm Conference was also the only CSCE meeting during the cold war where N+N third-party services were not vital in the final round for getting an agreement.[24]

Stockholm CSBM Regime

The Stockholm document was set in the context of Principle II of the Final Act, refraining from the threat or use of force, and established requirements for (1) the prior notification of certain military activities, (2) constraining provisions,

21. Grinevsky had raised the matter with Shevardnadze, who promised to speak to Gorbachev. Having been accused of state treason for proposing on-site inspection, it was a source of satisfaction to Grinevsky that Akhromeyev would "swallow his own words." Ambassador Oleg Grinevsky, interview by author, tape recording, Embassy of the Russian Federation, Stockholm, Dec. 20, 1994.

22. Swedish official, interview by author, tape recording, Stockholm, May 25, 1988; Swedish official, interview by author, tape recording, Foreign Ministry, Stockholm, May 20, 1988; and Swedish official, interview by author, tape recording, National Defense Research Institute, Stockholm, May 17, 1988.

23. Swedish official, interview by author, tape recording, National Defense Research Institute, Stockholm, May 17, 1988; Finnish official, interview by author, tape recording, Ministry of Defense, Helsinki, Apr. 20, 1988. See also Borawski (1988, 98).

24. Swedish official, interview by author, tape recording, National Defense Research Institute, Stockholm, May 17, 1988.

and (3) compliance and verification procedures. First, it required notification to all participating states forty-two days or more in advance of the start of notifiable activities[25] wherever this involved at least thirteen thousand troops and three hundred battle tanks (the Helsinki CBMs threshold was twenty-five thousand troops and was only applicable to a 150-mile zone of Western Russia). Second, and significantly, whenever troops exceeded seventeen thousand, the activities were subject to observation, and at the time of notification the host state was under the obligation to invite all CSCE participating states to attend. Moreover, the Stockholm document provided detailed specifications for arranging the inspection. As part of the compliance and verification regime, inspections could be demanded by any CSCE participating state that had doubts about compliance, although no state needed to accept more than three inspections per calendar year and more than one inspection per calendar year from the same participating state. In this case, it was agreed the host state would provide transportation, including aircraft, for the inspection.

The Stockholm Conference CSBMs substantially improved the CSCE security regime, with strengthened norms and accompanying rules of procedure, including the specification of the rights and duties of the participating states to (1) notify military activities that may have threatening effects on other states, (2) exchange observers and agree to on-site inspections, (3) not engage in large military activities close to borders, and (4) refrain from the threat or use of force—an elaboration of the corresponding principle of the Final Act. As Efinger and Rittberger note, these "norms [were] intended to enhance the transparency and calculability of the overall military situation in Europe and thus to strengthen confidence and reduce threat perceptions among the CDE states" (1991, 109). Explicit rules of procedure corresponded to each of these norms, including provisions for a review of implementation as part of the overall policy-making system within the CSCE follow-up process. Accordingly, in Annex III to the Stockholm Agreement it was stipulated that each participating state has the right "to raise any question consistent with the mandate of the Conference on Confidence and Security-Building Measures and Disarmament in Europe at any stage subsequent to the Vienna CSCE Follow-up Meeting." Significantly, no major problems with adherence to these stronger CSBM measures were found, and moreover, "no questionable practices or outright breaches of agreed CSBM provisions were discovered by any party as a result of these inspections" (Efinger and Rittberger 1991, 109).[26]

25. As Borawski (1988, 78) tells us, this was "not just coincidentally twice the Final Act CBM period."

26. See Efinger and Rittberger (1991, 111) for a summary assessment of notification for the period 1987–90.

From the outset of the post-World War II period, the Soviets had resisted efforts by the West to use on-site inspections as a means to move toward disarmament of atomic weapons. The Soviets insisted Western disarmament precede an inspection regime. For the West on-site inspection was a precondition to disarmament. In fact, Gromyko had described an inspection regime such as the Baruch plans for atomic disarmament after World War II as a menace to national sovereignty. The Stockholm CSBMs, however, paved the way for the 1987 Treaty on Intermediate Nuclear Forces (INF) between the United States and the Soviet Union—the first such agreement to use an intrusive on-site inspection regime as a means to verify the dismantling of intermediate-range nuclear weapons. Moreover, the Stockholm CSBMs also had an impact on Basket III negotiations, laying the groundwork for an intrusive CSCE regime to monitor compliance in the human dimension.

In accordance with the Madrid mandate, the progress achieved in the Stockholm CDE was to be assessed at the 1986 Vienna Follow-up conference to consider how to approach the next stage of the CDE. Gorbachev's initiative of June 1986, a new "Budapest Appeal" issued by the Warsaw Pact, proposed bringing the MBFR negotiations under the auspices of the CSCE. In 1989, NATO and the Warsaw Pact agreed to establish the negotiations on Conventional Forces in Europe (CFE) as legally binding, including only the members of the military alliances but set within the overall framework of the CSCE, and with provisions for informing the nonbloc states of the developments. At the same time, the Vienna Follow-up set out a mandate for an expanded CSBM regime. The Treaty on Conventional Armed Forces in Europe, the second CSBM regime, and the Declaration of Twenty-Two States—a statement of friendly relations among NATO and Warsaw Pact countries—were adopted along with the CSCE Charter of Paris at the November 1990 summit meeting of CSCE heads of state.

Human Dimension

Remarkably, the 1975 Helsinki Final Act was widely disseminated in the Eastern bloc. The Soviets reproduced it in such presses as *Pravda* and *Izvestia*, declaring it a foreign-policy victory. While Soviet officials stressed in public statements and authoritative commentaries that the inviolability of frontiers was the most important of the ten principles of interstate relations,[27] citizens of

27. Stressing the importance of Principle III over the other principles was a violation of the obligation to hold all principles of the Final Act of "primary significance," to be "equally and unreservedly applied." Moreover, the Soviets followed this pattern in the Soviet-GDR treaty of Oct. 7, 1975, and also "described the GDR's borders as immutable"—Soviet terminology which had been

the USSR and elsewhere in the Eastern bloc learned of their rights of emigration, religious association, and of their "human rights and fundamental freedoms." In contrast to the Universal Declaration on Human Rights, the language of the Final Act was specific and unambiguous. It applied equally to each state, and each was obligated to adhere to its principles and put them in practice in their relations with all other participating states "*irrespective of their political, economic or social systems*" (emphasis added).[28]

As Kirk Laux notes, the Final Act "called for specific changes in practice rather than claiming universal and thus somewhat theoretical applicability" (1984, 261). Because the Helsinki Final Act was a political agreement, not a treaty with legally binding commitments, the domestic postagreement processes did not present the typical ratification requirements. There was no need for the usual domestic bargaining among governmental agencies, political leaders, parties, lobbyists, or other interest groups with a stake in bringing the agreement into force (cf. Spector and Zartman 2003). Nevertheless, the Helsinki Accords had an impact on domestic society in Eastern Europe and eventually on the socialist regimes themselves. By "confirming the right of the individual to know and act upon his rights and duties" in the area of human rights,[29] the Final Act provided a legitimizing framework around which groups throughout the Eastern bloc could mobilize and monitor their government's compliance and submit systematic reports of violations both to their own government and to the governments of other participating states (Thomas 1991; Chilton 1995).

There were at least four kinds of groups in East European societies that reacted positively to the Helsinki Final Act. The most visible were the leading intellectuals. However, they represented concerns more widely held among the new socialist middle class of professionals, the religious believers, ethnic minorities, and university students (Mastny 1986, 143–52). In May 1976, Yuri Orlov and ten others founded the first Helsinki monitoring group, the Public

---

specifically rejected in Helsinki in favor of inviolability. *First Semiannual Report by the President to the Commission on Security and Cooperation in Europe*. Dec. 1976, p. 16.

28. Preamble to the Decalogue § 5. See *Conference on Security and Cooperation in Europe. Stage III—Final Act.*

29. Principle VII § 7. The primary focus on implementation was in regard to Eastern bloc compliance. The Western liberal democracies generally took the position that their political and legal systems and foreign-policy doctrine and practices were already in compliance. Nevertheless, it is interesting to note that the Final Act was never widely disseminated in the West, as stipulated in the Final Act. See *Conference on Security and Cooperation in Europe. Stage III—Final Act.* Kirk Laux (1984) notes that some Western states like Canada, Great Britain, and Spain had to deal with separatists movements, and it was therefore in their own interest to limit awareness of the Final Act, particularly given its inclusion of the principle of self-determination.

Group to Promote Observance of the Helsinki Agreement in the USSR,[30] an action followed by the emergence of groups in the Ukraine, Lithuania, Armenia, and Georgia. Eastern European opposition formed primarily in Poland and Czechoslovakia. Of these, Charter 77 received the most widespread recognition (Kirk Laux 1984, 262). Pointing to the human rights and freedoms underwritten in international covenants, confirmed again in the Helsinki Final Act in 1975, and brought into force in Czechoslovakia on March 23, 1976, Charter 77 signatories declared that "our citizens have the right, and our state the duty, to abide by them" (Skilling 1981, 209).[31] Charter 77 pursued constructive dialogue with the political and state authorities and sought to draw the attention of their own states, other monitoring groups, and dissidents in the Eastern bloc, as well as peace activists, monitoring groups, and governments in the West to individual cases of human and civil-rights violations. They prepared documentation and suggested solutions, drawing up proposals and appeals to reinforce their rights and guarantees.

Helsinki monitoring groups met with state repression and were declared illegal throughout the Eastern bloc based on a misrepresentation of the Final Act and often flagrant violation of the domestic laws.[32] The Czech authorities' justification for repression of the Charter 77 dissidents illustrates the type of argument to which governments in the East took recourse. As reported in the Czechoslovak News Agency, even if there are constitutional guarantees for the "right to freedom of expression in all spheres of life of society," and constitutional rights for citizens to submit proposals, suggestions, or complaints to their representatives and states bodies, these rights had to be exercised according to the "interest of the working people." Charter 77 signatories were branded antisocialist, and their efforts were characterized as a "hypocritical pretext of the defence of human rights" to "intentionally and grossly falsify the truth about life and the real situation in Czechoslovakia, and hatefully defame our state and social system and its organs." In contravention of the Czechoslovak authorities' obligation to treat all CSCE principles with equal consideration, the Charter 77 activities were deemed "in direct conflict with the interests of the working people, with Czechoslovak laws and with the principles of the Final Act of the Helsinki Conference, which also stresses the principles of noninterference in the

30. *First Semiannual Report by the President to the Commission on Security and Cooperation in Europe*. Dec. 1976, 16 n. 28.

31. Charter 77 took its name from the year of its founding, proclaimed the Year of Political Prisoners by Amnesty International; it was also the year in which the Belgrade conference was due to review the implementation of the obligations assumed at Helsinki (Skilling 1981, 212).

32. See also "Soviet Law and the Helsinki Monitors." *Hearing Before the Commission on Security and Cooperation in Europe. Ninety-Fifth Congress, Second Session on Implementation of the Helsinki Accords*, vol. VI, June 6, 1978.

internal affairs of individual states and respect for the laws of each country" (as quoted in Skilling 1981, 212–13).

The monitoring and advocacy activities of Eastern bloc human-rights groups were enhanced through the transnational linkages with human-rights and peace groups in the West and the creation of more formal monitoring agencies, such as the U.S. Commission on Security and Cooperation, or the Council of Europe's subcommission on the CSCE. However, there was never any formal organizational structure connecting the various monitoring groups and peace movements between East and West. Moreover, the Western peace movements were more focused on disarmament than on human rights, which was central to the platforms of more conservative parties (Weaver, Lemaitre, and Tromer 1989).

Nevertheless, groups like END (European Nuclear Disarmament) were lobbied by dissident movements in the East, such as Charter 77, to include in their agenda the right of East European citizens to fundamental rights and freedoms (Chilton 1995, 200).[33] As Chilton notes, "the relationship between this 'détente from below' and the persistence, in Europe at least, of policies of 'détente from above' is paradoxical. Many of the contacts could not have been made without some relaxation of travel procedures agreed between East and West authorities" (1995, 200). However, the impetus for these transnational linkages arose as much from détente's failures as from its success.[34]

As dissident movements used the Helsinki Final Act to legitimize their human-rights demands, they sought to challenge the deeply ambiguous meaning of the Helsinki Final Act—that it ratified the status quo but also contained the seeds for changing Europe. Thus, within the ranks of the Soviet dissident movements there was always some difference of opinion about the CSCE: some were critical of the West for signing CSCE documents that did little to ameliorate the abuse of human rights, the repression of dissidents, or sanction Soviet violations. Nevertheless, the Final Act provided an alternative source of norms and authority for these groups to promote the transformation of domestic soci-

33. See also Charter 77's 1985 "Prague Appeal." Addressed to the European peace movement END, the appeal argues that "the demand that governments live up to the obligations they themselves have undertaken appears to us a hitherto little utilized opportunity for the peace movement." This was a call for the West to recognize that no democratic and autonomous Europe could arrive through disarmament alone, as long as "any citizen group or nation is barred from participation in the decisions that affect not only their daily life, but their very survival." See "The Prague Challenge" in Roussopoulos (1986, 257–59).

34. Chilton (1995, 200) notes that "the most significant contacts were not meetings at all, but invitations—i.e. 'empty chairs'—and the exchange of ideas in samizdat"—underground correspondence channels. Empty chairs were poignant reminders of East Europeans invited but not accorded visas by their government. Samizdats led to the 1985 Prague Appeal.

ety. Appeals such as those made by Alexander Solzhenitsyn in his article "Live no longer the Lie" were highly influential. Even though the dissident movement in the Soviet Union consisted of a small group of individuals, their views impacted widely on Soviet society; they helped develop an alternative way of thinking that distinguished the private views from the official, and thus laid the groundwork for Gorbachev's "new thinking" to flourish when it was introduced nearly a decade after the emergence of the Helsinki monitors.[35]

Many Eastern European and Soviet dissidents came to share the view that, without the strengthening of civil society across the bloc divide *from below,* the Helsinki Final Act was a "dead letter" (Chilton 1995, 201). Documents and appeals such as the *Helsinki Memorandum* were presented to delegations at CSCE follow-up meetings.[36] For example, the Memorandum argued that "détente policy, to achieve permanent results, must have a firm basis not only on the governmental level, but within societies. Grass roots contact and common activities between groups and individuals across frontiers can dissolve the structure of cold war. . . . Official détente policy should create a framework which encourages the process of 'détente from below' " (as quoted in Chilton 1995, 201).[37]

From the late 1970s the notion prevailed that a viable alternative for transforming East-West relations was "a shared migration away from official politics and into parallel political structures based on emerging civil societies" (Chilton 1995, 201). The challenge was to act as " 'if the blocs no longer existed,' "[38] as " 'if a united, neutral and pacific Europe already exists' " (as quoted in Chilton 1995, 201). The bottom line was that "politically active citizens must be the agents of system transformation" (201). Jan Patocka argued, in an elegant exposition of the purposes of Charter 77, that " 'the effort of the chartists is aimed exclusively at cleansing and reinforcing the awareness that a higher authority does exist, to which they are obligated, individually, in their conscience, and to which states are bound by their signatures on important international covenants.' " Politics had to be made subject to law, not law subject to politics (as quoted in Mastny 1986, XXX).

For groups such as Charter 77, the CSCE was an alternative source of au-

35. I owe this point to Lena Jönsson.

36. The full title is "Giving Real Life to the Helsinki Accords: A Memorandum" (Berlin: European Network for East-West Dialogue, April 1987). Chilton (1992, 7) notes "it was written in common by independent groups and individuals in Eastern and Western Europe" and was presented in December 1986 at the Vienna Follow-up meeting.

37. Chilton writes that "shock waves" were sent through the communist leadership as their official peace groups, church liaison groups, women's organizations, youth groups, ecological projects, and citizens' initiatives were increasingly passed over in the West in favor of independent activists and dissidents (1995, 203).

38. See END's Response to the Prague Appeal, in Roussopoulos (1986, 260).

thority and "court of appeals." Delegations to the Belgrade Follow-up meeting received a letter from the Polish Workers Defence Committee, set up in 1976 to protect strikers from state reprisals, citing Basket III provisions on free flow of information and invoking International Covenants on Human Rights to justify its protests against the arrest of committee members (Kirk Laux 1984, 262). The efforts of these groups were also directed toward the expansion of CSCE substantive commitments and norms and inclusion of new humanitarian issues. Soviet dissidents, for example, cited the Final Act's reference to the International Covenants on Human Rights, which outlaws forced labor, to argue that the widespread use of forced labor in places of detention in the USSR is a violation of the CSCE agreements and therefore constituted grounds for their examination at the Belgrade Conference (Kirk Laux 1984, 262).

At the Madrid Follow-up, dissidents from all over Eastern Europe and the Soviet Union, along with ethnic and human-rights groups, converged to hold their own parallel conference, grant interviews, issue press releases, and convene their own press conferences. Thus, transnational linkages provided another means for monitoring and advocacy at the intergovernmental levels. These activities resulted in the founding of the International Helsinki Association (later Federation) under the honorary presidency of Dr. Sakharov. With headquarters in Vienna its objective was to monitor the CSCE agreements and receive complaints of violations, as well as to mobilize assistance for those persecuted and seek amnesty for them (Skilling 1984b, 318–19).[39]

Intergovernmental and Governmental Monitoring Agencies

In support of these domestic-CSCE linkages, several intergovernmental and governmental monitoring agencies began to carry out their own monitoring and reporting on (failures of) CSCE implementation. From an early stage of the development of the CSCE, the Council of Europe sought a role in the consultations among its member states in preparation for the Geneva negotiations and also in monitoring the follow-up to the CSCE, particularly within the domain of cultural cooperation. However, these objectives proved politically unrealizable (Ghebali 1989, 66). Despite these failures, the Council decided in 1975 to retain the question of CSCE follow-ups in the order of the day of its special commissions and its plenary meetings. The Council continued to make its own

39. See also Commission Security and Cooperation in Europe (March 1985). *The Helsinki Process and East West Relations: Progress in Perspective. A Report on the Positive Aspect of the Implementation of the Helsinki Final Act 1975–84,* 12. The New York-based Helsinki Watch Committee is one of ten such monitoring groups located in the United States, Canada, and Western Europe.

assessments of the CSCE in preparation for follow-up meetings (Ghebali 1989, 65–69).

Two other intergovernmental bodies played a role in relation to CSCE monitoring: the North Atlantic Assembly (NAA) and the Interparliamentary Union. The NAA created the Subcommission on the Free Circulation of Information and Persons, which was charged with analysis of the implementation of Basket III and compiling East-West agreements on these issues. Starting in May 1976 and continuing through March 1989, the NAA published a trimester publication, "The Bulletin," which surveyed essentially Western press on Basket III issues and information. The Interparliamentary Union has a longer history with the CSCE, originating in the 1960s efforts of several of its members to launch an IPU Conference on Security and Cooperation in Europe (see chapter 3). Eventually, the IPU organized six regional conferences on the CSCE, the first parallel to the Helsinki consultations (January 1972). Subsequent conferences were held in Belgrade (1975), Vienna (1978), Brussels (1980), Budapest (1983), and Bonn (1986) (Ghebali 1989, 67–70).

The U.S. Commission on Security and Cooperation in Europe, signed by Congress into law in 1976, was authorized "to monitor the act of the signatories which reflect compliance with or violation of the articles of the Final Act of the Conference on Security and Cooperation in Europe, with particular regard to the provision relating to Human Rights and Cooperation in Humanitarian Fields," and to report to members of the U.S. House of Representatives and the Senate on its findings and to provide them with information. The origins of the Commission lie in the increasing tension in East-West relations palpable by the mid-1970s, along with the growing concern in the U.S. Congress and throughout the country that the United States "was granting the Soviets significant concessions regarding post-War borders and military security, with no means to enforce Soviet compliance with the human rights commitments of the Final Act."[40] While on a working trip to the Soviet Union and Romania in the fall of 1975 shortly after the Final Act was signed, U.S. Representative Millicent Fenwick and a delegation of House members met with a number of dissidents, refuseniks, and representatives of religious communities, including Dr. Yuri Orlov (who only months later would found the first Soviet monitoring group). The courage of these individuals in the face of state-led persecution inspired Fenwick to push for a bipartisan commission to monitor and encourage compliance with the Final Act. Henry Kissinger, the State Department, and the Ford administration expressed their objection to such "an encroachment on the pre-

40. See the Commission on Security and Cooperation in Europe. Informational folio on the Creation of the Helsinki Commission.

rogatives of the executive branch to conduct foreign affairs." Reflecting his reluctance, President Gerald Ford took the unusual step of signing the bill creating the commission in a private ceremony, without inviting any press and without making any public statement as the bill became law (Mastny 1986, 117).

But the commission set out to encourage Soviet compliance (by bringing individual cases to the attention of the administration) and to enhance the ability of the State Department to press for higher human-rights standards. Representative Fenwick determined to raise awareness within the U.S. Congress and the incoming Carter administration of the importance of the Final Act and the moral issues at stake. The fact that there was a natural constituency for such issues in the form of the American electorate's Eastern European emigré communities—particularly those from captive nations—injected domestic political capital into the issue of Eastern bloc human-rights violations of the Helsinki Final Act and made Congressional oversight politically attractive, if not imperative. The Soviet interpretation of the Final Act as enshrining the principle of nonintervention in internal affairs could not stand uncontested by the West in the CSCE follow-up process.

The Commission's efforts to document East-West compliance with the CSCE focused immediately on the systematic repression of Eastern bloc Helsinki monitors before the opening of the 1977 Belgrade conference. Starting with this first follow-up, the commission also assumed a vital role preparing U.S. positions and providing commission members for U.S. delegations to CSCE conferences and expert meetings. The commission also channeled the energies of ethnic communities in the United States who were from captive nations, like the Baltic states and other Soviet republics including Armenia, which became a key constituency in the United States for the CSCE process. At the same time, "through the vehicle of this Commission's Semiannual Reports the United States opened a new and important channel of communication to the East European signatories of the Final Act," keeping the issue of human rights at the forefront of public attention in the United States and Europe (Mastny 1986, 145–46).

Expanding the Human Dimension

At the first CSCE follow-up in Belgrade, discussions became mired in controversy over the West's efforts to hold the East politically accountable for its human-rights violations and the East's refusal to consent to any final agreement that would make any reference to them. Ultimately, no substantive agreement could be made to extend the normative commitments of the CSCE in this area or dealing with human contacts (see also chapter 8). By the time of the 1980–83 Madrid Follow-up, the initial disappointment in the West with the minimal compliance by the Eastern bloc states to the Helsinki CBMs, and outrage over the blatant violation of these in the context of the Polish crisis during the Madrid meeting, was also coupled with growing Western concern over the lack of Soviet and Eastern European compliance with the CSCE human-rights commitments. In the review of implementation at Madrid, the Soviet Union received the largest share of criticism. Western delegations questioned the drastic reductions in Soviet Jewish emigration in 1980 and "deplored" the rise of anti-Semitism.[41] The West protested the Soviets' use of bureaucratic and procedural obstacles to emigration as a form of harassment. Furthermore, the United States was disturbed with the Soviet's misuse of Basket III provisions on the reunification of families to restrict rather than facilitate emigration. Similarly, the records of the GDR, Romania, and Czechoslovakia were also scrutinized concerning emigration and bilateral family reunification cases. The United States brought attention to the "absurd" Romanian practice of requiring a would-be emigrant to request an application in order to receive an application for emigration; and the Federal Republic of Germany criticized the imposition of higher currency-exchange requirements for Western citizens traveling to the GDR.

Western delegations pointed to several other breaches of the CSCE commitments. After the imposition of martial law in Poland in December 1981, travel abroad was restricted, while Solidarity activists who were detained were pressed to leave the country for good. Czechoslovakia and Romania were criticized for imposing an education tax on emigrants, "ostensibly to recover the costs of their secondary and university education" (Dowdy 1987, 214). Jamming of Western radio broadcasts was an object of sustained discussion throughout the Madrid meeting, as was the deterioration of working conditions for Western journalists in the Eastern bloc. The GDR had even made it a possible crime for citizens to speak to Western journalists.[42] During the 1982 Olympic Games hosted by Moscow, the Soviet authorities arrested many prominent dissidents to avert close contact between visitors (of whom many

41. For example, the U.S. Helsinki Commission reported that there were "no profound adjustments" in the Soviets procedures to grant exit visas, and although emigration increased initially, it reached its peak in 1979. Korey (1993, 216) reports that Jewish emigration increased during 1975–79, with 1975 figures at 13,221, 1976 at 14,261, 1977 at 16,736, and 1978 at 28,864. Although the initiation of Gorbachev's reformist policies in 1987 resulted in a 700 percent increase in emigration compared with the beginning of the year, this increase still only amounted to 8,000 Jews that year. The new January 1987 regulations requiring an affidavit from a first-degree relative proved a powerful constraint (Korey 1993, 235).

42. For other violations cited by the West during the first phase of the Madrid review of implementation see report by the Staff of the Commission on Security and Cooperation in Europe, "The Madrid CSCE Review Meeting: An Interim Report," Jan. 6, 1981, 16–18.

were from the Western media) and the political opposition (Helgesen 1990, 253). By the mid-1980s, most Helsinki monitors in the Soviet Union were either imprisoned or, along with other dissidents, forced into exile. And it was estimated that as many as 250,000–400,000 Soviet citizens who had applied to exit were denied. The applications of these refuseniks were pending often up to ten years and sometimes longer (Dowdy 1987, 200).[43]

While the dissidents used the CSCE as a vehicle to press for changes, their protests and the repression they suffered from communist authorities were used instrumentally by the West to press for new human-rights provisions (Mastny 1986, 64–70). For example, in response to the declaration of martial law in Poland during the Madrid meeting, the West insisted and succeeded in returning to a review of implementation, even though the period for review had already passed according to the agenda. The West also introduced new substantive proposals, including trade union rights, again illustrating the way the CSCE was able to respond rapidly and "legislate" new measures in response to ongoing cases of violation of civil and political rights.

The post-Madrid expert meetings on human-dimension issues, on which the United States had insisted as a quid pro quo for its agreement to the CDE, did not yield very encouraging results. No concluding document was reached in the 1985 Ottawa meeting on Human Rights and Fundamental Freedoms, the 1985 Budapest Cultural Forum, or the 1986 Bern meeting on Human Contacts. The lack of results from these meetings fueled doubts in the West about the Soviet's intention to implement in good faith CSCE commitments. Western officials also realized that, given the expert meetings' separate standing from the other CSCE baskets, substantive progress was "virtually impossible"; they afforded no opportunity to create tradeoffs that would induce concessions from the Eastern bloc in the human-rights area.

Around this time, some exiled Soviet dissidents began to criticize the West for abandoning the human rights and security linkage by continuing to cooperate with the Soviet Union despite its record of human-rights abuses. They pointed to the West's signing the Belgrade and then Madrid document without mention of the ongoing repression and to the separation of security and human rights in further review conferences that the CDE threatened to introduce. In particular, they drew attention to the deaths of imprisoned Helsinki monitors

43. See the testimony of exiled and founding member of the Moscow Helsinki Monitoring Group, Ludmilla Alexeyeva, and the U.S. Helsinki Watch Committee brochure, "Where Are They Now? Human Rights Monitors in the U.S.S.R. Ten Years After Helsinki" (August 1985), both reproduced in *Hearing Before the Commission on Security and Cooperation in Europe, Ninety-Ninth Congress,* Oct. 3, 1985, *First Session, Human Rights and the CSCE Process* (Washington, D.C.: Government Printing Office, 1986).

and to long terms in prison and labor camps spent by others, underscoring the impotence of the Final Act "to protect its most sincere supporters."[44]

In light of increasing Soviet violations of human rights during the period from the late 1970s to the mid-1980s, U.S. policymakers also began to reconsider the U.S. approach to the CSCE and détente with the Soviet Union more generally. In the first two follow-up meetings, the United States had attempted to link progress on military-security issues to stricter human-rights commitments, giving primary importance to a review of implementation and to public diplomacy emphasizing the East's noncompliance. By 1986, however, serious debates and even studies on a unilateral renunciation of the Helsinki Accords were carried out by the U.S. Congress, the Helsinki Commission, and the U.S. State Department. With progress lacking across the board also in the MBFR negotiations, along with the Soviets' largely declaratory approach to the Stockholm CDE during the first year of negotiations, some exiled dissidents appealed to Congress for the United States to withdraw unilaterally from the CSCE.[45]

Congressman Hoyer, cochairman of the Helsinki Commission, expressed concern with such a course of action, however, lest "we let off the hook those violating human rights by reducing the forums at which our concerns can be raised and discussed."[46] The executive director of the Helsinki Watch Committee, Jeri Laber, similarly stressed that "the Helsinki process can be an instrument for restoring human and civil rights in Poland and in other East European countries. The Final Act of the CSCE and the Final Declaration of the Madrid meeting still remain an essential basis for claims set forth by the societies of these countries. . . . The societies' awareness that one normative standard exists helps give social demands a rational form and increases the chances of a peaceful resolution of the conflict."[47] Withdrawal, in contrast, would not bring about any tangible results.

In spite of the failure of post-Madrid expert meetings on human rights to produce any final documents, some positive results could be noted. First, by using the 1985 Ottawa forum to bring attention to homelessness, joblessness, and lack of medical care as criticism of the United States for human-rights violations, the Soviets in effect acknowledged that human-rights compliance by a

44. "Exiles: Nullify Helsinki Pact," *Wall Street Journal,* May 8, 1985 (signed by twenty-two exiled dissidents).

45. *Hearing Before the Commission on Security and Cooperation in Europe, Ninety-Ninth Congress,* 6.

46. Testimony by Congressman Hoyer, Cochairman of the Helsinki Commission, *Hearing Before the Commission on Security and Cooperation in Europe, Ninety-Ninth Congress,* 4.

47. *Hearing Before the Commission on Security and Cooperation in Europe, Ninety-Ninth Congress,* 30.

specific country is a legitimate concern of all Helsinki signatories.[48] Second, the West had been able to use the Ottawa forum to derive a broad-based consensus among all the West European allies and the N+N on a basic human-rights agenda (although the United States withheld its support), which was useful to prepare for the Vienna Follow-up. Likewise, the 1985 Budapest Cultural Forum yielded some tangible benefits. Although the Eastern bloc would not agree to allow NGOs access to the meeting, the West succeeded in bringing sufficient pressure to bear on the Hungarian government so that the Helsinki Federation was able to carry out its parallel NGO meetings in private apartments without disruptions. Through the bilateral exchange of lists of outstanding humanitarian cases, the 1986 Bern meeting on Human Contacts also led to the release of several hundred divided families, although no progress on the status of the thousands of refuseniks, prisoners of conscience, or Jewish emigration was made. In the meantime, the Reagan administration used bilateral contacts with the Soviets to resolve directly human-rights questions, and here, too, CSCE norms and commitments came into play (Korey 1993, 249).

Instead of unilateral renunciation of the CSCE, U.S. policymakers began to explore ways of maximizing leverage on human rights in the upcoming Vienna Follow-up Conference. Pointing to the success of the Jackson-Vanik Amendment, some experts argued for the United States to use Soviet aims in the areas of security, scientific exchange, and economic cooperation to leverage compliance on human rights as well. They called for a pragmatic approach, taking advantage of the deepening crisis in the Soviet economy and the possibility for change in orientation with the new leadership of Mikhail Gorbachev. Given the strong Soviet interests in reducing military spending, enhancing economic ties, and increasing the exchange of scientific and technological information, they argued that economic tools of state craft could be a useful mechanism—such as what West Germany pursued with its policy of Ostpolitik.

Nevertheless, the United States did not use trade relations as a leverage for obtaining human-rights concessions (Hassner 1991). Instead, the decision was made to use a more complex linkage strategy that would require the Eastern bloc's fulfillment of concrete human-rights measures as a precondition for achieving a balanced agreement in the Vienna Follow-up. The U.S. dual linkage strategy would use progress on military-security issues to induce Soviet bloc cooperation in the area of human rights. The approach was shaped in part by lessons the United States had learned from lifting sanctions on Poland in the mid-1980s. The main objective was to assure the Soviets really were internalizing or "domesticating" CSCE norms—not just chasing instrumental and op-

48. *Hearing Before the Commission on Security and Cooperation in Europe, Ninety-Ninth Congress*, 31.

portunistic changes.[49] Adopting recommendations that Scharansky and other Soviet exiled dissidents and experts had urged on the U.S. Helsinki Commission in Congressional hearings,[50] Ambassador Warren Zimmerman specified that, at the Vienna Follow-up, the United States would look for results measured by Soviet performance and deeds on such issues as "the full release of political prisoners, resolution of the family reunification cases, a steep increase in emigration and an end to jamming." He insisted that " 'we are asking the Soviets to provide credible assurances that compliance will continue to improve beyond the Vienna meeting. Examples would be: abolition of Articles 70 and 190 of the Criminal Code, abolition of the psychiatric hospitals run by the Interior Ministry . . . mechanism to ensure higher levels of emigration and unambiguous commitments in the Vienna final document' " (as quoted in Korey 1993, 239).

Because dual linkage was premised on positive inducements rather than threats, Ambassador Frowick (deputy to Ambassador Zimmerman) sought to keep security negotiations in Vienna one step ahead of human rights, thus using progress there to generate movement on human rights (Korey 1991, 90). The Soviets' anxiousness at the Vienna meeting to move quickly to a final document and proceed with negotiations on the reduction of conventional forces in Europe also became an important source of leverage for the United States in the negotiations (Korey 1991, 1993). Because the adoption of a mandate at the Vienna Follow-up for a conference on conventional-force talks was subordinate to consensus on all three CSCE baskets, the United States made it clear to the Soviets that they would have to be forthcoming on Western human-rights demands in order to gain the West's consent to a final document.

Human-Dimension Mechanism

Thus, it was not until the Vienna Follow-up that major breakthroughs on human-rights agreements were achieved in the CSCE. This turn of events cannot be understood without reference to Gorbachev's leadership of the Soviet

49. As soon as U.S. sanctions on Poland were lifted, many Solidarity activists were simply rounded up and sent off to prison again. See *Hearing Before the Commission on Security and Cooperation in Europe, Ninety-Ninth Congress.*

50. Secretary of State George Schultz, in his address at the commemoration of the tenth anniversary of the signing of the Final Act of the CSCE in Helsinki, July 30, 1985, hinted at this policy. He asserted that "sustained improvements are vital, but concrete steps—to improve emigration, to allow spouses and dual nationals to unite with loved ones, to release human rights activists and religious teachers—*these concrete steps are also important*" (emphasis added). See *Hearing Before the Commission on Security and Cooperation in Europe, Ninety-Ninth Congress,* Appendix 5, 78–79.

Union and introduction of glasnost and perestroika in the mid-1980s. The fact that profound changes were underfoot in the Soviet approach to the CSCE was immediately made apparent in Foreign Minister Shevardnadze's opening statement to the Vienna Follow-up in November 1986. Emphasizing that "the strength of any society lies in its ability to perfect itself, to improve itself," Shevardnadze affirmed that the "Soviet Union attaches paramount significance to the seventh principle of the Helsinki Final Act, concerning respect for human rights and fundamental freedoms, including the freedom of thought, conscience, religion or belief." He also pointed to major legislative and administrative measures being adopted in his country to further the development of international contacts and to resolve in a humanitarian spirit problems relating to family reunification and mixed marriages, underscoring the Soviets readiness to be guided in practice by the draft document of the Bern Meeting of Experts on Human Contacts. While also drawing attention to the importance of the International Covenants of Human Rights (and to U.S. violations of its rules of conduct for safeguarding individual rights, i.e. work, housing, rest, free education, medical care, and social welfare), he nonetheless stunned Western delegations (as well as his own) with a proposal to convene in Moscow "a *representative conference of the CSCE participating States* . . . to consider the whole range of such problems, including human contact, information, culture and education" (emphasis original). The Soviets expected a "comprehensive discussion oriented towards a practical result, a mutual understanding that would make it possible to improve the situation in the humanitarian area in all countries participating in the CSCE process."[51]

A leading Austrian newspaper, *Die Presse,* editorialized that this would be like " 'a debate in the fox den about raising chickens' " (as quoted in Korey 1991, 91). In response to the Soviet initiative, the United States required that principles and operating procedures that applied to the organization and hosting of other expert meetings be similarly upheld by the Soviets. Recalling key positions advocated in the West's draft concluding document for the 1985 Budapest Cultural Forum,[52] the United States insisted the Soviets guarantee several conditions: entry and exist visas for prospective attendees, including human rights activists and Soviet emigrés; the right to organize meetings, demonstrations, book fairs, and press conferences by such individuals or NGOs; Soviet citizens' access to public meetings, to all journalists, delegations,

51. Eduard A. Shevardnadze, CSCE/WT/VR.3. *Vienna Meeting 1986 Verbatim Record of the Opening Statements,* Nov. 4–7, 1986, 11–21.

52. For the Western draft proposal, see *Hearing Before the Commission on Security and Cooperation in Europe, Ninety-Ninth Congress.* See also Marit Ingves, "KSSE Wien: 'Förhandlingarna igång på allvar,' " *Huvudstadsbladet,* July 26, 1987.

and foreign press; and last but not least, unhindered access to these fora by foreign press (Korey 1993, 92).[53]

Along with the United States, Great Britain and Canada also held out on agreeing to a Moscow human-rights meeting. However, the United States eventually assured the Soviet Union it would approve holding the meeting in Moscow if its conditions were met. To this end, the United States also worked to gain British support for the Moscow meeting so that by November 9, 1988, British demands were added to the U.S. list. Thus, before the end of the Vienna meeting, the Soviet Union had to free all political prisoners (including Helsinki Monitors) from prisons, labor camps and psychiatric institutions; permit a significant increase in emigration; bring an end to jamming; grant visas to long-term refuseniks; and finally provide assurances that these changes would be institutionalized (Korey 1993, 253; Lehne 1991b, 127–28). Britain, in particular, sought changes in Soviet law for the abolition of laws to harass and imprison human-rights activists. As a further safeguard, the United States presented to the Vienna meeting a paper specifying host country requirements for guaranteeing access to CSCE expert meetings. This paper was met without protest from the Soviet Union and was eventually included in the Vienna Concluding Document as Annex XI (Korey 1991, 98).

With assurance that, if these preconditions were met, the United States would approve holding the meeting in Moscow and encourage its allies to do likewise, the Soviet Union made considerable strides during the last two months of 1988 in each of these areas. Decisive negotiations on U.S. conditions were carried out bilaterally between the United States and the Soviet Union. Despite some shortcomings, Schultz struck a deal with the Soviets to bring pressure to end the negotiations in January 1989 during his "watch" and before the change of presidential administration in the United States, which could introduce new complexities (Lehne 1991b, 129; Korey 1991, 101).

The Vienna meeting of the CSCE marked a crucial turning point in the development of consensual understanding on human rights, on the formal observance and domestication of the CSCE principles in the legislative practices, as well as in foreign-policy initiatives and treaties of the participating states. By the conclusion of the Vienna meeting, "the idea of human rights as one of the elements uniting Europe was taking shape" (Lehne 1991b, 152). Considerable attention had been focused on human-rights issues because there was a general appreciation in the West that too much progress and emphasis had been placed

53. These points were addressed by Ambassador Zimmerman in a July 1987 speech to the Soviet delegation. Commission on Security and Cooperation in Europe. United States Congress. *Phase III and IV of the Vienna Review Meeting of the Conference on Security and Cooperation in Europe.* May 5–July 31, 1987, and Sept. 22–Dec. 18, 1987, 10.

on the military dimension since the Madrid Follow-up meeting and the Stockholm CDE without parallel progress and attention to the human dimension of the CSCE.

To balance this situation, the Vienna Concluding Document enhanced the instrumentality of CSCE human-rights principles and commitments by creating a linkage between these commitments and national legislation and by securing the right of individuals and groups to monitor the implementation of human rights. This change led to provisions for "the right to know one's rights," the dissemination of information on human rights, and the elaboration of two principles of the Final Act: Principle VII, concerning Respect for Human Rights and Fundamental Freedoms, and Principle IX, on cooperation among States (Lehne 1991a, 155). This included the participating states' recognition of their duty to "respect the right of their citizens to contribute actively, individually or in association with others, to the promotion and protection of human rights and fundamental freedoms" (§13.5). In an acknowledgment of the importance of monitoring in the implementation of these rights, the participating states also confirmed that "governments, institutions, organizations and persons have a relevant and positive role to play in . . . the full realization of the Final Act" (§26). The participating states committed themselves to "facilitate direct contacts and communication among these persons, organizations and institutions within and between participating States *and remove, where they exist, legal and administrative impediments inconsistent with the CSCE provisions*" (§26, emphasis added).[54] The language is specific and incontrovertible. The strengthening of these commitments illustrates the diachronic aspects of rule making and the incremental development of CSCE regime governance and institutional competence.

The Vienna Concluding Document was a milestone in East-West negotiations, codifying the "human dimension" of the CSCE (a concept in informal use in the CSCE for some time). This term brought under one conceptual roof the distinct elements of the Final Act that had protected the rights of individuals in what otherwise was a political agreement largely predicated on interstate relations (Brett 1992a). Strictly speaking, Principle VII of the Decalogue, which provides for "respect for human rights and fundamental freedoms, including the freedom of thought, conscience, religion or belief," is the only part of the Final Act that covers human rights. In contrast, "Basket III fits comfortably within the inter-state framework of the CSCE" (Brett 1992a, 14), since it *regulates the behavior of states* as regards their citizens, particularly on matters with

54. *Concluding Document of the Vienna Meeting 1989 of Representatives of the Participating States of the Conference on Security and Cooperation in Europe, Held on the Basis of the Provisions of the Final Act Relating to the Follow-up to the Conference*, in Annex III in Lehne (1991).

transfrontier dimensions such as freedom of movement and information, the right to leave and return to one's country, reunification of families, binational marriages, human contacts, family ties, travel for personal or professional reasons, etc. While these provisions clearly relate to human rights and "may be considered specific instances of more general human rights such as freedom of movement and information," they are not expressed in terms of human rights in Basket III (Brett 1992a, 14).

The Human Dimension subsumed both the human-rights and Basket III aspects of the Final Act and subsequent CSCE agreements under its monitoring functions. These functions include the Vienna Human Dimension mechanism, a landmark achievement. The objective was to create a binding instrument for both individual "cases" and more general "situations" or practices (Brett 1992a, 19).[55] Approximating a system of interstate complaints procedure, the Vienna mechanism allowed for a system of supervision that could function permanently whenever any state wished to apply the mechanism to obtain information from another state (on possible violations) relating to the human dimension of the CSCE. This provision included a binding commitment to hold bilateral meetings with other participating states to examine the situation and provide notification about the situation to all CSCE states.

The precise scope of the Human Dimension was, however, a question open to different interpretations. According to the Vienna Concluding Document, the Human Dimension encompasses "the undertakings entered into in the Final Act and in other CSCE documents concerning respect for all human rights and fundamental freedoms, human contacts and other issues of a related humanitarian character."[56] Thus, the substantive scope of the Human Dimension may be considered to cover all issues of Basket III. This interpretation would encompass Eastern conceptions of human rights as socioeconomic rights (information, culture, education, welfare, etc.). But in practice the Vienna Mechanism was used only by Western states against Eastern states—extensively during the transition period to the post-cold war era and at least seventy times during 1989 to counter human-rights abuses. Hence, its use fell within the scope of the Western conception of human rights as based on fundamental freedoms.

On the other hand, because the Final Act commits states to act in conformity with the purposes and principles of the Charter of the United Nations and with the Universal Declaration of Human Rights, these provisions also fall within the parameters of the Human Dimension. Furthermore, it is also possi-

55. The adoption in Vienna of this first, nonvoluntary CSCE human-rights mechanism was inspired by the breakthrough achieved in the Stockholm CDE for an intrusive, on-site inspection regime.

56. *Concluding Document of the Vienna Meeting 1989,* in Annex III in Lehne (1991).

ble for states unilaterally to expand the scope of coverage of the Human Dimension, since Principle VII of the Final Act calls on them to fulfill also their obligations to other international declarations and agreements in the field of human rights. This broader interpretation can also be substantiated by the mechanism's review functions. They provide for oversight of the Human Dimension of the CSCE, including relevant CSCE commitments. This wording suggested "the CSCE commitments do not exhaust the human dimension" (Brett 1992a, 20). The fact that subsequent CSCE documents have a codicillary function in relation to the Final Act has provided a means for enhancing the area of application of the Human Dimension (Brett 1992a, 21).

The CSCE expert meetings leading up to the Vienna Follow-up as well as the Vienna meeting itself, along with the expert meetings held shortly thereafter, all provided the West with important opportunities to judge the social transformation under way in the Eastern bloc and the Soviet Union, which Gorbachev had initiated under his policies of perestroika and glasnost. The first CSCE expert meeting to be held in a Communist bloc country, the 1985 Budapest Cultural Forum, was only the second CSCE meeting open to nondiplomats. The participation of leading cultural figures from across the CSCE states "gave the meeting a unique atmosphere." More than 900 persons were accredited, which was a CSCE record. Parallel to the Cultural Forum, the International Helsinki Federation organized its own forum held in private apartments to bring together leading Eastern and Western intellectuals. Lehne concludes that it had an "impact on the international debate on reform in Eastern Europe that equaled or even exceeded that of the official forum" (1991a, 31).

By 1989, dissidents and opposition groups used the Vienna Follow-up meeting and the subsequent CSCE expert meetings in the Eastern bloc countries to pressure their governments for greater change. President Todor Zhivkov offered to host in Sofia the October 16-November 3, 1989, CSCE Meeting on the Protection of the Environment. By allowing opposition movements more latitude, he sought to impress the Western press and enhance his image. But the meeting was used by activists as a "protective cover for unprecedented public protest activity against the Communist regime."[57] Zhivkov's strategy backfired when the groups took to the streets and were met with police brutality, bringing great criticism on the regime and leading shortly thereafter to his ouster (Lehne 1991a).

For his part, Honecker attempted to live up to the CSCE commitments as a "passport to greater international respectability" (Brown 1991, 144); but this

57. See report prepared by the staff of the Commission on Security and Cooperation in Europe, *Human Rights and Democratization in Bulgaria. Implementation of the Helsinki Accords* (Washington, D.C., September 1993) 2.

did little to stem the tide of East German vacationers in Hungary seeking to exit the Communist bloc. Hungary permitted them to travel to the West, citing its obligations to the CSCE and to United Nations principles on freedom of movement. By September 1989, when Czechoslovakia and Poland adopted this policy, "one of the basic functions of the Berlin Wall ceased to exist" (Wallender and Prokop 1993, 71). These decisions unleashed a series of events leading to the fall of the Berlin Wall in November 1989, "velvet revolutions" throughout the Eastern bloc, and the rapid unification of the divided Germany.

Perestroika and glasnost also brought a new Soviet approach to the law of peaceful coexistence, because the earlier distinction regarding international law between socialist and capitalist states—the former governed by socialist internationalism and the latter international law—was dropped. As Hoedt and Lefeber note (1991, 2), "the repudiation of this distinction in Soviet ideology has enabled the Soviet Union to recognize the primacy of international law in all international relations. In fact, it removed the legitimacy of socialist international law as a separate, regional, category of international law."[58] On November 21, 1990, the thirty-four members of the East-West community of nation-states, including a united Germany, gathered in Paris for the signing of the Charter of Paris for a New Europe. The occasion marked the end of East-West confrontation and the beginning of what they hoped would be a new era of democracy, peace, and unity. The Charter reaffirmed the fundamental role of the Ten Principles of the Final Act in guiding the CSCE participating states toward a future shaped by "a steadfast commitment to democracy based on human rights and fundamental freedoms; prosperity through economic liberty and social justice; and equal security for all our countries."

Conclusion: Toward Consensus on Comprehensive Security

Using the review of implementation not only as a means of monitoring compliance and sanctioning offenders but also for rule interpretation helped bridge the gap between the various starting points East and West brought to their arguments. The review process stimulated intense debates over the *implications* of the Final Act for cooperation on security and human rights and for *determining* how the further development of these understandings related to the norms, principles, and rules of the CSCE process, as well as objectives to strengthen détente and international peace. Eventually, these debates forged a meeting of minds between East and West on the causes of their conflict and on possible solutions. The debates allowed the two sides to elaborate a code of

58. However, the 1977 Soviet Constitution, amended in 1990, continued to refer to the principle of socialist internationalism in Article 30. See Hoedt and Lefeber (1991, 2 n. 4).

conduct that guided the development of new understandings and practical ideas for cooperation.

The cornerstone of CSCE cooperation was the principle of the indivisibility of security. First, this meant that security cooperation in the CSCE had to be based on enhancing all participating states' security. This was a different starting point from superpower arms-control talks and BPA principles. Thus, in the CSCE regional security concerns were a part of the whole picture and were not incidental to any agreement. Participating states agreed to work on CSBMs as the main approach to the subject and search for formulas premised on controlling the means to bloc confrontation. This situation mitigated the extent to which such negotiations would involve questions of status and prestige between the military alliances; there was no need for evaluating strict reciprocity. Therefore there was a referent point that was entirely different from maintaining the status quo, which had motivated superpower arms-control negotiations. This reasoning also helped the parties to reframe the issues at stake so that fears about such matters as the threat of surprise attack could be dealt with cooperatively and in ways more amenable to the development of confidence and trust. As a result, the CSCE offered an important alternative for developing international peace and cooperation to the rules that guided the superpowers' détente relationship. In fact, the CSCE helped diminish in importance the weight of the negative aspects of East-West confrontation by building up areas of constructive engagement through its multilateral endeavors.

Moreover, the CSCE addressed directly the problem of the perception of insecurity that existed between East and West through its CSBM regime. By encouraging the notification of military activities, exchanging observers and agreeing to on-site inspections, and desisting from large-scale military activities close to borders, the CSCE promoted greater transparency and calculability in the overall military situation. These provisions entailed not just limitations on behavior—as was the objective in arms control—but concrete, cooperative steps to strengthen confidence and reduce threat perceptions. In this sense, the CSCE was more important than were other arms-control fora. Indeed, from the experience of having U.S. inspectors on Soviet soil, "Russian military officials could confirm first hand that nothing bad happened by opening up and cooperating; they could see Soviet Union still existed, and everyone was OK." Psychologically, this was a profound breakthrough. It was also politically imperative; Gorbachev could not introduce economic and democratic reforms without a reassessment of the threat from the West first. It was therefore important to ask whether the threat was real or just imaginary. Glasnost opened the way to these developments, releasing social pressures from below and stimulating democratization of the Soviet system in general. Grinevsky concluded that "the importance of the CSCE was in changing the psychological situation in the Soviet

Union, so that for the first time, it was possible to say, we are the same people in the West and the East. We have the same problems. Practically that was the beginning of the end of the cold war. That started the whole process." [59]

The decision of the United States in the mid-1980s to stay in the CSCE and to use a dual linkage strategy was also important. The new strategy was better suited than the earlier "sticks" approach to take advantage of the changes under way in the Soviet Union. Linkage works better if it accelerates or is aimed at orienting an evolution that is already under way, rather than attempting to change completely the other side's orientation to a problem. Linkage is more likely to be effective when the outcome sought is itself presupposed by the terms of the linkage, i.e. "natural linkage." As Hassner explains, coexistence does not presuppose convergence, but cooperation presupposes communication (1991, 60–61).

The dual linkage strategy was also important for the changes it signified in terms of the U.S. approach to the CSCE and to the Soviets. First, the dual linkage strategy signaled a departure from the traditional U.S. détente politics of the Kissinger era, where progress in superpower relations was subordinate to improvements in Soviet behavior on any number of (unrelated) fronts. Indeed, the breakdown in superpower bilateral talks in 1983 in the MBFR and on START left the CSCE as the only forum for East-West dialogue, and this situation also had the effect of releasing the CSCE from the subordinate position it had earlier occupied vis-à-vis U.S. strategic objectives. In fact, to some extent the obverse took hold: that is, in light of the achievements of the Stockholm document and Soviet interest to bring the MBFR talks under the umbrella of the CSCE, the Helsinki process began to serve as the overarching framework for East-West cooperation. France actively supported such developments and in fact encouraged the neutral and nonaligned countries who demanded that as a minimum there be an exchange of views and information between the twenty-three (former MBFR) states and thirty-five (CSCE) states on the Negotiations on Conventional Armed Forces in Europe and the possibility of establishing a common forum in the future, terms which were eventually agreed upon in Vienna despite U.S. resistance.[60]

Second, these developments led the United States to pursue a more organic linkage between security and progress in human rights in the CSCE. Several factors help explain the increased leverage that the United States gained with this new approach. For the first time in February 1986, there were signs of political

59. Ambassador Oleg Grinevsky, interview by author, tape recording, Embassy of the Russian Federation, Stockholm, Dec. 20, 1994.

60. Swedish official, interview by author, tape recording, Foreign Ministry, Stockholm, May 25, 1988.

change that could lead to the domestication of CSCE norms and principles in the practices of the Soviet regime. On the occasion of the 27th Communist Party congress, Gorbachev "declared a fundamental principle of 'an all-embracing system of international security' would be the 'resolution in a humanitarian and positive spirit of questions related to the reuniting of families, marriage, and the promotion of contacts between people and between organizations' " (as quoted in Korey 1993, 189). The Soviets' acceptance of the verification and on-site inspection regime in Stockholm in July 1986 was also taken as evidence of a fundamental shift in thinking (Korey 1993, 222). While Gorbachev's proposal to bring MBFR under the CSCE auspices played into France's interests, it also gave the West as a whole the possibility of using this Soviet objective as a means of leveraging compliance on human rights. Even though the United States was reluctant to see the bilateral negotiations on conventional forces subject to the consensus decision-making process of the multilateral CSCE process, gaining leverage on human rights was clearly in its interests. U.S. Ambassador Rozanne Ridgeway stressed that a strategy of leverage and linkage was essential to achieve progress in all three baskets at Vienna.

Third, this approach marked a shift in the U.S. cold war détente policy where its multilateral cooperation with the Soviets was largely conditioned to the superpowers' strategic relationship. This shift brought the U.S. policy on the CSCE more closely in line with its West European partners, whose relations had been disrupted as late as 1986 by the refusal of the United States to adhere to the N+N draft concluding document at the Bern meeting on Human Contacts. Along with the policy positions the West and the N+N had outlined in the Ottawa and Budapest meetings, the new U.S. policy opened the way for a more united and concerted Western stand on human-rights issues in the approach to the Vienna conference and throughout the meeting. This development was also facilitated, however, by evidence in Vienna of the Soviets' willingness to adhere to the more far-reaching commitments the United States had pushed in Bern, thus also legitimizing the U.S. stance vis-à-vis its allies. Finally, the dual linkage strategy was organic also in the sense that the United States now used in a concrete way the rules and norms of the CSCE process to achieve specific results in Soviet compliance on human rights. This approach diminished the importance of public diplomacy as mere propaganda and enhanced the enforcement aspect of the CSCE. Further legitimacy was thus given to the notion of comprehensive security, so that international peace and cooperation came to embrace the protection of human rights and the right of states' to intervene in other states' internal affairs in defense of those rights. Finally, the dual linkage strategy tied the United States into multilateralizing its own approach to East-West security—an outcome that also helped to strengthen the notion of cooperative security as a way out of cold war confrontation.

8 Institutionalizing Peaceful Change

THE PROBLEM OF PEACEFUL CHANGE in international politics is finding a way to transform conflict and solve political problems without war—whereas in national politics it is a question of renewing the domestic political system without violent revolution. In both cases the concept embraces a notion of agency—a set of actors effecting political change, and instrumentality—the mechanisms and tools they use. Peaceful change concerns both the standards and methods of managing relationships that allow adversaries and partners to continue to work out problems. There is also a close relationship between the principles and instruments of peaceful change. Principles of peaceful change shape expectations about acceptable and appropriate ways to govern behavior and manage change. Whereas in domestic society principles of peaceful change sanction practices such as free, democratic elections, in international relations the equivalent kind of peaceful governance can be achieved by institutionalizing mechanisms and procedures to work out differences and resolve disputes between states (Holsti 1991).

But the institutionalization of the CSCE posed numerous challenges for CSCE participating states in the aftermath of the signing of the Final Act. This difficult task had been left to work out at the first follow-up conference in Belgrade in 1977. Yet increasing superpower tensions amid the East's flagrant violations of Basket III ensured a less-than-propitious atmosphere. The first post-Helsinki gathering seemed more destined to foul up than follow-up the Final Act.

To prevent such a suicide theory from becoming reality, the N+N continued to intervene as third parties. They provided the catalyst that helped to underpin the institutionalization of the CSCE process, when there were no mechanisms yet in place to govern the process and secure its durability. Their contributions included the assumption of key organizational responsibilities, including the forging of consensus on procedural solutions to the institutional structure and modalities of the CSCE follow-up process. This meant getting consensus on the purpose of the review of implementation and justification for new commitments. Both of these procedural considerations were politically explosive because they were shrouded in debate about how to deal with violations of CSCE commitments. The N+N also helped keep East and West at the table when tensions led to a new cold war. In effect, they endeavored to protect the rule effectiveness of the nascent institution.

Dearth of Institutional Guidelines

According to the minimalist approach set forth in the Final Act, the first follow-up to the CSCE was to be held in 1977 in Belgrade, where the participating states were to commit themselves to three broadly construed endeavors: (1) to pay due regard to and implement the provisions of the Final Act unilaterally, bilaterally, and multilaterally; (2) to proceed to a thorough exchange of views on the implementation of the provisions of the Final Act and, in this context, to deepen their mutual relations; and (3) to continue the multilateral process. Unilateral, bilateral, and multilateral implementation depended respectively on self-enforcement, negotiations with other participating states and meetings of experts of the participating states, and also on their cooperation within the framework of existing international organizations.

This sketchy mandate left many questions about the institutional development of the CSCE to be worked out in preparation for the Belgrade Follow-up. For example, the Final Act was nonspecific about whether a contingent relationship was implied between the review of implementation and the possibilities for the parties (given the results of the review) to proceed to "the deepening of their mutual relations, the improvement of security and the development of co-operation in Europe, and the development of the process of détente in the future."[1] Nor was there any CSCE precedent for making these practices operational. For example, should review come first, as implied by the order of the tasks enumerated in the Final Act? How long should a review go on? If there were serious shortcomings in the implementation of already-existing CSCE commitments, should there be any discussion of new substantive commitments? How long should the conference last? Should a closing date be set in advance? What criteria should be used to distinguish the impact and success of the CSCE from its outputs (additional agreements or new and deeper commitments)?

The absence in the Final Act of explicit rules and operating procedures for developing the follow-up process also left the CSCE vulnerable to increasing East-West tensions and a return to cold war polemics. From the late 1970s to the early—to mid-1980s, the external environment as well as the atmosphere at

1. See the section titled "Follow-up to the Conference," § 2 (a) in *Conference on Security and Cooperation in Europe. Stage III-Final Act.*

the negotiating table was hardly conducive to securing the governing capacity of the CSCE. The Eastern bloc anchored on old positions, having no intention in 1975 or afterwards of recognizing or implementing the human-rights agreements of the Helsinki Final Act (Korey 1993, xxi). Indeed, they had resisted the elaboration of these commitments at every step of the negotiation process during the multilateral preparatory talks in Dipoli in 1972–73 and throughout the negotiation rounds in Geneva leading up to the signing of the Helsinki Final Act. They were less than enthusiastic about the outcome of the agreement. They sought to "pigeonhole" the human-rights obligations, and thus practically disregard the conceptual political content of the Final Act as it related to the human dimension (Korey 1993, xxi). They had little interest in the Belgrade Follow-up having as its main responsibility a thorough review of implementation, as outlined in the Final Act. For the East, a CSCE with supervisory capabilities would turn the follow-up process into a zero-sum game.

Zbigniew Brzezinski, Carter's national security adviser, was influential in shaping the U.S. approach to the Belgrade conference. The architect behind the U.S. bridge-building policy toward Eastern Europe in the mid-1960s, Brzezinski viewed détente as inevitably challenging Soviet control of Eastern Europe. Seeing the Nixon-Kissinger strategy as one that ratified the division of Europe, Brzezinski brought to the Carter administration the policy that U.S. relations with Eastern Europe should not be subordinate to U.S.-Soviet relations. Carter's visits to Poland and Romania early in his administration underscored these intentions (Nathan and Oliver 1989, 354). Brzezinski sought to open channels for East European countries to develop closer ties to Western Europe. His method of liberating them was by isolating the Soviet Union and bringing the West to bear against the Soviets as a bloc (Jowitt 1977, 9–12).

Brzezinski's central objective was to make the Soviets really pay for the Helsinki Accords, to question the Soviets' internal regime publicly and "loudly proclaim [it] illegitimate, irrelevant, and even pernicious to the tide of progress sweeping the globe" (Nathan and Oliver 1989, 354). In his view, a truly comprehensive détente would be a challenge to the Soviet Union and would jeopardize their very existence. Thus, international moralism took sides with cold war confrontation, becoming indistinguishable in Carter foreign policy (Nathan and Oliver 1989, 357; Hoffman 1983, 76). As Brzezinski later explained, "I pushed hard and I believe effectively for a more assertive U.S. posture in the CSCE" (1985, 297).

The United States took the lead among the Western states in approaching the Belgrade review of implementation as an opportunity to punish the East for noncompliance (Mastny 1986, 155–61), for which the repression of dissident groups across many parts of the Soviet Union and Eastern Europe was ample motivation. The United States was prepared to use the CSCE as a club even at the cost of undermining delicate compromises that established CSCE procedural rules, and apparently at the risk of ending the CSCE. In his opening statement at Belgrade, U.S. Ambassador Arthur Goldberg, personally designated by President Carter to deliver the address, noted the wholehearted commitment of the United States to détente and stated the country's "considered view that a deepening of détente, a healing of the divisions in Europe, a relaxation of tensions in Europe, cannot be divorced from progress in humanitarian matters and human rights. The pursuit of human rights does not put détente in jeopardy." This was followed by references to specific Eastern bloc violations of the Final Act.[2] After the speech, Goldberg proceeded with a press conference (a practice the United States adopted at Belgrade) in order to elaborate in detail the names and situations of the cases raised. This was considered a serious breach of the rules of procedure, which called for the representatives to respect the confidentiality of the negotiations (Davy 1980, 9).

The politicized nature of the U.S. approach to Belgrade was also reflected in the composition of its delegation, in which the professional diplomats held a subordinate position. Goldberg, chief of the U.S. delegation, commanded considerable stature as a former ambassador to the United Nations and as a justice of the U.S. Supreme Court who was formerly active in Jewish affairs and the civil-rights movement. Along with this personal envoy, the U.S. team also included twelve senators and congressmen who were members of the Commission on Security and Cooperation in Europe, and numerous other officials both public and governmental (Davy 1980, 7). Their participation and the tactics employed by Goldberg introduced into the diplomatic setting both polemics and the competition between the State Department and the U.S. Congress over the country's policy in the negotiations. In fact, Goldberg "reported directly to the White House and could (and did) appeal to the president over the heads of his own delegation" (Skilling 1984, 297).[3] While interventions by U.S. senators flying into Belgrade to make statements were perhaps important politically for their constituency,[4] they also jeopardized the principle of consensus decision making, the mechanics of which other delegations felt these newcomers did not appreciate. No decision could be reached by forcing one's own view upon the other parties.[5]

2. Goldberg (United States), CSCE/BM/VR.6, *Belgrade Meeting 1977,* Verbatim Records of Opening Statements, Oct. 4–10, 1977, 27.

3. A Swedish official makes the same argument, noting that Goldberg was acting on a high level, as a personal representative to the president. Swedish official, interview by author, tape recording, Office of the Prime Minister, Stockholm, May 27, 1988.

4. The Canadians followed a similar practice.

5. Swedish official, interview by author, tape recording, Office of the Prime Minister, Stockholm, May 27, 1988.

The confrontational approach of the United States was at odds with some of its West European allies, and particularly West Germany. In contrast to U.S. efforts to isolate the Soviets, Helmut Schmidt continued West Germany's Ostpolitik through visits to Eastern Europe and with a "policy of small steps" to further engage East Germany. Secretly at the outset, the new administration paid ransom in Deutsch marks to secure the release of East German political prisoners. Trade between the states increased, as did amounts of interest-free credit to the GDR (Turner 1987; Clemens 1990). The West German objective was to use détente to make the separation of the two Germanies more humane and to stabilize relations with the East, including with the Soviet Union—without abandoning the hope of unification some day. Undermining Soviet relations with its own allies would put at risk these improvements in inner-German cooperation and would potentially destabilize German-Soviet relations.[6]

Thus, the change of administration in the United States did not help to advance policy coordination among the Western alliance members on the way to Belgrade. Even the NATO meetings held in Brussels before each negotiating phase at Belgrade served little more than to work out "a common general strategy" (Skilling 1984a, 294). During the Belgrade meeting, NATO accommodated itself to the EC positions, mostly reacting to them. Cooperation on the Western side between NATO and the EC was often strained, and during certain periods the EC did not want to include the United States in its position taking. There were also a number of solo performances. Within the EC, the French maintained their own views, while French President Giscard d'Estaing sought for France a special relationship with the Soviet Union. The United States was often on its own in attacking the Soviet Union for human-rights abuses and in its negotiating strategy.

If the N+N had worked throughout Dipoli and Geneva to sustain dialogue across bloc lines in an attempt to overcome the divided Europe, at Belgrade their challenge was to prevent renewed superpower confrontation from driving the CSCE to its end station. This thrust the N+N into a more formalized intermediary role at Belgrade. The N+N realized the lack of Western cohesion made it more important for them to take an active role. In his opening statement prior to the main Belgrade meeting, Austria's representative, Mr. Steiner, cautioned that it would be a mistake for one side to use the process of détente to obtain unilateral advantage over the other. He argued that détente means "a realistic estimate of possibilities" and declared that "détente has become indivisible" in a world where time and space are getting shorter and shorter.[7] Jaakko Iloniemi,

6. I am also indebted to Patricia Davis for this point.

7. Steiner (Austria), CSCE/BM/VR.4, *Belgrade Meeting 1977,* Verbatim Records of Opening Statements, Oct. 4–10, 1977, 138–39.

on behalf of the Finnish delegation, expressed what soon became the N+N's principle objective at Belgrade:

> We believe, Mr. Chairman, that we should organize our co-operation in such a manner that spells of colder winds in our political environment could not freeze our long-term achievements or actions. We should secure the preconditions for further multilateral efforts so that we could confidently rely on their solidity even if there might be some adverse developments in one area or another. This we can do by agreeing to continue our co-operation building on the basis laid down in the Final Act. If there were no such arrangements to secure continuity, how could we take stock of our experiences or learn from our mistakes?[8]

Sweden's representative, Leif Leifland, similarly emphasized the long-term goals: "it cannot be taken for granted that the present pattern of European security will remain unchanged in the long range. We do not want to exclude that one day it will be possible to dismantle the pact system on which our security is based today. This goal may of course seem very remote but it would be absurd and dangerous to get used to regarding it as unattainable." In Sweden's view, the follow-up meeting should be so conducted that future meetings were a natural outcome.[9]

The N+N were prepared to intervene as third parties to mitigate the effect of the East's intransigence, which threatened to void the CSCE of substantive and politically relevant outcomes—despite their national interests (promoting arms reduction and disarmament in particular). At the same time, they determined to disabuse both the West and East of manipulating the rules of procedure without regard to the destabilizing effect of their tactics on the negotiating process.

Paradoxically, the minimalist approach probably afforded greater flexibility for developing the CSCE follow-up process and safeguarding its continuity under difficult international conditions than if rigid institutional mechanisms had been explicitly developed in the Final Act. Necessity being the impetus behind invention, the N+N assumed two basic responsibilities; first, they endeavored to forge a consensus on procedural solutions to the organizational structure and modalities of the CSCE follow-up process. Consensus on two separate but related considerations had to be shaped: the function of the review of implementation where monitoring and sanctioning were at stake and the relationship of these activities to the consideration of new commitments. In addi-

8. Iloniemi (Finland), CSCE/BM/VR.4, *Belgrade Meeting 1977,* Verbatim Records of Opening Statements, Oct. 4–10, 1977, 102.

9. Leifland (Sweden), CSCE/BM/VR. 3, *Belgrade Meeting 1977,* Verbatim Records of Opening Statements, Oct. 4–10, 1977, 70–71.

tion, the N+N sought to secure these results against backsliding and other adverse contingencies in future follow-up meetings. Adherence to these procedural arrangements was fundamental for the rule effectiveness of the CSCE. At stake was the establishment of an historic precedent: using internationally agreed norms and standards to hold a state politically accountable for the treatment of its own citizens. In the CSCE accountability meant demonstrating through an open debate among the thirty-five participating states that noncompliance could bring political costs.[10] The first crucial test came at the opening of the Belgrade preparatory talks. The N+N interventions helped to secure the key institutional functions of the CSCE.

N+N as Precursors

In the 1977 Belgrade meeting, the N+N helped make operational the "minimalist approach" set out in the Final Act as the basis for continuing the CSCE. They facilitated agreement on both the agenda for the main meeting and the concluding communiqué, which together set the parameters for the institutional development of the CSCE. The continuity of the CSCE was predicated on the follow-up meetings and its governing capacity on the review of implementation, for example, the right of participating states to examine the record of implementation and to raise issues to this effect with the other participating states. Participating states could not claim that scrutiny was an infringement or illegal intervention into their internal affairs of state. This hard-won interpretation was a product of the considerable bargaining that went into making the agenda for the Belgrade meeting (the Yellow Book), which was put to the test throughout the very difficult Belgrade negotiations.

The organizational structure of the CSCE follow-up process stems from the precedents set in Belgrade and the final communiqué that the participating states agreed on. First, the organizational structure of the CSCE follow-up reflected the phases through which the negotiations would progress (preparatory meeting, opening speeches, review of implementation, tabling proposals and general debate, drafting in smaller groups, etc.). Second, the Dipoli rules of procedure (from the Blue Book) were reaffirmed and adopted in the Yellow Book, thus ensuring continued adherence to consensus decision making. Furthermore,

10. Skilling (1984, 286) makes this point, adding that these mechanisms produced stronger machinery for dealing with violations than were available to the United Nations human-rights covenants. The criticism was open and public—a fact underscored by the practice followed by the U.S. delegation in the Madrid Follow-up meeting and by other Western delegations to grant interviews with the press regarding specific individual human-rights abuses that had been (or were to be) raised in the negotiations.

Belgrade established that among the tasks of the follow-up was the drafting and attainment of consensus on a final, concluding document, which, for example, would specify the place and date of the next follow-up. The agenda for the 1980 Madrid meeting weakened this provision somewhat, but by the 1986 Vienna Follow-up there were no longer any questions about "whether to meet at all." The question was rather "where, when and under what conditions follow-up meetings will occur."

Belgrade also institutionalized the use of "expert meetings" as a means of sustaining East-West contact between sessions and for providing an exchange of views and the development of substantive documents on more specialized issues. In fact, the East sought to get more expert meetings in their capitals (citing the rotation principle and the need to balance the trend of hosting CSCE meetings in the West). The West refuted this idea, since the concept of blocs was alien to the Final Act and the question was instead one of consensus. The West argued that the choice of sites was conditional on favorable working conditions for journalists and nongovernmental organizations and "the host state having an exemplary record in the area to be discussed." [11]

By facilitating work according to the consensus decision-making rule, the N+N played face-saving roles that helped make it politically possible for East and West to sustain their commitment to the CSCE process. Given the destabilizing negotiating strategies of the bloc participants, the N+N were indispensable in their effort at Belgrade to produce a "fair" and balanced, though admittedly meager, substantive document. In the Madrid Follow-up, the N+N defended the political viability of the CSCE, both by promoting concrete, and significant substantive results, and by providing face-saving interventions to obtain long recesses when good results were in jeopardy. Finally, they helped secure the linkage promoted by the West between progress on human rights and disarmament, thus contributing to a multifaceted conception of security in East-West relations.

Setting the Agenda: 1977 Belgrade Preparatory Meeting

Even before the modalities for the follow-up negotiations could be discussed at the preparatory meeting in Belgrade, NATO and the EC tabled a complete proposal for a working program to the follow-up. This action prompted the Soviets to counter with their own proposal, and a hardening of positions ensued.[12]

11. See Commission on Security and Cooperation in Europe, United States Congress, *Phase II of the Vienna Review Meeting of the Conference on Security and Cooperation in Europe,* Jan. 27–Apr. 10, 1987 (Washington, D.C.: Government Printing Office) 21.

12. Swedish official, interview by author, tape recording, Office of the Prime Minister, Stockholm, May 27, 1988. See also "USA:alta ja EEC:ltä malli jatko Etykille," *Suomenmaa,* June 17,

For the West a thorough review of the implementation of the provisions of the Final Act was a precondition to "deepening relations." Thus, the West argued that extending cooperation in new directions should be carried out in light of the review. To this end, the West took the position in the preparatory talks that the agenda set no deadline for a conclusion to the meeting. On the other hand, the East declared it wanted to emphasize discussing new ideas and improving cooperation. In fact, the Soviets intended simply to quote the Final Act and diminish the part of checking up on the implementation—which for the N+N and the West was the main idea behind the follow-up meeting. Moreover, the Soviets expected the main meeting to conclude before the Christmas holidays.[13]

Although the N+N countries had their own interests in pursuing disarmament and the CBM regime,[14] the confrontational approach of East and West to this first follow-up rendered the N+N's participation as third parties essential for reaching an agreement on the Belgrade agenda. Initially the four neutrals commenced close cooperation, but because of the heavy workload Yugoslavia was brought in because it was the host country; then the other N+N delegations took part, too.[15] Amid appeals from the East and Yugoslavia that all sides sustain a constructive climate, Austria hinted that the neutral and nonaligned would be prepared to act as an intermediary in an effort to create an agenda for the main meeting.[16]

While consulting the two blocs separately, the N+N also took care that their own aims were among the points of the working program, in particular (1) that the continuity of the CSCE process be ensured, including the mechanism of expert meetings, and (2) that specification of the date and place of the next follow-up meeting be agreed upon.[17] Only after repeated attempts at a compromise, all of which were rejected by the Soviet Union, the N+N found a solution they felt was good—although it clearly indicated that the N+N had thrown

---

1977, UILA. On the Soviet-bloc position see "Etyk-asialista eteni," *Aamu Lehti,* June 18, 1977, UILA.

13. Swedish official, interview by author, tape recording, Office of the Prime Minister, Stockholm, May 27, 1988.

14. For a summary of their substantive positions and proposals, see chapter 7.

15. Swedish official, interview by author, tape recording, Office of the Prime Minister, Stockholm, May 27, 1988. See also Veikko I. Pajunen, "Sveitsin Etyk-ujostelu asteittain häviämässä," *Helsingin Sanomat,* June 4, 1977, UILA.

16. Heikki Aarnio, "Suomi valmiina välittäjän osaan," *Helsingin Sanomat,* June 21, 1977, UILA.

17. See for example, "Puolueettomat sovittelivat idän ja lännen näkemyksia esityksessään," *Helsingin Sanomat,* July 2, 1977; "Uusi Etyk-ehdotus ei tyydytä itää," *Uusi Suomi,* July 10, 1977; "Sitoutumattomat esittävät: Yhdeksän kohdan ohjelma ETYK-seurannan pohjaksi," *Kansan Uutiset,* July 17, 1977, UILA.

their weight toward the West. The solution was presented by Spain, which the N+N believed to be a good tactical move, and it was accepted.[18]

The Belgrade agenda, or the Yellow Book, called for a thorough exchange of views, specifically an examination of the implementation of the Final Act, to be followed by the presentation of new proposals, the drafting of a concluding document, and the determination of the future follow-up conference including its date and place. The rules of procedure adopted in Geneva on the basis of the Blue Book were again adopted at Belgrade, mutatis mutandis. In accordance with decisions read into the Journal (No. 66) on August 5, 1977, it was also noted in the Yellow Book that "nothing in these decisions, or in the other decisions adopted by the Preparatory Meeting, can prejudice the principle of consensus." [19]

Like the initial CSCE negotiations, the Belgrade meeting progressed through three stages: presentation of opening statements, implementation and drafting, and presentation of concluding statements. The controversial aspect of the follow-up concerned the organization of work in the second stage. The N+N solution called for eight weeks of debate, followed by work in subsidiary bodies to be concluded by December 16 so that the plenary could make every effort to have the concluding document drafted no later than December 22, 1977. If this were not possible, then the plenary could set up drafting groups to resume work in mid-January to last until mid-February to reach a concluding document.

The agenda gave the negotiators a general framework and referent principles, ensuring balanced treatment of the baskets, a review of implementation, and the drafting of new proposals in light of this review. However, procedurally, this formula favored the West. For the first time in the history of diplomacy, governments' compliance with a multilateral instrument was scrutinized, giving way to open criticism of others' failure to implement the agreement (Skilling 1984a, 286). The Soviet Union and its allies, especially East Germany and Czechoslovakia, were subject to considerable attack, with specific cases of human-rights violations raised, as well as other issues pertaining to the free flow of information, treatment of journalists, etc. While the West and the N+N viewed the implementation debate as "a genuine achievement," they were concerned with Soviet threats that continuation of the debate would lead them to call off the conference. Furthermore, they were not pleased with the way the

18. Swedish official, interview by author, tape recording, Office of the Prime Minister, Stockholm, May 27, 1988. See also Heikki Aarnio, "Beograd päätyi kompromissiin," *Helsingin Sanomat,* Aug. 4, 1977, UILA.

19. *Decisions of the Preparatory Meeting to Organize the Belgrade Meeting 1977 of Representatives of the Participating States of the Conference on Security and Cooperation in Europe, Held on the Basis of the Provisions of the Final Act Relating to the Follow-up to the Conference* (Belgrade: Sava Centre, 1977).

"exchange of views" turned into East-West confrontation, and especially the way the Soviets countered criticism with "*tu quoque* arguments against the West" (Skilling 1984a, 286–87). The Soviets also refused to accept the principle that new proposals and drafting reflect or be carried out in light of a review of implementation, further polarizing the meeting.

N+N's "Fatherless, Motherless, Nameless Child"

In the main Belgrade meeting, formal drafting groups were set up with regular meetings with a fixed chairman for the whole time, because it was realized that there were problems with the rotating chairman system (some simply did not facilitate the process). Because of the polemics and bloc dynamics that added to the complexity of the negotiations, different subsidiary bodies or working groups were set up at different stages in Belgrade. Nevertheless, the basic distribution of coordinating responsibilities resulted in Austria chairing Basket III, Finland Basket II, Switzerland Basket I, and Sweden the follow-up. Malta characteristically attended to the Mediterranean issue.[20] This distribution was determined internally by the N+N themselves; agreement of the other delegations was sought by silent acceptance, carefully negotiated in the corridor. The selection process took account of the personalities, as well as the name of the country and the image, because each of these played an important role. Chairing the working groups was challenging, because those appointed were also heads of delegation and needed to keep abreast of developments within their own negotiating team, hold meetings with other heads of delegation, and generally keep well informed as to the direction of the conference as a whole. The role required above all that the delegate coordinating know the material and keep track of details not only on all the proposals but also on the amendments.[21] In Belgrade it became more and more customary for the N+N to head up the drafting, too, because, as one Swedish official recalls, "otherwise one could not have a balance between the two blocs."[22]

By late November 1977, there was little cause to warrant optimism that consensus on a final document would be attained in time for the target December deadline set out in the Yellow Book; there were still more new proposals to be considered. As a holiday recess loomed inevitable, in the main meeting the

20. Swedish official, interview by author, tape recording, Office of the Prime Minister, Stockholm, May 27, 1988.

21. Finnish official, interview by author, tape recording, Foreign Ministry, Helsinki, May 12, 1988.

22. Swedish official, interview by author, tape recording, Office of the Prime Minister, Stockholm, May 27, 1988.

negotiation process became very complicated. Realizing their target date might not be reached, the Eastern bloc accused the West of having used up time by expounding endlessly on human rights, thereby distorting the tasks of the follow-up process. To bring the process to a speedy end, they proposed that a single drafting group take charge of pulling the proposals together in a concluding document (Skilling 1984a, 287). The Western delegations, as was typical of their approach, insisted that it was important for each of the proposals to be carefully examined, pressing instead for the discussion and negotiating work to proceed in the separate drafting groups.

Nonetheless, prior to the Christmas break several efforts were made to commence the drafting work. In early December, France proposed a general outline for a final document;[23] to this project Western delegations submitted more detailed documents,[24] but these were not acceptable to the Soviet Union. Among other things, in reviewing the freer movement and contacts among individuals, the West's draft document "expressed concern at the number of cases in these areas which remain unresolved, despite expectations that the general practice would reflect the favourable, positive and humanitarian spirit of the . . . Final Act."[25] In sum, the impasse centered on how much and what could be said about the implementation debate in the final document. The Soviets wanted an agreement that would say the discussion "has been good, useful, constructive." But this was not the case, and the N+N, not to say the West, would not entertain any formulation to this effect.[26]

To facilitate the drafting, the N+N introduced their first jointly sponsored N+N compromise document, BM. 65. It was the first draft paper to cover the whole field of proposals discussed at Belgrade. Although the text was more general, it was intended to give momentum to the negotiations. In the view of its sponsors, BM. 65 presented a viable zone of agreement within which the negotiators could work for a final document.[27] On the delicate issue of the imple-

23. "Outline of Concluding Document of the Belgrade Meeting 1977 of Representatives of the Participating States of the Conference on Security and Co-Operation in Europe, Held on the Basis of the Provisions of the Final Act Relating to the Follow-up to the Conference, Submitted by the Delegation of France," CSCE/BM/61, Belgrade, Dec. 2, 1977.

24. "Proposal Submitted by the Delegations of Belgium, Canada, Denmark, France, Federal Republic of Germany, Ireland, Italy, Luxembourg, The Netherlands, Norway and the United Kingdom," CSCE/BM/69, Belgrade, Dec. 16, 1977.

25. Ibid., 4.

26. Swedish official, interview by author, tape recording, Office of the Prime Minister, Stockholm, May 27, 1988. See also "Suomi Etykistä: Varovaista optimismia," *Aamu Lehti,* Dec. 21, 1977, UILA.

27. Swedish official, interview by author, tape recording, Office of the Prime Minister, Stockholm, May 27, 1988.

mentation debate, the N+N attempted to state as a matter of fact that "a thorough exchange of views on the implementation . . . was carried out" and that "divergent views were expressed as to the degree of implementation." They also noted there was "encouraging progress in the process of implementation, but shortcomings, including cases of nonimplementation, called for further action."[28] Nevertheless, in a conversation with the Swedish coordinator, Soviet Ambassador Vorontsov made it clear the Soviets could never accept a document of the type the N+N had proposed. It was politically unacceptable because the N+N draft document, which had attempted to describe the implementation debate, would demonstrate to everyone else that the United States had shown how bad the Soviets behaved in the human-rights field.[29]

While the West was not especially satisfied with the N+N's December working paper because it did not give any "special emphasis" to human rights, it would have been willing to proceed on this basis. However, Ambassador Goldberg wanted specific points on human rights included in a final document, which took into account the individual cases raised by the West in the implementation debate. Ambassador Vorontsov replied that, if this were the case, then the Soviets would insist the document include their proposal for a "programme of action with a view to the consolidation of military détente in Europe." This program included a call for a treaty on the "no first use" of nuclear weapons to be reached in an "all-European conference," and an appeal to convene a special joint consultation among all CSCE participants to discuss disarmament and to agree that the military alliance and political groupings and alliances confronting each other in Europe should not be enlarged by the addition of new members.[30] These positions were entirely unacceptable to the West, not the least because "first use" constituted one of the doctrinal pillars of the NATO strategy in Europe. The Soviet proposal also hailed back to the early decades of Soviet efforts to convene an all-European conference at the expense of the United States' leading role in Western Europe through NATO.

As these attempts in December failed, a crucial opportunity to establish a turning point of seriousness in the negotiations and a general framework for drafting the final document were lost. Because of time pressures set out in the Yellow Book, the endeavor to reach agreement had been accelerated before the possibility of sufficient debate, a careful examination of positions, and the

28. "Proposal Submitted by the Delegations of Austria, Cyprus, Finland, Liechtenstein, Sweden, Switzerland and Yugoslavia," CSCE/BM/65, Belgrade, Dec. 7, 1977, 4.

29. Swedish official, interview by author, tape recording, Office of the Prime Minister, Stockholm, May 27, 1988.

30. "Proposal of the Union of Soviet Socialist Republics presented by the USSR Delegation," CSCE BM.5, Belgrade, Oct. 24, 1977.

arrangement of a setting amenable to serious drafting and the building of consensus. Moving quickly from the presentation of (comprehensive) proposals to drafting a premature concluding document led to intransigence and worked against a problem-solving and consensus building approach between the blocs.

After the Christmas break, several other attempts at a final document followed much in the same vein as those in December. The first of these was a Soviet document, received by the West and the N+N as a short and uninspired document, which did not even take into account positions the Soviets had themselves introduced. The only encouraging point reached in January 1978 was Soviet acceptance of the position held by all delegations in the West and among the N+N that the next CSCE conference be held in Madrid and that its opening date be specified. Yet even here agreement was limited. Still at stake was consensus on principles and procedures for the next review of implementation. The West wanted to affirm in the Belgrade final document that the Yellow Book would serve as the basis for the modalities of the Madrid meeting. This plan was unacceptable to the Soviets, who had no interest in agreeing to a process that could lead to a repeat performance of the Belgrade implementation debate.

The impasse over this issue turned into a serious crisis. In light of the meager Soviet document, Ambassador Goldberg even threatened the other delegations by bringing out his own thirty-page final document, which could not help but irritate the Soviets in particular. This brash tactical move, and Goldberg's insistence on reviewing human-rights violations in detail, further diminished any possibilities for a common stand among the allies; even Norway and West Germany questioned the advisability of the U.S. approach.[31] Finally, Goldberg turned to the N+N and asked them to come up with a draft for the concluding document,[32] and the Soviets signaled likewise.[33]

On the first of February, the N+N circulated unofficially their final draft, which omitted positions wholly unacceptable to both superpowers while trying to find common ground around the remaining points.[34] It was the last compre-

31. Swedish official, interview by author, tape recording, Office of the Prime Minister, Stockholm, May 27, 1988. Skilling notes that this was an example of how Goldberg sometimes acted independently "without the prior knowledge, and to the embarrassment, of his own delegation as well as of the State Department." Skilling also notes that "this 'undiplomatic' behavior was . . . also [disturbing] to other allied and NNA [neutral and nonaligned] delegations, not to mention those of the Soviet bloc" (1984, 297). See also Heikki Aarnio, "Suurvaltojen jurkkyys lukitsi Etykokouksen," *Helsingin Sanomat,* Feb. 1, 1978, UILA.

32. Swedish official, interview by author, tape recording, Office of the Prime Minister, Stockholm, May 27, 1988.

33. "Puolueettomien Etyk-ehdotus vaikeuksissa: Itäryhmä epäroi edelleen," *Helsingin Sanomat,* Feb. 4, 1977, UILA.

34. Heikki Aarnio, "Loppuasiakirjasta oma ehdotus sitoutumattomilta," *Helsingin Sanomat,* Feb. 2, 1978, UILA.

hensive attempt to produce a document with substance, although the work was "very tough, very trying." The Western countries in Europe could have accepted this five-thousand-word document, but the Soviets could not because of human rights and because the N+N spoke too much about the implementation debate. On this matter the Soviets did not permit any critical comments whatsoever.[35] The Soviets now signaled they would push for a short communiqué.

Nonetheless, work proceeded in smaller drafting groups convened among the participating states that had been most active and had presented the most proposals, i.e., the United States, the Soviet Union, Denmark (for the EC), and typically some of the N+N countries (Sweden, Switzerland, Yugoslavia, and Malta because of the Mediterranean issue).[36] Throughout February, only more failed attempts at a final document followed—first by the Soviets, later the French, and then the Americans. The drafts by the latter two were wholly unacceptable even to the Western alliance members. Various attempts to exert influence over the process came also from outside the negotiation setting. From a meeting in Copenhagen, the EC signaled its support for the N+N draft for a concluding document, satisfied the latter were closer to their position than the other participants; but support for the N+N draft was really a measure of its own internal disarray, a consequence of French determination to go its own way.[37] In the meantime, Keijo Korhonen, head of the Finnish Foreign Ministry, visited Belgrade and met with heads of delegation from all sides. Korhonen explained (along the lines of the "suicide theory") that, in working to achieve the necessary compromise, the idea continuously guiding the former host was to ensure that Belgrade does not become "the CSCE end station." [38]

Finally, after an EC-NATO draft (excluding France) also failed to meet the test of consensus, it was decided that a short communiqué would be issued. To this end, the N+N contributed a paper that they termed a "fatherless, motherless and nameless child." In their view it was not a proposal that they could present as their position, but rather an "instrument" in order to continue the CSCE follow-ups.[39] After revisions and some insistence from Malta, a final communiqué was devised that did, at least, ensure the continuity of the CSCE, if not the basis of its modalities for Madrid. The communiqué secured three ex-

35. Swedish official, interview by author, tape recording, Office of the Prime Minister, Stockholm, May 27, 1988.

36. The Swedish delegation, working together with Yugoslavia, was still trying to get more concrete measures included on CBMs; it was eventually accepted that such matters of substance would not be addressed at Belgrade. Switzerland continued to insist that it would not agree to a document without an expert group on the free flow of information.

37. "EEC:ltä ei vielä Etyk-aloitetta," *Helsingin Sanomat,* Feb. 14, 1978, UILA.

38. "Korhonen: Suomella ei tärkeysasteita," *Helsingin Sanomat,* Feb. 11, 1978, UILA.

39. Pentti Suominen, "Sitoutumattomien esitys saamassa N-liiton tuen," *Helsingin Sanomat,* Feb. 25, 1978, UILA.

pert meetings in the meantime, thus fulfilling to some extent the Swiss and Maltese expectations on this point. It also established expert meetings as part of the follow-up mechanism to the CSCE process.

Madrid Preparatory Meeting

On September 9, 1980, the preparatory meeting commenced in Madrid, in spite of doubts during preceding months that the Madrid meeting would be held at all. France was intent on reaching a substantive outcome for its CDE proposal (see chapter 7) and argued that the international conditions were unfavorable for an East-West meeting. But the other alliance members determined to proceed with the conference as scheduled, arguing that the Madrid meeting was opportune to review CSCE violations, including the Soviet invasion of Afghanistan.[40] At Madrid, the superpowers' initial restraint in keeping out the polemics that predominated in Belgrade gave way within a few weeks to an air of confrontation. The Soviets' opening tactic was to test the competence of the main meeting to take up the implementation debate. The West wanted to carry out monitoring on an ongoing basis, rather than have the review limited to the opening phase and separated from the new drafting (as had been agreed in the Yellow Book). Spain, on behalf of the West, proposed that the Yellow Book serve as the primary basis for devising the Madrid agenda. This proposal was unacceptable to the East, because the Belgrade formulation had resulted in an "optical division" (Sizoo and Jurrjens 1984, 136–37). A blank line of text made clear the separation between instructions for a "thorough exchange of views," both on the implementation of the provisions of the Final Act and of the tasks defined by the conference and the deepening of these provisions. Dividing the implementation debate and drafting of new proposals into two distinct phases had proved an expedient maneuver for the West at Belgrade to get a full implementation debate.

However, at Madrid the West insisted on expanding the review functions. If new violations of the Final Act should come to light, the West retained the right to return to the implementation debate, even after the allotted period for debate had passed. With the East insisting the agenda specify a "cut-off" to the implementation debate at the very least, the preparatory meeting reached an impasse. There was a real possibility that the hour of the opening to the main meeting would arrive without agreement on how to proceed. The West judged the Soviet tactics a ploy to make it the *demandeur* on the issue of a follow-up and thus responsible for collapse of the CSCE in the event of no agreement. For their part, the N+N, like the West, emphasized the importance of adhering to the principle

40. See "Ranska yrittää lykätä Madridin Etykiä," *Helsingin Sanomat,* Mar. 22, 1980, UILA.

of debating the implementation as a basic aspect of the follow-up and a precondition for shaping substantive texts.

Taking into account the various proposals presented by Spain, Hungary, Czechoslovakia, and East Germany, Finland made the first third-party initiative to arrive at a pragmatic solution. Warning of the difficulties negotiators would inevitably face with too-specific instructions on the organization of the working program and the various working groups, the Finnish proposal was an implicit criticism of the modalities proposed by the East. With this effort received favorably but reservedly by all parties, the deadlock continued and led to considerable drama during the last week of the preparatory meeting. Sweden attempted to orchestrate a joint N+N proposal for the agenda but failed mainly because of Switzerland's more western position. In this instance, as was often the case, it was an issue of the Swedish between the Swiss and the Finns ideologically speaking.[41]

Thus, a week before the scheduled start of the main Madrid meeting, Sweden presented its own compromise proposal. There had been some debate between the Swedish and Finnish delegations concerning the wisdom of one individual N+N country going it alone rather than trying some bilateral solution, because it was clear that the Swiss did not want to join in this effort. While Finland was predisposed to working bilaterally with Sweden, Swedish officials took the view that it should be either a national effort, or include at least the four neutrals, or possibly the entire N+N. Sweden was in fact reluctant to compromise its position within the N+N as a key interlocutor by emphasizing bilateral initiatives with Finland. For these reasons, Sweden went it alone with a proposal for the agenda, but it failed "to buy everything the East wanted."[42]

With the Swedish initiative rejected, and East and West standing by their points of departure going into the weekend before the conference was to open, the Soviets proposed that an honest broker be selected to go between the East and West delegations to see if a solution could be found.[43] Although the West proposed Sweden, the Soviets proposed Switzerland. Ideologically speaking the Swiss were much further from the Soviet position, but they were proposed in light of Switzerland's long-standing neutrality and diplomatic experience mediating. Maintaining constant contact with the N+N caucus, the Swiss delegate's efforts as a go-between failed during that weekend, too. Finally, on the day before the conference was to commence, there was an opening for another N+N attempt, which also failed. In the end, the only way out of the difficulty was

41. Swedish official, interview by author, tape recording, Riksdag, Stockholm, May 18, 1988. See also Sizoo and Jurrjens (1984, 169).

42. Swedish official, interview by author, tape recording, Riksdag, Stockholm, May 26, 1988.

43. Ibid.

procedural, which led to a period of stopping the clocks (Sizoo and Jurrjens 1984, 196).[44]

With the successful launching of the Madrid conference and the continuity and integrity of the CSCE hanging in the balance, the foreign ministers of the N+N came to Madrid. During the rest of the week things were solved by various means, one being stopping the clocks and the other—thanks to the efforts of the Spanish delegation and their foreign minister—letting the main meeting start "on time," although the preparatory work had not yet finished.[45] The appearance by several of the N+N foreign ministers (from Austria, Cypress, Sweden, and Yugoslavia), along with the verbal support of the delegations from Liechtenstein, Malta, and San Marino, lent political prestige behind what was then finally an N+N/Spanish foreign ministry proposal for the solution to the main problems.[46] After six weeks of review of implementation, the deliberations should be closed and debate on new proposals commenced. However, the West stuck to its principle that the implementation debate could be reopened—and in fact did so after martial law was declared in Poland in December 1981 (Sizoo and Jurrjens 1984, especially 133–39). The agenda (the Purple Book) then called for the presentation of proposals and debate, to be followed by three weeks of work at the drafting level to commence on February 12, 1981. Thereafter, "every effort" was to be made to bring the Madrid meeting to a concluding document by March 1981.

The issue of the continuity of the CSCE process as agreed in the preparatory meeting's Purple Book proved more troubling. The West had been surprised at the Eastern bloc's refusal to accept as a matter of course that the Madrid conference would reach an agreement on the date and place of the next follow-up meeting—what was already established in the Yellow Book at Belgrade as among the key tasks of the follow-up meeting. In fact, the Soviet bloc attempted to condition agreement for a post-Madrid CSCE follow-up on the specification also of the date and place for a European disarmament conference, on which issue the Soviets emerged as *demandeurs*. The Soviets wanted to ensure that Madrid would produce concrete results rather than reproduce the Belgrade ex-

44. Swedish official, interview by author, tape recording, Riksdag, Stockholm, May 26, 1988.

45. The meeting actually "began" at 11:40 in the evening and "lasted no more than three minutes." See Sizoo and Jurrjens (1984, 196).

46. Finland, however, did not add its name to the compromise, pointing to its concern that the solution was a delicate one and insisting that the modalities of the work and the task of reaching a final document should be an integral aspect of the follow-up process. Finland did not send its foreign minister because it determined the situation did not merit that level of attention, a position that was consistent with its policy of avoiding "the occasional show and political opportunism" of which other participants availed themselves. Swedish official, interview by author, tape recording, Riksdag, Stockholm, May 26, 1988.

perience of endless attacks on its human-rights record and that of its Eastern bloc allies.

Thus, as part of its agenda for the main Madrid meeting, the Purple Book called (in ambiguous language) for the "definition of the appropriate modalities for the holding of other meetings in conformity with all the provisions of the chapter of the Final Act concerning the Follow-up to the conference." However, a statement by the chairman included in the Purple Book took note of the "general understanding of the Meeting that the definition in the concluding document of the appropriate modalities for the holding of other Meetings includes setting the date and place of the next Meeting similar to the present one." Thus, although the language was less incontrovertible than agreed in Belgrade (which had used the phrase in two parts of the Yellow Book that "the Belgrade Meeting would 'in any case' fix the date and place of the next similar meeting"), the West felt it had gotten a Soviet commitment on the matter. Nevertheless, the Soviets persisted in their attempt to link the question of the follow-up to Madrid with the issue of the NATO countries' "amenability" on the mandate for a European disarmament conference (Sizoo and Jurrjens 1984, 140–41). Hence, the Madrid meeting was a test of rule compliance also in terms of Soviet accession to the principle of the (unconditional) continuity of the CSCE process as a basic task of the follow-up meetings.

N+N and the Madrid Follow-Up

As the main Madrid meeting unfolded, the N+N assumed their now-customary role as coordinators, dividing among themselves the responsibilities for heading up the work in what were called the "contact groups," which had been established informally in relation to the four baskets. In this particular instance, there was some controversy between Finland and Sweden over who should take coordinatorship of Basket I and the working group on the proposed Conference on Disarmament in Europe. Sweden wanted this coordinatorship precisely because it had "sacrificed" its own CDE proposal at Madrid. However, Finland countered that this was why Finland was in a better position to build consensus.

The matter reached the presidential level in Finland because Kekkonen wanted to use the Madrid Follow-up to enhance the country's profile on military-security issues. He saw this as a means to counter pressures from the East, which resulted from the development of Eurostrategic nuclear weapons, especially cruise missiles. These were threatening to upset the delicate balance in the Nordic region, especially because of their technical capabilities: flying at altitudes of a few hundred meters high, these missiles could make use of third countries, and particularly neutral air space, to reach targets on the other side. The Soviets did not fail to pick up on this theme as a reason to bring political pressure to bear on the neutrals, and through them presumably to influence Denmark and Norway's position in NATO's decision to deploy the missiles. A prominent Soviet commentator of Finnish foreign policy argued that " 'any flight by American cruise missiles through the air space of countries like Sweden and Finland would very urgently prompt the question not only of whether the belligerent parties should be allowed to use the territory of countries not involved in the conflict, but also of the latters' right and obligation to defend their territorial inviolability.' " To this end he recalled Finland's military obligations under the terms of the 1948 Treaty of Friendship, Co-operation and Mutual Assistance with the Soviet Union, by which he meant Finland would defend its territory with the assistance of the Soviet Union (as quoted in Härkönen 1979, 24).[47] Kekkonen aimed to alleviate these political pressures in part by reviving his earlier proposals for a Nordic nuclear weapons-free zone to isolate the Nordic region from the consequences of a new round of arms escalation.[48] However, assuming the coordinatorship of the CSCE was also an opportunity for Finland again to use this multilateral context to strengthen its profile as a neutral and to reassure other countries (especially those in the West) about its intention to meet the country's own defense needs in the new circumstances. However, Finland eventually conceded the coordinatorship of the CDE to Sweden. In any case, of the two countries, Sweden more so than Finland had the confidence of the West.[49]

With this matter resolved, the coordinators proceeded to organize the work of the conference according to two referent principles that emerged in the process of sorting through the eighty-seven proposals introduced through March 1981: that the participating states would reach a "substantial and balanced concluding document" and that this would be based on "meaningful commitments." The Madrid conclusions were to constitute a step forward in relation to Belgrade and the Final Act, and thus underscore the political viability of the CSCE process. The concluding document would show that the participating states meant what they said, did what they meant, and could

47. The quote is from an article by J. Komissarov (a pseudonym) in the Finnish weekly magazine *Kuvalehti*. Komissarov, who had been commenting on Finnish foreign policy for more than a decade, had spurred controversy over a book he published (with T. Bartenyev) in 1976, which gave a stricter interpretation than had Finnish officials of Finland's obligations under the military articles in the Finnish-Soviet treaty (Härkönen 1979, 24).

48. "Tasavallan Presidentin esitelmä Ruotsin Ulkopoliittisessa Instituutissa Tukhomassa 8. 5. 1978." ULA 1978, 23.

49. Swedish official, interview by author, tape recording, Riksdag, Stockholm, May 26, 1988. There was also an element of political accommodation in that apparently it was agreed that Finland would have the military-security coordinatorship in the subsequent CSCE Follow-up meeting—which in fact it did.

thus use the CSCE to improve security and cooperation between East and West.

Because of the rather sensitive nature of questions relating to European security under discussion, the negotiations became even more polarized than in previous CSCE meetings.[50] The Soviets insisted on an extremely inductive working method. The West and the N+N interpreted this insistence as a tactical move to get early agreement on their proposals in Basket I on military-security issues and then stonewall on the West's demands on other issues, as they had done in Geneva (Sizoo and Jurrjens 1984, 231). A Finnish delegate warned that the working method was prolonging the negotiations without "a clearly foreseeable beneficial impact on the quality of our end result,"[51] and this was having a "negative political effect on the credibility of the CSCE process as a whole." As he explained, "it is often very difficult to find solutions and compromise formulas within the framework of a single sentence or a short paragraph. Sometimes the solutions that may be acceptable to everybody have to be found on a much broader basis."[52] These difficulties led to an effort spearheaded by the Finnish delegation to find comprehensive solutions in each of the baskets. A large number of meetings were held within the N+N, within their whole Madrid delegations, and within submeetings of experts on the different basket areas. On March 31, 1981, the N+N paper was the first covering the whole field at Madrid. The paper formed the basis of the drafting work, which then continued after the Easter break from May 5-July 27, 1981. This effort produced thirty pages of agreed text—eighty percent of what would be the final agreement. Despite the slow progress in the spring of 1981, a number of factors conspired to elevate the importance of an early CSCE agreement, and this situation promised to propel the negotiations forward. By the summer of 1981, the CSCE was the West's sole forum for daily dialogue with Moscow at a time of political crisis. In light of the tensions in Poland, the EC attached greater importance now to the CSCE as an informational forum. For their part, the Soviets gave renewed urgency to reaching a final document encompassing Brezhnev's Peace Programme, and they even made concessions on passages dealing with other areas of the concluding document (Sizoo and Jurrjens 1984, 233–34).

Nevertheless, by the end of July there was little possibility of agreement on the remaining obstacles. The N+N moved to schedule a long break rather than undermine accord on what had already been achieved. In response to a Finnish

50. "Suomen valtuuskunnan puheenjohtajan, osastopäällikkö Klaus Törnuddin puheenvuoro Madridissa 20. 3. 1981," ULA 1981, 203.

51. Ibid., 203–4.

52. Ibid., 204.

initiative, it was agreed the work would not resume until late October.[53] In the interval, all sides held consultations. The N+N foreign ministers met in New York on the opening of the UN General Assembly, expressing their commitment to work together both as a whole and separately to influence the superpowers and military alliances to come closer to each other's position on the outstanding questions. Furthermore, the N+N countries explored the remaining unresolved questions and, among other things, met in October at an expert level in order to be ready to present a compromise solution, should the political conditions arise.[54]

Despite the difficult international situation, when the delegations returned to the negotiating table for the fourth round in October 1981, the atmosphere in the conference hall itself was somewhat improved. Although the Madrid Follow-up would still require delegates' concerted efforts to agree on a final document before Christmas, it was now felt this possibility could not be excluded. Above all, the N+N countries insisted that one should not look to the international circumstances to explain why an agreement was difficult to reach, but rather should see these circumstances as the reason why it was so important in Madrid to take a positive step forward, to put East and West on the track toward disarmament, to preserve the process of détente, and to work from this point toward better relations.

New impetus came from the West, too, when the Reagan administration, almost a year after the U.S. presidential elections, finally announced in mid-November 1981 a comprehensive arms-negotiation policy. Now the CSCE and a Madrid mandate for a CDE figured as key components, alongside proposals for negotiations on intermediate-range nuclear forces, START, and the ongoing negotiations in Vienna on MBFR. Shortly thereafter, a visit to Bonn by Brezhnev resulted in the November 25, 1981, West German-Soviet communiqué. They committed themselves to bringing the Madrid negotiations for a Conference on Confidence and Security Building Measures and Disarmament in Europe to a satisfactory conclusion before the end of the year (Sizoo and Jurrjens 1984, 234). Progress on a disarmament forum was the main concern for both East and West. The Soviets and other East European delegations pointed to the mass marches for peace in Western Europe as a sign that " 'the peoples of Europe wanted disarmament,' a desire the Soviet Union claimed was frustrated by the Reagan administration and its closet allies" (as quoted in Sizoo and Jurrjens 1984, 234).

To propel the negotiations to a conclusion in time for a December finish, Finland circulated a proposal outlining a package deal. The central objective

53. "Ulkoasianministeri Paavo Väyrysen lausunto lehdistölle 6. 10. 1981," ULA 1981, 206.
54. Ibid., 206.

was to strike a balanced document. This depended on securing the linkage between human rights and disarmament. The key formulas dealt with the tough human-rights questions and a mandate for the CDE. The latter included a definition for a new area of application of CSBMs ("from the Atlantic to the Urals" as France sought) and a means for incorporating the air and sea activities related to troop maneuvers, at least as a functional aspect of the latter if not as a separate regime, which had been the N+N objective since Geneva. In the meantime, delegations in East and West held out on responding to the Finnish document, perhaps on tactical grounds, waiting until they came closer to the target date in December to reveal their final positions. For a while, all the N+N delegations continued to support the Finnish proposal in the expectation that agreement might be forthcoming on this basis.

Spurred by Austria, the N+N moved in December 1981 to produce a N+N compromise proposal. On December 16, after a meeting of the N+N foreign ministers in Madrid and unofficial negotiations (Krokfors 1985, 90), the N+N officially introduced their draft for a final concluding document, RM. 39. As the N+N countries had said of their earlier framework, the document was "not the ideal text but the only one that seemed likely to be achieved" (Sizoo and Jurrjens 1984, 235). They did not intend it as a final document, but one which should have led to an end game, or final round of concessions, and then to a final document. Even the N+N delegations were by this time running out of patience and possibilities, because the room for compromises from their side had been essentially exhausted in lieu of new movement from the blocs. Mr. Müller, the Finnish ambassador, urged the blocs to take the proposal seriously and expressed in an interview with the press that the N+N did not intend to draft papers as a serial production.[55] In spite of the fact that the agreement itself was now seen " 'as a positive good in the eyes of the parties, to be defended against loss just like the other demands of the parties,' " external conditions intervened to put all this on ice (Sizoo and Jurrjens 1984, 409, citing Zartman and Berman 1982). Indeed, the N+N's RM. 39 had been introduced just three days after the declaration of martial law in Poland.

Polish Crisis and the Long Recess

As a Swedish official recalls, "that was bad luck, but the Polish crisis had been linked to the whole Madrid meeting, on the mind of the delegates. By January, there was again great uncertainty whether one should simply leave the Madrid

55. Asko Mattila, "KSSE tar julpaus: De neutrala lade fram slutförslag," *Huvudstadbladet*, Dec. 17, 1981, UILA.

meeting at all—as after Afghanistan."[56] For the West the meeting reverted to the purpose of reviewing the implementation of the Final Act. Contrary to the working schedule of the Purple Book, which technically limited the implementation debate to the first six weeks of the main meeting, the West held to its conviction that such a debate could be reopened as circumstances warranted. To back up this argument, they cited evidence of new CSCE violations, including the Soviets' use of military exercises as a threat of the use of force, the imposition of martial law in Poland, and detention of Solidarity activists. After an N+N meeting in Vienna and under strong pressure from Switzerland and Austria, the N+N too decided that debate on the Polish crisis was necessary because it concerned more than just domestic issues: it also put at stake the CSCE principle of nonintervention in other states' internal affairs (Mastny 1986, 244–45).

During the session that lasted from February 9 to March 12, 1982, the EC, NATO, and even the neutral foreign ministers ventured to Madrid to give statements in the plenary sessions. After a new round of polemics, and crises inside the conference halls, it was finally determined on the basis of a proposal that Switzerland presented on behalf of the N+N that a long break was imperative. Finnish intervention secured the understanding that in November, when they returned to Madrid, RM. 39 would be the basis of their deliberations.[57]

During the recess, the N+N countries met in Stockholm for the first time in official consultations at the foreign-minister level. They signaled to both NATO and the Warsaw Pact countries their expectation that the negotiating process would be speeded up on their return to Madrid. Domestic political consideration intervened for some of the N+N states. Swedish Foreign Minister Ullstén explained that "Madrid could not be left everlasting." With elections upcoming in Sweden, and Olof Palme in the opposition, it was also understood that Ullstén needed his own feather in the foreign-policy area. Moreover, there were still a number of countries competing for the CDE besides Sweden, including Poland, France, Yugoslavia, and Romania. For its part Finland supported Sweden, although—assuming that it would be at least a two-phase conference—it was understood that the second phase could be held in a second capital, selected according to the rotation principle.[58]

In mid-October, the N+N countries met at the expert level in Helsinki, where they examined the alternatives for concluding Madrid. The N+N preferred a substantive, significant document, as provided in RM. 39. A second possibility was concluding with a short communiqué, as had been done in Bel-

56. Swedish official, interview by author, tape recording, Riksdag, Stockholm, May 26, 1988.

57. Ibid.

58. Vesa Santavuori, "Ruotsi yrittää vauhdittaa Eytk-seurantaa: Puolueettomien ja sitoutumattomien maiden ulkoministerit koolle Tuklholmaan," *Helsingin Sanomat,* Aug. 27, 1982, UILA.

grade. However, they pointed out that this would hardly be acceptable to the Eastern bloc, because it would show the CSCE had once again served to attack human rights. For the N+N, ending the conference like this hardly sufficed to uphold the integrity of the CSCE process. Third, there could be some compromise between these two positions, securing a follow-up meeting and perhaps an expert meeting to take up the CDE concept.[59]

Limits to Third-Party Credibility

On the return to Madrid in November 1982, it was clear that a speedy conclusion to the second follow-up would not be easily attained. In response to the declaration of martial law in Poland and the crackdown on Solidarity, the West introduced new proposals to strengthen the final content of the human-rights commitments for the Madrid agreement. This act opened some new ground on which to develop compromise proposals. But in November and December, Finland failed in its attempts to work out solutions on these issues that would be acceptable to all parties. After still another Christmas recess, the N+N returned to Madrid cohesive and offering their mediation services for the last time. As Sizoo and Jurrjens recount, "the common urge to save the CSCE now drove [the N+N] more than ever towards a communal policy" (1984, 239). Because discussions had simply dried up in the meetings scheduled in the official working program, they were "convened" and then adjourned immediately. In their place, small contact groups or minigroups were set up and headed by the neutral coordinators, who attempted to promote dialogue to get over the last hurdles to an agreement. Each coordinator took one chapter of the draft concluding document, RM. 39, to resolve the remaining questions. At the end, the formal coordinating process broke down and consultations ensued among all the N+N, France, the Soviet Union, the United States, and Great Britain. Many efforts were made in order to work out an agreement, with contacts going on between such states.[60] Inclusion of the West's new demands on human rights introduced in the autumn, along with agreement on key definitional aspects of the mandate for a CDE in Stockholm, still had to be worked out.

The Finnish and Swedish delegations divided various aspects of the CDE mandate between them, which may have strengthened the N+N's possibilities to build consensus on this matter given Sweden's strong role as intellectual entrepreneur at the outset of the Madrid meeting on the CDE. The solutions they proposed included a transitional formula between the first phase and second phase of the CDE when the mandate would be reformulated, whereby the goal

59. "Kansainvälinen kireys vaikeuttaa Etyk-työtä," *Aamu Lehti*, Oct. 13, 1982, UILA.

60. Finnish official, interview by author, written notes, Minneapolis, Minn., May 11, 1990.

of disarmament was preserved in the agreement. Thus, the N+N third-party role allowed them to ensure that at least some of their basic interests were included in the final, compromise text.

Getting an agreement on the transitional formula required "tough negotiations" with the Americans, French, and Soviets, but Finland and Sweden eventually felt they had struck a reasonably good compromise. They also secured agreement on the terms of reference for the Stockholm conference, which included a number of breakthroughs and facilitated the presentation of quite advanced, ambitious papers from the start of the Stockholm conference. Of particular significance was the so-called "Laajava formula,"[61] which worked out the geographical scope of application of the CBMs and how to include naval and air activities. The East insisted on independent air and naval activities of a certain magnitude, to which the West was adamantly opposed. The Finnish compromise formula entailed a "functional approach" such that naval and air activities were included to the extent that they were connected with military activities affecting security in Europe and taking place within the whole of Europe. However, independent naval exercises, an important aspect of the U.S. commitment to defend Europe, remained outside the scope of military activities to be dealt with in the Stockholm negotiations on a CSBM regime.

While the N+N initiatives in promoting a final round of negotiation were greeted with "enthusiasm" by the other delegations, external factors again weighed on the timing of the conclusion to the conference. In the West, there was interest in starting a CDE before the end of 1983 so that it would coincide with the NATO "track two" decision of December 1979 to begin deploying intermediate-range ballistic missiles in Western Europe in the event the INF talks in Geneva failed (Sizoo and Jurrjens 1984, 239). Finally, on March 15, 1983, the N+N presented a revised RM. 39, which excluded the West's demands for the termination of radio jamming and the deportation of journalists but did include a clause on trade-union rights as well as the times and places of the next follow-up and expert meetings (Krokfors 1985, 90). This was presented not simply as a mediated proposal but rather as the basis for the final document. The Soviet Union determined that the document satisfied its interests for a CDE and that it could manage with the rest of the compromises; the Soviets would accept the agreement as the N+N had presented it and as their final position. However, the United States found the revised draft did not buy everything it wanted in the way of human rights, and it withheld acceptance. Spurred by President Koivisto, the N+N heads of state (excepting Switzerland, Liechtenstein, and Malta) issued an appeal to leaders of the CSCE states to work soon to a favorable conclusion to Madrid.[62]

61. This is a reference to Finnish delegate Jaakko Laajava, who contributed this formulation.

62. "Koivisto teki puolueettomille aloitteen: Kuusi maata vetosi Etykin puolesta," *Aamu Lehti*, Apr. 19, 1983, UILA.

Madrid End Game

Finally, the stage was set for the end game, which lasted from April 19 to July 15, 1983, and included a long, although characteristic, final round of demands from Malta. For its part, the West proposed amendments to the N+N proposal, which embraced four words in the draft and included the addition of two passages—one on the prohibition of radio jamming and one for a meeting of experts on human contacts (to take up emigration policies), as well as a request for clarification on one phrase in the mandate for the European Disarmament Conference, which it felt was susceptible to two interpretations (Sizoo and Jurrjens 1984, 241). The problem with the proposal "to convene a meeting of experts of the participating states on questions concerning respect—in their states—for human rights and fundamental freedoms" centered on the turn of phrase "in their states," about which there had been hints from the Soviet Union and some of its allies in particular, including Czechoslovakia and Bulgaria, that they would interpret this to mean that diplomats have to limit their discussion of human-rights problems to their own countries. Thus, the West wanted it to read, "in those states." The second matter concerned agreement on workers' rights freely to establish and join trade unions and the right of trade unions to freely exercise the activities laid down in relevant international instruments. According to the text under consideration, "these rights will be exercised in compliance with the law of the state—and—in conformity with the state's obligations under international law." To avoid Eastern bloc claims of exclusions based on national laws, the West insisted on changing the "and" to a comma (see Mastny 1986, 263).

Again the issue of who was a *demandeur* for a CDE and for a final agreement to the CSCE meetings turned into a test of wills. If the West seemed to be now ready to end the Madrid meeting—as long as its last demands were met—the Soviets made it apparent that "the continuation of Madrid into the autumn would provide an ideal forum for Moscow's complaints against deployment of INF missiles." Political opportunism threatened one more time to link the achievements of the CSCE to other problems and to undermine an agreement that was almost in hand. Sizoo and Jurrjens write that some neutral and nonaligned as well as Western delegations were "impressed by this line of argument," but most were not, believing the Soviets to be the real *demandeur* on the CDE (1984, 241).

The N+N had by now exhausted their resources as mediators. They could hardly maintain credibility by going back and asking again for those items that they had excluded in an attempt to build a balanced and acceptable compromise. At the same time, they would stand to lose much politically if an agreement could not be found. This was the only substantive East-West agreement in a number of years, and the situation on other fronts was not encouraging. It was truly imperative to mark the Madrid meeting as a positive step forward, and one in a new direction. Thus, in the end as in the beginning, it was the Spanish who found compromises on the remaining four issues, not the N+N. As a Swedish official recalled, these four, small sections were easily edited and drafted, but were politically difficult. The Spanish government acted in the capacity of host country. Some feared the Eastern bloc would see this compromise as too favorable to the West because, out of the four unresolved issues, the Spanish solution was westerly in three. A Canadian delegate informed his Swedish colleague he was gloomy about the likely Eastern reaction. Nevertheless, it seems that the Soviets, too, had decided that it was time now to end the conference, and so they accepted the Spanish initiative in its entirety. It was a surprise. The Spanish compromise efforts in the end represented two percent of the whole package. The N+N had already done their share. Finland, Sweden, and the other N+N did not intervene at the very last, primarily because they had locked their national positions, and as intermediaries their credibility had already been exhausted on these remaining issues. This small final matter had to be done by someone else, and it was the host country that should do it.[63]

Evaluating Third-Party Strategies

Throughout the Belgrade and Madrid meetings, the N+N provided a key combination of third-party strategies, as both facilitative and instrumental third parties, laying the groundwork for more regularized, cooperative relations and promoting alternative approaches especially in the area of security. In the absence of institutional mechanisms, these third-party functions extended into the postagreement phase of the CSCE negotiations. They were critical for securing the further development of cooperation and for mitigating the destabilizing effect of the superpowers' return to more competitive, and often confrontational, behaviors.

In the aftermath of the Geneva negotiations, the N+N role as coordinators in the CSCE became customary. During the Belgrade and Madrid meeting, their third-party efforts encompassed both the procedural and substantive aspects of the negotiating process. In addition to their normal functions of facilitating the organization of the working committees, drafting texts, identifying the potential zone of agreement, and devising compromises, at Belgrade and Madrid the N+N also worked to stabilize the negotiating process. Supplying a mechanism of continuity when none existed institutionally, the N+N defended the integrity of the CSCE rules of procedure, the credibility of commitments, and the CSCE's viability as a multilateral political process. They also worked to keep the super-

63. Swedish official, interview by author, tape recording, Riksdag, Stockholm, May 26, 1988.

powers' threatening tactics from bringing the CSCE to an end, assumed responsibility for negotiating failures, and made it politically possible for East and West to accept the other's demands. In so doing, they contributed face-saving interventions at numerous crisis-ridden junctures.

In sum, the N+N worked as guardians of the Final Act to ensure the durability of the CSCE. Their influence stemmed not from the leverage of a coercive mediator, but rather from their use of practical reasoning: they tried to find solutions that embraced starting points or referent principles that both East and West could accept. However, by accepting the importance of upholding the CSCE human-rights commitments and the necessity of a thorough review of any violations of these, the N+N (led by Switzerland and Sweden, along with Austria) also helped assure the East could not diminish this aspect of the follow-up conference. As a result, the Soviets were also compelled to accept agreements favorable to the West's liberal conception of human rights.

Through their role as facilitative mediators, the N+N served as guarantors of the CSCE process. Their contributions underscore the important role third parties can have in laying the groundwork for institutionalized outcomes, not only in reaching an initial agreement, but also in the postagreement negotiations that ensue. Throughout these negotiations the N+N endeavored to prevent any backsliding on the basic aspects of the CSCE process, i.e. the procedural modalities that called for a review of implementation at the outset of the follow-up meetings and the right to return to it. This is where to a great extent they secured the continuity and integrity of the CSCE, which eventually permitted its institutionalization.

Beyond the Madrid meeting, there is only one instance of the neutrals offering to serve in a formal guarantor capacity. This came at the very end of the Stockholm CDE negotiations, when the neutrals offered air support for the aerial-inspection provisions of the CSBM regime. This offer was ultimately rejected by the Soviets and was not pursued by the United States, either.[64] A study carried out by Swedish officials determined that the neutrals did not have the military resources to fulfill such a role in its entirety. In any event, their oversight was not needed, because the superpowers, along with the other CSCE participating states, were able to implement the terms of the inspection agreement on their own accord, in compliance with the agreed procedures. This in itself attests to the degree of institutionalization achieved.

Situational demands on the N+N to promote consensus on final agreements in order to preserve the integrity and continuity of the CSCE especially during the Belgrade and Madrid meetings limited the N+N's opportunities to intervene

64. Swedish official, interview by author, tape recording, National Defense Research Institute, Stockholm, May 18, 1988.

as agenda setters and push for their own substantive demands. This limitation proved most problematic in Madrid, when Sweden sought to promote its own national proposal for a disarmament conference. When Sweden found it necessary to emphasize instead its role as a coordinator in the group drafting the text on such a conference, Finland in particular among the N+N questioned its advisability. Ultimately, the matter was resolved in Sweden's favor. However, the controversy highlights the tradeoffs in instrumental third-party intervention: the greater the emphasis on advocacy, the less well positioned the mediator is to promote consensus building and facilitate compromises. This being the case, how did Sweden manage to act effectively? N+N delegations always maintained a distinction between those delegates (usually heads of delegation) who were serving as coordinators (thus technically not representing national positions), and the rest of the delegation members advocating national positions; this was a distinction with a difference, and allowed Sweden to minimize its role constraints. Second, in any event, both Sweden and Finland along with the N+N as a whole cooperated in building consensus on all the elements of a final agreement, of which important elements of the CDE mandate were in fact worked out by a Finnish delegate. Thus, the joint efforts by different types of third parties contributed to positive results.

The results of the Stockholm CDE helped to strengthen the role of the CSCE as a supervisory body in the military-security domain. Meanwhile, the practice of holding expert meetings on human-dimension issues continued by the Madrid Follow-up also helped to cast a shadow of the future on cooperative endeavors leading to the opening of the 1986 Vienna Follow-up. As we saw in chapter 7, these meetings helped the West keep abreast of and judge the cultural and social transformation in the East that had been under way since as early as the Brezhnev era, which Gorbachev's policies of glasnost and perestroika began to unleash after he came to power in 1985. The existence of a "second society"—the samizdat publications, informal networks, political and intellectual groups, labor, peace and ecological movements that arose in the Soviet Union and other Eastern European countries like Hungary, Poland, and Czechoslovakia (Kaldor 1990, 234–36; Chilton 1995)—pointed to the penetration of an institutionalized CSCE and demonstrated its interfacing character.

The end of the Vienna Meeting of the CSCE in January 1989 essentially closed the cold war chapter on the CSCE and its institutional development. By that time, there was no longer any question about "whether to meet at all." The question was rather "where, when, and under what conditions follow-up meetings will occur." The CSCE had first promoted and than tapped into the forces of change. Opposition groups placed their governments under increasing pressure to uphold CSCE commitments. CSCE states invoked the human-dimension mechanism some seventy times in 1989 alone, primarily against

Warsaw Pact countries. Lehne reports (1991b, 188) that "virtual waves of requests for information were addressed by the [CSCE] to Czechoslovakia (imprisonment of Vaclav Havel), Bulgaria (expulsion of members of the ethnic Turkish minority), GDR (repressive measures against dissidents), and Romania (general human rights situation and specific cases)." Most of the CSCE states respected the procedures of the mechanism, although Romania refused. The Bulgarian leadership hoped to gain respectability by hosting the CSCE ecological conference in Sophia, but plans backfired when protesters who took to the streets were met with police brutality. But it was Hungary's decision to allow East German vacationers the right to leave in contravention of its bilateral agreements with East Germany that set into motion a series of cascading events.

The cascade, which lasted throughout the fall of 1989 and spring of 1990, led to the overthrow of communist regimes throughout Eastern Europe, the rapid unification of Germany, and eventually the breakup of the Soviet Union. Hungary based its decision on its obligations to the CSCE and to United Nations instruments to respect everyone's right to the freedom of movement (Lehne 1991b, 188) and maintained that these took precedence over bilateral commitments (i.e. principles of relations between socialist states). Ultimately, the internalization and domestication of CSCE commitments were achieved with dissident groups and their members assuming leadership positions, including Lech Walesa and Solidarity in Poland and Vaclev Havel and Charter 77 in the former Czechoslovakia.

Thus, after Vienna the continuity of the CSCE no longer depended on the N+N but rather on the rule effectiveness of the institution, including its supervisory and sanctioning capabilities. But the CSCE's hour of triumph with the end of the cold war brought its own consequences, for which the institution was neither designed nor prepared.

Conclusions

The institutional development of the CSCE generally worked to the advantage of the West, as did the elaboration of increasingly intrusive commitments in both the military-security and human-rights areas of the CSCE. However, the West's strategy of using the CSCE for monitoring compliance and sanctioning violations through public diplomacy, and for linking progress on human rights and military-security issues, could not have succeeded without the N+N. Why was their role crucial for these outcomes?

The N+N third-party interventions secured agreement between East and West on the basic parameters of the CSCE's working methods. This ensured periods for a review of implementation, the right to return to a review of implementation when developments warranted, and the principle that new commitments be developed in light of the review. In this sense the N+N were indispensable to the West. The N+N also defended the political viability of the CSCE by promoting concrete, significant substantive results in Madrid and by providing face-saving interventions to obtain long recesses when good results were in jeopardy. Thus, they helped make the CSCE agreements an instrument of political accountability (Kampelman 1982).

The role of the neutral and nonaligned centered on building and sustaining diffuse reciprocity. They fomented communication and helped build common ground to bridge bloc-based antagonism. Even though simultaneous exchanges and tit-for-tat bargaining between East and West did take place on occasion, in general the N+N services allowed the superpowers to make concessions without losing face and without requiring the strict equivalence in outcomes. As a result, failure to reach agreement could be attributed to the N+N rather than superpower intransigence. This also helped keep the parties at the table by making defection more difficult politically. The overall contribution of the N+N was to build a common basis for final agreement and a framework within which the parties could generate sequential exchanges. They helped establish trust, a code of conduct, and a set of obligations to which all parties would commit themselves.

On balance, the N+N added their weight to the West's position more than that of the East. They also helped secure the linkage promoted by the West between progress on human rights and disarmament, which contributed to the development of a multifaceted conception of security cooperation in East-West relations. The N+N compromise proposals were important in achieving this because they afforded a possibility for the Soviets to agree to a final document without having to formally accept Western demands. Thus, the N+N also helped shape common understandings on human rights and cooperative security across the ideological divide.

Eventually, institutional practices and CSCE mechanisms proved their rule-effectiveness so that, by the end of the Vienna Follow-up meeting in 1988, the N+N services were no longer critical to the durability of the institution. But if the CSCE had finally found a way to point the participating states out of the cold war mindset and structures of a divided Europe, it also sent them into largely uncharted waters, for which there would soon be many new, daunting challenges to respond to.

9 Promoting Democratic Peace

THE TWENTIETH CENTURY came to an early close in the late 1980s and early 1990s as monumental political change swept across Central and Eastern Europe and the Soviet Union, ushering in a new international era. The toppling of communist regimes, the reunification of the two Germanies, the breakup of the Federal Republic of Yugoslavia, the independence of the Baltic states, and eventually the implosion of the Soviet Union brought about new opportunities as well as unanticipated challenges. The moment was ripe for the introduction of democracy and free-market economies across the former communist bloc and, with the demise of the Warsaw Pact, the development of new security relations. But this same political, economic, and security vacuum also signaled instability and new dangers. The problems were quick to manifest. Ethnic tensions and political movements based on competitive nationalism and separatism in such places as Nagorno-Karabakh and the Federal Republic of Yugoslavia were warning signs of more conflict to come as political authority eroded from within states at the same time that the communist bloc structure collapsed from without. The upheavals led to the creation of almost twenty new member states for the CSCE, many of them in the midst of political crises. Whereas in 1989 there were just two armed conflicts in Europe, by its peak in 1993 there were ten such conflicts in six different locations, including eight in the newly independent states of Azerbaijan, Bosnia-Herzegovina, Croatia, Georgia, and Russia. Protracted conflicts such as in Chechnya have proved among the most difficult for enforcing regional codes of conduct and human rights norms (Bloed 2000). (The only armed struggles outside the former communist bloc were in Northern Ireland and the Basque country in Spain.) Many other transitional states faced conflict as well but managed to keep them nonviolent, including Hungary, Romania, Estonia, Latvia, and Czechoslovakia, which steered its way clear by means of a peaceful divorce between the Czech and Slovak regions (Berthelsen 1997, 9).

The response of the CSCE participating states to the changed political landscape was to focus on the consolidation of a common normative framework around democratic norms. This was a post-cold war project that involved both negotiating a new "constitutional basis" for the CSCE and finding ways to diffuse and domesticate the new norms, particularly to the former communist states. Over the course of the 1990s, the CSCE (renamed the Organization for Security and Cooperation in 1995) became specialized in the early warning and prevention of conflict, largely in response to the threat of violence erupting in transitional states. By 1999 the OSCE had nineteen missions deployed throughout Europe and parts of the former Soviet Union. By then its largest operation was the Verification Mission first deployed to Kosovo in October 1998, which numbered some fourteen hundred observers before war broke out the following spring. In 2000 the OSCE had missions in Albania, Bosnia and Herzegovina, Croatia, Kosovo, the Republic of Macedonia, Estonia, Latvia, Belarus, Chechnya, Georgia, Moldova, and Tajikistan. In addition, it was represented in the Minsk Conference dealing with the situation in Nagorno-Karabakh; had offices in Central Asia, Almaty, Ashgabad, and Bishkek; and had a project coordinator in the Ukraine. These efforts were complemented by other OSCE initiatives and programs, including the work of the High Commissioner on National Minorities, who during 2000 made visits and offered recommendations on minority issues to Croatia, Estonia, Hungary, Kazakhstan, Kyrsgyzstan, Latvia, the Former Yugoslav Republic of Macedonia, Moldova, Romania, Russia, Slovak Republic, Turkey, Ukraine, and the Federal Republic of Yugoslavia, while also working with the Roma and Sinti, and issuing recommendations on the effective participation of national minorities in public life (OSCE 2000b).

The shift from cold war conflict regulation and transformation to the management of intrastate conflicts marked an important change in regime governance for the CSCE. But the CSCE was not the only East-West institution that, having fulfilled its basic purpose, had to find a new reason to exist after the revolutions in Eastern Europe in 1989 and 1990. The Council of Europe, NATO, the Warsaw Pact, and also the European Union faced similar challenges, and this situation gave rise to considerable positioning among the member states and competition among institutions to carve out a new space (Liebich 1999; Yost 1998; Benoît-Rohmer and Hardeman 1994). Nevertheless, the CSCE's evolution leading up to the 1990s was in the direction of legitimizing norms of comprehensive security, including security of individuals and the rights of the international community to enforce them—even if doing so imposed limitations on state sovereignty and principles of nonintervention. Although the 1975 Final Act contained no references to democracy (except in the name of the Democratic German Republic), its provisions for respect of human rights and fundamental freedoms became "a driving force for change" (Höynck 1996, 14). Furthermore, the OSCE's history as a multilateral process based on political agreements also "gave it a special advantage in dealing with sensitive internal issues after the end of the cold war, for which judicial or enforcement processes would neither be appropriate nor feasible" (Chigas, McClintock, and Kamp 1996, 33). In sum, the OSCE's cold war history was shaped by an approach to dealing with conflict that was fundamentally different. In contrast to more traditional methods, the OSCE was "based on complexity and comprehensiveness rather than simplification of issues, on politics and dialogue rather than law and enforcement, and on moral rather than legal authority" (Chigas, McClintock, and Kamp 1996, 34).

While making the transition from a multilateral conference process to an international organization, the OSCE internalized key functions of instrumental mediation, especially as a norm entrepreneur, enabler, and diffuser (see also Finnemore and Sikkink 1998). At the same time it has developed a plethora of third-party mechanisms designed to build trust, understanding, and ultimately consensual arrangements based on democratic practices. Both in conflict prevention and in the rehabilitation of war-torn societies, the OSCE has carved out a niche for itself in the political arena, focusing on promoting the elements of soft security that underpin an international regime of democratic peace. On the one hand this circumscribed role came of necessity to the OSCE, given the path of its institutional redesign in the post-cold war era and the limited resources it has had to work with; on the other, the new mission seems to have emerged organically from the normative evolution of the OSCE that led up to the end of the cold war. In the conclusions we will reflect on the overall significance of the OSCE, particularly in light of its contributions to a post-Westphalian international order.

Developing New Institutional Structures

At a June 1990 meeting of the Warsaw Pact in Moscow, member states recognized the irreversibility of the developments in Europe overcoming the bloc security system, the division of the continent, and the ideological enemy image (Rotfeld and Stützle 1991, 153). Similarly, NATO allies meeting a month later in London declared that Europe had entered a new, promising era. The Soviet Union had embarked on the long journey toward a free society. Europe was choosing freedom, economic liberty, and peace—it would be "a Europe whole and free" (Rotfeld and Stützle 1991, 150). Both alliances immediately called for making the Conference on Security and Cooperation in Europe more prominent in Europe's future, regularizing and further institutionalizing the diplomatic process that emerged out of the 1975 Helsinki Final Act.

The "London Declaration on a Transformed North Atlantic Alliance," issued in conjunction with the July 5–6, 1990, NATO summit meeting, proved decisive not only in setting the parameters for the CSCE's restructuring but also and more generally in establishing the context for the post-cold war European security architecture.[1] Intended to reassure the Soviets that the alliance no longer represented a threat to the Soviet Union, the Declaration opened the door to East European states and the Soviet Union to become partners with the West by establishing "regular diplomatic liaison" with NATO (through the North Atlantic Cooperation Council—NACC). The London Declaration also set out key parameters for developing CSCE institutions, albeit again along the lines of a "minimalist" approach. The NATO parameters, and in particular U.S. insistence on sustaining the process aspect of the CSCE over French-led demands for a more legal approach, "predetermined" the substance of the negotiations leading up to the November 1990 Charter of Paris and the CSCE's subsequent development (Lehne 1991b, 6–8; Heraclides 1993; Bloed 1994; Borawski 1995).

On November 19–20, 1990, the thirty-four participating states of the CSCE gathered in the French capital and adopted the Charter of Paris, a carta magna for Europe heralding the dawning of a new era of democracy and unity and celebrating the achievement of the CSCE.[2] The Charter provided for the establishment of a Council of Ministers for Foreign Affairs to meet at least once a year; a Committee of Senior Officials to support the Foreign Ministers; a purely administrative secretariat in Prague; an Office for Free Elections, set up in Warsaw; and a Conflict Prevention Center, which at the time hardly lived up to its name. In contrast to the more far-reaching Soviet, German, and Czech calls to make the CSCE into a pan-European security organization, for which the Conflict Prevention Center would have played a central role, the French, British, and Americans succeeded in limiting it to supporting the implementation of CSBMs and assuming responsibilities for a procedure for the conciliation of disputes. It was also a measure of the success of Western countries (strongly committed to NATO's long-term survival) that CSCE efforts remained focused on confidence building and crisis management rather than collective security or defense (Greco 1994, 7).

Ultimately, the United States agreed to support the development of a CSCE with a minimal bureaucratic structure because key Central European countries like Poland and Czechoslovakia saw it as a substitute security forum; giving the CSCE some bureaucratic structure was also a means of mitigating fears in the wake of the Warsaw Treaty's collapse in 1991. Furthermore, unlike other East-West or West European institutions, the CSCE counted on comprehensive

1. "London Declaration on a Transformed North Atlantic Alliance" was issued by heads of state and government participating in the Meeting of the North Atlantic Council, London, July 5–6, 1990.

2. See Commission on Security and Cooperation in Europe, "Charter of Paris for a New Europe" (Washington, D.C.: 1990).

membership, including both the United States and the Soviets. Giving it some institutional structures was also a means of keeping the Soviets from feeling isolated, after they had initially sought to convene a "Helsinki II" conference as a way to develop it into a pan-European security organization to replace the military alliances.[3]

Gorbachev had argued for such a solution, lest "the Soviet Union . . . become irrelevant to Europe as the European Community gains in political and economic strength and as the coin of Soviet military strength declines in value." Soviet security interests could be better managed and would be less costly if they were protected within "a European framework in which German energies are contained and channeled" (Goodby 1990).[4] In fact, the Kohl-Gorbachev agreement of July 16, 1990, resolved the principal question over German unification in favor of continued German membership in NATO. The "Two Plus Four Agreement" was the multilateral instrument the Great Powers used to work out the details. Thus, all that was left to the CSCE states was to affirm the results in the 1990 Charter of Paris.

When the CSCE participating states failed to reach agreement during the Charter of Paris negotiations to create a strong Conflict Prevention Center (CPC) as part of the new CSCE institutional structure, the smaller, weaker Central European countries were left without what they perceived to be adequate security guarantees (Weitz 1993, 380). These concerns, coupled with U.S. reservations, the lack of Soviet influence, and German unification with continued adherence to NATO membership, helped to shape a post-cold war CSCE that was based on a minimal organizational structure, along with a mixture of continuation of old practices regarding follow-up and expert meetings and new practices related to the emerging CSCE institutions.

These provisions were set out in the Charter of Paris, but the 1992 Helsinki Follow-up meeting was the first opportunity to begin to systematize them (see figure 6). In a short time span, the CSCE was transformed from an institutional process largely devoted to promoting consensus on managing a divided Europe to one with new responsibilities for "guid[ing] international change, including the disintegration of authoritarian empires, and oversee[ing] disputes among antagonistic nationalities" (Weitz 1993, 346). Along with democratization, the prevention, management, and resolution of conflicts became central objectives as the stronger provisions for collective security were ruled out.

The post-cold war OSCE decision-making process has included summits,

3. See "General Secretary Mikhail Gorbachev's Speech to Central Committee," Dec. 9, 1989, in Freedman 1990, 9.

4. See also Adomeit (1993) on the evolution in Gorbachev's thinking concerning the question of German unification, particularly in relation to the reorientation of Soviet policy toward Eastern Europe.

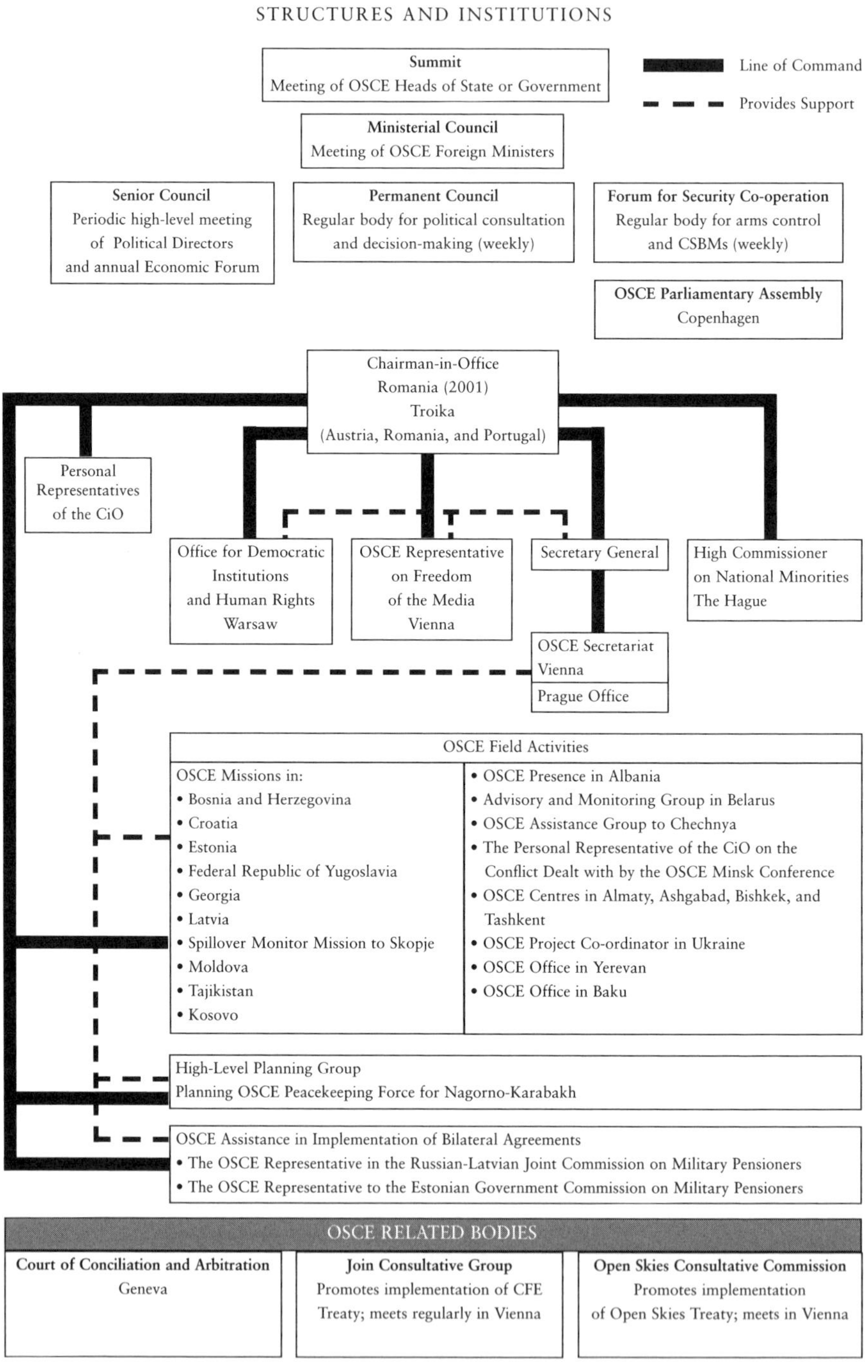

STRUCTURES AND INSTITUTIONS

Source: OSCE Handbook, www.OSCE.org

Figure 6. Organization for Security and Cooperation in Europe Organigram

which represent the highest level of political engagement, as well as political and administrative leadership posts. The Chairman-in-Office (CiO) is the key political officer, a post that rotates annually and is held by the foreign minister of the participating states. The CiO "is vested with overall responsibility for executive action and the co-ordination of current OSCE activies," including coordination of OSCE institutions, and their programs for conflict early warning, prevention and post-conflict rehabilitation (Kemp 2000, 30). Between summits, the central governing and decision-making responsibilities rest with the Ministerial Council, which is charged with seeing that the OSCE fulfills its main political goals. Originally, the Charter of Paris established a Committee of Senior Officials (CSO) to meet at least twice a year to prepare the meetings of the Ministerial Council. However, since 1997 the Senior Council has met only as the Economic Forum, and instead, along with the greater institutionalization of the OSCE, the Permanent Council has assumed its duties and become the regular body for daily consultations and decision making on the OSCE's ongoing business.

According to decisions made during 1993 to streamline OSCE operating procedures and structures, the newly created Permanent Council and the Secretary General's office of the OSCE have assumed day-to-day oversight of OSCE third-party activities (Greco 1994; Ghebali 1994). Since then, the Secretary General has come to act as the representative of the CiO, managing the overall operational activities of the OSCE, including such tasks as preparing the OSCE meetings, ensuring implementation of OSCE decisions, publicizing its work, maintaining contacts with other international organizations, serving as the OSCE chief financial officer, overseeing OSCE missions in the field, reporting to OSCE political bodies, and preparing annual reports on the OSCE (Kemp 2000, 31).

The OSCE Secretariat, first established in Prague, has operated out of Vienna since 1993 (although it continues to receive some assistance from the Prague office). Its main functions are to support the OSCE field operations and activities, including cooperation with other international organizations, and provide administrative, personnel, and information technology services. After decisions made by the June 2000 Permanent Council, the Secretariat encompasses the Office of the Secretary General, the Conflict Prevention Center, the Department for Support Services and Budget, and the Department of Human Resources. Also housed within the Secretariat is the Coordinator of OSCE Economic and Environmental Activities, who is charged with enhancing the OSCE's capacity to address economic, social, and environmental problems that have security implications (Kemp 2000, 32–34).

The Office on Free Elections (in Warsaw) was set up under a mandate from the 1990 Charter of Paris to monitor elections, but it subsequently became the Office on Democratic Institutions and Human Rights (ODIHR). It has promoted the rule of law; hosted diplomatic seminars open to NGO participation on issues like national minorities, migration, and free media; assumed certain supervisory functions in the human dimension, including in relation to the Moscow Mechanism; and established guidelines and procedures for creating democratic electoral systems (Rotfeld 1997, 146). It has also been charged to contribute to the early warning and prevention of conflict, especially through monitoring the implementation of human-dimension commitments.

The OSCE also has both an Economic Forum and a Security Forum. The Economic Forum (strongly advocated by the United States as a means of averting the rise of pan-European economic cooperation through the European Union) contributes to stability and cooperation by overseeing the monitoring of economic and environmental developments, with an eye to alerting OSCE states of any threat of conflict, as well as by facilitating economic and environmental policies of participating states with transitional economies. It is intended to enhance the OSCE interaction with other international organizations, NGOs, and the private sector. The Security Forum engages in arms-control negotiations, disarmament, and confidence and security building measures, as well as regular consultations on security matters, and oversees implementation of agreed measures.

The OSCE parliamentary body provides another avenue for political dialogue, although it has no enforcement powers over national legislatures. Its main role is to advise the OSCE Council and participating states. The Parliament has favored enhancing the OSCE's collective security functions and creating its own third-party missions. It has presented extensive recommendations for improving the overall capabilities of the OSCE (Weitz 1993; Bloed 1993a, 116–18), and more recently has helped promote consensus building on new OSCE norms and cooperation leading up to the 1999 Istanbul summit meeting (Courtney and Helwig 1999, 109).

In sum, promoting democracy across a once-divided continent must count as one of the central purposes of the post-cold war OSCE. Beginning with the Copenhagen Human Dimension meeting, the CSCE has given a "ringing endorsement of democratic pluralism," thus imbuing the Final Act's refrain about respect for each other's political and social systems with new meaning and eliminating any ambiguity about the undemocratic and oppressive communist regimes as sources of human-rights violations (Buergenthal 1990, 6). While retaining the Ten Principles of the Final Act as a guide to the future, the Charter of Paris set forth unambiguously the unity of Europe as based on the CSCE states' commitment to "build, consolidate and strengthen democracy as the only system of government of our nations," to abide by human rights and fundamental freedoms, and to root democracy in the respect for the human person and the rule of law. This is further strengthened in the CSCE Helsinki Summit Declaration 1992, which emphasizes that "the protection and promotion of human rights and fundamental freedoms and the strengthening of democratic institutions continue to be a vital basis for our comprehensive security." Thus, as Gaertner notes (1992, 10), "the documents imply that democracy promotes compliance with international law and peace building." In effect, "domestic democracy is vital for effective international peace" (Gaertner 1992, 10).

Creating Mechanisms for Peaceful Change

As ethnic conflict escalated in Yugoslavia and elsewhere in the former communist states, the secretary general of the United Nations, Boutros Boutros-Ghali, called on the CSCE to respond with a new strategy of conflict prevention, management, and rehabilitation. This required a new definition of the "problem" to be dealt with among CSCE participating states, which had originally developed in response to inter—not intra—state conflict.

The OSCE has faced these challenges by creating an institutional framework of democratic norms and tools for promoting their domestication, most urgently in transitional states facing civil strife and war. Developing a normative framework for the rights of national minorities was part of this effort—a topic that had not figured in Cold War CSCE agreements. The CSCE first addressed this gap in the 1990 Copenhagen Report of the Conference on the Human Dimension of the CSCE.[5] Despite that agreement's limitations, it still constitutes groundbreaking work (see Blischenko and Abashidze 1990, 205–6). Later, the matter of national minority rights was also raised at the July 1991 CSCE meeting, in Geneva, of Experts on National Minorities. Through the establishment of the ODIHR, the OSCE also supported the search for solutions to national minority questions (Bloed 1993a, 1993b). These efforts led to renewed interest at the Council of Europe and the European Union to regain the initiative in ths arena, which they did by pursuing essentially legal remedies (Liebich 1999, Rönqvist 1995). However, consistent with its own development, the CSCE focused on a strategy for promoting political and social change using a multifaceted, and multitiered program for conflict early warning, prevention, crisis management, and eventually, postconflict reconstruction.

The main responsibilities for this strategy are charged to the Chairman-in-Office (CiO) and the Permanent Council. The CiO, whose term generally lasts one year, has the primary responsibility for executive action and may draw on personal representatives to take full advantage of his or her mandate. The CiO is assisted by the OSCE Troika (previous, current, and following CiO), as well

5. For the 1990 Copenhagen report see "Document of the Second Meeting of the Conference on the Human Dimension of the CSCE," in Bloed, ed. (1993, 439–66).

as by the Secretary General, who is also actively involved in the management of the OSCE and participates in the Troika ministerial meetings. In addition, the OSCE has a number of tools and methods for the political management of conflicts, including promoting steps by the state or states concerned to avoid any action that could aggravate the situation. The CiO or the Permanent Council may recommend procedures or mechanisms to resolve disputes peacefully. The OSCE's comparative advantage over other international organizations lies especially in the early warning of conflict and its mechanisms for early action (Lucas 1994, 17).

Although the OSCE's main mission after the cold war became one of conflict prevention, OSCE documents offered little definitional basis for what was meant by "early warning" or "preventive diplomacy" and no *explicit* operational method for determining what it is about a developing conflict that requires preventive action or what the threshold for early warning is. In practice, however, the OSCE's commitment to preventive diplomacy has come to embrace four principal objectives: (1) to prevent disputes from arising, (2) to prevent disputes from developing into more serious conflicts, (3) to eliminate conflicts when they occur, and (4) to contain and limit the spread of conflicts that are escalated (i.e. prevent the spillover of conflict into other regions of a state or across national borders) (af Ugglas 1994).

The primary function of the OSCE's early warning system is to gather information on which basis political judgments can be made about whether or not to issue an early warning and to coordinate political decision making on appropriate preventive action. As Max van der Stoel (1994) argues, "*early warning* should provide the relevant CSCE bodies with information about escalatory developments, be they slow and gradual or quick and sudden, far enough in advance in order for them to react timely and effectively." This warning would leave diplomats with time "to employ preventive diplomacy, and other noncoercive and nonmilitary preventive measures."

It follows that "early" differs from "late" preventive diplomacy. Early preventive diplomacy is aimed at "encouraging and supporting efforts by contenders to seek accommodation." The objective of late preventive diplomacy is "to persuade parties to abstain from violence when eruptions seem imminent." Late preventive diplomacy aims at finding ways of averting the escalation of conflict or thwarting inadvertent conflict. Its functions include containing and de-escalating tensions and other negative developments. This may be accompanied by efforts to promote dialogue, confidence, and cooperation among the parties (Van der Stoel 1994).

The early warning of conflict depends on regular monitoring of potentially dangerous situations and access to adequate information about their development. The Permanent Council provides the key setting for in-depth political consultations and the backbone of the early warning system. The Permanent Council carries on some of the traditional review of implementation functions of the CSCE, but it does so in a way that ensures regular and timely review and more proactive responses to egregious violations.

One innovative tool the OSCE uses in the area of minority relations is the High Commissioner on National Minorities (HCNM)(Zaagman 1994). According to his mandate, the High Commissioner can gather information, carry out visits, and promote dialogue over situations that could develop into conflicts (Foundation on Inter-Ethnic Relations 1997, 18–24). The 1992 Helsinki Decisions (chapter 2) describes the High Commissioner as "an instrument of conflict prevention at the earliest possible stage." It calls on the High Commissioner to "provide 'early warning' and as appropriate, 'early action' at the earliest possible stage in regard to tensions involving national minority issues which have not yet developed beyond an early warning stage, but, in the judgment of the High Commissioner, have the potential to develop into a conflict within the CSCE area, affecting peace, stability or relations between participating States." [6]

The High Commissioner's role is to enhance security more than to defend human rights. This fact limits the overall early warning capacity of the OSCE (where violations of human rights are concerned). A second limitation concerns provisions in the mandate that preclude the High Commissioner from engagement in situations in which organized acts of terrorism are involved. But the High Commissioner is not about acting as an ombudsman; nor can he or she influence situations where governments perceive conflict or violence resulting from terrorist group activities (Huber 1993, 17; Foundation on Inter-Ethnic Relations 1997, 24).

The HCNM also plays a vital role in gathering information and bringing potential conflicts to the attention of the CiO and Permanent Council. The HCNM may become involved at his or her own discretion and has the competence to enter a CSCE participating state without formally needing that state's consent or the support of other participating state. Thus, the HCNM becomes involved as an external third party and as a nonstate entity (Zaagman 1994). This nongovernmental aspect of its role is also enhanced by the cooperative relationship established between the High Commissioner and the Foundation on Inter-Ethnic Relations, and other nongovernmental organizations, by which means the High Commissioner may consult informally with parties and intervene in unofficial capacities.

The efforts of the High Commissioner on National Minorities have been singled out in particular as helping diffuse tensions in a variety of instances, in-

6. See "Helsinki Document 1992: The Challenges of Change," 701–78 in Bloed, ed. (1993).

cluding in Estonia and Latvia, Macedonia, and Slovakia and Hungary. Like the facilitative mediator, Chigas, McClintock, and Kamp (1996, 63) argue that the High Commissioner, along with the OSCE missions of long duration, act as an "insider third party"—they become insiders to the local situation, developing insider relationships and understandings. The High Commissioner and the missions are intended to work in a mutually reinforcing way to promote cooperation with local officials. For example, after an initial exploratory trip to the Ukraine by the HCNM and a personal representative of the CiO in 1994, the CSCE dispatched a mission to facilitate dialogue between the central government of the Ukraine and Crimean authorities concerning the autonomous status of the Republic of Crimea within Ukraine, and to formulate specific recommendations toward the solution to these problems.[7]

The CiO may also send a personal representative to carry out a fact-finding mission and make recommendations for follow-up activities to resolve conflicts that have escalated to a crisis. The OSCE may deploy missions of long duration to assist in mediating solutions or overseeing the implementation of agreements, with which the HCNM has also often liaisoned. In 1999, these included an OSCE presence in Bosnia and Herzegovina, Croatia, Albania, the Republic of Macedonia, Kosovo, Chechnya, Nagorno-Karabakh, Moldova, the Ukraine, Belarus, Estonia, Latvia, Tajikistan, and other states in Central Asia. There has been a growing recognition that efforts to apply these third-party tools must be coupled with the promotion of democratization, economic development, consistency in human-rights monitoring, and post-conflict peace building to ensure a comprehensive approach to the construction of a peaceful civil society and unity across Europe (cf. Commission on Security and Cooperation in Europe 1999; Blank 1999).

Peacekeeping forces are also a tool for crisis management; but, lacking its own capabilities, the OSCE must rely on inter-institutional coordination, including the resources of the UN, NATO, WEU, the EU, and the Common Wealth of Independent States (CIS) to carry out its mandate. It must also be noted that OSCE provisions for peacekeeping are more restrictive than those of the UN[8] and provide no mandate for "peacemaking," i.e. enforcement action of any kind. The first OSCE peacekeeping exercise would involve enforcing a cease-fire in Nagorno-Karabakh, but conditions have not yet permitted its de-

7. CSCE 27th Meeting of the Committee of Senior Officials, Prague 1994, Journal No. 3, Annex 3.

8. As Schlager (1993, 6) contends, "the peacekeepers are strictly prohibited from being assigned enforcement operations, and there are stringent requirements for the existence of an effective and durable cease-fire as well as security guarantees for personnel before any peacekeeping mission can be mandated."

ployment. Elsewhere OSCE missions have been active seeking solutions to crises in Moldova (Transdniester), Georgia (South Ossetia and Abkhazia), Tajikistan, and Chechnya, and in rebuilding civil society in Bosnia-Herzegovina and Kosovo.

Building Democracy Through Socialization

The OSCE has promoted peaceful change by socializing transitional states to democratic norms and practices. Its key objective has been to enhance the institutional capacity within OSCE states to manage political change and social tensions peacefully, while helping those states torn apart by war recover. The OSCE norms establish the parameters for how the new game in town—democracy and peaceful change—is to be played. OSCE mechanisms provide the tools for socializing leaders and citizens to these new practices and expectations. The OSCE officials engaged in conflict early warning and prevention, crisis mediation, and post-conflict reconstruction have worked together across many levels of society and in conjunction with other international organizations to promote these developments. But so too has the Office on Democratic Institutions and Human Rights with its work in the field of electoral assistance and its training seminars on organizing civil society and setting up democratic institutions. The OSCE Code of Conduct and the 1999 Charter for European Security set out the norms and principles, as well as monitoring mechanisms for promoting democracy in civil-military relations. Altogether, the OSCE system socializes states to new norms and principles of transparency, accountability, and solidarity. By establishing regional governance approaches to the control of violence and by promoting a new openness in the context of a multifaceted conception of security, the OSCE has replaced bloc-based confrontation in a divided Europe, and its traditional Westphalian principles of interstate secrecy and state monopoly over the tools of war, with an emergent, democratic, security community.

The contribution of the High Commissioner on National Minorities to social learning and consensual change stems from five aspects of the High Commissioner's role that set it apart from other types of third-party intervention: (1) the degree of independence of the High Commissioner, (2) the noncoercive and low-key form of intervention, (3) a mandate that ensures confidentiality and discretion, (4) a process orientation as opposed to one that is substantive or outcome focused, and (5) the High Commissioner's ongoing involvement, as opposed to ad hoc forms of mediation or "one shot" interventions (Chigas 1994, 31–37).

At the same time, the constant consultations between the HCNM and the CiO and Permanent Council have gained the High Commissioner greater latitude in his or her own activities. This change has been important, because it improves the opportunities to intervene early and informally. As Chigas concludes, "frequent consultation with the Chairman-in-Office and the CSO [presently the Permanent Council] has effectively allowed the High Commissioner to engage in a de facto program of early action without diluting his accountability to the CSCE as a whole" (Chigas 1994, 33). Informal intervention allows the parties to come together with a greater sense of confidentiality, and also without feeling pressured to raise the political stakes, as happens in more formal mediation.

The OSCE High Commissioner's mandate, however, provides a division of labor in the use of carrots and sticks that allows for an innovative solution to constraints on his or her role. The mandate implies that the HCNM "should act as the 'carrot,' working cooperatively with the government and providing positive incentives for actions to reduce tensions. The CSO's [Permanent Council] 'stick' of public censure and diplomatic pressure is implicit in the background" (Chigas 1994, 33). Thus, the High Commissioner attempts to devise recommendations "in a way that builds incentives for positive action by the government with respect to its relations with national minorities" (Chigas 1994, 34). Diplomatic pressure, when needed, can be obtained through the CiO or through interventions by other states in parallel; this pressure is, in effect, independent of the High Commissioner's own efforts (Chigas 1994, 34).[9]

Without compromising confidentiality, the High Commissioner endeavors also to create positive incentives for the parties to adhere to their commitments by making some of these part of the public record. This action helps also to clarify the situation and build public confidence in the process. Putting their reputation on the line is a means of leveraging their continued cooperation. This approach has helped to encourage positive results in the Baltic states, for example, along with pressure in the form of carrots and sticks from the international community (see Lähelma 1999; OSCE 2000b; Hurlburt 2000).

The means for leveraging change differs for other types of OSCE third-party interventions that are less independent than the High Commissioner and thus more constrained by any negative fallout from their actions. For example, there is a close link between the activities of OSCE missions of long duration and the CiO and the Permanent Council. Most missions are established by authority of the OSCE chair or Permanent Council, whose responsibility it is to decide when and where a mission is needed, what its mandate will be, and when its work is completed. Thus, the effectiveness of OSCE missions can be more easily compromised by the action (or inaction) of the Permanent Council, the CiO, or individual member states. In fact, Hurlburt argues that, because host

9. OSCE official, interview by author, written notes, Office of the High Commissioner, The Hague, the Netherlands, Mar. 16, 1995.

states are aware the OSCE "missions are not followed carefully by the sending states, the CSCE loses the leverage needed to bring about compromise settlements" (1994, 35).

The greater degree of openness of the missions' work (as opposed to confidentiality and discretion of the High Commissioner) is also a potential source of constraint on their effectiveness. One of the tasks of the missions is to monitor and report on local situations. These reports are sent (often weekly) to all OSCE states and, depending on the case, to other associated international organizations as well as to certain nongovernmental organizations. The reports play an important role in bringing to light developing problems, or contrariwise, in reporting on improvements in conditions. This role contributes to the OSCE's capacity for early warning of conflict and ability to shape appropriate responses to the conflict dynamics. Although the reports are not part of the public domain, their dissemination especially among OSCE states can in itself lead to pressures on governments or opposition parties to change. But there are tradeoffs here. Once problems are made public, the parties may be less likely to back down. At the same time, any lack of discretion in the reporting can also undermine the parties' confidence in the mission. Finally, reporting also gives the other party in the conflict an opportunity to exploit its adversaries' shortcomings.

For example, as host to an OSCE mission of long duration, the Estonian government has complained repeatedly not only about the OSCE criticisms of Estonian policies toward the non-Estonian minorities but also of Russia's tendency to magnify the problems the OSCE reports point out.[10] Some Estonian officials went so far as to claim that the OSCE mission was representing Russian interests through its intervention more than serving as an impartial third party. Thus, diminished confidentiality of the process can also undermine the host government's trust and good faith in the mediation initiatives. In fact, the improved relations between the Latvian government and the OSCE mission seemed to be partly due to the latter's decision to limit its reporting activities.

Despite these problems, the missions' work in channeling information through the OSCE and to the High Commissioner also enhances their effectiveness. Moreover, the long-term commitment to promoting dialogue and problem solving of both types of OSCE mediators ultimately creates more opportunities to build up trust and confidence in the third parties and facilitate the implementation of agreed procedures and solutions. In addition, it allows the mediators to bring follow-up measures to the attention of the OSCE officials and ensure

10. It must also be recognized that there were some instances in which the OSCE mission did not exercise sufficient judgment in reporting, and thus contributed unnecessarily to the worsening of relations with the host government. Official of the Estonian Foreign Ministry, interview by author, written notes, Foreign Ministry, Tallinn, Estonia, Nov. 25, 1994. Confidential Documents.

they are acted on. Thus, as we have seen in the examples of mediation by the neutral and nonaligned states in the CSCE, the continued involvement of OSCE third parties beyond the initial phase of solving conflicts helps stabilize relations between adversaries and build durable institutional procedures for working out solutions over the long run.

In addition, the tensions that emerged in Estonia in relation to the OSCE mission of long duration also underscore the fact that the availability of multiple mediators, even mediators with different mandates, can improve the chances of international organizations finding acceptable solutions to conflicts. This fact is important especially if the credibility of one of the mediators has been undermined or exhausted through its various initiatives. However, the initiatives must be coordinated and competition avoided. While the international community's efforts along these lines faltered during much of the mid-1990s in its dealings with the crisis in the former Yugoslavia, it was somewhat more successful in the case of the Republic of Macedonia—at least until the spillover of violence from Kosovo finally brought the armed struggle to this successor state in February 2001 (Ackermann 2000; Williams 2000).

Finally, the long-term presence of the OSCE missions raises questions about the criteria that should be used for determining when a mission's tasks have been completed and the mission should be withdrawn. Already by mid-1994, the Estonian government began raising questions about the continued presence of the OSCE mission of long duration in the country. The problems with designing an exit strategy have been at least twofold: "first of all, democratization is not a one-time event, but a long and very complex process, and relevant tasks, therefore, require considerable time and efforts. Secondly, while it is relatively easy to assess the ending of a [overtly violent] conflict situation, it is simply impossible to assess when exactly the democratization mandate can be considered to have been accomplished" (Abadjian 2000, 29–30). The Charter for European Security, adopted in Budapest in 1999, attempted to redress this situation. The approach centers on promoting the transfer of tasks to the host country, but this process needs elaboration and, in any event, still invites judgment calls about when democratization has been accomplished (Abadjian 2000, 29–30).

Another factor mitigating the OSCE's contribution to social learning stems from its organizational development during the 1990s, which has moved the OSCE away from the cold war conference process. In contrast to the old OSCE, the new intergovernmental structure of the OSCE has tended to isolate officials and national delegation members from the public and NGOs, thus curtailing the type of interaction that had become a characteristic feature of the CSCE from the 1975 Helsinki Final Act through the 1989 conclusion of the Vienna Follow-up conference. This situation was aggravated by the greater focus the main OSCE decision-making bodies have given to the security aspects of preventing, managing, and resolving post-cold war conflicts in the early 1990s than to the specific problems related to the human dimension. Nonetheless, the ODIHR, the OSCE High Commissioner on National Minorities, and the extensive use of OSCE third-party missions have all provided avenues for making the OSCE relevant at the national and local levels.

The basis for the ODIHR's involvement in preventive measures was established at the 1993 Rome Council meeting. There it was decided that "in order to further political consideration and action under the human dimension, the decision-making bodies of the CSCE will consider human dimension issues on a regular basis as an integral part of deliberations relating to European security" (CSCE Documents 1994). This included a commitment to emphasize human-dimension issues in mandates of OSCE missions as well as in the follow-up of mission reports. This also meant linking the ODIHR more closely with the work of the Secretary General in Vienna and with the OSCE political bodies and other institutions. The Rome decisions also specifically included an enhanced role for the ODIHR in the preparation of OSCE missions (in providing information and advice to missions). In the context of conflict prevention and crisis management, the Rome Council determined that greater attention should be given by (what is now) the Permanent Council of the OSCE to the issue of mass migration, namely displaced persons and refugees.

The ODIHR functions and operations were also strengthened in terms of ODIHR supervisory and advisory role in the human-dimension area. The Rome Council decisions called for the ODIHR to request participating states and nongovernmental organizations to inform it of experts available in the fields relevant to the human dimension, enhance its role in election monitoring, strengthen cooperation with other international organizations, and receive information provided by NGOs with relevant experience in the human-dimension field. In effect, the Rome decisions allowed for NGOs to alert the OSCE through the ODIHR of human-rights violations.

Seminars on human-dimension issues organized by the ODIHR during the 1990s have provided important opportunities for the joint participation of diplomatic representatives and the NGO community in the consideration, review, and exploration of new commitments in the human dimension. Indeed, the post-cold war OSCE provisions for the annual review of implementation under the auspices of the ODIHR also allowed for direct participation by NGOs in the various working groups, as well as the possibility of making oral interventions. The reports coming out of these meetings were not adopted formally, however.

Monitoring compliance with CSBMs and the "Code of Conduct on Politico-Military Aspects of Security" agreed at the 1994 Budapest Summit have also helped to strengthen the OSCE's promotion of democracy-building.

The Code of Conduct enumerates democratic procedures and principles to guide national security and military decisions, with a special emphasis on democratic political control of the military, paramilitary, and internal security forces, as well as of intelligence services and the police. It underscores the importance of the effective guidance of these forces by "constitutionally established authorities vested with democratic legitimacy" and the political neutrality of armed forces.

The principal aim of the Code is to "strengthen the restrictions on the use of military force by the OSCE states and substate-parties" and to oblige them to "use political procedures in the framework of the OSCE and other international bodies for settling conflicts." As Lucas concludes, the Code should be viewed as "a monitoring and investigative mandate and an instrument to be used to uncover, document, and criticize the violations of OSCE principles in the military political sphere by miscreant states and sub-state actors" (1995, 33). In addition, the OSCE Forum for Security Cooperation has other measures for promoting consultations among military forces and exchanging information on defense planning on an annual basis—as well as mechanisms for clarifying potentially dangerous situations—all of which contribute to greater transparency and warning of impending conflict.

From 1995 to 1999 the OSCE states maintained an ongoing dialogue aimed at strengthening further the organization's role in promoting common and comprehensive security for its member states. The debate on a new OSCE charter revisited many of the competing visions and suspicions (that Russia would use the fashioning of a new charter to weaken NATO and U.S. influence while playing the allies off each other) that attended the launching of the CSCE in the early 1970s and its transformation in the early 1990s (Borawski 1998, 7). Thus, the United States continued to push for NATO to emerge as the center of gravity in Europe, seeing no military role for the OSCE even in peacekeeping. But Russia refused to accept NATO centrism and instead advocated a collective security system, which would help support its vision of a multipolar Europe and also block further NATO enlargement (Borawski 1998, 7).

The result of the four years of debate was the 1999 Charter for European Security. Adopted at the November 8–10, 1999, Istanbul OSCE summit, the Charter is more of a declaratory, political document than a program for new operational capabilities. The Charter aims to contribute to the formation of a common, indivisible, and comprehensive security space, based on principles of democracy, transparency, tolerance, and solidarity. It is an elaboration of the normative consensus achieved in the Charter of Paris, but—with the advantage of hindsight—also an acknowledgment that the outbreak of many violent conflicts during the 1990s involved the gross violation of OSCE norms and principles. The 1999 Charter lays forth a conception of comprehensive security based on a governance regime rooted in transparency and nonhierarchical relations among states and international organizations, equal partnership, equal security, and shared responsibilities. It does so by recognizing both the dangers of intrastate conflict to international security, and other forms of violence from below (e.g. terrorism, violent extremism, organized crime and drug trafficking, the accumulation and uncontrolled spread of small arms and light weapons), as well as the threats to stability from neighboring regions in direct proximity to OSCE states. The Charter contributes conceptually to a more democratic security system also by calling for enhanced networking and collaboration among international organizations and a greater role for the Parliamentary Assembly.

Conclusions

The collapse of the communist bloc and the end of the division of Europe held the promise of a new era of democracy, unity, and fundamental freedoms. Instead the 1990s gave rise to ethnic violence, separatism, terrorism, and the spread in instability in many transitional states. While the CSCE provided an overarching framework of norms and principles that helped guide states out of the cold war, it failed to anticipate the unintended consequences of systemic change. In particular, it lacked tools to manage conflicts within states and contingency planning.

Because key states were opposed to turning the CSCE into a collective security organization, its main postwar mission was limited to the further enhancement of cooperative security measures and (gradually) the prevention, management, and resolution of intranational conflicts—all aimed at supporting democratic development. After initially creating legal instruments for third-party dispute resolution, the OSCE has come to rely mostly on the use of politically flexible, ad hoc missions. These missions, together with the work of the HCNM, characterize the OSCE third-party involvement as being focused more on instrumental mediation and facilitation, monitoring, and fact finding than enforcement or peace making with muscle.

Rather than using a diplomacy of criticism regarding human-rights abuses, the OSCE has more typically focused on helping transitional states develop democratic institutions and processes. In all these endeavors, Europe probably has the richest set of institutional resources of any region in the world. But overlapping mandates and bureaucratic interests among such organizations as NATO, the Council of Europe, the European Union, and the OSCE in particular also create competition in the field and the danger of competing goals (see Liebich 1999 and Rönquist 1995). These problems also point to the need for more effective division of labor and use of resources among international organizations; this objective figured in the 1999 OSCE Charter for European Security under its Platform for Security and more recently in the OSCE's *Annual Report 2000 on Interaction between Organizations and Institutions in the OSCE Area.*

Undoubtedly the period since 1989 has forced a rapid pace of change on international institutions like the OSCE while demanding immediate, innovative, and varied institutional responses. Assessing the effectiveness of the post-cold war OSCE response to conflicts in Eastern Europe and the former Soviet Union is complicated by the fact that many of these conflicts began to escalate before 1992, when the participating states met in Helsinki to work out the new CSCE tools for third-party intervention. Thus, between 1991 and 1993, many CSCE interventions were largely of an ad hoc character, such as the Minsk group dealing with Nagorno-Karabakh. But where the CSCE has intervened early in the conflict cycle, it has fared somewhat better. The Baltic States and Republic of Macedonia may be cited as encouraging examples, although, as regards the latter, the withdrawal of the United Nations peacekeeping forces in spring 1999 in the midst of the war in Kosovo was ill-timed. It proved all the more premature in light of the spillover of tensions from Kosovo into Macedonia beginning in February 2001, helping to bring the country to civil war in the spring and summer.

The post-cold war experience of the OSCE leads us to several insights about the possibilities and challenges of promoting democratic peace. The end of the cold war has resulted in a plethora of new states. Studies indicate that violence is most frequent among the newest states in the system, in part because they are likely to perceive fewer policy alternatives (Brecher, Wilkenfeld, and Moser 1988, 73). Linz and Stepan (1996) also show the dangers for war in newly democratizing states. Institutionalized approaches to preventing conflict and managing crises can provide important policy alternatives, contribute political pressure for states to invoke them, and enhance the opportunity for domestic actors to advocate them.

In many respects, the OSCE is the antithesis of traditional power politics and mediation with muscle, which usually are top-down approaches that call, if necessary, for imposing political solutions rather than engendering democratic development (Lederach 1997, 44–45). In contrast, a culture of peaceful change associated with the promotion of democracy in regional organizations can aid in building institutional capacity within member states. As Raymond notes (1997, 215), "international norms tell us who shall play the political game, what the playing board will look like, and which moves are acceptable." Flynn and Farrell also speak to the enabling capacity of a normative framework, meaning that "it allows, or greatly facilitates, actions that would otherwise be impossible or unlikely to occur" (1999, 511). A normative framework provides the collective legitimation that regulates and constitutes the way a social system is to function. But it is important to have mechanisms that facilitate implementation as well as ensure enforcement (Scherrer 1999, 168). Such tools give opposition groups political means to pressure their governments to commit themselves to internationally accepted approaches and standards for managing conflicts (Lehne 1991b, 188; Brown 1991).

Institutions both domestic and international help members make credible commitments and adhere to agreements. By virtue of their participation in the OSCE, states are under certain obligations to uphold their commitments to resolve disputes peacefully.

As Lederach notes (1997, 133), "peacebuilding in deeply divided societies is, above all, the task of establishing an infrastructure for sustaining initiatives." International mechanisms may be most helpful if the working relationships they foster cut across the levels of society, linking community work with higher levels, and also "cut across the lines of identity that mark the central divisions of the society" (Lederach 1997, 142). Flynn and Farrell (1999, 50) argue that such a system has emerged in the post-cold war OSCE, where member states' agreement on norms underpinning a democratic framework of consensual change has enabled the OSCE "to intervene in the transformation process in the states of the former Eastern bloc to control conflict as well as to help consolidate democratic systems of government." Thus, the normative framework operates with respect to both international peace and security and problems related to intrastate transitions and crises.

The enabling function of norms is enhanced by mechanisms of conflict transformation that can assist parties in reframing conflict and searching for solutions. This may be especially helpful in societies that lack appropriate mechanisms or that are testing out newly adopted procedures. In effect, instead of building democratic peace in the international system from the ground up as suggested by the democratic peace theory (Raymond 1997, 209), a regional normative framework like the OSCE facilitates this process from the outside in.

Because institutions have the capacity to generate and disseminate new ideas, establish new norms and expectations for behavior, and create opportunities for new courses of action, their presence can affect the calculation of alternatives and consequences that actors make. One of the key sources of power of international organizations is their role in diffusing norms. Barnett and Finnemore (1999, 713) argue that "IOs are eager to spread the benefits of their expertise and often act as conveyor belts for the transmission of norms and models of 'good' political behavior. There is nothing accidental or unintended about this role. Officials in IOs often insist that part of their mission is to spread, inculcate, and enforce global values and norms. They are the 'missionaries' of our time." OSCE third-party missions of long duration, special envoys, meetings and seminars convened by the High Commissioner on National Minorities and NGOs, diplomatic seminars on democratic practices, and review conferences on military-security issues as well as human-dimension concerns are among the many mechanisms available that can serve as the transmission belt for norm diffusion and learning (cf. Pentikäinen 1998; Plomb 1993; 1994; Brett and Eddison 1993). These mechanisms can also be effective in creating or linking epistemic communities (cf. P. Haas 1992; E. Haas 1990). In sum, promoting democratic approaches to conflict resolution also depends on actors learning about and becoming socialized into new patterns of behavior and creating a set of reinforcing expectations.

In conclusion, what contribution does the OSCE's democracy-building efforts make to the post-cold war world and era of globalization? One of its main contributions is defining a new basis for legitimate governance at both the national and regional levels. The OSCE represents a transparent, transregional institution promoting governance, democracy, and accountability concerning the behavior of its member states toward both their own people and other states. Moreover, those community members have obligations to hold each other accountable, including for the treatment of their own citizens. The OSCE is also embedded in a regional pattern of governance that consists of layers of institutions (many with overlapping memberships) and mutually reinforcing norms and expectations. Democracy, transparency, and accountability provide for a new test of legitimacy, displacing Westphalian norms that justified nonintervention and secrecy. Along similar lines, the trend to develop norms and mechanisms for control at the transregional level of organized violence represents another break with one of the chief prerogatives of the Westphalian state—exclusive monopoly of force (Kegley and Raymond 2002).

Kaldor (2000, 285) argues that legitimacy is "the extent to which people consent to and even support the framework of rules within which political institutions function, either because the political institutions are seen having gained authority through some legitimate process, and/or because they are seen to represent ideas or values widely supported."

What is striking about the institutional development of the OSCE is not the changes so much as the continuities. What began in 1973 as an odd diplomatic bargain wrapped in an ideological conflict but waged over traditional Westphalian principles of sovereignty, territorial integrity, security, and nonintervention, versus the primacy of liberal conceptions of human rights, turned into a unique consensus building exercise that fused security and the human dimension in the OSCE.

But, as Kaldor notes, the real challenge of the 1990s and beyond is to develop forward-looking approaches for understanding the future. Instead, for many transitional states, much of the past decade has been spent on backward-looking strategies, trying to define the basis for legitimacy and security on exclusive nationalist claims to territory, culture, and identity. The current crises in

Europe are really more than just the erosion of political authority from the demise of communism. There are also challenges from globalization and the attending political, economic, and cultural changes it imposes (Kaldor 2000, 296).

Following Falk (1995), Kaldor calls for an international order established on the basis of humane governance. From this perspective, the democracy imperative calls for reconstructing security around principles of humanity—universalistic goals of comprehensive rights for everyone and the elimination of war (Kaldor 2000, 296). The core rule of governance cannot just focus on the nation-state monopoly of violence but must also look transnationally. We see this type of wide lens defining OSCE goals for the new millennium, focusing on problems relating to the drug trade, terrorism, and the illicit trafficking of small arms and light weaponry, as well as women and children, etc. Kaldor (2000, 298) argues "traditional statist concepts of security assumed a fragmented world order, and an integrated domestic order. Today, integration at a global level has been accompanied by fragmentation at a local level." Reconstructing statist conceptions of security may well slow globalization without providing solutions to local fragmentation.

Thus, there is a need to create humane governance that ensures social justice, norms, and principles as much as democracy and security. The most important lesson of the end of the cold war may well be that Western conceptions of human rights, centered as they are on the individual and on political and civil rights, owe too much to their own cold war formulas of political legitimacy. The era of globalization, coupled in Europe with the transitions to democracy, challenge us to conceive of humane governance that does not leave societies and people scoured from war and social upheavals and decades behind economically. Meeting these challenges, not just normatively but operationally as well, would go a long way toward alleviating the sources of crises that have fueled violence in the post-cold war era. It would put the OSCE more squarely on the path to creating a new form of democratic governance and order for the future.

Appendix

Glossary

References

Index

Appendix

Government of Finland's European Security Conference Memorandum of May 5, 1969

THE GOVERNMENT OF THE SOVIET UNION approached recently the Governments of European countries in the matter of the arrangement of a European security conference and of its preparations. This proposal concerning a special preparatory meeting was extended to the Government of Finland on April 8, 1969.

The Government of Finland has on several occasions stated that Finland considers a well prepared conrefence [*sic*] on European security problems useful. The Government of Finland considers well-founded the view of the Soviet Union that such a conference should be convened without any preliminary conditions. The participants should have the right to present their views and to make their proposals on European questions.

Furthermore, the Government of Finland is of the opinion that all Governments concerned should participate in such a conference. This opionion [*sic*] was expressed, e.g., in the Finnish-Soviet Communique in June 1966 on the occasion of the visit to Finland of the President of the Council of Ministers of the USSR, A. N. Kosygin. At the Foreign Ministers' metting [*sic*] of Finland, Denmark, Iceland, Norway and Sweden, held in Copenhagen on April 23 and 24, 1969, a joint position was defined according to which "preconditions for conferences on security problems are that they should be well prepared, that they should be timed so as to offer prospects of positive results, and that all states, whose participation is necessary for achieving a solution to European security problems, should be given opportunities to take part in the discussions."

The Government of Finland is, consequently, favourably disposed to the convening of a conference on European security problems. The success of such a conference requires careful preparations in advance. This is necessary to assure both a sufficiently representative participation and the technical arrangement of the conference. Considering the great importance of European security problems the prerequisites for success of the conference should be guaranteed as well as possible. The Government of Finland considers that the preparations for the conference should begin through consultations between the Governments concerned and, after the necessary conditions exist, a preparatory meeting for consideration of the questions connected with the arrangement of the conference could be convened.

Finland has good relations with all the countries which are concerned with European security and her impartial attitude towards the most vital problem of European security, the German question, has been appreciated by different interested parties. This is why the Government of Finland is willing to act as the host for the security conference as well as for the preparatory meeting provided that the Governments concerned consider this as appropriate.

The Government of Finland will send this memorandum to the Governments of all European states, to those of East and West Germany and to the Governments of the United States of America and Canada and will instruct her representatives to sound the position of these countries on the European security conference and to consult them on questions connected with the preparations of such a conference.

In view of this, the Government of Finland will closely follow this matter and consider what real possibilities it may have in order to take new measures on its part.

Glossary

ABM: Anti-Ballistic Missile Treaty signed between the United States and the Soviet Union in 1972.

Basket: A term used in the CSCE to designate different areas of cooperation under negotiation. Essentially a procedural, rather than substantive formula, the 1975 Helsinki Final Act was negotiated around three main "baskets": Basket I embraced principles and military security issues; Basket II the economic, scientific, technology, and environmental aspects of cooperation; and Basket III what came to be known as human-dimension issues—humanitarian concerns such as human contact and human rights. Basket IV concerned follow-up conferences.

Blue Book: The 1972 document laying out the modalities for the first Conference on Security and Cooperation in Europe, also referred to as the Final Recommendations of the Helsinki Consultations.

BPA: Basic Principles Agreement of 1972, a bilateral agreement between the United States and the Soviet Union establishing ground rules of their détente relationship.

Charter of Paris: The 1990 CSCE agreement that put this multilateral process on the path to becoming an international organization, heralding the end of a divided continent.

CiO: Chairman-in-Office, the key political officer of the OSCE, a post that rotates annually and is held by the foreign minister of the participating states.

CBMs: Confidence Building Measures, first negotiated in the Helsinki Final Act and later named Confidence and Security Building Measures in the 1983 Madrid Concluding Document.

CSBMs: Confidence and Security Building Measures, negotiated in the 1983 Madrid Concluding Document of the CSCE as part of the mandate for the 1984–86 Stockholm Conference on Disarmament in Europe.

CDE: Conference on Disarmament in Europe held in Stockholm under the CSCE process during 1984–86.

CSCE: Conference on Security and Cooperation in Europe, the original name of the OSCE.

EEC: European Economic Communities, also referred as the EC (European Community), and which became the EU (European Union) in 1993.

EPC: European Political Cooperation, a mechanism established by the EC for cooperation in foreign affairs among the EC member states.

ESC: European Security Conference, a Soviet proposal for achieving a collective security arrangement in Europe, which they promoted in 1954.

EU: European Union. Under the Maastricht Treaty, which took effect in November 1993, the EU became the successor to the European Community.

FCMA: Treaty of Friendship, Cooperation, and Mutual Assistance, signed in 1948 between Finland and the Soviet Union.

Final Act: The 1975 Concluding Document of the first Conference on Security and Cooperation in Europe. It was signed in Helsinki, Finland, at the level of heads of state and was politically, though not legally, binding. Sometimes referred to as the Helsinki Final Act, or the Helsinki Accords.

Finnish Memorandum: A 1969 initiative by President Kekkonen to invite interested parties from Eastern Europe and Western Europe, and the United States and Canada, and the neutral and nonaligned states of Europe to Helsinki to explore the convening of a European security conference.

GDR: German Democratic Republic or East Germany.

Group of Nine: Loose coalition of nine small European states from East and West that cooperated in the 1960s to promote a European security conference and cross-bloc cooperation.

Harmel Report: 1968 NATO policy for improving relations with Eastern Europe and the Soviet Union, while maintaining alliance cohesion.

HCNM: High Commissioner on National Minorities. Located in The Hague, the Netherlands, the OSCE Commissioner's mandate is focused on matters concerning national minorities.

Human Dimension: This aspect of the CSCE/OSCE refers to its commitments in the area of human rights and fundamental freedoms, human contacts, and issues of a humanitarian character, as well as mechanisms to enforce the Human Dimension.

INF: Intermediate Force Reduction talks held between the United States and the Soviet Union and focused on intermediate-range nuclear missiles, which led to the INF Treaty in 1987.

IPU: Interparliamentary Union. It was the focus of efforts of the Group of Nine between 1969 and 1970 to launch a European Security Conference.

MBFR: Mutual Balanced Force Reductions. NATO and the Warsaw Pact countries' negotiations on conventional-arms reductions initiated in Vienna in 1973 and subsumed by the CSCE in 1992 under the Vienna Forum for Security Cooperation, thus bringing the Conventional Armed Forces in Europe negotiations (which encompassed only NATO and Warsaw Pact countries) with the CSBM negotiations under the umbrella of the CSCE.

NAA: North Atlantic Assembly, intergovernmental body of NATO.

NACC: North Atlantic Cooperation Council, established in 1991 by NATO and replaced in 1997 by the Euro-Atlantic Partnership Council (EAPC).

NGOs: Nongovernmental Organizations.

N+N: Neutral and Nonaligned states that served as intermediaries in the CSCE negotiations.

NATO: North Atlantic Treaty Organization.

ODIHR: Office on Democratic Institutions and Human Rights, established at the Paris CSCE Summit in 1990 (originally named the Office on Free Elections); the ODIHR is located in Warsaw, Poland. It oversees democratic elections, the rule of law in the OSCE, and other aspects of the Human Dimension.

OSCE: Organization on Security and Cooperation in Europe, the new name of the CSCE which has been in use since January 1995.

OSCE Troika: The previous, current, and following CiO of the OSCE.

Purple Book: The informal term for the preparatory document of the 1980 CSCE Madrid Follow-up. Purple was in reference to the color of the document's cover, thus following the practice established in Helsinki, which had created the Blue Book in 1972; and Belgrade, the Yellow Book in 1977.

SALT I and II: Strategic Arms Limitation Talks. Bilateral agreements on nuclear arms between the United States and the Soviet Union.

START: Strategic Arms Reductions Talks, which superseded the SALT treaty negotiations between the United States and the Soviet Union in the 1980s beginning with the Reagan administration.

UILA: Ulkopoliittisen instituutin leikelmäarkisto (Finnish Institute of International Affairs Newspaper Clippings Archive).

ULA: Ulkoasianlausuntoja ja Asiakirjoja (Finnish Foreign Affairs Statements and Documents).

UMSLT: LK: Ulkoaisiainministeriö Sanomlehtiasiantoimisto: Lehdistökatsaus (Finnish Foreign Ministry Office of Press Affairs).

UM: LKEV: Ulkoasiainministeriö Lehdistökatsaus Edustustoja varten (Finnish Foreign Ministry Press Review for Parliamentarians).

UN: United Nations.

Yellow Book: The informal term for the preparatory document of the 1977 CSCE Belgrade Follow-up. Yellow was in reference to the color of the document's cover, thus following the practice established in Helsinki, which had created the Blue Book in 1972.

References

Abadjian, Vahram. 2000. "OSCE Long-Term Missions: Exit Strategy and Related Problems." *Helsinki Monitor* 11, no. 1: 22–36.

Aćimović, Ljubivoje. 1981. *Problems of Security and Cooperation in Europe.* Alphen aan den Rijn: Sijthoff and Noordhoff.

Ackermann, Alice. 2000. *Making Peace Prevail: Preventing Violent Conflict in Macedonia.* Syracuse: Syracuse Univ. Press.

Adomeit, Hannes. 1991. "Gorbachev and German Unification: Revision of Thinking, Realignment of Power." In *The Soviet System in Crisis,* edited by Alexander Dallin and Gail W. Lapidus, 530–55. Boulder, Colo.: Westview Press.

af Ugglas, Margaretha. 1994. "Conditions of Successful Preventive Diplomacy." In *The Challenge of Preventive Diplomacy,* edited by the Ministry for Foreign Affairs, 11–32. Stockholm, Sweden: Ministry for Foreign Affairs.

Andrén, Nils. 1967. *Power-Balance and Non-Alignment: A Perspective on Swedish Foreign Policy.* Uppsala, Sweden: Almqvist and Wiksell.

Apunen, Osmo. 1972. "ETYKin kabinettipolitiikkaa." *Ydin* 7: 8–9.

———. 1977. *Paasikiven ja Kekkosen Linja.* Helsinki, Finland: Tammi.

———. 1984. *Tilinteko Kekkosen Aikaan: Ulkopoliittinen Valta ja Vallankäyttö Suomessa.* Helsinki, Finland: Kirjayhtymä.

Axelrod, Robert. 1986. "An Evolutionary Approach to Norms." *American Political Science Review* 80: 1095–1111.

Ayer, R. William. 1994. "Mediated International Conflicts and Conflict Resolution: Is Image Change Necessary?" Paper prepared for the Annual Meeting of the American Political Science Association, New York, Sept. 1–4.

Babbitt, Eileen F. 1997. "Contributions of Training to International Conflict Resolution Training." In *Peacemaking in International Conflict,* edited by I. William Zartman and J. Lewis Rasmussen, 365–88. Washington, D.C.: United States Institute of Peace.

Baring, Arnulf. 1984. *Machtwechsel: Die Ära Brandt-Scheel.* Munich: Deutsche Taschenbuch Verlag.

Barnet, Richard. 1983. *Allies: America, Europe, and Japan Since the War.* London: Jonathon Cape.

Barnett, Michael, and Martha Finnemore. 1999. "The Politics, Power, and Pathologies of International Organizations." *International Organization* 53, no. 4: 699–734.

Barnett, Michael, Martha Finnemore, and Emanuel Adler. 1998. *Security Communities.* New York: Cambridge Univ. Press.

Benoît-Rohmer, Florence, and Hilde Hardeman. 1994. "The Pact on Stability in Europe: A Joint Action of the Twelve in the Framework of the Common Foreign and Security Policy." *Helsinki Monitor* 5, no. 4: 38–51.

Bercovitch, Jacob. 1984. *Social Conflicts and Third Parties: Strategies of Conflict Resolution.* Boulder, Colo.: Westview Press.

———. 1986. "Problems and Approaches in the Study of the Incidence, Strategies, and Conditions of Successful Outcomes." *Cooperation and Conflict* 21: 155–68.

———. 1992. "The Structure and Diversity of Mediation in International Relations." In *Mediation in International Relations,* edited by Jacob Bercovitch and Jeffrey Z. Rubin, 1–29. New York: St. Martin's Press.

Bercovitch, Jacob, and Robert Langley. 1993. "The Nature of the Dispute and the Effectiveness of International Mediation." *Journal of Conflict Resolution* 37, no. 4: 670–91.

Bercovitch, Jacob, and Jeffrey Z. Rubin. 1992. *Mediation in International Relations.* New York: St. Martin's Press.

Bercovitch, Jacob, M. Theodore Anagnoson, and Donnet L. Wille. 1991. "Some Conceptual Issues and Empirical Trends in the Study of Successful Mediation in International Relations." *Journal of Peace Research* 28: 7–18.

Berthelsen, Ole. 1997. "This is the OSCE." In *Conflicts in the OSCE Area,* edited by Sven Gunnar Simonsen, 7–10. Oslo, Norway: International Peace Research Institute.

Bilder, Richard B. 1999. "Kosovo and the 'New Interventionism': Promise or Peril?" *Journal of Transnational Law and Policy* 9, no. 1: 153–78.

Bindschedler, Rudolf L. 1976. "Neutralitätspolitik und Sicherheitspolitik." *Österreichische Zeitschrift für Aussenpolitik* 16: 339–54.

Binter, Josef. 1985. "The Actual and Potential Role of Neutrality in Search of Place and Security." *Bulletin of Peace Proposals* 16: 387–98.

———. 1989. "Neutrality, European Community, and World Peace: The Case of Austria." *Journal of Peace Research* 26, no. 1: 413–18.

Birnbaum, Karl E. 1970. *Peace in Europe: East-West Relations 1966–1968 and the Prospects for a European Settlement.* London: Oxford Univ. Press.

Blacker, Coit. 1993. *Hostage to Revolution: Gorbachev and Soviet Security Policy, 1985–1991.* New York: Council on Foreign Relations Press.

Blank, Ann-Catherine. 1999. *Three Years after Dayton—Lessons Learned in Bosnia and Herzegovina.* Report by Ann-Catherine Blank, Working Session Rapportuer, Organization for Security and Cooperation in Europe, Working Session 1, May 17.

Blischenko, I. P., and A. H. Abshidze. 1990. "National Minorities and International Law." In *Human Rights in a Changing East-West Perspective,* edited by Allan Rosas and Jan Helgesen with the collaboration of Donna Gomien, 202–15. New York: Pinter Publishers.

Bloed, Arie. 1993a. "The CSCE and the Protection of National Minorities." *CSCE ODIHR Bulletin* 1, no. 3: 1–4.

———. 1993b. "The First CSCE Human Dimension Seminar: Tolerance." *Helsinki Monitor* 4: 15–21.

———. 1993c. "Monitoring the CSCE Human Dimension: In Search of its Effectiveness." In *Monitoring Human Rights in Europe,* edited by Arie Bloed, Liselette Leight, Manfred Nowak, and Allan Rosas, 45–92. Dordrecht, The Netherlands: Martinus Nijhoff Publishers.

———, ed. 1993. *The Conference on Security and Co-operation in Europe: Analysis and Basic Documents, 1972–1993.* Dordrecht, The Netherlands: Martinus Nijhoff Publishers.

———, ed. 1994. *The Challenges of Change: The Helsinki Summit of the CSCE and its Aftermath.* Dordrecht, The Netherlands: Martinus Nijhoff Publishers.

———. 2000. "The OSCE and the Conflict in Chechnya." *Helsinki Monitor* 11, no. 2: 58–62.

Bloed, Arie, Liselette Leicht, Manfred Nowak, and Allan Rosas, eds. 1993. *Monitoring Human Rights in Europe.* Dordrecht, The Netherlands: Martinus Nijhoff Publishers.

Blomberg, Jaakko. 1969. "Suomen lännenpolitiikka." *Ydin* 43: 7–9.

———. 1970. "Suomenlännen politiikka puolueettomuus pyrkimys johtuu Suomen tarpeestä suhteita Neuvostoliiton kanssa." *Ydin* 44: 5–7.

———. 1972. "Ulkopolitiikkamme sivutavoitteista." *Ydin* 1: 4–6.

Blomberg, Jaakko, and Pertti Joeniemi. 1971. *Kaksiteräinen miekka.* Finland: Huutomerkki.

Borawski, John. 1988. *From the Atlantic to the Urals: Negotiating Arms Control at the Stockholm Conference.* New York: Pergamon-Brassey's.

———. 1995. "The Budapest Summit Meeting." *Helsinki Monitor* 6, no. 1: 5–17.

———. 1998. "Towards an OSCE Charter: A Question of Identity." *Helsinki Monitor* 9, no. 4: 5–8.

Borawski, John, and Bruce George. 1993. "The CSCE Forum for Security Cooperation." *Arms Control Today* (Oct.): 13–16.

Borawski, John, Stan Weeks, and Charlotte E. Thompson. "The Stockholm Agreement of September 1986." *Orbis* 30, no. 4: 643–62.

Boutros-Ghali, Boutros. 1992. *An Agenda for Peace.* New York: The United Nations.

Breslauer, George W., and Philip E. Tetlock, eds. 1991. *Learning in U.S. and Soviet Foreign Policy.* Boulder, Colo.: Westview Press.

Brett, Rachel. 1992a. "The Development of the Human Dimension Mechanism of the Conference on Security and Co-operation in Europe (CSCE)." Papers in the Theory and Practice of Human Rights, no. 1, Univ. of Essex.

———. 1992b. "Non-Governmental Organizations and the CSCE." *Helsinki Monitor* 3, no. 3: 19–24.

Brett, Rachel, and Elaine Eddison. 1993. "The CSCE Human Dimension Seminar on National Minorities: Can National Minorities be Considered Positively?" *Helsinki Monitor* 4, no. 3: 39–43.

Brown, J. F. 1991. *Surge to Freedom: The End of Communist Rule in Eastern Europe.* Durham, N.C.: Duke Univ. Press.

Brzezinski, Zbigniew. 1985. *Power and Principle.* New York: Farrar, Straus, and Giroux.

Buergenthal, Thomas. 1990. Copenhagen: A Democratic Manifesto. *World Affairs* 153, no. 1: 5–8.

———. 1991. "The CSCE Rights System." *George Washington Journal of International Law and Economics* 25: 333–86.

———. 1993. "The CSCE Rights System." *CSCE ODIHR Bulletin* 1, no. 3: 5–7.

Bunce, Valerie. 1985. "The Empire Strikes Back: The Transformation of the Eastern Bloc from a Soviet Asset to a Soviet Liability." *International Organization* 39, no. 1: 1–46.

Burton, John W. 1985. "World Society and Human Needs." In *International Relations: A Handbook of Current Theory,* edited by M. Light and A. J. R. Groom, 46–59. London: Francis Pinter.

———. 1988. "Conflict Resolution as a Function of Human Needs." In *The Power of Human Needs in World Society,* edited by Roger Coate and Jerel Rosati, 187–204. Boulder, Colo.: Lynne Rienner.

———. 1990. *Conflict: Human Needs Theory.* New York: St. Martin's Press.

Buzan, Barry. 1981. "Negotiating by Consensus: Developments in Technique at the United Nations Conference on the Law of the Sea." *American Journal of International Law* 75: 324–48.

Buzan, Barry, and R. J. Barry Jones, eds. 1981. *Change and the Study of International Relations: The Evaded Dimension.* London: Frances Pinter.

Caballero-Anthony, Mely. 1998. "Mechanisms of Dispute Settlement: The ASEAN Experience." *Contemporary Southeast Asia* 20, no. 1: 38–66.

Caporaso, James. 1993. "International Relations Theory and Multilateralism: The Search for Foundations." In *Multilateralism Matters,* edited by John Ruggie, 51–90. New York: Columbia Univ. Press.

Checkel, Jeffrey T. 1993. "Ideas, Institutions, and the Gorbachev Foreign Policy Revolution." *World Politics* 45, no. 2: 272–325.

———. 1997. *Ideas and International Political Change: Soviet/Russian Behavior and the End of the Cold War.* New Haven, Conn.: Yale Univ. Press.

Chernenko, K. 1975. "The Conference in Helsinki and International Security." *International Affairs* (Moscow) 11: 4–14.

Chigas, Diane. 1994. "Bridging the Gap Between Theory and Practice: The CSCE High Commissioner on National Minorities." *Helsinki Monitor* 5, no. 3: 27–41.

Chigas, Diane, Elizabeth McClintock, and Christopher Kamp. 1996. "Preventive Diplomacy and the Organization for Security and Cooperation in Europe: Creating Incentives for Dialogue and Cooperation." In *Preventing Conflict in the Post-Communist World,* edited by Abram Chayes and Antonia Handler Chayes, 25–98. Washington, D.C.: Brookings Institution.

Chilton, Patricia. 1995. "Mechanics of Change: Social Movements, Transnational Coalitions, and the Transformation Processes in Eastern Europe." In *Bringing Transnational Relations Back In,* edited by Thomas Risse-Kappen, 189–226. New York: Cambridge Univ. Press.

Chomsky, Noam. 1999. *The New Military Humanism: Lessons from Kosovo.* Monroe, Maine: Common Courage Press.

Clemens, Walter C. 1990. *Can Russia Change? The USSR Confronts Global Interdependence.* Boston: Unwin Hyman.

Commission on Security and Cooperation in Europe. 1995. The OSCE at Twenty: Its Relevance to Other Regions. Seminar presented by the CSCE. Washington, D.C., Nov. 13–14.

Conflict Management Group. 1994. Methods and Strategies in Conflict Prevention. Report of an Expert Consultation in Connection with the Activities of the CSCE High Commissioner on National Minorities. Rome, Italy, December 2–3.

———. 1999. "Human Rights: The Role of Field Missions." Report prepared for the OSCE/ODIHR Seminar, Washington, D.C.

Cortell, Andrew P., and James W. Davis, Jr. 2000. "Understanding the Domestic Impact of International Norms: A Research Agenda." *International Studies Review* 2, no. 1: 65–87.

Cortright, David. 1993. *The Citizen's Role in Ending the Cold War.* Boulder: Westview Press.

Cortright, David, and George Lopez. 2000. *The Sanctions Decade: Assessing U.N. Strategies in the 1990s.* Boulder, Colo.: Lynne Rienner.

Courtney, William H., and Janice Helwig. 1999. "OSCE Summit Held in Istanbul." *CSCE Digest* 22, no. 12: 109–11.

Cox, Robert. 1987. *Production, Power, and World Order: Social Forces in the Making of History.* New York: Columbia Univ. Press.

CSCE Documents. 1994. "Decisions of the Rome Council Meeting." *Helsinki Monitor* 5 no. 1: 99–110.

Davidson, Alan. 1972. "The Role of the Uncommitted European Countries in East/West Relations." Center for Contemporary European Studies, Research Papers, no. 3. Univ. of Sussex.

Davy, Richard. 1980. "The United States." In *Belgrade and Beyond: The CSCE Process in Perspective,* edited by Karl Birnbaum and Nils Andrén, 3–15. The Netherlands: Sijthoff and Noordhoff.

Defarges, Philippe Moreau. 1986. "The Political Role of the European Community in the CSCE." In *Ten Years After Helsinki,* edited by Kari Möttölä, 129–36. Boulder, Colo.: Westview Press.

Deng, Francis Mading, and I. William Zartman. 2002. *A Strategic Vision for Africa: The Kamapala Movement.* Washington, D.C.: Brookings Institution Press.

Deudney, Daniel, and G. John Ikenberry. 1991–92. "The International Sources of Soviet Change." *International Security* 16, no. 3: 74–118.

Dowdy, Alan. 1987. *Closed Borders: The Contemporary Assault on Freedom of Movement.* New Haven, Conn.: Yale Univ. Press.

Efinger, Manfred, and Volker Rittberger. 1991. The CSBM Regime in and for Europe. In *European Security—Towards 2000,* edited by Michael C. Pugh, 104–21. New York: Manchester Univ. Press.

Einhorn, Robert. 1985. *Negotiating from Strength: Leverage in U.S.-Soviet Arms Control.* New York: Praeger.

Evangelista, Matthew. 1993. "Source of Moderation in Soviet Security Policy." In vol. 2 of *Behavior, Society, and Nuclear War,* edited by Philip E. Tetlock, Charles Tilly,

Robert Jervis, Paul Stern, and J. L. Husbands, 254–354. New York: New York Univ. Press.
———. 1999. *Unarmed Forces: The Transnational Movement to End the Cold War.* Ithaca, N.Y.: Cornell Univ. Press.
Falk, Richard. 1995. *On Humane Governance: Toward a New Global Politics.* Cambridge: Polity Press.
Ferraris, Luigi Vittorio, ed. 1979. *Report on a Negotiation. Helsinki-Geneva-Helsinki.* Translated from the Italian by Marie-Claire Barber. Alphen aan den Rijn: Sijthoff and Noordhoff International Publishers.
Finnemore, Martha, and Kathryn Sikkink. 1998. "International Norm Dynamics and Political Change." *International Organization* 52, no. 4: 887–917.
Fisher, Roger, and William Ury. 1991. *Getting to Yes.* 2d ed. New York: Penguin.
Fisher, Ronald J., and L. Keashly. 1991. The Potential Complementarity of Mediation and Consultation Within a Contingency Model of Third Party Intervention. *Journal of Peace Research* 28: 29–42.
Flynn, Gregory, and Henry Farrell. 1999. "Piecing Together the Democratic Peace: The CSCE, Norms, and the 'Construction' of Security in Post-Cold War Europe." *International Organization* 53, no. 3: 505–35.
Foundation on Inter-Ethnic Relations. 1997. *The Role of the High Commissioner on National Minorities in OSCE Conflict Prevention.* The Hague: Foundation on Inter-Ethnic Relations.
Gaddis, John Lewis. 1989. "Hanging Tough Paid Off." *Bulletin of Atomic Scientists* 45 (Jan.): 11–14.
Gaertner, Heinz. 1992. "Small States and Concepts of European Security." Paper presented at the First Pan-European Conference on International Relations, Heidelberg, Sept. 16–20.
Galtung, Johan. 1972. "Europe: Bipolar, Bicentric, or Cooperative?" *Journal of Peace Research* 9: 1–25.
Garfinkle, Adam. 1978. *Finlandization: A Map to a Metaphor.* Philadelphia, Pa.: Foreign Policy Research Institute.
Garthoff, Raymond L. 1985. *Détente and Confrontation.* Washington, D.C.: Brookings Institution.
George, Alexander. 1988. "Incentives for U.S.-Soviet Security Cooperation and Mutual Adjustment." In *U.S.-Soviet Security Cooperation,* edited by Alexander L. George, Philip J. Farley, and Alexander Dallin, 641–54. Oxford: Oxford Univ. Press.
George, Alexander, Philip J. Farley, and Alexander Dallin. 1988. "Research Objectives and Methods." In *U.S.-Soviet Security Cooperation,* edited by Alexander L. George, Philip J. Farley, and Alexander Dallin, 3–18. Oxford: Oxford Univ. Press.
———, eds. 1988. *U.S.-Soviet Security Cooperation.* Oxford: Oxford Univ. Press.
Geyer, Alan. 1982. *The Idea of Disarmament.* Elgin, Ill.: The Brethren Press.
Ghebali, Victor-Yves. 1989. *La Diplomatie de la Détente: La CSCE D'Helsinki a Vienne.* Bruselles: Établissements Émile Bruylant.
———. 1993. "Towards a CSCE in the Mediterranean: The CSCM." In *The CSCE in the 1990s,* edited by Michael R. Lucas, 334–44. Baden-Baden, Germany: Nomos.

———. 1994. "The CSCE after the Rome Council Meeting: An Institution Still in the Making." *Helsinki Monitor* 5, no. 1: 75–81.

Goodby, James. 1987. "To Reduce the Risk of War: The Stockholm Negotiation." In *Confidence-Building Measures and International Security,* edited by R. B. Byers, F. Stephen Larrabee, and Allen Lynch, 39–54. New York: Institute for East-West Security Studies.

———. 1990. "To Make Europe 'Whole and Free.' " *New York Times,* July 21.

Gorbachev, Mikhail. 1987. *Perestroika: New Thinking for Our Country and the World.* New York: Harper and Row.

Gouldner, Alvin W. 1960. "The Norm of Reciprocity: A Preliminary Statement." *American Sociological Review* 25: 161–78.

Greco, Ettore. 1994. "The Role of the Conflict Prevention Center in the Security System of the CSCE." *Helsinki Monitor* 5, no. 1: 5–15.

Grosse-Juette, Annemarie. 1977. "Peace and the Structure of the East-West Conflict." In *Détente and Peace in Europe,* edited by Ruediger Juette, 48–68. New York: Campus Verlag.

———. 1991. "Reassurance in International Conflict Management." *Political Science Quarterly* 106: 431–50.

Haas, Ernst. 1990. *When Knowledge is Power: Three Models of Change in International Organizations.* Berkeley, Calif.: Univ. of California Press.

———. 1991. "Collective Learning: Some Theoretical Speculations." In *Learning in U.S. and Soviet Foreign Policy,* edited by George W. Breslauer and Philip E. Tetlock, 62–99. Boulder, Colo.: Westview Press.

Haas, Peter M., ed. 1992. "Knowledge, Power, and International Policy Coordination: International Organization." Special Issue. *International Organization* 46.

Haass, Richard, ed. 1998. *Economic Sanctions and American Diplomacy.* New York: Council on Foreign Relations.

Haftendorn, Helga. 1985. *Security and Détente: Conflicting Priorities in German Foreign Policy.* New York: Praeger.

Hakovirta, Harto. 1983. "Effects of Non-Alignment on Neutrality in Europe: An Analysis and Appraisal." *Cooperation and Conflict* 18: 57–75.

———. 1988. *East-West Conflict and European Neutrality.* Oxford: Oxford Univ. Press.

———. 1975. "Odota-ja—Katso: Analyysi Suomen läntinsenintegraatio politiikan perusmallista." In *Suomen Ulkopolitiikka,* edited by Harto Hakovirta and Raimo Värynen, 407–40. Jyväskylä: Gaudeamus.

Hampson, Fen. 1996. *Nurturing Peace: Why Settlements Succeed or Fail.* Washington, D.C.: United States Institute of Peace.

Handrieder, Wolfram. 1989. *Germany, America, Europe: Forty Years of German Foreign Policy.* New Haven, Conn.: Yale Univ. Press.

Härkönen, Seppo. 1979. "Eurostrategic Weapons, Northern Europe, and Finland: New Weapons Technology as a Finnish Security Problem." *Yearbook of Finnish Foreign Policy,* 20–26.

Haslam, Jonathan. 1990. *The Soviet Union and the Politics of Nuclear Weapons in Europe, 1969–87.* Ithaca, N.Y.: Cornell Univ. Press.

Hassner, Pierre. 1991. "A Time for Linkage? Western Leverage for Human Rights and Security in Eastern Europe." In *Human Rights and Security: Europe on the Eve of a New Era,* edited by Vojtech Mastny and Jan Zielonka, 57–76. Boulder, Colo.: Westview Press.

Helgesen, Jan. 1990. "Between Helsinkis—and Beyond? Human Rights in the CSCE (Conference on Security and Co-operation in Europe) Process." In *Human Rights in a Changing East-West Perspective,* edited by Allan Rosas and Jan Helgesen with the collaboration of Donna Gomien, 241–63. New York: Pinter Publishers.

Heraclides, Alexis. 1993. *Helsinki-II and Its Aftermath: The Making of the CSCE into an International Organization.* New York: Pinter Publishers.

Herman, Robert G. 1996. "Identity, Norms, and National Security: The Soviet Foreign Policy Revolution and the End of the Cold War." In *The Culture of National Security,* edited by Peter J. Katzenstein, 271–316. New York: Columbia Univ. Press.

Hermann, Margaret G. 1993. "Leadership and Foreign Policy Change: When Do Leaders Choose to Change Course?" Paper prepared for the Workshop on International Crisis Decision and Management in a Turbulent, Interdependent Political Setting. European Consortium for Political Research Joint Sessions at Leiden Univ., Apr. 2–7.

Hermann, Richard. 1992. "Soviet Behavior in Regional Conflicts: Old Questions, New Strategies, and Important Lessons." *World Politics* 44, no. 3: 432–65.

Heymann, Philip B. 1973. "The Problem of Coordination: Bargaining and Rules." *Harvard Law Review* 86: 797–877.

Hill, Christopher. 1983. *National Foreign Policies and European Political Cooperation.* London: George Allen and Unwin.

Hoedt, S., and R. Lefeber. 1991. "Europe: Divided We Stand." In *The Changing Political Structure of Europe: Aspects of International Law,* edited by R. Lefeber, M. Fitzmaurice, and E. W. Vierdag, 1–28. Boston: Martinus Nijhoff.

Hoffmann, Stanley. 1983. *Dead Ends: American Foreign Policy in the New Cold War.* Cambridge, Mass.: Ballinger Publishing.

Holsti, Kalevi J. 1984. "Who Got What and How: The CSCE Negotiations in Retrospect." *Canada and the Conference on Security and Co-operation in Europe,* edited by Robert Spencer, 134–68. Ontario: T. H. Best Printing.

———. 1991. *Peace and War: Armed Conflicts and International Order 1648–1989.* New York: Cambridge Univ. Press.

Howorth, Jolyon. 1984. "Consensus of Silence: The French Socialist Party and Defence Policy under François Miterrand." *International Affairs* 60, no. 4: 579–600.

Hoyer, Steny H. 1993. "The Future Role of the United States in the CSCE." In *The CSCE and the Turbulent New Europe,* edited by Louis B. Sohn, 31–36. Washington, D.C.: Friedrich Naumann Foundation.

Höynck, Wilhelm. 1996. *From CSCE to OSCE: Statements and Speeches by Dr. Wilhelm Höynck.* Vienna, Austria: Secretariat of the Organization for Security and Cooperation in Europe.

Huber, Konrad. 1993. "Preventing Ethnic Conflict in the New Europe: The CSCE High Commissioner on National Minorities." In *Minorities: The New Europe's Old*

Issue, edited by Ian M. Cuthbertson and Jane Liebowitz, 285–310. New York: Institute for East-West Studies.

Huldt, Bo K. A. 1984. "Swedish Disarmament and Security Policy from the 1920s to the 1980s." In *Neutrality and Defense: The Swedish Experience,* edited by *International Review of Military History,* 35–68. Swedish Commission Report no. 57. Translated by Gordon Elliot. Stockholm, Sweden: Wallin and Dalholm Boktr AB.

Huopaniemi, Jukka. 1973. *Parliaments and European Rapprochement.* Leiden: A. W. Sijthoff.

Hurlburt, Heather. 1992. "The CSCE Forum on Security and Cooperation: Creating an Arms Control Negotiation for Post-Arms Control Europe." *Helsinki Monitor* 3, no. 4: 21–32.

———. 1994. "CSCE Conflict Resolution in Practice." *Helsinki Monitor* 5, no. 2: 25–38.

———. 1995. "Russia, the OSCE, and European Security Architecture." *Helsinki Monitor* 6, no. 2: 5–20.

———. 2000. "Preventive Diplomacy: Success in the Baltics." In *Opportunities Missed, Opportunities Seized,* edited by Bruce W. Jentleson, 91–107. Lanham, Md.: Rowman and Littlefield.

Hyvärinen, Risto. 1969. "Suomen puolueettomuuspolitiikka." In *Suomi Kansainvälisen Jännityksen Maailmassa,* edited by Ilkka Hakalehto, 49–64. Porvoo, Finland: Werner Söderström.

Ikenberry, John G. 1996. "The Myth of Post-Cold War Chaos." *Foreign Affairs* 75 (May-June): 79–91.

Iloniemi, Jaakko. 1975. "Suomen Politiikka Euroopan Turvallisuus-ja Yhteistyönkonferenssissa." In *Urho Kekkonen: Rauhan Politiikko,* edited by Keijo Korhonen, 171–87. Keuruu, Finland: Kustannusosakeyhtiö Otava.

Independent Commission on Disarmament and Security Issues. 1982. *Common Security: A Blueprint for Survival.* New York: Simon and Schuster.

Jakobson, Max. 1968. *Finnish Neutrality.* New York: Praeger.

———. 1983. *38. Kerros: Havaintoja ja Muistiinpanoja vuosilta 1965–1971.* Helsinki, Finland: Kustannusosakeyhtiö Otava.

Jentleson, Bruce W., ed. 2000. *Preventive Diplomacy in the Post-Cold War World.* Lanham, Md.: Rowman and Littlefield.

Jervis, Robert. 1988. "Realism, Game Theory, and Cooperation." *World Politics* 40: 315–49.

Joenniemi, Pertti. 1978. "Political Parties and Foreign Policy in Finland." *Cooperation and Conflict* 13: 43–60.

———. 1987. "The Debate on European Security in Finland." Paper presented at a Conference on European Security—Its Non-Military Aspects from the Viewpoint of Various Nations. Organized by the Center of Peace and Conflict Research, Copenhagen, Sept. 25–27. Photocopied.

———. 1989. "The Peace Potential of Neutrality: A Discursive Approach." *Bulletin of Peace Proposals* 20, no. 2: 175–82.

Jönsson, Christer, and Bo Petersson. 1985. "The Bear and the Mouse That Roared: Soviet Reactions to Public Swedish Criticism—Czechoslovakia and Vietnam." *Cooperation and Conflict* 20: 79–90.

Jowitt, Kenneth. 1977. "Images of Détente and the Soviet Political Order." Policy Papers in International Affairs, Institute of International Studies, Univ. of California, Berkeley, no. 1.

Kahneman, Daniel. 1992. "Reference Points, Anchors, Norms, and Mixed Feelings." *Organizational Behavior and Human Decision Processes* 51: 296–312.

Kaldor, Mary. 1990. *The Imaginary War: Understanding the East-West Conflict.* Oxford: Basil Blackwell.

———. 2000. "Governance, Legitimacy, and Security: Three Scenarios for the Twenty-First Century." In *Principled World Politics,* edited by Paul Wapner and Edwin K. Ruiz, 284–99. Lanham, Md.: Rowman and Littlefield.

Kampelman, Max. 1982. "Negotiating with the Soviets in Madrid. Statements by Ambassador Max Kampelman Before the Madrid Conference on Security and Cooperation in Europe." *World Affairs* 144, no. 4: 267–512.

Kegley, Charles W. 1994. "How Did the Cold War Die: Principles for an Autopsy." *Mershon International Studies Review* 30, supplement 1 (Apr.): 11–42.

Kegley, Charles W., and Gregory A. Raymond. 2002. *Exorcising the Ghost of Westphalia.* Upper Saddle River, N.J.: Prentice Hall.

Kekkonen, Urho. 1977. *Nimellä ja Nimimerkkillä.* Vol. 1. Helsinki, Finland: Kustannusosakeyhtiö Otava.

———. 1982. *A President's View.* Translated by Gregory Coogan. London: Heinemann.

Kelman, Herbert C. 1972. "The Problem-Solving Workshop in Conflict Resolution." In *Communication in International Politics,* edited by R. L. Merritt, 168–204. Hobson, Ill.: Univ. of Illinois Press.

———. 1990. "Interactive Problem-Solving: Social-Psychological Approach to Conflict Resolution." In *Conflict: Readings in Management and Resolution,* edited by John Burton and Frank Dukes, 199–215. New York: St. Martin's Press.

Kemp, Walter C. 2000. *OSCE Handbook.* Vienna, Austria: OSCE Secretariat. Third Edition.

Keohane, Robert. 1984. *After Hegemony.* Princeton, N.J.: Princeton Univ. Press.

———. 1986. *Neorealism and Its Critics.* New York: Columbia Univ. Press.

———. 1989. *International Institutions and State Power.* Boulder, Colo.: Westview Press.

Kirk Laux, Jeanne. 1972. "Small States and Inter-European Relations: An Analysis of the Group of Nine." *Journal of Peace Research* 9, no. 2: 147–60.

———. 1984. "Human Contacts, Information, Culture, and Education." In *Canada and the Conference on Security and Co-operation in Europe,* edited by Robert Spencer, 256–82. Ontario: T.H. Best Printing.

Kleiboer, Marike. 1998. *The Multiple Realities of International Mediation.* Boulder, Colo.: Lynne Rienner.

Korbonski, Andrzej. 1973. "The United States and East Europe." *Current History* 64 (May): 226.

Korey, William. 1991. "Human Rights and the Policy of Leverage and Linkage: The Lesson of the Helsinki Process." In *Human Rights and Security: Europe on the Eve of a New Era,* edited by Vojtech Mastny and Jan Zielonka, 107–18. Boulder, Colo.: Westview Press.

———. 1993. *The Promises We Keep: Human Rights, The Helsinki Process, and American Foreign Policy.* New York: St. Martin's Press.

Korhonen, Keijo. 1978. "Finland and the Disarmament Negotiations." *Yearbook of Finnish Foreign Policy,* 15–19.

Kratochwil, Friedrich. 1989. *Rules, Norms, and Decisions: On the Conditions of Practical and Legal Reasoning in International Relations and Domestic Affairs.* New York: Cambridge Univ. Press.

———. 1993. "The Embarrassment of Changes: Neo-Realism as the Science of Realpolitik Without Politics." *Review of International Studies* 19: 63–80.

Kratochwil, Friedrich, and John Gerard Ruggie. 1986. "International Organization: A State of the Art on the Art of the State." *International Organization* 40, no. 4: 753–75.

Kressel, Kenneth, and Dean G. Pruitt. 1985. "Themes in the Mediation of Social Conflict." *Journal of Social Issues* 41, no. 2: 179–98.

Kriesberg, Louis. 1992. *International Conflict Resolution.* New Haven, Conn.: Yale Univ. Press.

Kriesberg, Louis, Terrel A. Northrup, and Stuart J. Thorson. 1989. *Intractable Conflicts and Their Transformation.* Syracuse: Syracuse Univ. Press.

Krokfors, Klaus. 1985. "Suomen toiminta ETYKissä." *Ulkopolitiikka* 2: 90.

Lähelma, Timo. 1999. "The OSCE's Role in Conflict Prevention: The Case of Estonia." *Helsinki Monitor* 10, no. 2: 19–38.

Larson, Deborah Welch. 1987. Crisis Prevention and the Austrian State Treaty. *International Organization* 41, no. 1: 27–60.

———. 1991. "Learning in U.S.-Soviet Relations : The Nixon-Kissinger Structure of Peace." In *Learning in U.S. and Soviet Foreign Policy,* edited by George W. Breslauer and Philip E. Tetlock, 350–99. Boulder : Westview Press.

———. 1997. *Anatomy of Mistrust: U.S.-Soviet Relations During the Cold War.* Ithaca, N.Y.: Cornell Univ. Press.

Leary, Virginia. 1980. "The Rights of the Individual to Know and Act upon His Rights and Duties: Monitoring Groups and the Helsinki Final Act." *Vanderbilt Journal of Transnational Law* 13: 375–95.

Leatherman, Janie, Raimo Väyrynen, Patrick Gaffney, and William DeMars. 1999. *Breaking Cycles of Violence: Conflict Prevention in Intrastate Crises.* West Hartford, Conn.: Kumarian.

Lebow, Richard Ned. 1994. "The Long Peace, the End of the Cold War, and the Failure of Realism." *International Organization* 48, no. 2: 249–77.

Lederach, John Paul. 1995. *Preparing for Peace: Conflict Transformation Across Cultures.* Syracuse: Syracuse Univ. Press.

———. 1997. *Building Peace.* Washington, D.C.: United States Institute of Peace.

Lehne, Stefan. 1991a. *The CSCE in the 1990s.* Vienna: Wilhelm BraumÅller.

———. 1991b. *The Vienna Meeting of the Conference on Security and Cooperation in Europe, 1986–1989.* Boulder, Colo.: Westview Press.

Lieber, Robert J., and Nancy I. Lieber. 1979. "Eurocommunism, Eurosocialism, and U.S. Foreign Policy." In *Eagle Entangled: U.S. Foreign Policy in a Complex World,* edited by Kenneth Oye, Donald Rothchild, and Robert J. Lieber, 264–89. New York: Longman.

Liebich, André. 1999. "Janus at Strasbourg: The Council of Europe Between East and West." *Helsinki Monitor* 10, no. 1: 9–18.

Linz, Juan, and Alfred Stepan. 1996. *Problems of Democratic Transition and Consolidation.* Baltimore, Md.: Johns Hopkins Univ. Press.

Lucas, Michael. 1994. "Russia and the CIS: The Role of the CSCE." *Helsinki Monitor* 5, no. 4: 5–37.

———. 1995. "The War in Chechnya and the OSCE Code of Conduct." *Helsinki Monitor* 6, no. 2: 32–42.

Mandelbaum, Michael. 1984. "The Anti-Nuclear Weapons Movements." *Political Science* 17: 24–32.

Maanpuolustustiedotuksen Suunnnittelukunta, ed. 1982. *Suomen Turvallisuuspolitiikka: Tasavallan Presidenti Urho Kekkosen Turvallisuupolittiisia Puheita Vuosilta 1943–1979.* 2d ed. Helsinki, Finland: n.p.

March, James G., and Johan P. Olsen. 1989. *Rediscovering Institutions: The Organizational Basis of Politics.* New York: The Free Press.

———. 1998. The Institutional Dynamics of International Political Orders. *International Organization* 52, no. 4: 943–70.

Maresca, John. 1985. *To Helsinki: The Conference on Security and Cooperation in Europe, 1973–75.* Durham, N.C.: Duke Univ. Press.

Mastny, Vojtech. 1972. *East European Dissent.* Vol. 2, *1965–70.* New York: Facts on File.

———. 1986. *Helsinki, Human Rights, and European Security: Analysis and Documentation.* Durham, N.C.: Duke Univ. Press.

Määttänen, Sakari. 1973. *Tapaus Jakobson.* Helsinki: Weilin and Göös.

Maude, George. 1976. *The Finnish Dilemma.* London: Oxford Univ. Press.

———. 1982. "The Further Shores of Finlandization." *Cooperation and Conflict* 17: 3–16.

Mayer, Peter, Volker Rittberger, and Michael Zürn. 1993. "Regime Theory: State of the Art and Perspectives." In *Regime Theory and International Relations,* edited by Volker Rittberger. Oxford: Oxford Univ. Press.

Moore, Christopher. 1996. *The Mediation Process: Practical Strategies for Resolving Conflict.* San Francisco, Calif.: Jossey-Bass Publishers.

Müller, Richard. 1981. "Etyk ja Madridin Kokous." *Esitelma Paasikivi-Seuran Kokouksessa* 19, no. 1. Paasikivi-Seuran monistesarja N:o 29. Helsinki, Finland.

Möttölä, Kari. 1982. The Politics of Neutrality and Defense. Finnish Security Policy since the Early 1970s. *Cooperation and Conflict* 17: 287–313.

Muñoz, Heraldo. 1998. "The Right to Democracy in the Americas." Translated by Mary D'León. *Journal of Interamerican Studies and World Affairs* 40, no. 1: 1–18.

Nathan, James A., and James K. Oliver. 1989. *United States Foreign Policy and World Order.* 4th ed. Glenview, Ill.: Scott, Foresman and Company.

NATO. 1967. The Future Tasks of the Alliance. Report of the North Atlantic Council. Brussels, December 13–14.

Nerlich, Uwe. 1976. "NATO, EEC, and the Politics of Détente: Regulative Frameworks of Western Foreign Policy-Making." In *Beyond Détente: Prospects for East-West Co-operation and Security in Europe,* edited by Nils Andren and Karl E. Birnbaum, 51–64. Leyden, The Netherlands: A. W. Sijthoff.

Neu, Joyce, and Vamik Volkan. 1999. *Developing a Methodology for Conflict Prevention: The Case of Estonia.* Atlanta, Ga.: The Carter Center.

Nevakivi, Jukka. 1975. "Urho Kekkosen Ulkopoliitisesta Toiminnasta Toisen Maailmansodanjälkeen." Eripainos. *Ulkopolitiikka,* 66–87.

Nolan, Janne E., ed. 1994. *Global Engagement: Cooperation and Security in the 21st Century.* Washington, D.C.: Brookings Institution.

OSCE. 2000a. *Annual Report 2000 on Interaction Between Organizations and Institutions in the OSCE Area.* The Secretary General. http://www.osce.org/docs/English/misc/anrep00e_org.htm.

OSCE. 2000b. *Annual Report 2000 on OSCE Activities.* The Secretary General. http://www.osce.org/docs/English/misc/anrep00e_activ.htm.

Ostrom, Elinor. 1990. *Governing the Commons.* Cambridge: Cambridge Univ. Press.

Oye, Kenneth. 1995. "Explaining the End of the Cold War: Morphological and Behavioral Adaptations to the Nuclear Peace." In *International Relations Theory and the End of the Cold War,* edited by Ned Lebow and Thomas Risse-Kappen, 57–84. New York: Columbia Univ. Press.

Palmer, Michael. 1971. *Prospects for a European Security Conference.* London: Chatham House.

Pentikäinen, Merja. 1998. "The 1997 Implementation Meeting on Human Dimension Issues of the OSCE." *The Helsinki Monitor* 9, no. 2: 18–37.

Pfetsch, Frank R. 1981. *Die Außenpolitik der Bundesrepublik 1949–1980.* Munich: Wilhelm Fink.

Plomb, Wouter. 1993. "The CSCE Human Dimension Seminar on Migration." *Helsinki Monitor* 4, no. 3: 26–30.

———. 1994. "The CSCE Human Dimension Seminar on Migrant Workers." *Helsinki Monitor* 5, no. 2: 85–88.

Princen, Thomas. 1992. *Intermediaries in International Conflict.* Princeton, N.J.: Princeton Univ. Press.

Project on Ethnic Relations. 1996. *Russia and Eastern and Central Europe: Old Divisions and New Bridges.* Princeton, N.J.: Project on Ethnic Relations.

Pruitt, Dean G., and Peter J. Carnevale. 1993. *Negotiation in Social Conflict.* Pacific Grove, Calif.: Brooks/Cole Publishing.

Rapkin, David. 1990. *World Leadership and Hegemony.* Boulder, Colo.: Lynne Rienner.

Raymond, Gregory A. 1997. "Problems and Prospects in the Study of International Norms." *International Studies Review* 41, supplement 2: 205–46.

Ries, Tomas. 1988. *Cold Will: The Defence of Finland.* London: Brassey's Defence Publishers.

Risse-Kappen, Thomas. 1994. "Ideas Do Not Float Freely: Transnational Coalitions, Domestic Structures, and the End of the Cold War." *International Organization* 45, no. 3: 185–214.

———. 1995. "Bringing Transnational Relations Back In: Non-State Actors, Domestic

Structures, and International Institutions." In *Bringing Transnational Relations Back In,* edited by Thomas Risse-Kappen, 3–36. New York: Cambridge Univ. Press.

Rittberger, Volker. 1990. "International Regimes in the CSCE Region: From Anarchy to Governance and Stable Peace." Paper prepared for the Annual Meeting of the International Studies Association, Washington, D.C.

Rittberger, Volker, and Michael Zürn. 1990. Editor's Introduction. In *International Regimes in East-West Politics,* edited by Volker Rittberger and Michael Zürn, 1–6. New York: Pinter Publishers.

———. 1991. "Regime Theory: Findings from the Study of East-West Regimes." *Cooperation and Conflict* 26: 165–83.

———, eds. 1990. *International Regimes in East-West Politics.* New York: Pinter Publishers.

Rönquist, Anders. 1995. "The Council of Europe Framework Convention for the Protection of National Minorities." *Helsinki Monitor* 6, no. 1: 38–45.

Rotfeld, Adam Daniel. 1993. "Introduction: Parameters of Change." In *SIPRI Yearbook 1993: World Armaments and Disarmament,* 1–12. Oxford: Oxford Univ. Press.

———. 1997. "Europe: In Search of Cooperative Security." In *SIPRI Yearbook 1997: Armaments, Disarmament, and International Security,* 127–49. Oxford: Oxford Univ. Press.

Rotfeld, Adam Daniel, and Walther Stützle, eds. 1991. *Germany and Europe in Transition.* New York: Oxford Univ. Press.

Rothstein, Robert L., ed. 1999. *After the Peace: Resistance and Reconciliation.* Boulder, Colo.: Lynne Rienner.

Roussopoulos, Dimitrios I. 1986. *The Coming of World War Three: From Protest to Resistance.* Vol. 1. Montreal: Black Rose Books.

Rubin, Jeffrey Z. 1991. "Timing the Ripeness and Ripeness of Timing." In *Timing the De-escalation of International Conflicts,* edited by Louis Kriesberg and Stuart J. Thorson, 237–46. Syracuse: Syracuse Univ. Press.

Rubin, Jeffrey Z., Dean G. Pruitt, and Sung Hee Kim. 1994. *Social Conflict: Escalation, Stalemate, and Settlement.* 2d ed. New York: McGraw Hill.

Rubin, Jeffrey Z., and Bert R. Brown. 1975. *The Social Psychology of Bargaining and Negotiation.* New York: Academic Press.

Ruggie, John G., ed. 1993. *Multilateralism Matters.* New York: Columbia Univ. Press.

Sandole, Dennis J. D. 1993. "Paradigm, Theories, and Metaphors in Conflict and Conflict Resolution: Coherence or Confusion?" In *Conflict Resolution Theory and Practice,* edited by Dennis J. D. Sandole and Hugo van der Merwe, 1–24. New York: Manchester Univ. Press.

Scherrer, Christian P. 1999. "Conflict Management and the Process of Escalation: Timing and Types of Responses." In *Ethnicity and Intra-State Conflict,* edited by Håkan Wiberg and Christian P. Scherrer, 165–84. Aldershot, England: Ashgate Publishing.

Schimmelfennig, Frank. 1993. "The CSCE as a Model for the Third World? The Middle East and African Cases." In *The CSCE in the 1990s,* edited by Michael Lucas, 319–33. Baden-Baden, Germany: Nomos.

Schlager, Erika. 1993. "Conflict Resolution in the CSCE." Occasional Papers. Kroc Institute for International Peace Studies, Univ. of Notre Dame.

Schmidt, Helmut. 1989. *Men and Powers*. Translated by Ruth Hein. New York: Random House.

Schoutheete, Philippe. 1980. La coopération politique européenne. Brussels: Editions Labor-Nathan.

Schramm, Friedrich-Karl, Wolfram-Georg Riggert, and Alois Friedel, eds. 1972. *Sicherheitskonferenze in Europa: Dokumentation 1954–1972*. Frankfurt am Main: Alfred Metzner Verlag.

Shevardnadze, Edvard. 1991. "Speech to the Congress of People's Deputies, December 20, 1990." In *The Soviet System in Crisis,* edited by Alexander Dallin and Gail W. Lapidus, 698–99. Boulder, Colo.: Westview Press.

Shifter, Michael. 1997. "The Challenge of Multilateralism: Intervention and Aid in the Americas." *The Brown Journal of World Affairs* 4, no. 2: 85–101.

Shikaki, Khalil. 1999. "The Internal Consequences of Unstable Peace: Psychological and Political Responses of the Palestinians." In *After the Peace: Resistance and Reconciliation,* edited by Robert L. Rothstein, 29–66. Boulder, Colo.: Lynne Rienner.

Sibenius, James. 1992. "Negotiation Analysis: A Characterization and Review." *Management Science* 38, no. 1: 18–38.

Simon, Sheldon W. 1998. "Security Prospects in Southeast Asia: Collaborative Efforts and the ASEAN Regional Forum." *The Pacific Review* 11, no. 2: 195–212.

Sipilä, Johanna Leena Tellervo. 1988. "Sosiaaliset Normit Ulkopolitiikan Säätelijöinä: Kolme Tapaustutkimusta Suomen ja Ruotsin Ulkopolitiikasta." Master's thesis, Univ. of Helsinki.

Sizoo, J., and R. Th. Jurrjens. 1984. *CSCE Decision-Making: The Madrid Experience.* Boston: Martinus Nijhoff Publishers.

Sjöstedt, Gunnar. 1994. "The Development of Long-Term Strategies of the European Union: 'Externalization' Through Consensual Knowledge." Paper presented at the Conference on the External Role of the European Union: Dynamics, Predictions, and Policy Needs, Swedish Institute of International Affairs, Stockholm, Sweden, Dec. 9–10.

———. 2003. "Regime Dynamics: An In-road to Environmental Governance. A Conceptual Framework." In *Getting It Done: The Post-Agreement Negotiation and International Regimes,* edited by Bertram Spector and I. William Zartman. Washington, D.C.: United States Institute of Peace Press

Skilling, Gordon. 1981. *Charter 77 and Human Rights in Czechoslovakia.* Boston: Allen and Unwin.

———. 1984a. "The Belgrade Follow-Up." In *Canada and the Conference on Security and Co-operation in Europe,* edited by Robert Spencer, 283–307. Ontario: T. H. Best Printing.

———. 1984b. "The Madrid Follow-Up." In *Canada and the Conference on Security and Co-operation in Europe,* edited by Robert Spencer, 308–50. Ontario: T. H. Best Printing.

Spector, Bertram I. 2003. "Post-Agreement Negotiation: Conflict Resolution Processes in the Aftermath of Successful Negotiations." In *Getting It Done: The Post-Agreement*

Negotiation Process and International Regimes, edited by Bertram I. Spector and I. William Zartman. Washington, D.C.: United States Institute of Peace Press.

Spector, Bertram I., and I. William Zartman, eds. 2003. *Getting It Done: The Post-Agreement Negotiation Process and International Regimes.* Washington, D.C.: United States Institute of Peace Press.

Spector, Bertram I., and Anna Korula. 1992. "Facilitative Mediation in International Disputes: From Research to Practical Application." Working Paper: 92–016. International Institute for Applied Systems Analysis, Laxenburg, Austria.

Spencer, Robert. 1984. "Canada and the Origins of the CSCE, 1965–1973." In *Canada and the Conference on Security and Co-operation in Europe,* edited by Robert Spencer, 20–101. Ontario: T. H. Best Printing.

———, ed. 1984. *Canada and the Conference on Security and Co-operation in Europe.* Ontario: T. H. Best Printing.

Stabreit, Immo. 1983. "Die Feierliche 'Deklaration zur Europäischen Union'—Eine Etappe auf dem Weg zu einem Vereinten Europa." *Europa Archiv* 15: 445–52.

Stanley, Timothy, and Darnell Whitt. 1970. *Détente Diplomacy: United States and European Security in the 1970s.* New York: Univ. Press of Cambridge, Mass.

Stein, Eric. 1983. "European Political Cooperation (EPC) as a Component of the European Foreign Affairs System." *Der Zeitschrift für ausländisches offentliches Recht und Völkerrecht* 43: 49–69.

Stein, Janice Gross. 1991. Reassurance in International Conflict Management. *Political Science Quarterly* 106: 431–50.

———. 1994. "Political Learning by Gorbachev as Uncommitted Thinker and Motivated Learner." *International Organization* 48, no. 2: 155–84.

Stern, Paul C., and Daniel Druckman. 2000. "Evaluating Interventions in History: The Case of International Conflict Resolution." *International Studies Review* 2, no. 1: 33–64.

Suomela, Kalevi. 1971. "Kaksiteräinen miekka." *Ydin* 45: 8–9.

Susskind, Lawrence, and Eileen Babbit. 1992. "Overcoming the Obstalces to Effective Mediation of International Disputes." In *Mediation in International Relations,* edited by Jacob Bercovitch and Jeffrey Z. Rubin, 30–51. New York: St. Martin's Press.

Tetlock, Philip E. 1991. "Learning in U.S. and Soviet Foreign Policy: In Search of an Elusive Concept." In *Learning in U.S. and Soviet Foreign Policy,* edited by George W. Breslauer and Philip E. Tetlock, 20–61. Boulder, Colo.: Westview Press.

Thomas, Daniel C. 1991. "Social Movements and International Institutions: A Preliminary Framework." Paper presented at the Annual Meeting of the American Political Science Association, Washington, D.C.

Thomson, Janice E. 1993. "Norms in International Relations: A Conceptual Analysis." *International Journal of Group Tensions* 23, no. 1: 67–83.

Törnudd, Klaus. 1982. "From Unanimity to Voting and Consensus: Trends and Phenomena in Joint Decision-Making by Governments." *Cooperation and Conflict* 17: 163–77.

Touval, Saadia. 1982. *The Peace Brokers.* Princeton, N.J.: Princeton Univ. Press.

———. 1989. "Multilateral Negotiation: An Analytic Approach." *Negotiation Journal* 5: 159–73.

Touval, Saadia, and I. William Zartman, eds. 1985. *International Mediation in Theory and Practice*. Boulder, Colo.: Westview Press.

Turner, Henry Ashby, Jr. 1987. *The Two Germanies since 1945*. New Haven, Conn.: Yale Univ. Press.

Ulam, Adam. 1974. *Expansion and Coexistence: Soviet Foreign Policy 1917–1973*. 2d ed. New York: Praeger.

Underdal, A. 1994. "Leadership Theory: Rediscovering the Arts of Management." In *International Multilateral Negotiation,* edited by I. William Zartman, 178–97. San Francisco, Calif.: Jossey-Bass Publishers.

Vaky, Viron P. 1993. "The Organization of American States and Multilateralism in the Americas." In *The Future of the Organization of American States,* edited by Viron Vaky and Heraldo Muñoz, 1–66. New York: Twentieth Century Fund.

Van der Stoel, Max. 1994. Plenary Meeting—Keynote Speech by Ambassador Max Van der Stoel, CSCE High Commissioner on National Minorities. Seminar on Early Warning and Preventive Diplomacy. Consolidated Summary. Warsaw, Poland, Jan. 12–21. Document Courtesy the Ministry for Foreign Affairs, The Netherlands.

Väyrynen, Raimo. 1972. *Conflicts in Finnish-Soviet Relations: Three Comparative Studies*. Tampere, Finland: Tampereen Yliopisto.

———. 1973. "Towards a More Secure Europe: An Analysis of Problems in European Security and Cooperation." *Coexistence* 10: 99–118.

———. 1982. *Stability and Change in Finnish Foreign Policy*. Research Report, no. 60. Department of Political Science, Univ. of Helsinki. Helsinki: Helsingin Yliopiston Monituspalvelu.

———. 1991. "To Settle or to Transform? Perspectives on the Resolution of National and International Conflicts." In *New Directions in Conflict Theory,* edited by Raimo Väyrynen, 1–25. London: Sage.

———. 1992. "Security Regime in Europe: Conceptual and Empirical Issues." Paper presented at the First Pan-European Conference on International Relations, Heidelberg, Sept. 16–20.

Vladimirov, Viktor. 1993. *Näin se oli. Muistelmia ja Havaintoja Kulissientakaisesta Diplomaattitoiminnasta Suomessa 1954–84*. Translated from the Russian by Arnold Hiltunen. Keuruu, Finland: Otava.

von Groll, Götz, and Berthold Meyer. 1996. "Noch Eine Chance Für den Verhandlungsfrieden: Lehren aus der KSZE für eine Konferenz über Sicherheit und Zusammenarbeit im Nahen Osten." Frankfurt am Main: Hessische Stiftung Friedens-und Konflikt-Forschung Report, July.

Wallander, Celeste A., and Jane E. Prokop. 1993. "Soviet Security Strategies Toward Europe: After the Wall, with their Backs up Against It." In *After the Cold War,* edited by Robert O. Keohane, Joseph S. Nye, and Stanley Hoffmann, 63–103. Cambridge, Mass.: Harvard Univ. Press.

Weaver, Ole, Pierre Lemaitre, Elzbieta Tromer, eds. 1989. *European Polyphony: Perspectives Beyond East-West Confrontation*. New York: St. Martin's Press.

Weber, Steven. 1991. "Interactive Learning in U.S.-Soviet Arms Control." In *Learning in U.S. and Soviet Foreign Policy,* edited by George W. Breslauer and Philip E. Tetlock, 784–824. Boulder, Colo.: Westview Press.

Wehr, Paul, and John Paul Lederach. 1996. "Mediating Conflict in Central America." In *Resolving International Conflicts,* edited by Jacob Bercovitch, 55–74. Boulder, Colo.: Lynne Rienner.

Weiss, Thomas G., and Larry Minear. 1993. *Humanitarian Action in Times of War.* Boulder, Colo.: Lynne Rienner.

Weitz, Richard. 1993. "Pursuing Military Security in Eastern Europe." In *After the Cold War,* edited by Robert O. Keohane, Joseph S. Nye, and Stanely Hoffmann, 342–80. Cambridge, Mass.: Harvard Univ. Press.

Wilkenfeld, Jonathan, Michael Brecher, and Shiela Moser. 1988. *Crisis in the Twentieth Century.* Vol. II. *Handbook of Foreign Policy Crises.* New York: Pergamon Press.

Williams, Abiodun. 2000. *Preventing War: The United Nations and Macedonia.* Lanham, Md.: Rowman and Littlefield.

Wilson, Andrew. 1983. *The Disarmer's Handbook of Military Technology and Organization.* Middlesex, England: Harmondsworth.

Yost, David. 1998. *NATO Transformed.* Washington, D.C.: United States Institute of Peace.

Young, Oran. 1967. *The Intermediaries: Third Parties in International Crises.* Princeton, N.J.: Princeton Univ. Press.

———. 1991. "Political Leadership and Regime Formation: On the Development of Institutions in International Society." *International Organization* 45: 281–308.

Youtz, David, and Paul Midford. 1992. *A Northeast Asian Security Regime.* Boulder, Colo.: Westview Press.

Zaagman, Rob. 1994. "The CSCE High Commissioner on National Minorities: An Analysis of the Mandate and the Institutional Context." In *Challenges of Change: The Helsinki Summit of the CSCE and Its Aftermath,* edited by Arie Bloed, 113–76. Dordrecht, The Netherlands: Martinus Nijhoff Publishers.

Zagorski, Andrei V. 1993. "The New Republics of the CIS in the CSCE." In *The CSCE in the 1990s,* edited by Michael Lucas, 279–92. Baden-Baden, Germany: Nomos.

Zartman, I. William. 1988. "Alternative Attempts at Crisis Management: Concepts and Processes." In *New Issues in International Crisis Management,* edited by Gilbert Winham, 199–224. Boulder, Colo.: Westview Press.

———. 1997. "Negotiating Regime Evolution in the Environmental Field: The Dynamics of Regime Building." American Political Science Association Annual Conference, Aug. 30.

———. 2003. "The Dynamics of Regime Building." In *Getting It Done: The Post-Agreement Negotiation Process and International Regimes,* edited by Bertram I. Spector and I. William Zartman. Washington, D.C.: United States Institute of Peace Press.

———, ed. 1994. *International Multilateral Negotiations.* San Francisco, Calif.: Jossey-Bass Publishers.

Zartman, I. William, and Maureen R. Berman. 1982. *The Practical Negotiator.* New Haven, Conn.: Yale Univ. Press.

Index

Abkhazia, 237
Adenauer, Konrad, 64
Afghanistan, 164, 208, 216
Agenda for Peace, 23
Akhromeyev, Sergei, 168
Albania, 226, 236
Ankara Review Conference (1999), 2
Armenia, 173, 178
Austria: at Belgrade Follow-up Meeting, 201, 203; bid to host CSCE, 125; and elements of neutrality policy, 51, 78, 125; as facilitative mediator, 167; and Group of Nine, 70; institutionalizing the CSCE, 158; issuing of July 24, 1970, Austrian Memorandum, 107; at Madrid Follow-up Meeting, 210, 215; position on Mutual Balanced Force Reduction Talks, 107–8; as possible host for CSCE, 92n. 32; proposals for political and military security, 123; response to Budapest Appeal, 91; stand on human rights, 221; State Treaty (May 1955), 55, 78; third-party role in CSCE, 49. *See also* détente; neutral and nonaligned states; neutral countries
Azerbaijan, 225

Basic Principles Agreement (1972): limitations of, 53n. 1; and Nixon administration, 133; provisions of, 7–8; and superpower competition, 53. *See also* détente; Soviet Union; United States
basket, 2; Dutch inspiration for, 119; importance of, 121–22; organizational structure for, 112; origins of, 118–23; principle of equality of texts and baskets, 121, 164; as procedural formula, 119; relation to NATO proposal, 109
Basket I: designation of, 121; and Geneva Talks on, 144–48; negotiation impasses in, 140–44; negotiations on Madrid Follow-up Meeting, 213; Soviet negotiating strategy for, 134–35
Basket II: designation of, 121; substance of in Final Act, 153
Basket III: designation of, 121; Eastern bloc violations of, 179–81, 195–96; human rights content of, 19–20, 153, 155; impact of Follow-up on, 149; negotiating impasses in, 144–45; Nixon's position on, 133; relationship to interstate framework of CSCE, 186–88; relevance to Polish Defense Committee, 176; and Soviet bloc dissidents, 16; Soviet negotiating strategy for, 131–32, 134; U.S. position on, 16; and Vienna Follow-up Meeting, 16–17
Basket IV: at Geneva Talks, 148–51; neutral and nonaligned position on, 136; substance of in Final Act, 153. *See also* Conference on Security and Cooperation in Europe
Belarus, 226, 236
Belgium, 96; and CBMs proposal, 142–43; efforts with Group of Nine, 70, 72; at Helsinki Consultations, 118–19; institutionalizing the CSCE, 158; proposals for European Security Conference by, 105; and third-party interventions, 139. *See also* Group of Nine

Belgrade Follow-up Meeting (1977–78), 2, 159, 176; accountability for human rights violations, 178–79, 202; attempts at final document, 203–8; consensus decision making jeopardized at, 197; controversy over review of implementation, 198–99, 200–201; Eastern bloc negotiating strategy at, 195; Eastern bloc objectives at, 158–59, 220; East-West tensions at, 202–3; follow-up, 194, 198–99, 463–67; initial use of expert meetings, 200; N+N as coordinators at, 197–99; N+N intermediary role at, 200–208; N+N objectives for, 158–59, 197–99, 201; opening of, 159; precedents set by, 199; preparatory meeting for, 200–203; results of, 160–61; Soviet proposals at, 205–6; stages of, 202; and United States, 195–97; U.S. proposal at, 206; West European objectives for, 158, 197; West's objectives at, 200–202; and Yellow Book, 200–203. *See also* Conference on Security and Cooperation in Europe; neutral and nonaligned states

Berlin Conference of Four Great Powers (1954), 55

Berlin Wall, 52, 62, 180

Bern Meeting on Human Contacts (1986), 20, 180, 182, 184, 192

Blue Book: continuity of process, 128–29, 148–51; CSCE agenda for, 103, 111–12, 131; definition of consensus, 115–16; lasting significance of, 199, 202; as normative foundation, 104, 112; and rule of rotation, 140; structuring of, 138–40. *See also* Belgrade Follow-up Meeting; Conference on Security and Cooperation in Europe; Finland's third-party role; Geneva talks

Bosnia-Herzegovina, 226, 236–37

Boutros-Ghali, Boutros, 233

Brandt, Willy, 62

Brandt Initiative, 64–65

Brezhnev, Leonid, 105, 160, 493; and Peace Program, 213; and strengthening of Warsaw Pact, 57; view of détente, 8

Brezhnev Doctrine, 6, 59; implications for Final Act, 154; significance for Geneva talks, 146; West's opposition to, 133

bridge-building policy, 65. *See also* détente

Brzezinski, Zbigniew, 195

Bucharest Declaration on Strengthening Peace and Security in Europe (1966): Eastern-bloc tensions concerning, 59–60; key objectives of, 58–59, 76; origins of, 58; Polish objectives for, 59n. 5; and preconditions for West, 132–33; Soviet position on, 59–61

Budapest Appeal (1969): Austria's response to, 91–92; Finland's response to, 91; provisions of, 98; Soviet aims, 105n. 5; Warsaw Pact's position on, 91

Budapest Cultural Forum (1985), 20, 180, 182, 184, 188, 192

Budapest Review Conference (1994), 2

Bulgaria, 70, 219, 223

Canada, 96, 158; and continuity of CSCE, 129; as coordinator of Basket I, 141n. 20; monitoring compliance in CSCE, 158; and NATO positions on Helsinki Consultations, 109

Carter, Jimmy: and Basket III, 16, 195–96; linkage politics, 160; policy for Belgrade Follow-up Meeting, 160; policy on human rights, 160; position on U.N. Special Session on Disarmament, 162; relations with Soviet Union, 160; and SALT II, 160–62; support of Commission on Security and Cooperation in Europe, 178; and Soviet bloc dissidents, 6–7. *See also* human rights

Ceausescu, Nicolae, 57–58

chairman-in-office, 231, 233–36

Charter for European Security (1999), 237, 240, 242–44

Charter of Paris: basis in Helsinki Final Act, 232; and end of cold war, 2, 157, 171; key elements of, 228; negotiations on, 228–29; origins of, 1; signing of, 1, 228

Charter 77, 173–76, 223. *See also* Czechoslovakia; dissidents; Helsinki Final Act

Chechnya, 226, 236, 237

Code of Conduct, 237, 242
coercive mediator: definition of, 32, 34; and enforcement of agreements, 38–40; as norm enforcer, 24, 26, 32–34, 38–39; 43–44; objectives of, 32; resources of, 32; strengths and weaknesses of strategy, 34, 45–56; use of carrots and sticks by, 39
cold war: and division of Europe, 50–51; end of, 226–27; ideological dimension of, 51; as "imaginary war," 50–51; impact of Cuban Missile Crisis on, 52; means of pursuing, 51; origins of, 50; second cold war, 158; transformation of, 2–7, 222–23
Comecon, 51
Commission on Security and Cooperation, 177–78, 181, 196; meeting with dissidents by, 177–78; and study of unilateral renunciation of Helsinki Final Act, 181–82
Committee of Senior Officials, 231. *See also* Permanent Council
Conference on Disarmament in Europe (CDE; 1984–86), 2; achievements of, 189–92; bids to host, 216; and CSBMs, 21; endorsement to be host of, 163; importance of results of, 222; key elements of final document, 170–71; limited N+N role in, 169; Madrid mandate for, 162, 166n. 18, 166–67; neutral proposal for air support by, 169, 221; and on-site inspection, 17, 168–69; origins of, 162; as precedent for monitoring Basket III, 171; and Reagan administration, 21; Soviet proposal for air inspections at, 168–69
Conference on Security and Cooperation in Europe: as alternative to détente, 189–90; and body of human dimension commitments, 19; change in regime governance, 226–27; and compliance issues at Madrid Follow-up Meeting, 179; credibility of commitments, 158–59; and early warning and prevention of conflict, 23; impact of process on change in East, 190–92; institutional development of, 9–12, 148–50, 157, 193, 210–11, 220–23, 223–24; issue linkage of human rights and security, 152–54; and limited cross-bloc ties, 134–35; and monitoring of human rights, 20; naming of, 68n. 22; as norm entrepreneur, 227; and on-site inspections, 7; origins of, 1, 50; post-cold war challenges confronting, 233, 243; and Reagan administration, 21; and review of implementation, 152, 158; rule-making, 19–21; test of rule effectiveness, 189, 198–99, 212–13, 220, 221–24; transparency of process, 20, 190, 246; unintended consequences of system change, 243; and violations of Basket III commitments, 178–81, 219. *See also* Basket I; Basket III; Belgrade, Helsinki Final Act; human rights; Madrid Follow-up Meeting; Vienna Follow-up Meeting
Conference on the Human Dimension (Moscow Meeting), 184–88
confidence- (and security-) building measures (CBMs): and elements of democracy building, 241–42; and Geneva talks, 141–44; and Madrid concluding document, 166–67; NATO promotion of functional approach, 166–67; N+N promotion of 40, 135–38; origins of, 143n. 22, 165–66; problems of compliance with, 166–67, 179; shortcomings of Helsinki CBMs, 167
conflict prevention, 226, 234–35
Conflict Prevention Center, 228, 231
conflict transformation: management of intrastate conflicts, 226; and normative change, 43; and peaceful change, 193; under way in Eastern Europe, 189–92
consensus: CSCE principle of, 7; as defined in CSCE, 115–16, 127; impact on multilateral decision making, 126–27, 289; and importance of neutral and nonaligned role, 126–27; problems with at Belgrade Follow-up, 193; Romania's position on, 115; West's position on, 115
Conventional Forces in Europe (CFE), 171, 183
cooperative security: comprehensiveness of, 189; CSCE principle of, 1; development of, 22; Final Act and multidimensionality

cooperative security (*cont.*)
of, 151–53; indivisibility of, 189–90; 242; N+N role in developing, 224
coordinator. *See* facilitative mediator
Copenhagen Report of Conference on the Human Dimension of the CSCE (1990), 233
Council of Europe: competition with other international organizations, 243; and end of cold war, 226; monitoring Final Act, 174, 176–77; national minorities in, 233
Crimea, 236
crisis mediation, 233
Croatia, 225, 226, 236
CSCE Meeting on Protection of the Environment (Sofia, Bulgaria, 1989), 188
Cypress, 210
Czechoslovakia, 222; at Belgrade Follow-up Meeting, 202; and border issues, 51; and Brezhnev doctrine, 59; dissidents of, 173–75; and end of cold war, 222; freedom of movement, 189; at Madrid Follow-up Meeting, 209, 219; nonaggression treaty with West Germany, 64; proposal for follow-up at Geneva Talks, 149; proposals for post-cold war CSCE 228; response to human dimension mechanism, 223; Soviet intervention in, 70, 73, 85; transitional state of, 225; violations of Basket III, 179

de Gaulle, Charles, 63, 84–85, 89, 162
democratic peace, 1
Denmark, 70, 149, 151, 158, 207, 212
détente: Austrian conception of, 197; and Berlin Wall, 63; and Blue Book, 124; Carter administration policy of, 195–96; changes in U.S. policy on, 191; and conflict transformation, 22; and Cuban Missile Crisis, 62, 73; and Finnish neutrality, 87; from above versus from below, 174–75; and human rights violation, 139; and limitations of Basic Principles Agreement, 8–9; multilateral agreements on, 54–55; neutral and nonaligned states' position on, 69–70; origins of, 51–52; and policy on Kennedy administration, 62; SALT I and II, 53–54; Soviet perspective on, 158–59; at a stalemate, 74–76, 85; and U.S.-Soviet relations, 9; Western conception of, 133. *See also* dissidents; Soviet Union; United States; West, the
dissidents: criticism of West for abandoning linkage politics, 180–81; and CSCE commitments, 512; and CSCE follow-up meetings, 16; impact of Final Act on, 155–56, 172–73; importance of to Belgrade Follow-up Meeting, 195; monitoring of Helsinki Final Act by, 20, 157; 171–78, 179–80; transnational linkages, 172–73; under Gorbachev, 222; at Vienna Follow-up Meeting and afterward, 188–89. *See also* Helsinki Final Act; International Helsinki Federation; Madrid Follow-up Meeting

early warning, 226, 233–36, 237, 241. *See also* chairman-in-office; high commissioner on national minorities; missions of long duration; preventive diplomacy
East, the: and bloc positions in Geneva, 131–32, 144; lack of compliance to Final Act, 158; negotiating strategy for CDE, 167; proposals for European Security Conference, 57–62. *See also* Soviet Union; Warsaw Pact
East-West conflict, 13, 52, 189–90. *See also* cold war
Economic Forum, 232
Eden, Sir Anthony, 55
Enckell, Ralph, 95, 106
Erhard, Ludwig, 64
d'Estaing, Valery Giscard, 162, 197
Estonia: and high commissioner on national minorities, 236; as host of CSCE/OSCE mission of long duration, 226, 239–40; and role of multiple mediators, 573; as transitional state, 225
European Community (EC): and CDE, 162; at Dipoli, 128; enlargement of, 85; and European political cooperation, 54, 73, 85, 133; Geneva talks and follow-up,

150; importance of Madrid Follow-up Meeting, 213; interventions at Madrid, 216; and NATO, 133; relations with Nordic countries, 85. *See also* European Union; West, the
European Nuclear Disarmament (END), 174
European Security Conference: Austria's bid to host, 91–92; and division of Germany, 155; Eastern bloc proposals for, 57–62; Finnish Memorandum on, 89, 90–91; Finnish objectives for, 77, 101–2; first Soviet proposal for, 51; obstacles to, 74–76; origins of, 15, 54, 55; as precursor to CSCE, 50; West's objections to, 54–55
European Union (EU), 226, 236. *See also* European Community; Finland; West, the

facilitative mediator: at Belgrade Follow-up Meeting, 201, 203; and consensus decision making, 43; coordinating substantive negotiations, 41; as cue-taker 36; definition of, 32, 35–9, 40, 41–43; evaluating effectiveness of, 9, 97–98; examples of at Madrid Preparatory Meeting, 209–10; gaining acceptance of, 15; institutionalizing cooperation, 13, 26, 38; at Madrid Follow-up Meeting, 213–14, 219–20; as mechanism for socialization, 44–45; in multilateral negotiations, 41–42; and N+N in CSCE, 12–13, 12n. 3, 136–38, 141n. 20, 145–48, 154; normative impact of, 38–43, 45; and potential for conflict transformation, 40–42; in prenegotiations, 42; at preparatory meeting for the CDE, 167; process orientation of, 36–8; resources of, 35; sensitivity to political context of dispute, 32; strengths and weaknesses of strategy, 45–8; and Sweden as example of, 168; and transitional formula, 41. *See also* Finland's third-party role; neutral and nonaligned states
Fenwick, Millicent, 177–78
Finland: bid to host CSCE, 124–25; and CBMs, 135–36; concerns with détente, 85–89; at CDE, 167; CSCE follow-up, 149, 150–51; and East-West relations, 85–86; FCMA Treaty (1948), 79, 81, 98, 212; Finlandization, 80, 120; and France, 92; gaining entry, 89; and German Question, 81–82, 84, 87, 88, 97, 98, 108–9; Group of Nine, 69–74, 94; as host of SALT talks, 80; launching CSCE, 6, 103; and (1969) Memorandum, 15, 89, 92–97, 103, 106; neutrality of, 77–82, 128, 151; neutrality policy, 77–82, 101–2; Nordic Council, 92–93; nuclear free zone, 135; relations with Austria, 91, 107, 280; relations with Soviet Union, 80–81, 89, 90–91, 95, 101; relations with Western Europe, 85–86; role of facilitative mediator, 15, 76, 89–95; and Sweden, 91, 92; and Treaty of Paris (1948), 78, 78n. 2; withdrawal of Soviet base from, 51. *See also* Conference on Security and Cooperation in Europe; Finland's third-party role; Group of Nine; neutral and nonaligned states; neutral countries
Finland's third-party role: agenda setting, 93; at Belgrade, 203, 211–13; in building consensus, 104, 108; and CBMs, 143; and commitment to CSCE's continuity, 124–25; and disarmament, 164; engendering commitments, 100–102, 103–4, 108; in facilitative mediation, 76, 89–95, 107–8, 209–10, 211, 217–18; gaining entry as mediator, 89; and initiatives to launch CSCE, 6, 15, 37, 89–95; as process-oriented, 103, 107–8. *See also* Conference on Security and Cooperation in Europe; facilitative mediator; Finland
Ford, Gerald R., 6, 155, 374, 161
Forum for Security Cooperation, 21, 242
France: bid to host CDE, 216; border disputes of, 51; on bringing MBFR under CSCE, 192; and European political cooperation, 128; and Geneva Summit (1955), 56–57; at Madrid Follow-up Meeting, 217; monitoring compliance to CSCE, 158; and NATO, 66; policy of rapprochement, 50, 54, 63–64, 84–85; positions at Belgrade Follow-up Meeting,

France (*cont.*)
197, 204, 207; post-cold war objectives for CSCE, 228; proposals for CDE, 162–63, 207; proposals for Helsinki Consultations, 116; and Soviet Union, 197; and U.N. Special Session on Disarmament, 162
Frowick, Robert, 183

Geneva talks (1973–75): Basket III negotiations, 144–45; CBMs, 141–44; neutral package deal, 145–48; East and Basket III, 146; impasses at, 140; organizational structure of, 138–40; proposals on follow-up, 148–51; trade-offs between Baskets I and III, 145–48
Georgia, 173, 225–26, 237
German Democratic Republic: at Belgrade Follow-up Meeting, 202; border issues of, 51; and exodus of Hungarian vacationers from Hungary, 223; human dimension mechanism invoked against, 223; at Madrid Follow-up Meeting, 209; nonaggression treaty with West Germany, 64; recognition of, 60, 131–32; Soviet control of, 74–75; Soviet policy of two Germanies, 56; violations of Basket III by, 179. *See also* East, the; German Question; Germany; Soviet Union
German Question, 63–64, 74. *See also* Federal Republic of Germany; German Democratic Republic
Germany, Federal Republic of: at Belgrade Follow-up Meeting, 206; border disputes of, 51; and Brandt Initiative, 64–65; and Carter's human rights policy, 161; and European Security Conference, 96; Hallstein Doctrine (1955), 64; institutionalizing the CSCE, 158; and Moscow Treaty, 108; and NATO Track Two decision, 161–62; and neutralization, 65; objectives for détente, 197; *Ostpolitik,* 50, 54, 84, 182, 197; relations with East Germany, 179, 197; relations with Soviet Union, 60, 197; reunification of, 6, 63, 146, 197; and Warsaw Treaty, 108. *See also* European Union; German Democratic Republic; German Question; Germany; Soviet Union, West, the
Germany, 51, 225, 228. *See also* Federal Republic of Germany; German Democratic Republic
glasnost, 16, 19, 183–84, 189, 222
Goldberg, Arthur, 160, 196, 205–6
Gorbachev, Mikhail: on bringing MBFR into CSCE, 191; and CDE, 168–69; "new thinking" and the CSCE, 18, 182, 183–84, 192; proposals for post-cold war CSCE, 229; response to on-site inspections, 17, 168, 190; social and cultural transformation 222; views on common security, 17–18. *See also* glasnost; perestroika; Soviet Union
Great Britain. *See* United Kingdom
Grinevsky, Oleg, 167–69
Gromyko, Andrei: and Budapest Appeal, 171; and CDE, 167–68; policy of Americocentrism, 161; and SALT II, 161; and Soviet objectives for CSCE, 132, 133; and United Nations, 98
Group of Nine: cooperation with Interparliamentary Union, 72–73; cross-bloc initiatives of, 69–75; dissolution of, 73; and foreign ministers' meeting, 72; origins of, 70; and U.N. General Assembly Resolution, 72; Yugoslav initiative on behalf of, 72–73

Harmel Report, 66–67
Havel, Vaclav, 223
Helsinki Consultations (1972–73): agenda for, 116–18; debate on institutionalizing CSCE, 129–30; host of, 108–9, 111; impasse in, 117, 119; interstate principles and modalities, 112–15, 119; and NATO conditionality, 111; and NATO objectives, 107–8; opening statements, 112; origins of basket structure, 118–23; participation at, 111; phases of, 103, 104, 105–8, 108–11, 111–12; Soviet objectives for, 117; structuring work at, 116–18. *See also* basket; Finland; Finland's third-party

role; neutral and nonaligned states; neutral countries
Helsinki Decisions (1992), 235
Helsinki Final Act (1975): follow-up to, 148–51, 193–94; importance of neutral package deal, 145–48; and interdependence of principles, 152–53; on inviolability of frontiers, 58, 75, 119, 132, 134, 140, 146, 153, 155, 171–72; main principles of, 2, 151–55, 157; monitoring agencies for, 176–78; normative importance of, 182, 189; peaceful settlement of disputes in, 143; ten principles reaffirmed, 189; treatment of human rights in, 6, 153–55; and violations of commitments, 179, 196. *See also* Commission on Security and Cooperation in Europe; Council of Europe; dissidents; Interparliamentary Union; North Atlantic Assembly; neutral and nonaligned states; neutral countries; Soviet Union
Helsinki Follow-up Meeting (1992), 229
Helsinki monitors. *See* dissidents
Helsinki Summit Declaration (1992), 232–33
High Commissioner on National Minorities: and conflict early warning, 235; and consultations with CiO and Permanent Council, 236; leverage of, 238–39; mandate for, 235, 238; and social learning, 237–39; visits by to participating states, 226; work with Sinti and Roma, 226
Honecker, Eric, 188–89
Hoyer, Steny, 181
human dimension: CSCE rule-making, 19; development of, 178–83; mechanism for, 183–89; relations to Basket III, 187; and role of the Office on Democratic Institutions and Human Rights, 241; scope of, 187; and Soviet Union, 3. *See also* Basket III; human dimension mechanism
human dimension mechanism, 187, 222
human rights: CSCE approach to, 1, 134; monitoring of, 157, 176–78, 179–80, 188; and Principle VII of Final Act, 19, 187; and Principle IX of Final Act, 186; right to know one's rights, 186. *See also* European Security Conference; Helsinki Final Act; human dimension mechanism; linkage politics; norms
Hungary, 70, 189, 209, 222; and freedom of movement, 223; proposals for Helsinki Consultations, 116; as transitional state, 225; work in by high commissioner on national minorities, 226, 236
Hyvarinen, Risto, 98

Iloniemi, Jaakko, 197–98
instrumental mediator: definition of, 13–14, 32–34; evaluating effectiveness of, 217–18; 220–35; as element of OSCE, 227; gaining entry, 28; limitations of strategy, 13, 32, 222; mechanism for socialization, 44; in multilateral negotiations, 40, 44; N+N role as, 127–28, 136–37; as norm entrepreneur, 14, 26, 32, 40, 44; objectives of, 35; and potential for conflict transformation, 34, 40; resources of, 34–35; Sweden and CDE, 163–65, 217–18; Yugloslavia's role as, 164–65
intellectual entrepreneur. *See* instrumental mediator
Intermediate Nuclear Force talks (INF), 162, 167, 171, 214, 218
International Helsinki Federation (previously International Helsinki Association), 176, 188
international law: changing Soviet perceptions of, 189; and human rights negotiations at Madrid Follow-up Meeting, 220; socialist conceptions of, 7, 11, 117, 146, 147, 153; and Western universalism, 116, 146, 150
Interparliamentary Union, 177. *See also* Group of Nine
Ireland, 158
Italy, 120, 142, 158, 161

Jackson-Vanik Amendment, 182
Jakobson, Max: and Finnish neutrality, 80, 98; and German Package, 98; and (1969)

Jakobson, Max (*cont.*)
Memorandum, 89; and Nixon and Kissinger, 61n. 13, 105; in race for U.N. secretary general, 125; and United Nations, 80
Johnson, Lyndon, 50, 63

Karjalainen, Ahti, 81, 90, 101, 111, 136
Kazakhstan, 226
Kekkonen, Urho: and CSCE diplomacy, 105–6; defense policy of, 81; and European Security Conference, 77, 80; and FCMA Treaty, 79, 81–82, 212; and Finnish foreign policy, 88, 91; and Finnish neutrality, 77–78, 82–84, 101–2; and Finnish objectives at Madrid Follow-up Meeting, 211–12; and "mandarins," 82–84; Memorandum (1969), 90–95, 95–97; and *naapulaliiga* ("little leaguers"), 83–84; and Nordic Nuclear Weapons Free Zone proposal, 80, 212; and "Paasikivi-Kekkonen line," 79, 83; relations with West, 96; and United Nations, 80; and "Westpolitik," 80. *See also* Finland; Finland's third-party role; neutral countries; Soviet Union
Khrushchev, Nikita, 50
Kissinger, Henry, 195; CSCE, 133; détente, 8, 9, 133; opposition to CSCE in Europe, 177; and proposed European Security Conference, 61, 106
Koivisto, Mauno, 81, 218
Korhonen, Keijo, 207
Kosovo, 226, 236, 237, 240, 244
Kyrsgyzstan, 226

Laber, Jeri, 181
Latvia, 226, 236, 239
Leifland, Leif, 198
Liechtenstein, 164, 210, 218
linkage politics: effectiveness of, 191–92; and end of cold war, 21; linking human rights and security, 7; and N+N position on, 224; and results of Vienna Follow-up Meeting; and U.S. leverage with Soviets, 20, 96–97, 180–81; and U.S. position at Belgrade, 158
Lisbon Review Conference (1996), 2
Lithuania, 173

Macedonia (former Yugoslav Republic of), 226, 236, 240, 244
Madrid Follow-up Meeting (1980–83), 2, 157, 200; compliance failures (of Eastern bloc), 179–80; concluding document of, 180; and dissidents, 179–80; "end game" of, 219–20; impasses and East-West tensions in negotiations, 209–10, 213–14, 215–17; "Laajava formula" and CSBMs, 218; and mandate for CDE, 162, 214, 217–18; and normative importance of, 181–82; N+N preparation for, 163–65; N+N third-party interventions in, 209–16, 217–20; and Polish crisis, 166, 210, 213, 215–17; preparatory meeting for, 208–11; search for transitional formula, 217–18; Soviet objectives for, 208, 218; Spain's third-party interventions, 210, 219–20; "stopping the clock," 210; Swedish proposal for, 163–64; U.S. and NATO aims for review of implementation, 166; West's objectives for, 208–9. *See also* Poland
Malta, 210, 219; at Belgrade, 203, 207–8; blocking consensus in CSCE, 134n. 4, 219; proposals on Mediterranean, 123, 129, 135
Mansfield, Mike, 65
mediator: and emergent mediation, 28–29; interests of, 27–28; and multilateral negotiations, 29; political sensitivity of, 28; resources of, 27, 32
Mediterranean: cooperation in, 152, 159, 207; security community in formation, 23; security measures for, 123, 129, 135. *See also* Belgrade Follow-up Meeting; CSCE; Madrid Follow-up Meeting; Malta; neutral and nonaligned states
mini groups, 122, 145
Ministerial Council, 228
missions of long duration, 226, 236, 238–40
Mitterrand, François, 169

Moldova, 226, 236
Molotov, Vyacheslav, 55
Müller, Richard, 215
Mutual Balance Force Reduction Talks (MBFR): and Austria's position, 108; and CBMs and CSCE, 123; exclusion from of neutral and nonaligned states, 86; origins of, 67; proposed agenda for, 67; and Reagan's arms control policy, 214; in relation to CSCE, 21, 111, 131–32, 160, 191; and Soviet interests, 16, 167, 191; and West as *demandeur,* 67, 68, 97

Nagorno-Karabakh, 225, 226, 236; 244
NATO: compliance with CBMs, 166; competition with other international organizations, 243; coordination with OSCE, 236; and end of cold war, 21, 226; Finnish proposal of November 24, 1970, 108; London Declaration on a Transformed North Atlantic Alliance, 227–28; and MBFR, 86, 108; 1971 NATO Communiqué, 118–19; and nuclear weapons, 161; origins of, 51; positions on Belgrade Follow-up Meeting, 197, 205, 207; proposals for CDE, 162, 167, 214; role in Bosnia, 48; Rome Communiqué (1970), 68–69, 96–97; Track Two decision by, 161, 218. *See also* West, the
Netherlands, the, 138, 158–59
neutral and nonaligned states: at Belgrade Follow-up Meeting, 200–202; building consensus, 193, 198, 223–25; as catalyst for institutionalizing the CSCE, 193, 199; and CBMs, 124, 143–44, 159, 163–65; and Charter of Paris, 1; and compliance with CBMs, 166; and disarmament, 159; expanding CSCE normative commitments, 157; as facilitative mediators, 137–38, 207, 221; functions of coordinator role, 126; impact on CSCE, 12–13, 49; as intellectual entrepreneurs, 158; origins of coordinator role, 114–15, 137; origins of group, 12, 131, 136–37; position on follow-up, 148–51; position on human rights issues, 6, 219; positions at Geneva talks, 135–38; precedent-setting role, 239–40; and principle of nonintervention, 154; promotion of diffuse reciprocity, 224; and proposals for CDE, 163–65; relations with Soviet Union, 164; relations with superpowers, 12; role at Helsinki Consultations, 103, 120, 122–23; role in CSCE follow-up meetings, 15; role in Madrid Preparatory Meeting, 208–11; support of linkage politics, 224; third-party interventions at Madrid Follow-up, 212–13, 215, 216–17, 218, 219–20; third-party interventions at Vienna Follow-up Meeting, 16–17; third-party strategies of, 9, 12–15, 136–37. *See also* Austria; Finland; Finland's third-party role; Malta; Sweden; Switzerland; Yugoslavia
neutral countries: on Basket IV and follow-up, 136; and CBMs at Geneva, 142; and CDE, 221; as coordinators of Basket III in Geneva talks, 139–40, 144; and détente, 136. *See also* Austria; Finland; neutral and nonaligned states; neutral package deal; Sweden; Switzerland
neutral package deal: elements of, 131, 146–47; Finish formula for, 147–48; impasse in Geneva talks, 144; negotiations on, 145–48; and Spanish compromise, 146; sponsors of, 137; Swedish contributions to, 147; and Swiss efforts, 137. *See also* Finland's third-party role
Nixon, Richard, 195; détente policy of, 133; meetings with Kekkonen, 106; policy on CSCE, 7–8, 133; relations with the Soviets, 65; SALT I, 65
Nordic Council, 92–93
norms: of aversion, 10; and comprehensive security, 530; conflict transformation, 9, 245; and CSCE's democratic deficit, 226; definition of, 9; and diffuse reciprocity, 11; diffusion of, 245; enabling function, 245; and end of cold war, 4; expansion of, 158, 186–88, 189; and the Final Act, 151–55; institutionalization of, 10–11; internalization (domestication) of, 11, 184, 190–91; and learning, 226–27, 246;

norms (*cont.*)
and peaceful change, 4, 9, 243–47; role in reassurance agreements, 10; and third-party strategies, 12; violations of, 11
North Atlantic Assembly, 177. *See also* conflict transformation; détente; peaceful change
North Atlantic Cooperation Council, 21, 228
Northern Ireland, 225
Norway, 119, 158, 206, 212

Office on Democratic Institutions and Human Rights: coordination with UN secretary general, 241; main functions, 231–32, 241; and national minority questions, 233. *See also* human dimension
Office on Free Elections. *See* Office on Democratic Institutions and Human Rights
on-site inspections: 2, 7, 17; breakthrough on, 165–66, 168; importance of, 190–91; Stockholm regime provisions for, 170–71.
Organization on Security and Cooperation in Europe (OSCE): evaluating transparency of, 246; facing post-cold war challenges, 22–23; and institutionalizing cooperation, 15; as new normative framework, 233; origins of, 1; as post-Westphalian system, 227, 246–47; promoting humane governance, 247; renaming CSCE as, 1; and security communities, 23–4; social learning in, 237–43; as tool for peaceful change, 7
Orlov, Yuri, 173
OSCE Parliament, 232
OSCE secretary general, 231
OSCE Troika, 233–34
Ostpolitik ("eastern policy"). *See* Brandt, Willy; Germany, Federal Republic of
Ottawa Meeting on Human Rights and Fundamental Freedoms (1985), 180, 182, 192

Paasikivi, Juho Kusti, 79
Palme, Olof, 216
Partnership for Peace, 21
Patocka, Jan, 175–76
peaceful change: and democratic transitions, 237; impact on Westphalia system, 24, 246–47; institutionalization of, 193; lessons of, 21–24; as means to capacity building, 244; OSCE as means to, 7; and security communities, 23–24; third-party strategies for, 9, 13; unintended consequences of, 22–23
peaceful coexistence, 50, 60, 189
peacekeeping, 236–37
peace movements 161, 214, 222
perestroika, 19, 184, 189, 222
Permanent Council, 231, 233, 238
Poland: bid to host CDE, 216; border issues, 51; and Charter, 77, 173; economic riots, 59; Jimmy Carter's visit to, 195; lifting of U.S. sanctions on, 182; and nonaggression treaty with West Germany, 64; Polish Crisis, 179, 181–82, 210, 217; proposals for Helsinki Consultations, 116; proposals for post-cold war CSCE, 228; and "second society," 222; U.S. relations with, 182. *See also* Madrid Follow-up Meeting
post-conflict reconstruction, 236
preventive diplomacy, 234
Principle I (Final Act), 152, 154
Principle II (Final Act), 152, 186
Principle III (Final Act), 152, 170
Principle IV (Final Act), 152–53
Principle V (Final Act), 153
Principle VI (Final Act), 153
Principle VII (Final Act), 19; 153, 186, 188
Principle VIII (Final Act), 153
Principle IX (Final Act), 153, 186
Principle X (Final Act), 153–54
Purple Book, 210, 216

Quadrapartite Agreement on Berlin, 54, 154

Rapacki, Adam, 56
Reagan, Ronald, 21; 161, 182, 214
Ridgway, Rozanne, 192

Rogers, William, 133
Romania, 70; bid to host CDE, 216; and consensus principle, 115; at Geneva talks, 144; in Group of Nine, 70; Jimmy Carter's visit to 195; military security, proposals for, 119; as norm entrepreneur, 40; position on disarmament, 129; position on rotation principle, 114; on principle of sovereign equality, 113–14; proposals at Helsinki Consultations, 107; relations with Soviet Union, 81; response to Vienna mechanism, 223; as transitional state, 225; at U.N. General Assembly, 71; violations of Basket III, 179; visit to by high commissioner on national minorities, 226
Rotfeld, Adam, 168
Russia, 225, 242. *See also* Soviet Union

Sakharov, Andrei, 176
San Marino, 210
Scheel, Walter, 137–38
Schevardnadze, Eduard, 16, 184
Schmidt, Helmut, 197
Schröder, Gerhard, 64
Schultz, George, 185
Secretariat (CSCE/OSCE), 231
Security Forum, 232
Shcharansky, Anatoly, 183
Slovak Republic, 226
Solidarity, 217, 223
Solzhenitsyn, Alexander, 139, 175
South Ossetia, 237
Soviet negotiating strategy: arms control and Blue Book, 123; at Belgrade Follow-up Meeting, 161, 200–201, 202, 205; deductive, 116–17; and inductive approach, 213; at Madrid Follow-up Meeting, 207; at Vienna Follow-up Meeting, 183
Soviet Union: break-up of, 223, 225; and Brezhnev Doctrine, 117; continuity of CSCE, 149, 150; and disarmament, 164, 210; emigration from, 179; European Security Conference and the Finnish initiative, 1, 90, 101; evaluation of Helsinki Final Act, 155–56, 171–72; at Geneva Summit (1955), 56–57; and German Question, 56, 60, 82, 131; immutability of borders, 119, 146; impact on Gorbachev's new policies, 222; invasion of Afghanistan, 164; invasion of Czechoslovakia, 6, 81, 87; objectives for CDE, 164; objectives for CSCE, 6, 15–16; peaceful co-existence, 50, 60, 189; political-legal significance of CSCE, 42; position on détente, 133, 142, 158, 161; principle of sovereign equality, 114; promotion of Bucharest Declaration, 58–59; proposals for Helsinki Consultations, 116; proposals for post-cold war CSCE, 228; tensions with China, 90. *See also* Belgrade; Conference on Human Dimension (Moscow Meeting); CSCE; glasnost; Gorbachev; Helsinki Final Act; Madrid; on-site inspections; perestroika; Vienna Follow-up Meeting
Spain, 122; Basque country in, 225; third-party interventions, 119–20, 139, 202, 208–10, 220
Stalin, Josef, 51
Strategic Arms Limitations Talks (SALT I and II), 160–61. *See also* détente; Nixon, Richard; Soviet Union; United States
Strategic Arms Reduction Talks (START), 191, 214
Sweden: bid to host CDE, 163, 216; détente, 136; disarmament policies of, 128, 144, 154, 163, 165; as facilitative mediator, 154, 167; institutionalizing the CSCE, 369; as intellectual entrepreneur, 165, 379; neutrality policy of, 78; 128; as norm entrepreneur, 34, 40, 158; objectives for CSCE, 135; Palme Doctrine, 70; policies at Madrid Follow-up Meeting, 209, 211–12; position on human rights, 221; positions taken at Belgrade Follow-up Meeting, 198, 203, 207; proposal for neutral air support, 169; proposals for CDE, 163–65; proposals for military security, 119, 123–25; relation to European security, 128; third-party role in CSCE, 49. *See also* Group of Nine; instrumental

mediator; neutral and nonaligned states; neutral countries
Switzerland: at Belgrade Follow-up Meeting, 203, 207; contributions to Helsinki Consultations, 119, 122–23; and human rights, 221; at Madrid Follow-up Meeting, 209, 210; monitoring compliance to CSCE, 158; neutrality policy of, 78, 120–21; as norm entrepreneur, 40; overcoming impasses, 118; peaceful settlement of disputes, 119, 123, 124, 136, 144, 208; proposals for CDE, 165; third-party role in CSCE, 49, 120–21. *See also* neutral and nonaligned states; neutral countries

Tajikistan, 226, 236
third-party strategies: and end of cold war, 9; evaluating outcomes, 30–31; gaining entry, 14–15; importance of mediator readiness, 97–100; normative capacity of, 9, 12, 25–26, 32–34; as parallel mediation, 48; peaceful change, 21–23; in post-agreement negotiations, 14, 22; promoting learning, 26; socialization to new norms, 25–26; theoretical models of, 32–34. See also facilitative mediator; instrumental mediator; neutral and nonaligned states
Tötterman, Richard, 113–14
Transdniester, 237
Treaty on Conventional Forces in Europe, 171
Turkey, 226
"Two plus Four Agreement" (1990), 229

Ukraine, 173, 226, 236
United Kingdom, 116, 122, 157, 217
United Nations: coordination with OSCE, 236–37; efforts to overcome cold war, 54; freedom of movement, 189, 223; Group of Nine initiatives, 70, 71–72; importance for neutral member states, 70; Secretary General U Thant, 106; Special Session on Disarmament, 162; as third party, 48
United States: debate on withdrawing from CSCE, 181–83; diplomacy of public shaming, 158; and human contact issues, 6, 7; and INF talks, 161–62; interest in CSCE process, 20–21, 96–97, 178, 191–92; at Madrid Follow-up Meeting, 217; participation in CSCE, 6; position on CSCE continuity, 148; preconditions for European Conference, 55; proposals for post-cold war CSCE, 228–29; relations with Eastern Europe, 195–96; relations with Soviet Union, 197; and SALT I and II, 160–62; and timing of CSCE and MBFR, 111. *See also* CSCE; human rights; linkage politics; NATO; Soviet Union; West, the
Universal Declaration of Human Rights, 172, 187

Vance, Cyrus, 161
Vienna Follow-up Meeting (1986–89), 2, 16, 157, 222; and CDE, 171; consensus on human rights, 186–87; impact on change in East, 16–17, 188, 511, 222–23; importance of concluding agreement, 185–87; institutionalization of CSCE, 21, 200, 223–24; N+N position on conventional armed forces in Europe negotiations, 222; role of dissidents, 188–89; Soviet objectives for, 182–83; U.S. linkage politics, 182–83. *See also* human dimension; human dimension mechanism

Walesa, Lech, 223
Warsaw Pact: demise of, 225, 228; implementation of Helsinki CBMs, 166; invasion of Czechoslovakia by, 70, 73, 85; origins of, 51, 56; position on CDE, 164. *See also* Bucharest Appeal; Budapest Declaration; East, the; Soviet Union
West, the: bloc position at Geneva talks, 133–35, 146; expert meetings on human rights, 140, 216, 219; institutionalizing the CSCE, 150–51, 155, 157; linkage politics, 224; monitoring Final Act, 177; opposition to disarmament, 123; and